The Network Society
Economic Development and International Competitiveness as Problems of Social Governance

In memory of *Leopoldo Mármora*

His cheerful nature was infectious,
his optimism unshakable,
his human warmth inexaustible,
his intellectual creativity unsurpassed.

THE NETWORK SOCIETY
Economic Development and International Competitiveness as Problems of Social Governance

DIRK MESSNER

Routledge
Taylor & Francis Group
New York   London

Published in association with the
German Development Institute, Berlin

First published in 1997 by Frank Cass Publishers

This edition published 2012 by Routledge
2 Park Square, Milton Park, Abingdon, Oxon OX14 4RN
711 Third Avenue, New York, NY 10017

Routledge is an imprint of the Taylor & Francis Group, an informa business

Copyright © 1997 GDI/Frank Cass

British Library Cataloguing in Publication Data

Messner, Dirk
    The network society : economic development and
    international competitiveness as problems of social
    governance.- (GDI book series; no. 10)
    1. Competition, International   2. Economic development
    I. Title
    338.6'048

    ISBN 0-7146-4402-1

Library of Congress Cataloging-in-Publication Data

Messner, Dirk.
    The network society : economic development and international
    competitiveness as problems of social governance / Dirk Messner. p.
        em.-(GDI book series :no. 10)
    Includes bibliographical references (p.   ).
    ISBN 0-7146-4402-1 (pbk.)
    1. Industrial policy. 2. Free enterprise.   3. Conservatism.
    4. State, The.   5. Competition, International.   6. Economic
    development.   I. Deutsches Institut für Entwicklungspolitik.
    II. Title.   m. Series.
    HD3611.M448   1997   97-23233
    338.9-dc21   CIP

*All rights reserved. No part of this publication may be reproduced in
any form or by any means, electronic, mechanical, photocopying,
recording or otherwise, without the prior permission of
the publisher*

Contents

Preliminary Remarks   IX

Introduction and Formulation of the Problem   1

Part I   **The Concept of "Systemic Competitive-
                ness" - An Approach to the Development
                of National Competitiveness and Loca-
                tional Advantages**

1   The Four Levels of Systemic Competitiveness   10

2   Essential Requirements at the Macrolevel   16

3   New Demands at the Company Level   19

4   Shaping Structures in the Mesodimension - The
        Relevance of Selective Policies   21

4.1   The Significance of the Mesodimension   21

4.2   State, Business Enterprises, and Intermediary Institu-
        tions in the Mesodimension - Traditional Dichotomies
        under Attack   24

4.3   The National, Regional, and Local Dimensions of
        the Mesolevel   30

5   The Metalevel: Social Integration and Governance
        Capacity   33

5.1   Building Social Structures as a Condition of Eco-
        nomic Modernization   33

5.2   Social Organizational and Governance Capacity as a
        Dimension of Competitiveness   34

Part II   **Reconstruction of the Theories of Social
                Governance Capacity**

Chapter 1   Preliminary Remarks   38

1.1   The Social Dimensions of Development - A Neglect-
        ed Field   38

1.2   Search Directions in Governance Theories in the So-
        cial Sciences - An Initial Structuring of the Field of
        Research   42

Chapter 2   The State as the Governance Center of Society   47

2.1   The Modern Understanding of the State: The Internal-
        ly and Externally Sovereign Leviathan   47

2.2   Discussions of the State, Planning, and Governance in
        the Framework of Traditional Theory of the State   49

2.2.1   Pluralism Theories, Elitist-democratic Concepts and
        their Proximity to Liberalist-economic Approaches   49

2.2.2   Welfare State, Planned Capitalism, and Keynesian
        Global Management   54

2.2.3   Limitations of Regulative Policy and Initial Approach-
        es Seeking Solutions in the Project of "Rationalist
        Statism"   58

2.3   From the Planning Illusion to the Issue of the State's
        Governance Capacity: The First Relativization of the
        Modern Understanding of the State   68

2.4   The Neocorporatist Discourse on Patterns of Social
        Organization: Governance of Society via Networking
        be-tween State and Large-scale Organizations: The
        Second Relativization of the Modern Understanding
        of the State - The Discovery of the Governance Poten-
        tials of Society   70

**Chapter 3   Neoconservative and (Neo)liberal Discourses
        on the Crisis of the State: From the "Ungov-
        ernability Debates" to the "End of the Gov-
        ernance Illusion"   78**

3.1   The Antipluralist Core of the Neoconservative Cri-
        tique of the Modern State: An Attempt to Revitalize
        the Leviathan's Absolute Sovereignty   79

3.2   (Neo)liberal Models for Restructuring the Relation-
        ship between State and Society   81

3.2.1	Nozick: The Concept of the Minimal State	81
3.2.2	Olson: The "Decline of Nations" as a Result of the Organization of Social Interests	84
3.3	Résumé	94

Chapter 4   **The Systems-theoretical General Offensive against the Idea of any Governance Capacity of Societies**   **99**

4.1	Luhmann's View of the Problem of Social Governance	99
4.1.1	Objections to Luhmann's Orthodoxy	107
4.1.2	The Complex and Fragile Relationship between Social Interdependence and the Self-referentiality of Subsystems	115

Chapter 5   **Initial Responses to the "Demystification of the State**   **120**

5.1	The New Modesty in the Discussion on Governance Theory Following the Ungovernability Debates and the Insecurities Generated by Luhmann	120
5.2	Policy Research in the Political and Administrative Sciences in Search of a Realistic Discussion on the State: Empirical Search Processes	125
5.2.1	From the Leviathan to the "Cooperative State"	125
5.2.2	A Differentiated View of Governance Activities	128
5.2.3	Partial Loss of State Sovereignty or the State as *Primus Inter Pares*?	131
5.2.4	The Discovery of the "Third Sector" by the Theory of the State	132
5.2.5	Institutional and Organizational Pluralism Instead of Market Versus State	138
5.2.6	The Palette of Governance Media	139
5.2.7	Results of the Reorientation in the Administrative and Political Sciences	143

**Part III   The Network Society: Further Development
               of Theories of Social Governance Capacity**

**Chapter 1   Network Theories: An Innovative Look at
              Altered Organizational Patterns in Societies
              Marked by a High Level of Division of Labor   147**

1.1   Network Phenomena in Economy and Society as a
        Reaction to Processes of Social Transformation and
        a "Response" to Luhmann's Complexity Problematic   148

1.2   Network Phenomena and the Limits of Hierarchical
        Governance   153

1.2.1   The Complexity Trap as a Core Problem of Hierar-
        chical Coordination   154

1.2.2   The State as the Agency of Social Integration? Re-
        marks on the Demanding Normative Foundations of
        Hierarchical Governance   156

1.3   Social Integration in Societies Marked by Division
        of Labour: A Problem Rediscovered, not a New Prob-
        lem   164

**Chapter 2   Analytical Network Theories as a New Per-
              spective on the Problem Posed by Social
              Governance   167**

2.1   The Limited Contributions Provided by Descriptive
        Approaches to Networks   168

2.2   Strengthening Social Governance Potentials by De-
        veloping Network Structures - (Partial) Answers to
        New Demands on Society and the (Partial) Loss of
        State Governance Autonomy   171

2.2.1   Networks as Organizational Patterns for Dealing
        with Reciprocal Dependence   171

2.2.2   Networks: Emergent Patterns of Organization and
        Governance beyond Markets and Hierarchies, or Hy-
        brid Forms?   175

2.2.3   Social Modernization as the Motor behind the Formation and the Universalization of Networks   178

2.2.4   The "Art of Separation" and the "Art of Connection"
- Reflections on the Organizational Patterns Underlying "Network Societies"   181

2.3   Elements of a Definition of the Network Phenomenon   186

**Chapter 3   Network Failure: The Problem Dimensions
of the Organization of Networks   190**

3.1   The Problem of Numbers   190

3.2   The Time Dimension of Decisions   193

3.3   Institutional Consolidation of Networks: Conditions
of and Problem Facing their Operation   196

3.4   The Coordination Problem   202

3.5   The Bargaining Dilemma   207

3.6   Power in Network Relationships   208

3.7   The Tense Relationship between Conflict and Cooperation   214

3.8   Instead of a Résumé: The Five Core Problems of
Network Governance   218

3.9   Governance Problems Resulting from the Interaction between Networks   222

**Chapter 4   Dimensions of the New Pattern of Organiza-
tion and Governance Designed to Mobilize
the Governance Potential in Network Societies   228**

4.1   Interest Constellations, Action Orientations, Value
Patterns, and Decision Styles in Network Structures   229

4.1.1   Conditions for Mastering the Dilemma Posed by
Typical Interest Constellations: The Simple Cases
(Prisoner's Dilemma and Chicken Game)   232

4.1.2	Conditions under which Complex Conflicts of Interest can be Mastered in Networks: The Difficult Case (Battle of the Sexes)	235
4.1.3	Three Decision Styles and their Effects on the Governance Behavior of Networks	238
4.1.4	The Problem of Justice in Network Structures: Reflections against the Background of the Studies of Rawls, Walzer, and Honneth	241
4.1.5	Résumé: Action Orientations and Decision Styles Capable of Overcoming the Pitfalls of Network Governance	258
4.2	The Social Functional Logic of Networks	263
4.2.1	Reciprocity as the Functional Principle of Networks Geared to Problem-solving	264
4.2.2	Trust as a Functional Condition of Network Governance	267
4.2.3	Dimensions of the Strategic Capacity of Network Actors and Networks	278
4.2.4	The "Radical Individualist": A Network Actor Doomed to Failure - The "Public-choice Society": Unsuited to Mobilizing the Governance Potential of Networks	282
4.3	Procedures and Institutional Mechanisms for Strengthening the Problem-solving Orientation in Networks	286
4.4	"Openness" of Network Structures as a Motor of Innovation	294
4.5	The Significance of Networks in Phases of the Policy Process	297
4.6	The Network Cycle - The Efficiency of the Network Society with Reference to the Governance of Incremental and Radical Social Change	308
4.6.1	The Dynamic Phase of a Network Cycle	310
4.6.2	The Phase of Exhaustion of the Network Cycle	313

4.6.3	The Phase of Upheaval of a Network Cycle	315
4.6.4	Three Patterns of Acceleration of the Process of Change Leading to New Development Corridors	317
4.7	On the Complementarity of Network Coordination and State-level Governance in the Network Society	325

Part IV **Social Governance Capacity and International Competitiveness**

Chapter 1 **Attempt at a Résumé and an Outlook: Contours of a Synthetic View of a New Organizational and Governance Pluralism in Network Societies** — **332**

1.1	The State of Governance Theory in the Context of the Network Discussion	332
1.2	An Enlightened Systems-theoretical View - and its Black Holes: The Conception of Helmut Willke	339
1.3	Theoretical Search Process with an Eye to Jürgen Habermas and Bernhard Peters	346

Chapter 2 **Conclusions Drown from the Governance Discussion on the Concept of "Systemic Competitiveness"** — **357**

2.1	The Macrolevel as the Framework for the Development of Competitiveness: The Primacy of Hierarchical Governance	357
2.2	The Mesolevel as the Locus at which Dynamic Competitive Advantages are Created: The World of Network Governance	360
2.3	The "New Production Paradigm" at the Microlevel: The World of Clusters	365
2.4	Organizational and Governance Pluralism at the Metalevel: Social Governance Capacity as a Condition for Economic Efficiency and Development	366

Notes   **368**

Bibliography   **379**

Figures in the Text

1   Determinants of Systemic Competitiveness   15

2   Determinants of Systemic Competitiveness   36

3   The State as Governance Center ·   57

4   Sectors of Society   135

5   Governance Media   141

6   The Coordination Problem   204

7   The Social Functional Logic of Networks   266

8   Dimensions of the Processing of Political Problems
         in Highly Differentiated Societies   348

Overviews in the Text

1   Instruments of State Locational Policy in Germany   26

2   Governance Problems from the Perspective of Dif-
         ferent Authors and Theories   97

3   Demands on State-level Governance   128

4   Phases of the Policy Process   142

5   Problem Dimensions and Pitfalls in Networks   219

6   The Five Core Problems of Network Governance   221

7   Interest Constellations Relevant in Networks   231

8   The Problem Field of "Justice" in a Developing
         Market Economy - A Heuristic Overview   260

Preliminary Remarks

The globalization of the economy has become an irreversible mega-trend in the world society. Dynamic economic development of both nations and regions is proceeding within the context of the world market economy. The building of internationally competitive economic structures is for that reason a challenge with which industrialized and developing nations as well as countries in transformation are alike confronted.

In view of the globalization of the economy the current discussion in the economic and social sciences often jumps to the overhasty conclusion that societies are losing more and more of their political governance capacity due to social and economic development processes and that the market principle is gaining in autonomy - and the consequent response is not seldom to affirm, or to resign to, the lack of alternatives to the neoliberal policy project. The present study, however, shows that economic development and the creation of competitiveness are - contrary to the view dominant among neoliberal economists - not based solely on liberal economic policies and a strengthening of market forces. The development of efficient industrial locations and competitive economies constitutes a challenge to society as a whole and its ability to focus its governance and problem-solving potentials.

One of the central conclusions of the present analysis is that, at the end of the twentieth century, the societies most effective in economic, social, and ecological terms will not be unleashed market economies but active and continuously learning societies which solve their problems on the basis of a complex organizational and governance pluralism; the study analyzes its contours, functional logics, as well as creativity and blockade potentials. True, the loss of governance capacity so often bewailed is a reality insofar as the traditional governance of society and economy by an autonomous state is approaching its limits. The study links economic approaches to the determinants of competitiveness with theories on the governance of societies stemming from the social sciences, in this way outlining a model of the "network society" which is grounded both empirically and theoretically, but also in normative terms. The aim is to describe new forms of governance that make it possible to frame policy even under the conditions of the world market economy. In this sense the study is a contribution to the discussion over different types of market economies now that the competition between capitalist and socialist systems has come to an end.

If it is to unfold its productive forces, and if its potentially destructive social and ecological secondary effects are to be contained, the market is in need of regulation and must be imbedded in an institutional and normative framework. At the same time, traditional statist economic policies and blueprints of society have reached a state of depletion. In view of the globalization of the economy, the growing and ever finer differentiation of society, and the complexity of the problems facing it, the nation state is losing its autonomy of action and scopes to shape policy. The state that is the object of modern theory of the state, i.e. a state that is sovereign both internally and externally, is in reality long since obsolete. The question is how the process of building international competitiveness and promoting broadly effective economic development can be governed under these conditions.

The analysis presented makes it clear that industrial and developing nations as well as countries in transformation in search of their place in the world economy are in the midst of a process of radical structural change affecting their patterns of social organization and governance and their approaches to problem-solving; this process, it is argued, is in terms of its impact entirely comparable to the upheavals underway in the spheres of economy and technology. But while, during the 1980s, at least a differentiated picture of the contours of the "New Production Paradigm" after the end of Fordism emerged, the picture we have of the forms, scopes, and limits of the political governance of development processes is - in view of the apparent lack of competence on the part of the planning state - far less clear. The gamut ranges from those who - for instance with reference to the development successes met with in Asia - have rediscovered the charm of the strong state, autonomous vis-à-vis society - to authors who (like Niklas Luhmann) regard any and all attempts to selectively govern economic and social processes as doomed to failure.

The concept "network society" is based on the fundamental premise that the claim to frame and govern development processes may not and must not be abandoned. Network societies are characterized by "divided and shared sovereignties." Governance potentials seep into society. It is becoming evident that the state's loss of autonomy does not automatically translate out as a gain in autonomy for other groups of actors. For example, locational policy: In a great variety of policy fields, such as education/training and research policy, industrial and technology policy, regional or environmental policy, state institutions no longer have the governance resources (e.g. knowledge about complex effective contexts in specific sectors, implementation capacities, control capacity) required to formulate policy independently of social actors. In other words, the state is on the one hand losing its autonomy of action in the field of economic policy in view of the globalization of the economy and the growing complexity of industrial production. On the other hand, firms are reliant on efficient industrial sites, science systems, institutional structures, political stability, and stable long-term expectations - i.e. effectiveness of government, effective and efficient intermediary institutions, and cooperation with other social institutions and groups of actors. The situation marked by interdependence between firms, public and private institutions, and social organizations gives rise to a field of action for economic policy in which market, state, and a variety of network structures have complementary roles to play.

Modern and modernizing societies, but also firms, clusters of firms, and large-scale organizations are alike confronted with a core problem: there are dynamic processes of differentiation at work in economy and society. This differentiation enhances the effectiveness, self-responsibility, creativity, and autonomy of the subsystems, though it at the same time also poses the danger of fragmentation and atomization of the overall system, i.e. for the case that coordination between the subsystems should fail and effective social integration fail to materialize. Growing differentiation, decentralization, and the redistribution of governance resources and action potentials to a great variety of actors are thus the motors of "learning societies", while they at the same time jeopardize the reproduction of the overall system, the polity, or complex networks of firms.

The task of securing coordination between the subsystems as well as ensuring social integration - which, thanks to "divided sovereignties," can be guaranteed neither through hierarchical decision-making nor exclusively by decentral self-organization - is becoming one of the crucial challenges facing economies and societies; these are marked by a paradox noted by Niklas Luhmann: the trend toward an increasing independence of their subsystems, accompanied by a simultaneous interdependence of problem contexts. Network structures are on the one hand an expression of these processes of differentiation, and on the other hand they constitute organizational patterns capable of dealing with complexity and the phenomenon of independence-interdependence.

The network society is accordingly characterized by an organizational and governance pluralism that was not acknowledged in the dichotomist debate of the 1980s over the issue of "market versus state". Beside law, power, and money as the classical governance media, the flow of information, the skills involved in communication and the development of a problem-solving orientation shared by groups of social actors and policy arenas, and the ability to organize continuous social search and learning processes are gaining in significance for the governance capacity of societies.

It is also becoming evident that the functioning of market economies and network societies is reliant on specific action orientations on the part of actors as well as on systems of social values. Market economies need for their reproduction social resources and action orientations that the market itself is unable to create - and which it may at times even undermine. The market's competitive dynamics encourage innovative competition, creativity, and self-responsibility - but also egoism and the erosion of social solidarity. The social functional logic of networks is based on reciprocity, trust, a willingness to compromise on the part of actors, voluntary restriction of one's own freedom to act, and fair exchange. In the network society the relation between these action orientations is one of unresolvable tension, and its balance must constantly be worked out anew. One thing is becoming clear: the ideal type of the egoistic *homo oeconomicus* - stylized since the 1980s, in the context of neoliberal hegemony, as the maxim, as it were, governing all activity - is no longer adequate to the demands posed by the network society. And: it is not only institutional structures and organizations but also systems of social values and action orientations that will have to be cultivated, modernized and advanced.

The network society is a dynamic and at the same time fragile system. Market, state, and networks can complement each other productively and contribute to enhancing the learning and problem-solving capacities of societies, though they can also obstruct one another as a result of different types of failure on the part of market, state, and networks. The presentation of the structures and dynamics of the network society opens up a perspective on governance and problem-solving potentials - and the limits associated with them - that have their locus beyond the simplified logics of the planning state and the perfect market. Linkage of the concept of "systemic competitiveness" with the model of the "network society" leads to general propositions and conclusions on the institutional design of societies that are able, even under the conditions emerging at the end of the 20th century, to process complex problems and secure the future of politics and democratic control even over development processes in the context of global market economy. The concept of "systemic competitiveness" and the model of the "network society" can therefore offer an orientation for industrialized and developing nations as well as countries in transformation, all of which are faced with the challenge of linking economic efficiency with social justice and ecological sustainability.

January 1997   Dirk Messner

Introduction and Formulation of the Problem

"What we call the beginning is often the end. And to make an end is to make a beginning. The end is where we start from."
T.S. Eliot, quoted after: Azian/Nochteff (1994), p. 103

The present study is situated at the point of intersection of three fields of research. The **first point of departure** is the empirical fact of the failure of one-sidedly inward-looking and interventionist industrialization strategies in developing countries as well as in socialist states. The corollary is that in many countries of the South and the East, following years of orientation in terms of the concept of import-substituting industrialization, the time has come for a fundamental rethinking of economic policy.[1] The challenge facing these countries is that in the future they will have to reorient themselves in terms of the frame of reference defined by the world market, i.e. they will have to build up internationally competitive economies. This means that these countries are confronted with problems that have also assumed great significance in the industrialized countries and are the subject of intensive discussion.

We see in retrospect that the neoliberal structural adjustment programs of the 1908s were unable to show the developing countries a way out of the crisis. In the countries in transformation, i.e. in the process of transition form a planned to a market economy, similar projects are also proving to be undercomplex. The notion that even a correction of the macroeconomic framework could serve to strengthen the competitiveness of the economy and lead to dynamic economic and social development is an illusion. Also, policies one-sidedly geared to setting free the forces of the market have not infrequently intensified tendencies toward social disintegration.

In the 1980s, in the wake of the hegemony of neoliberalism, an interesting and unorthodox debate emerged on the determinants of international competitiveness after the end of Fordism. This search process, expressed in a number of studies published since the end of the 1980s, is the **second point of departure** of the present study. The new approaches to competitiveness are fed by a great variety of different

sources, and yet they all arrive at convergent and complementary results: industrial sociologists point to the increasing significance of in-
company decentralization and intracompany division of labor for the
efficiency of business enterprises. The catchword "systemic rationalization" sums up this discussion (see Altmann/Sauer 1989). Studies
based on innovation theory point to the specific character of the new
technologies and their effects on the determinants of competitiveness.
This view makes it plain that the foundation of viable economic development is constituted not by a country's static cost advantages or given
resources endowment but by dynamic, knowledge-based competitive
advantages that emerge in "national innovation systems" (see OECD/
TEP 1991, 1992, Lundvall 1992 and Nelson 1994; Hurtienne/Messner
1994, Messner/Meyer-Stamer 1993). The studies based on innovation
theory have, in particular, come from the surroundings of the OECD
Development Center. Michael Porter, originally more at home in the
field of microeconomics, has contributed a well-received approach to
the discussion on competitiveness. He sees the economic efficiency of
countries as localized in the existence of clusters of firms (and institutions) in which "national competitive advantages" emerge (Porter
1990). Finally, regional economic approaches geared to working out
the collective and geographically bound character of efficiency are cur-
rently experiencing a renaissance (see Schmitz/Nadvin 1994; Brusco
1990; Krummbein 1991). All these concepts emphasize the "man-
made" character of competitiveness and the importance of institutional
structures, the surroundings of firms (economic locations) for economic development. **Part I** of the present study presents the outlines of the
concept of "systemic competitiveness" (see Eßer et al. 1996). This concept is meant as a frame of reference for industrialized economies and
economies in the process of development and transformation, one that
can be used to develop their specific national competitive advantages.

The frame of reference of systemic competitiveness, developed at the
German Development Institute (GDI) in collaboration with the author
of the present study, does not represent a model in competition with the
unorthodox approaches to competitiveness addressed above. Rather, it
complements, expands, and synthesizes them, weighting the specific

determinants of competitiveness in a way that differs from the other concepts addressed.

In the course of the preliminary work that went into the making of the study on systemic competitiveness, it became more and more clear that the core of the challenge of strengthening and optimizing (national) competitive advantages and creating conditions favorable to a dynamization of economic and social development consists less in working out a highly differentiated package of economic and locational policy instruments - although, in view of the persistent dominance of neoliberal economic policies in many countries, we are no doubt also faced with a lack of creativity in this respect. The systemic character of competitiveness implies, rather, far-reaching social challenges: competitiveness emerges not only at the company level, supported by the innovation-friendly policies of an efficient state. If this were the case, competitiveness would emerge on the basis of programs designed to promote private industry and direct investment, in combination with efforts geared to modernizing the state ("good governance", in current development jargon) and implementing an economic policy devised with an eye to the "success cases in the world economy."

The fact of the matter is, however, that international competitiveness - owing to the increasing significance of industrial clusters, regional economic zones, and network structures between firms and their environment based on collective efficiency - results from *specific patterns of social organization and governance*, and that little is known about their structure, internal logic, and development dynamics. In successful economies it appears to be possible to better focus social creativity and learning potentials than is the case in weaker economic systems. But what, in fact, is it that characterizes successful countries and economies?

The discussion over the institutional-organizational and social factors crucial to an economy's competitiveness is nowhere near the state of maturity that has been reached by the studies on the contours of the "new production paradigm" at the company level or the state of the discussion concerning the fundamental orientation of macroeconomic policy. As far as the macro- and microeconomic dimensions of competitiveness are concerned, convergence can be observed in the positions advanced by the various theoretical approaches. There are, however, as yet no signs of an approximation to a common model or even of a broad-based controversy over the institutional-organizational and social dimension of competitiveness and economic development.

The present study foregrounds this issue. Its has set itself the task of defining, under the conditions of the "new production paradigm," the institutional designs, social rules, ways of limiting and optimizing the market and shaping the relationship between state and social actors that can serve to release economic and social dynamics. The analysis of the determinants of competitiveness and dynamic development lead into the issue of the organizational and governance capacities available in societies. The governance theories developed by the social sciences constitute the **third point of departure** of this study.

Parts II and III of the study, its nucleus, seek to reconstruct and further develop the governance discussion in the social sciences. Here it will become evident that it is hardly possible to use the reception of the literature in the social sciences on the issue of "governance capacities of and in societies" to derive directly any cogent answer to the question concerned with an optimal institutional design, political regulation patterns, and the determinants of a dynamic and learning society - as the foundations of competitive economies. What is to be observed here are theoretical search processes that have not yet come to a conclusion. The most extreme poles are on the one hand traditional statist approaches and on the other conceptions pointing to society's self-organizing capacity, the state's loss of significance as a central actor of governance, and the generally increasing loss of governance potentials in complex societies. This debate is looked into and analyzed as to its usefulness for developing a concept of systemic competitiveness.

We can note an interesting convergence here. The growing functional differentiation of societies, the emergence of an increasing number of efficient actors and institutions, and the growth in complexity associated with these factors are both an expression and a condition of modernization. This is also true, as is demonstrated by the theorists of competitiveness, for the economy: what has proven to be particularly efficient are clusters, i.e. firms integrated within networks, and/or industrial districts, which are marked by a high level of vertical and horizontal concentration of a variety of interacting firms and organizations. This is likewise true, as is shown by the analyses presented by governance theories, for the political arena: the increasing differentiation of the institutional system and society's organizational capacity are consequences of democratization and the will and ability of social actors to participate. In dynamic societies these elements combine to form growing collective problem-solving capacities.

There is general agreement on the trend toward increasing differentiation in modern societies in the course of their modernization, though this is not at all the case when the issue concerned is the implications this state of affairs has for the governance capacity of societies. What is surprising is the at time ambivalent relationship between the modernization of societies and the possibilities available to shape this process. The dilemma is that on the one hand the organizational capacity of society and the efficiency of a growing number of actors constitute motors of development, while on the other hand these motors can become obstacles to development to the extent that they (can) give rise to crippling divergencies of interests and pronounced vested group interests that may confront state actors during the process of policy formulation. Growing social differentiation and the formation of groups of efficient actors and institutions can heighten the rationality of subsystems, while at the same time increasing the irrationality of the whole. The study seeks to clarify the question under what conditions modernization gains are possible and when pathologies are apt to occur.

The study discusses in two respects the formation of new patterns of organization and governance in modern and modernizing societies. On the one hand it works out the dynamics inherent to changes of basic social structures, seeking in doing so to establish the reasons responsible for the fact that governance by the state sometime succeeds and sometimes ends up in a situation of overregulation and crippling bureaucratization. And why, the study asks, is it that close cooperative relations between the state and private actors lead in some cases to clientelism, corruption, and political blockades, while in other cases the same approach can be pinpointed as the foundation of social integration capacity and dynamic economic and social development? These "blind spots" and "gaps in our knowledge" are looked into, the aim being to set up a frame of reference that can help to understand, and to structure, the organizational and governance pluralism typical of post-Fordist societies. The further course of the argumentation presented here will have recourse to, and further develop, in particular studies by Dahrendorf, Elias, Honneth, Mayntz, Mancur Olson, Scharpf, Rawls, and Walzer. A critical discussion of public-choice theory forms the focal point here. On the other hand, in the course of the reconstruction of theories of governance changes affecting the institutional design of societies are viewed with reference to upheavals in the economic field. The study here develops the thesis that societies that gear their efforts one-sidedly to the institutional concept of and the normative system of rules and values stemming from the public-choice theory - dominant in many discussions in the field of social and economic sciences - will prove largely unable to deal effectively with the economic and social demands posed by the future. There are many indications that the radical-neoliberal theories at home in the theories of the social and economic sciences, and the political projects derived from them, will prove inadequate to meet the challenges posed by a globalizing world - at least as long as the goal is to retain the model of a democratically organized welfare state governed by the rule of law.

The final section, **Part IV**, seeks on the one hand to draw conclusions from the governance debate in the social sciences and to develop the contours of a synthetic view of "network societies". On the other hand, conclusions are drawn from the governance-theory debate for the concept of systemic competitiveness. The study notes that, and points out how, the challenge involved for countries aiming for international competitiveness, and the problem of social and economic development in general, can be conceptualized as a problem of social organizational and governance capacity.

Part I The Concept of "Systemic Competitiveness" - An Approach to the Development of National Competitiveness and Locational Advantages

The analyses of competitiveness presented by Porter (1990) and the OECD's innovation researchers (OECD/TEP 1991, 1992), and the theorists of industrial districts (Becattini 1989, 1990; Nadvi/Schmitz 1994; Pyke 1990) are marked by a basic pattern of argumentation that sets them off against both neoliberal and traditional structuralist concepts: the studies in question aim on the one hand at not restricting the discussion of international competitiveness solely to the firm level. They focus on the development of the competitive power of national economies and/or regional industrial locations that cannot be grasped as a simple aggregation of the positions assumed by individual firms in international markets. On the other hand, and in contrast to static textbook models, in their studies they go beyond the given factors and structures of comparative advantages and disadvantages and focus specifically on the development and dynamization of such determinants of competitiveness. The learning processes of the actors and institutions involved, concealed as they are behind the structure, are made into the subject of analysis. This perspective obviates any one-dimensional explanatory approaches, pointing instead to the complexity of determinants of international competitiveness, the interactions of which constitute a multidimensional system. Orientations hitherto understood as opposites are seen as structural characteristics of the "new paradigm": competition and cooperation (between firms as well as between institutions); globalization of the economy, and a new look at the role of regional or even local policies in improving locational quality; strengthening market forces (even within firms; see the establishment of profit centers) and politically governed coordination processes geared to improving external economies and shaping locational policies.

The concept *"Systemic Competitiveness"*, which will be sketched briefly in what follows, was developed at the German Development Institute (GDI) against the background of this innovative theoretical studies as well as a series of empirical investigations conducted by the GDI. The concept is not conceived as a model competing with the studies published by the OECD-researchers, Porter or the district theorists; it is instead intended to complement and extend the existing studies on competitiveness. The intention is a twofold one: on the one hand, the gain in knowledge brought about by the new theories of competitiveness as regards the cumulative, interactive, and nonlinear character of innovations and competitive advantages corresponds with a lack of concrete policy recommendations. The GDI-study entitled *"Systemic Competitiveness - International Competitiveness and Demands on Policy"* (Esser et al. 1996) explicitly aims at drawing from the ongoing debate over the determinants of competitiveness conclusions regarding economic and locational policy. On the other hand, it became more and more clear in the course of the study that the core of the challenge posed by the process of the development of (national) competitive advantages consists not so much in the availability of a package of economic- and locational-policy instruments (though, in view of the persistent dominance of neoliberal economic policy in many industrial and developing countries as well as in countries in the process of transformation, there is no doubt a lack here as well). Instead, the systemic character of competitiveness implies further-reaching social challenges: it is not only at the company level, supported by innovation-friendly policies devised by an efficient state, that competitiveness emerges. If this were the case, it would be possible for just about any country to generate competitiveness through a program designed to promote direct investment, combined with efforts geared to modernize the state (in the current jargon of development policy: *good governance*) and to implement an economic policy keyed to the "success cases in the world economy". But the fact is that, owing to the increasing significance of industrial clusters, regional economic zones, and networking between firms and their environment - emphasized by Porter or the district theorists - as the foundations of "collective efficiency", international competitiveness is based on specific patterns of social organization, on economic and social systems. Thus far little is known about their structures, internal logics, and development dynamics, for which reason, and due to the fact that complex forms of social organization always have their history and are slow to change, they are difficult to copy. In successful economies it seems to be possible to better focus social creativity and learning potentials than is the case in more weak economic systems. It is for this reason of course always advisable to learn from "formulas for success" of dynamic countries, though it is enormously difficult to transfer these formulas.

As far as the contours of the "New Production Paradigm" at the company level and the basic orientation of macroeconomic policy are concerned, convergent positions are emerging in the debate over competitiveness. There is still controversy over the significance of selective locational policies for the development of competitive advantages. As yet, there are no signs of any approximation to a common model, or even of a clear-cut controversy over the organizational, social dimension of competitiveness. The new concepts of competitiveness are linked without any theoretical foundation with relatively traditional notions of the state: the strong and planning state of the structuralist school appears (Porter's arguments on the problematic of developing countries thrust in this direction); neoliberal approaches to the function of the state as the agent responsible for defining the macroeconomic framework (e.g. Porter's remarks on the industrialized countries) and concepts emphasizing the self-organization capacity of society or more or less unspecified patterns of organization and governance "beyond market and state" (e.g. in the district studies; also in Porter in his comments on cluster formation; the OECD theorists) are presented; other studies focus on neocorporatist theories emphasizing the close linkage between the state and industrial federations (e.g. in the studies published by CEPAL; see Hurtienne/Messner 1994).

Accordingly, the question is: what institutional designs, sets of social rules, forms of delimitation and optimization of the market, and what relationship between state and social actors are, under the conditions of the "new production paradigm", apt to give rise to economic and social development dynamics. Analysis of the determinants of competitiveness invariably leads to the question as to the organizational and governance capacity of societies. This dimension of competitiveness is at the root of the GDI-concept on "Systemic Competitiveness"; the intention of the present study is to deepen it. The main outlines of the concept will first be discussed.

1   The Four Levels of Systemic Competitiveness

Industrial competitiveness comes about neither spontaneously as a result of a change in the macroframework nor solely through entrepreneurship at the microlevel. It is instead the outcome of a pattern of complex and dynamic interaction between state, firms, intermediary institutions, and the organizational capacity of given societies. And what is essential here is a competition-oriented incentive system that compels firms to engage in learning processes and step up their efficiency. In the end, however, the competitiveness of firms rests on a society's overall organizational pattern. Parameters relevant to competition at all system levels, and the interrelation of these levels, give rise to competitive advantages. The OECD refers to the competitiveness that emerges in this way as *"structural"* (OECD 1992, p. 243). The GDI gives preference to the concept *"systemic competitiveness"* in order to underline the following aspects: an economy's competitiveness is first based on targeted and interlinked measures at three system levels (the macro-, micro- and mesolevels). The activity and specific dynamics at these levels, and their interplay, are shaped by different institutional structures specific to individual countries, organizational patterns, the ability of groups of social actors to learn and adapt, and their integration within specific normative value contexts. The micro-, macro-, and mesolevels are imbedded in these social dimensions (the metalevel). Competitiveness emerges in firms, though it cannot be reduced to their activities; international competitiveness can be understood only within the context of social patterns of organization.

This view stands in contradiction to the underlying premises of mainstream economics. Neoliberal theorists proceed on the assumption that economic development is based on a pattern of social organization and governance which (apart from the state's framework-setting function) is characterized by the principle of the freedom of decision, individual scopes of action, and the uncoordinated competition of individual activities; from these result concrete economic outcomes that then, again, constitute the basis of economic activity. Seen from this perspective, competition and the price system are the decisive governance mechanisms of the *"method of discovery"* (Hayek) in market economies; these are otherwise characterized by *"basic anarchy"* (Röpcke). Michalski sums up this position in the following way: *"... a competition-oriented market economy represents the mechanism best suited to meet, constructively, flexibly, and without excessive costs, the challenges of constantly changing social, economic, and technical environmental conditions... A further important precondition for the satisfactory operation of the system of market economy is relatively stable international framework conditions and the confidence of market participants in the continued existence of a free multilateral system of trade and payment..."* (Michalski 1985, pp. 217 f.).

The option best suited to coming to terms with the process of structural change is seen above all in a macroeconomic policy *"in which governments rely primarily on the ability of the market economy to regulate itself and to coordinate decentral producer and consumer decisions. In this case the thrust of economic-policy activity is based on regulative economic policy (*Ordungspolitik*) and competition policy as well as on the macroeconomic measures of monetary, credit, and financial policy"* (Michalski 1985, pp. 224 f.).

The concept of systemic competitiveness differs clearly, in two respects, from neoliberal economic concepts: it on the one hand emphasizes the strategic significance of selective locational policies at the mesolevel, i.e. at the level of institutions and intercompany networks; it on the other hand points out that the alternative of "market versus plan", which is still current among the neoliberals and in which the advantages and disadvantages of specifically one-dimensional governance mechanisms are processed, fails to do justice to the core of the governance problematic in highly differentiated societies and economies, thus missing its chance to provide an interesting contribution to understanding the determinants of competitiveness. The task at hand is instead to decipher the structures and functional logics of the multidimensional organizational and governance mechanisms that have emerged in complex societies.

The concept "systemic competitiveness" constitutes a frame of reference for industrialized and developing countries alike. Its basic premise is that medium- and long-term perspectives (visions) and the intensive interaction among the actors involved should not merely aim at optimizing performance potentials at different system levels and mobilizing social creativity potentials so as to build national competitive advantages. A given country cannot simply pick out from the set of determinants (system levels and instruments of governance) the individual policies or elements it finds attractive. Particularly competitive countries have

- structures at the **metalevel** that promote competitiveness,

- a **macroframework** that exerts performance pressure on firms and a structured **mesospace** in which state and social actors negotiate targeted support policies and advance the formation of structures,

- at the **microlevel**, a variety of firms which aspire to efficiency, quality, flexibility, and responsiveness and many of which are integrated within networks.

By way of contrast, developing countries and countries in transformation generally display grave shortcomings at all four levels. What are the approaches open to developing countries that wish to build internationally competitive industries or convert existing industries into internationally competitive ones? What measures will have to be taken first? The experiences of a number of successful and less successful countries suggest the following propositions:[1]

1. It is above all important that the economic **macroframework** be **stable** (i.e. inflation, budget deficit, exchange rate, and debt be within manageable proportions and, in addition, the rules of economic policy

not be constantly altered; only in this way can investment security come about) and that the macropolicy send clear, unmistakable signals which indicate to firms that they will have to come closer to the **internationally usual efficiency level**. Trade policy can make a contribution here to the extent that protection against imports is reduced in successive and predictable stages. Competition policy can play an important part in preventing the emergence of monopoly situations.

2. Though **stabilization at the macrolevel** is a necessary precondition, it is **not a condition sufficient** for any sustainable development of competitiveness. It is equally important that **mesopolicies be put in place**. But it makes little sense to formulate such policies as long as the task of stabilizing the macroframework has not been tackled. Technology policy, for example, will attain its goal of strengthening the technological competence of firms only when entrepreneurs themselves have set their sights on competitiveness. Selective import protection can only contribute to strengthening industries when firms in fact make use of the time available to become competitive.

3. Many developing countries and ex-socialist economies that long had an inward-looking stance are marked by social development blockades and lack of consensus on the direction that a future development strategy should take (**blockades at the metalevel**). It was with this problem that, for instance, the Latin American countries were confronted in the 1980s. In the phase of upheaval leading the way to a world economy, it is essential that a growing consensus emerge on the direction of development in order to overcome social blockades. This is a precondition for the creation of competence in the spheres of policy and strategy on the part of the most important groups of actors, for social search processes geared to approaching the new rough pattern of industrial development, and for the development of state-level and intermediary institutions that make it possible to shape the macro- and mesodimensions (**consensus-building in the fields of politics and economic policy**). The dynamics of this process will, however, differ in terms of the sociocultural structures of the societies in question (traditions, values, fundamental social organizational and power structures), and these tend

to change only very slowly (**capacities for social organization and integration**).

Stabilization of the macroframework, consensus-building, and meso-policies place considerable demands on the organizational capacities of societies, on their political-administrative systems and intermediary institutions. The difficulty encountered in meeting these demands is the central characteristic of industrial backwardness; in many developing countries and countries in transformation incomplete nation-building processes, social polarization, disintegration phenomena, and other unfavorable factors at the metalevel inhibit, even over the medium term, any industrial development aiming at international competitiveness.

Aside from "inward-looking" efforts in the process of building competitive and locational advantages, the significance of regional cooperation and integration is also on the rise. Cooperation between neighboring states in regional trade and integration groups is becoming more and more important as a means of enlarging the market dimension - and with it the interest of potential domestic and foreign investors - and jointly improving the supply-side conditions for given economies, e.g. regional transportation, telecommunications, and energy networks, or the existing technology base.

What is required in the end also includes development of an international regulatory framework. Following the collapse of the socialist states and the failure of state-capitalist development strategies beyond the world market, a new world economy has been developing in the 1990s, and it embraces now - for the first time - all nations. Globalization of the economy calls for international rules to ensure a minimum level of governance of global market processes. The most important of these are agreements on a further reduction of trade barriers, in particular of the protectionist barriers put up by the industrialized countries against products from developing countries and regulation of the international financial markets. As a means of effectively countering the concomitant speculation in the areas of exchange rates and interest rates, in the face of which every national central bank is powerless,

James Tobin, for instance, proposed as early as 1978 to tax international financial transactions on a worldwide basis.[2]

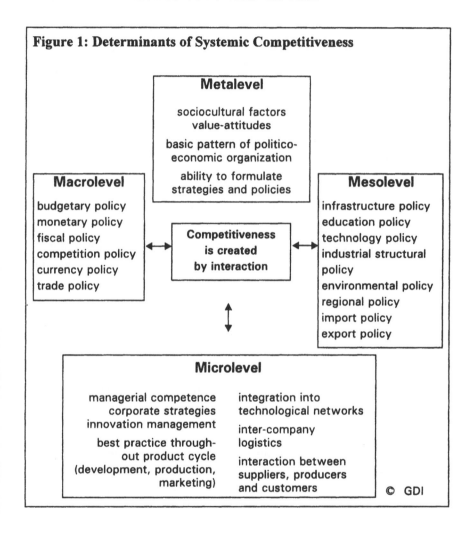

Figure 1: Determinants of Systemic Competitiveness

Metalevel

sociocultural factors
value-attitudes

basic pattern of politico-economic organization

ability to formulate strategies and policies

Macrolevel

budgetary policy
monetary policy
fiscal policy
competition policy
currency policy
trade policy

Competitiveness is created by interaction

Mesolevel

infrastructure policy
education policy
technology policy
industrial structural policy
environmental policy
regional policy
import policy
export policy

Microlevel

managerial competence
corporate strategies
innovation management
best practice throughout product cycle
(development, production, marketing)

integration into technological networks

inter-company logistics

interaction between suppliers, producers and customers

© GDI

In other words, the concept of systemic competitiveness is concerned not with *"rejecting the world-market perspective"* (Altvater 1994, p. 347) but with working out political scopes of action both within nation states and at the level of regional economic cooperation between countries under the existing difficult world-economic conditions. There is no disagreement on the fact that the world economy should develop a "regulative framework" to compensate for structural disadvantages faced by weaker economies and, in particular, to limit the instabilities stemming from the international financial markets. Nevertheless, the concept of systemic competitiveness focuses on working out the demands on and scopes open to national locational policies.

2   Essential Requirements at the Macrolevel

The whole structural adjustment debate in the 1980s over developing countries focused on macroeconomic reforms. The result today is that there is in the discussion of development policy a large measure of consensus on the point that a permanently unstable macroeconomic framework has a negative impact on the functioning of factor and commodity markets, inhibits investment, and reduces the chances of growth. If they are to safeguard their macroeconomic stability, many developing countries and countries in transformation need to reform their fiscal and budgetary policies, their monetary and exchange-rate policies, and, in particular, their exchange-rate policies in order to stabilize their economies and pave the way for a successive orientation in terms of the frame of reference defined by the world market. Transition from an unstable to a stable macroframework is difficult for the following reasons:

-       Fighting **inflation** by means of a restrictive budgetary, fiscal, and monetary policy often leads to a retrenchment of both consumption and investment, and thus to a further reduction of the economy's scope for growth.

-       Macroeconomic **stabilization measures** will as a rule bite only when they are accompanied by protracted parallel structural reforms, for instance a reform of the public economic sector, development of an efficient financial sector, and reform of foreign-trade policy.

- There are often **goal conflicts** between individual reform measures, which protracts the period of time needed for the reforms to
  become effective.

- **Adjustment costs** are felt immediately, while adjustment gains
  take time to materialize, so that production, investment, and employment start out, in the initial phase, by developing negatively.

- The **social groups** involved are not uniformly affected by the impacts of macroeconomic stabilization measures and the structural
  reforms accompanying them. Instead, there are in this process
  winners and losers, and this, accordingly, gives rise to internal
  conflicts.

The "early" structural adjustment programs of IMF and World Bank,
initiated at the beginning of the 1980s, in many cases failed due to the
fact that these economic goal conflicts and political and social costs
were not perceived. In the 1990s the same phenomenon has surfaced in
many countries in transformation: the reform strategies geared to short-
term correction of macroeconomic data neglected the time dimension
of structural adjustment, necessary social and environmental reforms,
which as a rule require large financial transfers from outside,[3] and the
social character of the reform programs. It is, however, in the end only
reform-minded national coalitions that that are capable of implementing any far-reaching macroeconomic reform. The idea that structural
adjustment "from outside", i.e. conducted through international financial institutions, can be governed successfully has proven to be an illusion (Hübner 1992, Khan/Knight 1985, Wade 1990).

If an internal balance is be secured, it is necessary to consolidate the
state budget and to run a nonexpansive monetary policy. It is, however,
not seldom that, under the conditions of underdeveloped financial and
capital markets, monetary-policy efforts run up against tight limitations, since the instruments usually deployed, such as credit rationing,
selective credit allocation, and arbitrarily fixed interest rates, tend more
to further distort financial and capital markets than to influence the
volume of credit in the manner intended. In the last analysis, any effec-

tive monetary policy presupposes comprehensive reform of the financial sector.

In terms of external economic activity, the concern must be to reform
trade and foreign-exchange policies. The experience made during the
1970s and 1980s indicates that sharply overvalued exchange rates invariably lead to high current-account deficits, since, above all, they
place obstacles in the way of exports, while at the same time encouraging imports. Countries that permit an overvaluation of their currency
over the long term are obstructing the development of their production
capacities. An exchange-rate level tending toward a sharp anti-export
bias must therefore be avoided at all costs. The exchange rate is not
merely one price among many others. Indeed, it must be seen as a strategic variable that determines whether an economy will be able to create the macroeconomic framework required to build internationally
competitive industries. There are, however, strict limits to any national
controls on exchange rates, since flows in the international financial
markets have been deregulated and are for the most part speculative in
nature. It is here that international regulations would be required to
restrict the allocative efficiencies of an untrammeled market.

As in the case of exchange-rate policy, it is essential that firms be given
clear signals from trade policy, signals that induce them to gear their
strategies to the world market as a frame of reference. Here we are
faced with two fundamentally different concepts. More orthodox neoliberal economists call for general liberalization of imports. This approach aims at bringing about a low and unified tariff applicable to all
categories of goods. It places its trust in the validity of the principle of
comparative cost advantages and accepts the fact that only those industries will survive that are in tune with a country's given factor endowment. This approach thus aims more for a liberalization of exports that
is not only nondiscriminatory but at the same time very rapid as well.

The experience of newly industrialized countries (NICs) in Asia as
well as the results of the structural-adjustment policies of the 1980s
suggest, in contrast, that it could make more sense to liberalized imports selectively and on a step-by-step basis. Imports should be liberal-

ized along the lines of a liberalization schedule developed on the basis of an analysis of the actually predictable response potentials of existing industries or devised with an eye to the development requirements of new industrial cores. Trade policy in this way becomes a component of a policy focusing on an active shaping of industrial structures. Selective import liberalization aims at avoiding any excessive adjustment strain on firms and providing industries the time they need for learning processes. Counties like Korea or Taiwan have been pursuing this approach for some thirty years now (Hillebrand 1991, Wade 1990, Messner 1994).

3   New Demands at the Company Level

In the 1980s the industrialized countries as well as the advanced developing nations implemented far-reaching company-level restructuring processes that caused them to question the wisdom of the traditonal Fordist production paradigm. A new best practice is emerging, and its contours worked out, in the context of the Japan discussion, in a number of studies from the fields of innovation theory (see Dosi et al. 1990, and Lundvall 1988) and industrial sociology (see Womack et al., Meyer-Stamer 1990 and 1991).The picture that emerges is largely consonant with Porter's work on the development of firm clusters, and thus the matter need not be looked into in any more depth at this point.

It can be noted here that the concept of the fully automated, computer-controlled factory as the optimal organizational model has run aground. As Womack, Jones, and Roos noted in their much-discussed study comparing the Japanese and the North American auto industries: "... *high-tech plants that are improperly organized end up adding about as much indirect technical and service workers as they remove unskilled direct workers from manual assembly tasks. What's more, they have a hard time maintaining high yield, because breakdowns in the complex machinery reduce the fraction of the total operating time that a plant is actually producing vehicles"* (Womack/Jones/Roos 1990, p. 94).

The new production paradigm is no longer characterized by the Babbage principle and Taylorization, with their advantages in terms of specialization and securing in-plant power structures. It is based, as Meyer-Stamer shows, on thrusts in innovation at three levels:

- on in-plant organizational innovations (e.g. logistic concepts, order-related final assembly, just in time, reduction of cycle times, new forms of quality control) and intercompany innovations (e.g. intercompany logistics, development of relatively stable supplier relationships);

- on social innovations (e.g. flexibilized deployment of labor, group work, reduction of levels of hierarchy, return of responsibilities to the shopfloor level);

- on technical innovations (e.g. digitalization and electronic networking of machinery, computer-aided design, computer-aided planning, computer-aided manufacturing) (Meyer-Stamer 1991 and 1995).

Seen from the perspective of governance and organization theory, it is interesting that the hierarchical governance of firms by a corporate headquarters - as the classical Fordist management concept - is undergoing modification. Firms are strengthening their horizontal levels; the basic challenges consist in developing functioning forms of horizontal and vertical networking and providing for good lines of communication between more and more autonomous corporate divisions. Corporate headquarters is no longer responsible for the central guidance of the overall corporate organization. In many areas it instead assumes moderator functions as a means of mobilizing the creativity and performance potentials of different corporate divisions and promoting and optimizing the coordination between in-company subsystems, the task of headquarters being to develop and implement an overall strategy.

More and more significance is accruing to the "external relations" of firms, a growing number of which are organized in interfirm networks or clusters. Reduction of manufacturing depth and specialization in terms of segments of the "value-added chain" evidently contribute to boosting productivity and accelerating collective learning processes, though it at the same time also steps up the demands placed on the organizational competence of the firms concerned. Organizational know-how is becoming a key factor of competitiveness, while, as late as the end of the 1980s, the discussion over the "new production paradigm" was still restricted to technical innovations.

4 Shaping Structures in the Mesodimension - The Relevance of Selective Policies

4.1 The Significance of the Mesodimension

In connection with structural adjustment in the 1980s, macroeconomic reforms and the company-level modernization measures made possible and forced through via these reforms were seen as the key to strengthening competitiveness. This view neglects the significance of building and expanding economic locations and constantly optimizing the environment of firms. In contrast to neoclassical allocation and foreign-trade theory, which - with reference to properly functioning technology markets and the optimal nature of corporate decisions taken at decentral levels - rejects any active, anticipatory industrial and technology policies, those industrialized countries and NICs developed most dynamically in the 1980s, improving their position in the hierarchy of the world economy, that worked toward selectively optimizing the mesodimension situated between the macroeconomic framework and the microlevel.

The significance of locational policies is also addressed in Porter's studies and, in particular, by the OECD's researchers and the theorists of the industrial districts. The GDI's view differs from the above-discussed strands of the discussion insofar as it accords special significance to this dimension and points to the specific functional logic of this policy field. It is in the mesodimension that organizational patterns and forms of policy develop that on the one hand differ fundamentally from the classical top-down industrial and locational policies of the past and on the other hand point to far-reaching changes in basic social structures.[4]

The market alone does not provide for an optimal shaping of industrial locations. At the same time the "development state" called for by the structuralist school is overburdened when faced with the task of conceiving an efficient industrial structure. Novel patterns of social organization and more complex governance patterns are taking shape in countries that operate successful locational policies. Innovative networks consisting of banks, business firms, and public and private intermediary institutions make it possible to shape structures in the mesodimension with an eye to the longer term. It is in particular the Japanese success story that demonstrates that creative organizational forms in this "third arena of allocation" (Teubner 1992) provide a decisive contribution to building national competitive advantages.

Just how central this field, so neglected in terms of economic policy, is for the development of sustainable competitiveness is also shown by the fact that a number of developing countries (e.g. Bolivia) have, within the context of structural adjustment programs, managed quite well to stabilize their economic framework conditions, but without achieving the anticipated effect of a reactivation of their economies (Messner 1993). The reason for this is that their production sites are not developed and, in some cases, important locational factors were further weakened (e.g. education and training, research and development) within the framework of the adjustment measures devised with an eye to budget consolidation. Even in high-growth countries like Chile we find that the transition from a resource-based export phase to a technology-based growth sequence tends to meet with little success when macroeconomic policies are not selectively complemented by strategies in the mesodimension. Thanks to its high, albeit purely extensive, growth, Chile threatens to end up in a "success trap". The high growth rates experienced during the past decade occlude the fact that Chile's success in exports rests on a fragile foundation (see Castillo et al. 1994, Maggi 1994, Messner 1992, Messner/Scholz 1996).

Economic growth thus depends not only on stability-oriented economic policies and functioning markets (structuring of the macrodimension). Dynamic economic locations and zones are marked by general innovation-friendly framework conditions (elementary education, university system, etc.) and cluster- or sector-specific institutions that contribute to the development of cluster-specific competitive advantages (e.g. industry-specific technology institutes, specialized training institutions).[5] In the course of the past decade techno-organizational upheavals and the decline of the traditional, Fordist production paradigm have given a new significance to the mesodimension. Innovation has an increasingly interactive character based on exchange processes organized along both market and nonmarket lines. Cumulative learning effects and innovations on which systemic competitiveness are based develop through close networking at the microlevel and through formal and informal cooperative relations between firms and the cluster-related industrial landscapes in which they operate.

Under these conditions innovation and the building of technological competence assume a collective character, since processes involved in interactive learning and the exchange of information on a reciprocal or a market-oriented basis link a given firm's know-how production to that of its rivals and suppliers and are reliant on an innovation-friendly institutional structure. Technological competence as the foundation of the competitiveness of economies is based on stocks of knowledge and learning processes that are difficult to transfer, often not codified, and generally cumulative; and these in turn emerge in interplay between firms and institutions. It is in this way that country-specific competitive patterns and advantages are born.

Accordingly, the world economy is marked not by a face-off between isolated, decentralized firms in competition with one another but by industrial clusters, groups of firms organized in networks, and what is essential to their development dynamics is the efficiency of concrete **industrial locations** - i.e. the existence of universities, training institutions, R&D facilities, technology information systems, private industrial federations, etc.[6] Countries that decide against developing, in the mesodimension, a strategic perspective as a guideline for entrepreneurial and governmental action, opting instead primarily for ad hoc reactions and trial-.and-error processes, underestimate in particular

-   the significance of a timely and selective development of the physical and, above all, the nonphysical infrastructure required if firms are to be internationally competitive;

-   the amount of time needed to develop human capital and technological infrastructure, i.e. the central determinants of international competitiveness;

-   the negative impacts of insecurity and risk on offensive entrepreneurial strategies.

4.2   State, Business Enterprises, and Intermediary Institutions in the Mesodimension - Traditional Dichotomies under Attack

When firms manufacture more complex products, this intensifies the demands placed on the municipal, regional, and national environment. Both the notion that the state alone, as society's governance center, can direct and manage technological and economic processes and the dogma stating that the state's role vis-à-vis market processes is an exclusively subsidiary one miss the point in question. The success cases in the world economy demonstrate that there is a broad scope of action open for successful policies aimed at strengthening the competitiveness of industrial locations between the extremes of a dirigiste interventionism and a laissez-fair attitude that restricts itself to the establishment of framework conditions. Just as in the case of industrial production, the sociopolitical sphere is also experiencing the emergence of new forms of organization and governance.

In many cases competition-related supply conditions arise in connection with deregulation, privatization of state-owned enterprises, and external financial support. Another essential factor is the development of an export-related physical infrastructure (e.g. transportation and communications systems). What, however, proves far more difficult is the reform and competition oriented development of institutions in the fields of educational/training, research, technology policy, as well as other locational policies geared to supporting industry and conceived in such a way as to structure the mesodimension. The problem is not so much a matter of the possible instruments (see Overview 1);[7] the real issue is how to combine them and how, or on the basis of what decision-making process, locational policies adequate to the complexity of industrial production can be developed and implemented in the first place. In other words, the structuring of the mesodimension is first and foremost a problem of organization and governance. The concern is to devise an efficient institutional structure ("hardware") and, in particular, to develop close interactive skills among the private and public actors in a cluster ("software").

The new policy-level locational strategies differ fundamentally from the top-down approaches of traditional industrial policy, industrial planning, or investment guidance. The reasons why the latter are inappropriate are that, as far as locational policy and the development of mesopolicies are concerned, both the know-how required to formulate policies keyed to the long term and the implementation capacities required are distributed across a large variety of state-level, private, and intermediary institutions (firms, federations, science, state-level, private, and intermediary organizations, labor unions). If, during the phase marked by Fordism and highly standardized production patterns, it was still possible to build successful large-scale vertically integrated enterprises on the basis of centralized state-level industrial planning (in the USSR, India, or Brazil), one-dimensional, centralist patterns of regulation are today bound to fail when the concern is to develop and support complex networks of firms and specialized institutional landscapes.

"Soft governance media" (Krumbein 1991, p. 49) such as the flow of information, the integration of interests, and the definition of procedures are gaining in significance as a result of these altered structural conditions. They have two functions: on the one hand, state mesopolicy relies on the know-how resources of firms, science, and strategic actors; on the other hand, these new governance media correspond to the

Overview 1:	Instruments of State Locational Policy in Germany

1. Institutional promotion	3. Other infrastructure and technology transfer via
Major research institutions	Information and consulting
Fraunhofer-Gesellschaft	Demonstration centers
Max-Planck-Gesellschaft	Cooperation, networks, individuals
Technology transfer agencies	Technology centers
Universities	
Measuring, standards, testing, and quality	4. Public-sector demand
Other institutions	
2. Financial incentives	5. Cooperation of strategic actors
Indirect promotion	Targeting, long-term visions
Indirect-specific promotion	Technology assessment
R&D projects/networks	Technology advisory councils
Venture capital	
	6. Training/advanced training

After: Meyer-Krahmer/Kuntze (1992), p. 103

interactive character of innovation and the systemic character of competitiveness, since patterns of social organization that facilitate the rapid flow of information, promote open information channels, and encourage communication are themselves becoming factors of competition. What is becoming clear are the procedural character of meso-policies and the fact that the building of structures in the mesodimension (as opposed to macroeconomic policies) are not only advanced by public policies, but that firms, intermediary institutions, and federations (as individual organizations or working together) can and must provide contributions toward the goal of shaping a given location (e.g. in the form of training opportunities, the development of information systems, or the acceleration of the flow of information).

These new forms of governance have, for instance in Japan, gained in significance since the 1970s, when classical industrial policies (tariffs and nontariff trade barriers, export promotion via tax incentives, R&D subsidies, formation of compulsory cartels) dominated the field. The plans and visions presented by MITI, the Japanese Ministry for Industry and Trade, are conceived in a protracted communication process involving representatives of private industry and science. The plans, presented at regular intervals for periods of from three to ten years, bear no resemblance whatever to directives issued by a central administration, since they are not directly binding on either firms or state institutions. The visions conceived by the most important actors present an overview, regarded as realistic by many of those concerned, of the desired direction of the development of the overall economy and define for individual sectors medium-term goals based on a joint analysis of bottlenecks, strengths, and anticipated upheavals.

If medium-term industrial policy visions are concretized in a dialogue, these visions are - under the conditions of rapid technological change, great instability in the capital markets, and sharp international competitive pressure - of great significance for the allocative decisions of firms and the orientations of the state-level and public intermediary institutions in the mesodimension. They convey orientation aids for bank decisions on the allocation of credit, long-term investment decisions made by firms, the allocation of research resources in private industry, and reorientations and changes of course in intermediary institutions (such as training institutions and research centers). A locational policy of this type makes it possible for firms to pursue long-term strategies geared to growth and gains in market shares instead of primarily maximizing short-terms dividends.

A further example for the increased significance of soft governance media and the growing relevance of functioning communication channels between important social groups, institutions, and organizations are the "regional conferences" that have been constituted in some of Germany's *Laender*, particularly in crisis regions, and in which far-reaching restructuring measures have been, and continue to be, devised and implemented (see Jürgens/Krumbein 1991). In connection with these conferences a great number of the actors concerned seek to reach agreement on their region's future development chances, to identify bottlenecks in the modernization process, and to anticipate the costs of ecological and social modernization so as to be able to contain them and in this way to create orientations for political and entrepreneurial decisions. This entails the development in the regions of complex networks involving entrepreneurial organizations, labor unions, federations, local administrations, technology institutes, and universities. These networks are interposed between the state and the market (mesolevel), and they elaborate visions - or put in more pragmatic terms: scenarios - for regional development, prepare the groundwork for basic strategic decisions, and make possible a nonstatist governance of economic restructuring programs and an active shaping of structures at regional and national locational levels.

The search for future economic fields in industries with a high value-added potential and the development of anticipatory structural policies are demanding tasks. This form of targeting as a rule presents promising prospects only when it is undertaken in a cooperative effort including business firms, government, and science.

Targeting and selective mesopolicies go hand in hand with the development of a complex monitoring system. It is precisely in economic restructuring conducted in phases that a strategic, targeting-related vision is essential on the part of governmental institutions (economic affairs ministry, advisory groups). Business federations and lobbies will primarily represent particularist interests and seek to define their specific industries as strategic cores. In phases of radical change strategically oriented actors in public institutions should act in concert with independent consultants and experts with an eye to identifying industrial cores with development potential. In phases of economic consolidation the concern is to develop a broad-based monitoring system based on a pluralism of actors and institutions. A key contribution to improving the information base on the dynamics in the productive sector can be provided by economic research institutes, university research institutions, sector-specific technology and consulting institutions, business federations and research institutions of private industry, labor unions, and consulting firms. These institutions and actors interact via the publication of studies, the presentation of conflicting opinions at congresses, and joint research activities.

The know-how accumulated in institutions as well as the formal and informal forms of interaction between institutions (networking) pave the way for a continuous learning process on the part of all the actors concerned regarding issues of economic and locational policy, heighten transparency as regards the strengths, weaknesses, and challenges facing the economy, and improve the orientation capacity of the firms as well as the private and public institutions concerned. While many developing countries are initially concerned with creating new and viable institutions in which know-how on the productive sector can develop (type: Economic Planning Board / Korea), in advanced countries the accumulation of such knowledge is largely a self-impelled process: the above-named agents communicate by exchanging the results of studies, seminars, joint research projects, advisory councils, and the like. This horizontal self-organization is as a rule accompanied by institutions devised to promote research (type: Deutsche Forschungsgemeinschaft [German Research Council]).

Implementing this know-how in economic policy does, however, amount to a strategic decision. State institutions in the field of economic and locational policy here again have the important role of assembling and focusing the existing know-how, of illuminating development corridors, of formulating, in cooperation with strategic actors, visions for the medium term, and in this way of providing the basis on which a given location can be given the best possible shape.

These new network-like approaches to industrial and technology policy are clearly distinguished both from one-sidedly statist governance concepts (industrial planning) and from purely market-oriented solutions. The emergence in the mesodimension of patterns of social organization and intervention and regulation techniques conducive to autonomy facilitates the task of guiding and shaping market processes and diminishes the weaknesses inherent in purely market governance and statist planning.

4.3   The National, Regional, and Local Dimensions of the Mesolevel

Aside from generally innovation-friendly framework conditions (basic education, tax incentives for R&D), what is required to develop dynamic competitive advantages are specific, selective mesopolicies. Selectivity in the mesodimension, as opposed to the widespread pork-barrel principle, aims to "strengthen the strong" with an eye to building as rapidly as possible dynamic industrial cores and efficient industrial sites that generate spillover effects in less developed areas.

Selectivity aims at three levels:

-    concentration of mesopolicies on industrial (or, for instance, agricultural or service) clusters that show development potential;

-    development at the cluster level of an efficient cluster environment, i.e. cluster-related innovation-friendly framework conditions, instruments that can be used to promote best performers ("picking the winners"), so as to guide them as quickly as possible up to the international best practice, and the development of structures keyed to enabling firms with development potential to catch up with the group of best performers;

-    strengthening of development regions in which dynamic groups of firms or clusters can emerge.

Policies devised to shape the mesodimension have both a national and a regional/local dimension.[8] At the national level mesopolicies aim at developing infrastructures tailored to the clusters (transportation: ports, rail and road networks; telecommunications; supply and waste-disposal systems: energy, water/waste water, refuse) and nonphysical infrastructures (educational/training systems, etc.). Other important factors include selective and active foreign-trade policies (trade policy, market-development strategies), and an active representation of interests at the international level (e.g. those of developing countries vis-à-vis the protectionism of the industrialized countries).

Apart from these selective improvements of the national mesodimension, cluster-specific policies at the regional and local levels are also gaining in significance. This is important in that, as is emphasized in the studies on competitiveness cited above, it can be observed that the process of clustering is most dynamic in regionally limited areas. The change of the production paradigm from standardized mass production to production of a more flexible nature and the interactive character of innovation have perceptibly boosted the significance of industrial locations for the competitiveness of business firms. Competitive advantages are often geographically bounded.

The growing significance of spatial-structural factors for the competitiveness of firms points unequivocally to the need for decentralization policies and a redefinition of the competences of national, regional, and local policy-making authorities. Traditional industrial policies, formulated far from the sites concerned by the planning staffs in capital cities, are obsolete. What is instead gaining rapidly in significance is the expansion of the competence and the financial scopes of regional and local administrations. The objective is to build institutional structures that make it possible to shape the structures in local and regional industrial locations (bottom-up structuring). The shaping of structures at the regional level is geared to strengthening network-like structures between firms, shaping the intercompany dimension , creating close linkages between industry and services, and giving rise to interactive relationships between the regional and national level.

Decentralization should not be misunderstood as a schematic shift of responsibility to lower-ranking decision-making levels, or indeed as a process of decoupling between national states and their regions. Just as in modern corporations greater autonomy for profit centers does not in the least imply any sort of abolition of the top corporate levels, and indeed instead presupposes an expansion of controlling capacities and modified tasks for central management (networking and development of strategic visions for the overall enterprise instead of central management of all corporate divisions), any effective decentralization is reliant on complementary changes at the central level. In this sense the delegation of governance potentials from the national to the local level tends to increase the number of efficient actors, relieve the burdens of central government, make it possible to frame decision in close proximity to industrial sites, harness advantages stemming from agglomeration and close contact, and improve the opportunities for cooperative relations between central government and regions. The continuing significance of the latter factor is that is ensures the integration of dynamic agglomeration groups in the formulation of a national development strategy, contributes to initiating productive feedback loops between local and regional sites, encourages the building of a national industrial infrastructure, and promotes the implementation of an active foreign-trade policy.

The structuring of the mesodimension is a permanent task of the public and the private sector aimed at capability creation; mesopolicy must be understood as a cross-sectional task for public and private actors geared to continuously improving a given industrial location. In addition, a well-structured mesodimension its not only important to strengthen and secure international competitiveness, it also constitutes the groundwork on which flanking social and environmental policies are effectively implemented.

In summary, it is clear that building competitive advantages in the mesodimension relies on the activities of a variety of actors, that governance resources (e.g. governance-relevant knowledge) are often widely dispersed, and that new governance instruments (e.g. "soft governance") and different organizational patterns have emerged between governmental and private groups of actors. Analysis of the mesodimension shows that the task of building competitiveness represents a social challenge (Esser 1991, Esser et al. 1992, Hillebrand 1991, Hillebrand et al. 1992, Hillebrand et al. 1994, Messner 1993a/1993b/1994a, Meyer-Stamer et al. 1991). If the shape given to an industrial location is in fact as significant as it viewed in the concept of systemic competitiveness, then the dynamics of economic development is dependent on complex social and governance patterns to which the field of economics has as yet hardly addressed itself.

5 The Metalevel: Social Integration and Governance Capacity

5.1 Building Social Structures as a Condition of Economic Modernization

"Modern societies are integrated not only socially, through values, norms, and communication processes, but also systematically via markets and administratively applied power."
Jürgen Habermas, *Faktizität und Geltung*, Frankfurt 1992, p. 58

Two factors crucial to the optimization of performance potentials at the micro-, macro-, and mesolevels are the state's governance capacity and forms of social organization that make it possible to mobilize social creativity potentials. Formation of new social structures is the sine qua non of economic modernization and the development of systemic competitiveness. Many developing, industrialized nations and countries in transformation were and are characterized by centralist political decision-making processes and bureaucratized, inefficient government apparatuses with a low level of governance capacity. The latter are frequently also overlapped by rentist-corporatist structures that permit privileged groups to push through their particularist interests. These power-based and encrusted political structures correspond with forms of social disintegration and fragmentation that go hand and hand with the exclusion of broad segments of the population and are marked by political and social polarization.

Economic-policy strategies that seek to initiate processes of economic modernization by encouraging market forces and cutting back the scope of government often tend to underestimate the extent to which in particular developing countries are marked by weak markets and firms, an omnipresent and at the same time weak government, and weak social actors. If, in the process of macroeconomic reform, adequate regulatory and governance capacities (government reform, networking between strategic actors) are not developed and the formation of new social structures is neglected, tendencies working in the direction of social disintegration will intensify. Systemic competitiveness without social integration is a project doomed to failure. Building systemic competitiveness is for that reason a project entailing social transformation, one that goes far beyond simply correcting the macroeconomic framework.

Social integration is based on an institutional action context characterized by three central features:

- compatibility of the most important value orientations held first and foremost by the strategic actors, and subsequently marked by a growing group consensus (**minimal consensus**);

- the ability of social actors to respond quickly and effectively to the exigencies of adjustment (**learning and transformation capacity**); and, over the long term,

- the development of behavioral expectations on the part of the actors that are based on stable regulations, institutions, and habits (**stability**) and that are at the same time open to new challenges (**openness and change**).

Countries that are willing to accept the challenges posed by the world economy will find it essential to work on a basic social consensus on the direction to be taken by the changes aimed at. Medium-term orientations and visions are meaningful as a means of securing future interest against well-organized present interests and generating stable expectations. Should this not succeed - as was the case with several Latin American countries in the 1980s and possibly a number of former socialists states - the necessary process of structural change will be delayed and the process of social disintegration prolonged.

5.2   Social Organizational and Governance Capacity as a Dimension of Competitiveness

Once a minimal consensus on the direction of development has begun to take shape, one issue that remains to be addressed is the design of viable patterns of social organization and the institutional shape to be given to the state's role in economy and society. The state - limited by the *"inherent constraints of the world economy"*,[9] which extend into the core of national economies - is in a monopoly position as far as shaping the macroeconomic framework is concerned. It is essential to establish regulative and infrastructural framework conditions geared to imparting direction to economic and social development and creating the conditions needed to strengthen market forces. Below the level of macropolicy, dynamic societies display highly differentiated organizational patterns and forms of governance. Apart from the forms of governance that have until now dominated societies organized along the lines of a market economy - hierarchical coordination in firms and public institutions, market-governed coordination between firms, and hierarchical governance of society by the state - the mesodimension will display signs network-like forms of organization marked neither by simple market allocation (competition and price) nor by centralist mechanisms of governance (hierarchical governance by the state).

A question again arises that occupied the attention of, for instance, regulation theorists in the mid-1980s:[10] If the success of Fordism consisted in the combination of a specific production paradigm and the forms of social regulation compatible with it, what are the patterns of social organization in which the new production paradigm are imbedded? There are many indications that, at the level of society and in terms of the exigencies of regulation, the upheavals that are presently in the making, or indeed already making themselves felt, are just about as far-reaching as those in the sphere of production. While, in the age of standardized mass production, Keynesian global management instruments were used to steady the national economic cycle, the adequate regulation mechanisms and the levels of intervention involved within the framework of systemic competitiveness are as yet unclear. The nation state appears to be losing some of its governance capacity in the global economy, and at the same time new forms of interaction between the state, business firms, and intermediary actors are gaining in significance. The coherence of national industrial locations and the scope of national economic policies are being undermined by globalized markets, and at the same time the clusters integrated within institutional research and training landscapes are proving to be dynamic social systems in which the cohesion of industrial locations can be strengthened by interaction between firms, the state, and intermediary institutions. The structure and dynamics of these forms of organization not reducible to market relations and hierarchical governance by the state can be deciphered only by theories of competitiveness founded in a theory of society.

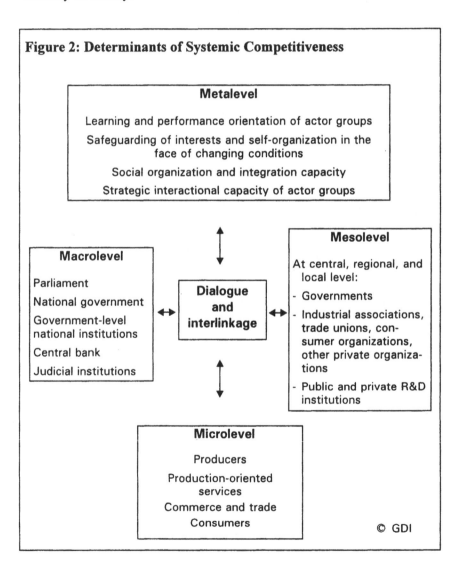

Figure 2: Determinants of Systemic Competitiveness

Metalevel

Learning and performance orientation of actor groups

Safeguarding of interests and self-organization in the face of changing conditions

Social organization and integration capacity

Strategic interactional capacity of actor groups

Macrolevel

Parliament

National government

Government-level national institutions

Central bank

Judicial institutions

Dialogue and interlinkage

Mesolevel

At central, regional, and local level:

- Governments

- Industrial associations, trade unions, consumer organizations, other private organizations

- Public and private R&D institutions

Microlevel

Producers

Production-oriented services

Commerce and trade

Consumers

© GDI

- How can the new forms of organization and governance be described precisely; in what way is the hierarchical governance of society by the state overlaid by new forms of horizontal self-coordination (in clusters, in the mesodimension)?

- What are the implications of the state's loss of autonomy for society's governance capacity?

- In what form do the new organizational patterns contribute to strengthening society's problem-solving capacities?

- How is the fact to be explained that, in different modern or modernizing societies subject to the same "dictates of the world economy", we see the emergence of sharply divergent social development trends which have very different and specific effects on their ability to build competitive advantages? What can be observed are disintegration tendencies (e.g. in Italy, in subsystems of American society, and in many countries in the process of development and/or transformation), obstructed societies in which it is precisely the close cooperation between the public and private sectors that leads to rent-seeking attitudes and structural blockades (e.g. in some countries in Latin America) as well as economically dynamic countries characterized by close networking between state and industry (e.g. Japan, South Korea, Taiwan) or between state, industry, and other social actors (e.g. in many western and northern European countries).

- What determinants of social organizational and governance capacity can be isolated which give rise to these wholly different social structures?

These issues will not be discussed on the basis of empirical research, although here too there is a need for research. Instead, the intention of this study is to consult theoretical approaches as to their applicability for the problematic outlined here.

Part II   Reconstruction of the Theories of Social Governance Capacity

CHAPTER 1   Preliminary Remarks

1.1   The Social Dimensions of Development - A Neglected Field

"The question of governability is becoming the central problem of the world."
Ignacy Sachs, Maison des Sciences de l'Homme, Paris; in a report to the UNESCO conference "The Two Americas, 1492-1992", Paris, November 1992 (quoted after: Das Argument, no. 199, 1993, p. 430).

The last chapter demonstrated that the new theories of competitiveness and the development of dynamic locational advantages converge in one basic point: as determinants of economic success, they emphasize the systemic character of competitiveness and with it the significance of the modernization capacity of societies, the efficiency of the social actors involved, and their strategic interaction. "Environmental factors", assigned by traditional neoliberal economists the role of external and marginal data, here become the object of analysis. Indeed, the question of the contours of the pattern of social organization that favors the emergence of competitiveness even acquires central significance here. In contrast to the theory of production factors and the neoclassical theory of allocation, which implicitly regard the production process as an a-social and mechanical utilization process, the approaches discussed here permit political and social institutions to step out of the "blind spot" of economic theorizing. It is only in this case that their innovative-stimulative and restrictive-prohibitive functions can be explicitly thematized. Competitiveness accordingly emerges in the process of synergism between firms and institutions at the mesolevel and macroeconomic regulations. If economic development is understood in this sense as a process anchored in society, the question is not, as it was in the mainstream discussion of the 1980s, simply whether there is too much or too little regulation (more or less state). The challenge consists in the development of innovative forms of social and economic organization and governance. What it is that constitutes efficient organizational patterns is, to be sure, a highly controversial issue in the majority of the approaches proposed by the social sciences.

In view of the fact that theories of competitiveness have rediscovered society, the state, and, in particular, the significance of the interaction between important groups of social actors (firms, science, private and public intermediary institutions), the next step is obviously to look carefully into the discussion in the social sciences over the possibilities of and limits to the governance of societies in order, building on them, to draft a more exact picture of viable patterns of organization and governance and forms of policy and regulation.

It proves impossible to derive from the literature in the social sciences on the governance potentials of and in societies any direct approach to an efficient institutional design, political patterns of regulation, and the determinants of a dynamic society capable of learning. What can be observed is an ongoing search process. Its extreme poles are marked on the one side by classical statist approaches and on the other by conceptions that point to society's capacity for self-organization, the state's loss of significance as a central actor in governance, and the generally growing loss of governance potentials in complex societies.

The following section attempts to reconstruct this debate and to scrutinize it with an eye to its immediate usefulness for the concept of systemic competitiveness. And if, beside the new theories of governance clustered around the term "network society", this analysis also briefly recapitulates concepts centered on the state and theories of pluralism, there are good reasons for doing so. The broad approach is justified inasmuch as, especially in the discussion on development theory, but also in large segments of the economic sciences open to the issues with which the other social sciences are concerned (such as, for instance, the approaches to competitiveness presented here), there is much confusion as to the question of the social determinants of development.

As was pointed out above for **theories of competitiveness**, there exist here very divergent notions of the role of the state and the significance of collective actors and social patterns of organization that are inserted into, or, as it were, built onto, the economic analysis without any recourse to the theoretical findings of the social sciences. Thus, on the one hand, Porter sometimes pleads for a strong "development state", while, on the other hand, he describes complex forms of interaction between the private and public sectors, without budging, in his conclusions concerning regulative policy, from a relatively orthodox (neoliberal) train of thought.

In the 1980s the **discussion in the field of development theory** was heavily dominated by the debate over structural adjustment programs. Accordingly, the controversy surrounding regulative policy (*Ordnungspolitik*) unfolded chiefly within the framework of a "market versus state" dispute. Beyond this discussion other approaches gained in significance that pointed to the efficiency of nongovernmental organizations as motors of economic and social development. Yet a discussion over the interlinkage between state, market, and social self-organization failed to materialize. At the beginning of the 1990s the sterile "market versus state" discussion ran out of steam. The schools of thought with a more statist orientation (e.g. CEPAL) came closer to free-market positions, but without being able to present any new model of society. Thus CEPAL's comments on the relationship between state, market, and social actors sometimes have the ring of neocorporatist approaches, sometimes recall neoliberal ideas.[1] At the same time the World Bank, after over a decade of structural adjustment, is beginning to take note of the fact that a reform perspective keyed solely reducing the activity of the state does not show a way out of the development predicament facing the Third World. The World Bank has for that reason launched a discussion on "good governance", one, however, that focuses one-sidedly on modernizing and streamlining the state and wholly neglects the issue of new forms of governance in a context of changing social structures.[2]

The discussion in the **industrialized countries** is likewise marked by some interesting turns of thought. Following the collapse of socialism and in connection with the more and more generally accepted insight that the neoliberal worldview dominant in the 1980s holds out no more than limited prospects for the future, models centering on the state as the key agent of governance of society are experiencing an unexpected renaissance. Perturbed by the economic success of countries in Asia, a good number of economic liberals are discovering the **charm of the strong state**, autonomous vis-à-vis society. The following analysis will show that this view cannot be adequate to the demands facing state and society.

It is also and precisely in the **countries in transformation** that the question arises as to what economic and social models are actually available for the transition to a market economy now that it has become clear that the macroeconomic "tricks" recommended to switch in the course of a few hundred days from a planned economy to a market economy tend more to end up in Mafia-like structures than in consolidated market economies. "Pluralism" is another catchword that has been revived since the end of the East-West conflict both in the transformation debate and, generally, in the field of development policy. Economic efficiency and political pluralism, so, with reference to the pluralism theories of the 1950s and 1960s, the argument goes, are the key to success in development. But do the pluralism theories of the 1950s and 1960s really hold the answer to the questions as to patterns of social organization that favor political and economic development?

In view of this confusion and lack of clarity regarding the role of state, market, and society in the development process, a systematic analysis of the governance debate seems called for if justice is to be done to the issue of "development of international competitiveness as a problem of social governance".

1.2   Search Directions in Governance Theories in the Social Sciences - An Initial Structuring of the Field of Research

Three development phases can be reconstructed in the theories of political governance in societies:

(1) The classical political science of the modern age was the theory of the political institutions of the central state.

(2) Pluralism and neocorporatism theories center on an analysis of the intermediary institutions and federations, i.e. the large-scale organizations, of society, but without questioning the state's dominant role as the central agency of governance.

(3) The more recent discussions have taken account of both these currents together; they note a blurring of the boundaries (*Entgrenzung*) between state and society which is interpreted by one strand of the discussion as the basis of the loss of governance capacity in modern societies and regarded by another strand as a trend that makes it possible to optimize potentials of political action and governance via the synergism of private and public actors and by shifting political decisions into intermediary arenas.

During the phase of reform and planning euphoria that dominated both West Germany and other industrialized Western states up to the beginning of the 1970s, the scopes open to governmental action were seen in an extremely rosy light. Then, during the course of the 1970s, it turned out that the various reform euphorias rested on an planning illusion. The discussion over neocorporatism envisaged political attempts to bring movement into the existing situation, based on cooperation between the state and the large-scale organizations of society (primarily labor unions and industrial federations), as auxiliary constructions of a concept of political governance that still, in one way or another, centered on the "state" as the key organ of governance. The theories of neocorporatism were closely bound up with the Keynesian project of global economic management and for that reason, at the beginning of the 1980s at the latest, ended up in crisis. In terms of economic policy, neoliberalism, with its penchant for deregulation, won ground. The debate in the social sciences over governance capacity experienced a radical reorientation due to the empirically observable crisis of the interventionist state, the erosion of national scopes of action stemming from economic globalization, and the general offensive against the state launched by systems theory. The discussion now centers of concepts such as "social", "societal", or "network-like" governance, all of which give expression to the fact that the state, in view of the high level of differentiation of society and the complexity of the problems awaiting solutions, can no longer be regarded as the governance and control center of society; politics, the argument goes, must be understood as a process that involves both public and private organizations. The traditional hierarchical governance of society by the (democratic) state seems to have reached the end of its tether. In this process of transition toward a view that sees the state, in the wake of a society growing ever more differentiated, losing more and more of its autonomy, the *concept of planning* is being successively supplanted by the *concept of governance*. Against this background the question arises how, under the conditions of increasingly differentiated, complex societies and the crisis of traditional governmental intervention policies, it is possible to reflect on the governance capacity of societies at all.

The growing functional differentiation of societies, the emergence of an increasing number of efficient actors, and the increases in complexity involved here are both the expression and the condition of modernization. This is, as the theorists of competition have demonstrated, true of economies as well: particularly efficient are clusters of firms integrated in networks or industrial districts, since these entail a high level of vertical and horizontal concentration on the part of a great variety of firms and organizations. This is holds true for the political arena as well: the growing differentiation of the institutional system and the organizational capacity of society are a consequence both of democratization and the will to participation and the participatory capacity of social actors. There is broad consensus on this general trend toward growing differentiation of modern societies in the course of their modernization, though there is very little agreement on the implications of this state of affairs for the governance capacity of societies and the chances and limitations of political governance.

Normal, everyday understanding is dominated by the notion that "everything is connected with everything else", and that it is thus becoming more and more difficult to arrive at "correct" political decisions. In fact, it has become a generally accepted fact that causal chains are becoming less and less transparent, that, in view of complex interdependencies, unintended side-effects of political interventions in social and economic subsystems are next to impossible to anticipate, and that the growing pluralism of interests can hamper the formation of political consensuses. In other words, there are, at first sight, many indications that the increasing complexity in modern societies leads to a disempowerment of the political sphere. Is, in other words, the strategic interaction of institutions and actors emphasized in recent theories of competitiveness as conditions for the emergence of competitive advantages the result of processes which are beyond control or governance and which, under auspicious conditions - but under what specific conditions? - produce synergy effects and otherwise give rise to various, unintended side-effects? There is an element of irony inherent in the fact that at the moment when important segments of the economic sciences are beginning to acknowledge, beside the invisible hand of the market, the significance of state governance and social organizations as important determinants of economic development, some of the social science are "reporting back" that any attempt to selectively shape social relations is bound to founder on the complexity of these relations and that any notion of an interlinkage of market and political governance is illusory.

The ambivalent relationship between the modernization of societies and the possibility of shaping this process is perplexing. The dilemma consists in the fact that on the one hand the organizational capacity of society and the efficiency of a growing number of actors constitute motors of development. On the other hand, however, these motors can turn into brakes on development in that they (can) at the same time give rise to paralyzing divergencies of interests and coalitions determined to defend their specific vested interests that confront state actors in the process of policy formulation and implementation. Accordingly, any obstruction of the state's governance capacity and loss of its potential to govern the process of reshaping society can prove to be *"a paradox consequence of increased scopes of social action, i.e. lead to a shrinking rather than a growth of any further increase"* (Streeck 1987, p. 483); the *"loss of scopes of action"* could thus be triggered by their very *"increase"* (Streeck 1987, p. 487). In social subsystems the process of modernization gives rise to a process of growing differentiation that increases the rationality of the subsystems, though it can at the same time increase the irrationality of the whole.

The interpretations of this paradoxical development as regards governance capacity in societies tend to be very contrary. The gamut extends from the assumption that the state must be strengthened vis-à-vis society as a means of countering particularist interests to the opposite position that contends that it is only a reduction of the role of the state that can prevent an increasing *"statification"* (*Verstaatlichung*) *of society.* We also encounter the thesis that any attempts at governance are, under the given conditions, bound a priori to fail; other authors opt for the optimistic perception that it is precisely the emergence and self-organization capacity of a variety of efficient actors and institutions that can contribute to compensating for the erosion of state governance potentials; the synergism of efficient actors, thus the core proposition of the governance optimists, leads to an increase in social coordination and problem-solving capacities.

One's initial inclination is to concur with all these completely divergent positions, or at least to concede their legitimacy, not least because empirical reality holds a store of valid examples to back each of them. There is no doubt that the state's governance capacity must be strengthened vis-à-vis powerful lobbies if the state is not to be "colonized", and thus, as it were, "refeudalized", by a number of small but powerful minorities. Often it is the more authoritarian Asian states that are seen as having this capacity, while, for instance, the more pluralist American society is perceived as lacking it. Is, in other words, the case such that the trajectory of liberal, pluralist societies automatically leads to *"strong societies and weak states?"* (Migdal 1988) But there is no doubt either that in many societies dynamic development is obstructed by exaggerated levels of state activity and forms of state overregulation. This is true of nearly all Western welfare states. In the field of economic policy, for instance, the thesis of the impossibility of any selective political governance seems convincing. Is it not the *"inherent necessities of the world market"* (Elmar Altvater) that are increasing restricting scopes of political action and governance? Nor can it simply be denied that it is precisely societies marked by highly differentiated institutional landscapes and close cooperation between public and private actors that are in a position to generate economic dynamism and run successful economic policies; here we need only think of the examples of the industrial districts in northern Italy, the Japanese organizational model, or the case of the German state of Baden-Württemberg which are again and again cited in theories of competitiveness.

But why is it that governance by the state sometime succeeds, while in other cases it ends up in overregulation and paralyzing bureaucratization? And why is it that close cooperation between the state and private actors on the one hand leads to cientelism, corruption, and political blockades, while on the other hand the same approach is seen as the basis of the capacity for social integration and development dynamics? The attempt to capture these paradoxes in language ends up in the formation of concepts like "the *'statified'* society" (Glagow 1984) or the *"socialized state"* (Glasmeier 1984), which express highly divergent views of the same state of affairs.

It would appear that the *"active society"* (Etzioni 1968) and the *"blocked society"* (Crozier 1970) are very close to one another, that the terms may describe one and the same phenomenon - namely, highly differentiated, *"institutionally rich societies"* (Streeck 1991, p. 27), that have enormous problem-solving capacities and know-how as well as great self-organization potentials anchored in many areas of society, and that nevertheless succumb to the danger of social disintegration, fragmentation, and social blockades. Is, in other words, the direction in which modernizing societies are moving a purely empirical question, or is it possible to define the determinants of this process? Can institutional designs be identified that stand for the one or the other of these directions of development? These "blind spots" and "gaps in our knowledge" will be addressed in the following section by reconstructing the governance debate in the social sciences.

CHAPTER 2   The State as the Governance Center of Society

2.1   The Modern Understanding of the State: The Internally and Externally Sovereign Leviathan

Even the question: What are we to understand by "the state"? is difficult to answer; there is no generally valid definition. The classical elements of the concept, as seen in terms of the theory of the state (state authority, national territory, the nation), are at best a point of departure for any inquiry into the state from the angle of the social sciences. The core of the modern concept of the state is, however, not put to the question. External sovereignty and the hierarchically superordinate position of state authority over all particular internal interests are the brackets that hold together modern theories of the state. The "unity" of the state and its autonomy vis-à-vis social actors are the basis for its acknowledgment as the central governance agency of society. Hermann Heller conceived of the state in the late phase of the Weimar Republic as *"the truly unitary center of action within the multiplicity of actual and autonomous centers of action, be they individual or collective"* (Heller 1983, p. 260); and Max Weber spoke of the *"state monopoly of the exercise of legitimate power"* (Weber 1956, p. 210). This sovereignty of the state was understood as the peak of a pyramid and the nerve center of an organism from which public affairs were regulated with the means of administration and power.

The separation of state and society in modern European theories of the state goes back to Hegel, who discovered civil society as *"the difference which imposes itself between the family and the state"*. Hegel -

with reference to the onset of industrialization and the social division of labor and the increasing differentiation associated with it (Hegel 1970, pp. 347 ff.) - broke radically with the Platonic-Aristotelian notion, hitherto dominant in the Western world, of the unity of the polis as the *"societas civilis sive politica"*. He defines "civil society" as the system of particular needs and interests, as the sphere of universal egoism. Hegel idealizes the state as the sovereign over society, the sphere of altruism and the agency instituting unity.[3]

Jörg Klawitter[4] has worked out the function which, according to Hegel, the state would have to assume in order to gain control of the centrifugal forces effective in society and safeguard the unity of society:

-    *"Society, grasped as a nexus of individual needs and particular interests (Hegel §188), is, in the action space defined by conflicting interests and power groups, in need of a regulative and stabilizing agency (state);*

-    *the state guarantees the existence of a formal means of channeling and coordinating the interests and needs present in society (Hegel §251 f. and §288) via a structure consisting of binding and coordinated behavioral and legal norms;*

-    *The state installs decision-making authorities that, autonomously and with superior jurisdictional power, oppose particularist social forces and exercise a binding power of arbitration (Hegel §219 ff.);*

-    *the state guarantees an internal law of state (constitution) and an external law of state that regulates the relations of the individual state with other states (Hegel §259)".*

This core of the modern understanding of the state (clear separation between state and society and the notion of the state as empowered to govern and to uphold unity and as internally and externally sovereign) has continued in currency in continental theories of the state up to and including the present day: the formula of the **state ruled by law** has made it possible to link the legitimatory aspects of the manner in which the state was grounded by Hobbes as the guarantor of internal peace with the emphasis placed by Locke on law as the foundation of a consensual social contract driven by utilitarian motives. The idea and the establishment of the constitutional state spelled the end of the media employed by the absolute state (arbitrary power and authority) in the exercise of power and conferred **legality** on the state. The **pluralism theories** that distance themselves from totalitarian theories of the state extend the idea of the state ruled by law above all by deriving state authority from popular sovereignty, thus endowing the leviathan with **legitimacy**. Pluralism theory - in connection with liberalist-economic notions - is concerned with the **form of decision-making in democratic societies**. The discussion on the **welfare state** and **planned capitalism** serves, among other things, to articulate critiques of the concept of the "free market economy". This entails a definition of the direction, i.e. the goal system, of state policy (social justice, equal opportunity), thus expanding the state's scope of tasks. Despite the advances that have been made in the discussion of the state, the state, sovereign vis-à-vis society, remains the center of society, legitimated and capable of governing the public sphere.

2.2 Discussions of the State, Planning, and Governance in the Framework of Traditional Theory of the State

2.2.1 Pluralism Theories, Elitist-democratic Concepts and their Proximity to Liberalist-economic Approaches

Pluralism theories, dominant in the 1950s and 1960s and born out of prewar discussions and discourses originating in the United States,[5] leave the core of the modern concept of the state untouched. They see the state as the organized center in which the public will is formed. The decisions it makes are in principle unrestricted and universally binding. As in classical theory, the state is here too the arena in which, in the broadest sense, society is shaped. Proceeding from the concept of popular sovereignty and the *contract social* and defining their terms *ex negativo* in terms of the predemocratic state, seen as an agency of governance and decision-making fully independent of society, the theorists of pluralism addressed themselves to the issues of the democratic **legitimation** of state policy and the **form in which decisions are made** in pluralist, competitive democracies.

They attempt to show how, in a parliamentary democracy, decisions come about through a process of interaction between individuals, social organizations, and state-level institutions and in what ways it is possible to secure the legitimacy of the leviathan. They succeed, within the scope of their concept, in discussing the links between society and the (democratic) state without questioning the state's role as the hierarchical peak of society.

Pluralism theories are based on the assumption that all relevant social interests are organizable, that they compete for political consideration of their particularist interests, and that in this way, at least in the long run, no socially relevant interests can be neglected. The interests of social actors are transformed - via the competition between parties and universal suffrage - into political power, which is allocated to government and opposition. The parliament initiates, on the basis of constitutionally defined competences, legislative processes that are implemented and executed by a governmental administrative apparatus. This process is complemented by the possibility enjoyed by groups of organized interests to exercise a consultative influence on the parliamentary process, which provides - in a way parallel to the transference of political power to parliament by citizens voting in elections - for feedback between state and organized society.[6]

The mutual control of organized and competing interests assumed by pluralism theorists generates a parallelogram of forces that, via conflicts and balance between social actors, continuously gives rise to a situational state of equilibrium. It is through this cyclical mechanism that competitive democracy succeeds in creating a social balance of power and attending to a broad spectrum of interests. These osmotic mechanisms that mediate between state and social actors lead to a situation in which decisions made by the state reflect the specifically dominant parallelogram of forces, in this way doing justice, in the long run, to the public interest: *"The will of the state can be nothing other than a universally binding decision formed and implemented by social forces".*[7]

In contrast to the classical theories of the state in the Lockean tradition, pluralism theories thus acknowledge the existence of organized interests beside the citizen-individual. This acknowledgment of the fact that the state is bound back to social interest structures at the same time distinguishes the representatives of pluralism from conservative theorists of the state, whose thinking has traditionally been premised on a complete independence of the state from society (e.g. Schmitt 1940 and 1969).

The proximity of pluralist approaches to economic liberalism is obvious: the competition of many individuals or groups is assumed to lead to the welfare of the whole. While in the marketplace economic agents act in competition to one another with an eye to maximizing their own utility, giving rise to an economic equilibrium via the mechanism of supply and demand and the free formation of prices, the competition of political citizens or social interest groups that finds expression in the election mechanism and the principle of vote maximization leads, almost in the sense of a natural process, to a compromise of political interests and a state of equilibrium (Esser 1985, p. 206). It is not by chance that studies in the field of pluralism theory at times draw analogies to Adam Smith's invisible hand.

The heroic assumption used by theorists of pluralism to ground their concept normatively consists in proceeding on the premise that all social interests can be organized in a balanced fashion, that all collective actors have roughly the same opportunities of influencing the decision-making processes relevant to them, and that the members of federations and organizations define their policies in such a way as to give rise to a social balance of power.

The Modified View of the Concept of Elitist Democracy

These almost romantic premises have been challenged above all on the basis of **elitist-democratic concepts**. It was Schumpeter who pointed out that, **in the first place**, the members of social organizations have hardly any influence on the policies of these organizations and that, **in the second place**, the preponderance of large-scale social organizations leads to a centralization of power which marginalizes interests that resist or organizations with weak resources, and that, **in the third place**, it is therefore unrealistic to assume that all political actors have comparable opportunities to exert influence on political parties and parliaments. In the end, Schumpeter reduced the democratic process to the plebicitary choice between competing elites. Schumpeter breaks with a democracy concept geared to emancipation and replaces it with a utilitarian concept of democracy. He understands democracy as an effective social technique for *"arriving at political, legislative, and administrative decisions"* (Schumpeter 1959, p. 384). While pluralism theory is concerned with reconstructing the interaction between state, organized groups, and individuals as a means of grounding society's democratic control over the state, Schumpeter insists on a strict separation between politics and nonpolitics (and thus between state and society).

But Schumpeter at least retained the normative principle that in a democracy the politics of elites are also obliged to satisfy the needs of nonelites. This gives rise to a normative problem: how and for what reasons can a state apparatus that is not governed via the articulation of social interests and has a very high level of autonomy be assumed to be willing and able to become sensitive to precisely these interests. Furthermore, for Schumpeter the elitist government system, largely shielded as it is from society, must also be able to detect problems and latent conflicts at an early point of time, since these are not (cannot be) articulated by society itself.

The state, for elite-based theories *per definitionem* autonomous, neutral, and omniscient , has about it a strong reminiscence of the all-powerful leviathan of the absolute state. While in pluralism theories the state is integrated within complexes of social relations and its policy reflects the results of the goals of social actors that have emerged in the democratic process, Schumpeter outlines a society in which the elites autonomously define and pursue political goal functions and are in a position to procure the mass loyalty required to do so.

If, in pluralism theories, the balancing of interests via election mechanisms and the principle of vote maximization recalls Adam Smith's invisible hand, Schumpeter's elitist state, largely decoupled from society, seems to be constructed on analogy to the Walrasian auctioneer. Just as Walras can imagine the creation of states of economic equilibrium only by means of the adjustments made by an auctioneer positioned above the market, for Schumpeter the task of bringing together all the special interests of individuals and organizations representing particularist interests to form a political equilibrium is not left to some wondrous invisible hand, but is assigned to the elitist state. The harmonistic equilibrium-based premises of pluralism theories rightly criticized by Schumpeter are replaced by notions of the functioning of complex societies and the efficiency and problem-solving capacity of the state and its elites that are equally remote from reality. Schumpeter solves the problem posed by the tense relationship between state and society by magnifying the role played by the state - and in doing so comes close to what has been described as the predemocratic absolute state.

Apart from these differences, it should be noted that, while variants deriving from democracy theory provide different answers to the question of the legitimation of state power and the scope of influence open to individuals and organizations, they nevertheless share some important features:

- Policymaking is derived from the intentions, strategies, and conscious acts of actors ("the elite" in Schumpeter; the sum total of social actors in pluralism theories) that are translated into sovereign acts of state via the mechanisms outlined above, but without according any attention to the unintended secondary effects of such acts or the structural determinants and functional re-

lations facing specific actors (e.g. power relations, contexts defined by the world market).

- The legitimacy of acts of state are based on the - more or less un-
substantiated - assumption of neutrality and welfare orientations
on the part of the state.

- In terms of the governance potential of societies, the approaches
are highly state-centered. The state apparatus is at the same time
seen as a black box inasmuch as these approaches turn a blind eye
to the modus operandi of state action and any possible ineffectivi-
ties or contradictions associated with it.

The essence of the modern understanding of the state (clear-cut separation of state and society, governance and decision- and policy-making
monopoly of a state positioned above society) is more or less uncriti-
cally adopted and supplemented with (different types of) set pieces
derived from democracy theory, without continuing the discussion over
the tense relationship between state and society that had already constituted an element of the Hegelian discourse.

2.2.2   Welfare State, Planned Capitalism, and Keynesian Global Management

In many countries the 1960s saw the emergence, in the context of the
prolonged period of economic prosperity in postwar Europe, of a
"vision of democratically governed capitalism" (Scharpf 1987, p. 17).
The discussions that dominated the period from the 1960s to the mid-
1970s centered on the concepts *welfare state* and *planned capitalism*
(e.g. Shonfield 1968). The transition to and connection between pluralism theories and the discussion over planned, welfare-oriented capitalism can be depicted in terms of the way in which the German term
Politik has been used. The term includes three dimensions that are kept
apart in English:

- *politics* - the processes of settling conflicts and forming consensuses, i.e. the struggle for shares of power, influence, and the realization of interests, claims, and plans;

- *policy* - political problem analyses, programs, projects, and plans geared to shaping social relations; and

- *polity* - the institutional framework, i.e. the political-administrative institutions within which politics and policies move.

Pluralism theory goes on from the modern understanding of the state, and in it the state and its institutions (*polity*) largely retain the character of a black box. The *politics* dimension constitutes the core of pluralism theories. The concern is to ground the legitimacy of the democratic state. This is done in the form of decision-making processes (elections, the principle of representation, realization of social interests via the state). The state's legitimation as the central decision-making actor of society and the harmonistic notion of a balanced compromise of interests between social actors that it entails are tacitly presupposed in the publications of the theorists concerned with the welfare state and planned capitalism: tacitly insofar as they fail to pursue *politics* issues at any length, in this way taking over the heroic premises underlying pluralism theories.

The center is now constituted by the goal system of politics (welfare state, creation of social justice and equal opportunity), i.e. the *policy* dimension, which is defined in the theoretical conceptions of pluralism as the open outcome of democratic conflicts of interests, and is thus not given any further attention (the invisible hand). The core idea is now to contribute to perfecting society by suitably organizing the activities of the state. As opposed to pluralism theories, which as a rule correspond with liberalist economic concepts, the significance of the state and its institutions are presented in a new, positive light as the decision-making and planning center of society, and the scope of the state's functions is expanded - which means devoting more attention to the shape given to the institutional landscape, the *polity* dimension. There is continuity between the core propositions of the theory of the state outlined above and the theories of pluralism in that the state is understood as the central governance actor of society, and to it is ascribed the capacity to comprehensively shape the social environment.

It might thus be said that the basic assumptions of the pluralism discussion as regards theories of democracy and the state are enlarged by addressing the issue of the direction taken by state policy and an expansion of the state apparatus seemingly suggested by it. The three pillars supporting the vision of democratically governed capitalism are thus:

- premises derived from the theory of democracy; these are based on the harmonistic ideas of decision-making processes and the balance of interests stemming from pluralism theories (*politics*) and include a notion of their opportunism as regards the unlimited governance capacity of the state;

- an interventionist and welfare-oriented state apparatus (*polity*) capable of building and/or expanding a system of social security (*policy*); and

- at the economic level, a Keynesian economic policy geared to overcoming the instability of capitalism and creating a greater measure of social justice and equal opportunity.

Keynesian global economic management made use in particular of macroeconomic and demand-oriented governance instruments such as expansive and restrictive financial policies, expansive and restrictive monetary policies, and exchange-rate policy to influence microeconomic decisions by altering the overall economic framework and in this way stabilizing the economic cycle. Less important were attempts to link a "global" cyclical policy with selective structural policies such as sectoral and regional technology and industrial policies. The discussions on the welfare state centered on the "humanization of work", equal participation of all in the services offered by a qualified educational and health-care system, and the improvement of public infrastructure. The welfare state was to provide for the progressive social utilization and the just redistribution of the welfare produced.

The state - positioned above society - is responsible for shaping an economically efficient and socially balanced society; it approaches this task by means of economic policy measures and social transfers. It is reliant on the financial resources generated in the economic system and the mass loyalty of the social actors. This project, aimed as it were at a *"social-democratic consensus"* (Dahrendorf 1979, pp. 147 ff.), was dominant until the mid-1970s even in western European countries in which social-democratic parties either seldom or never came to power, and it broadened the state's spectrum of tasks and at times considerably expanded the density of regulation in western European societies.

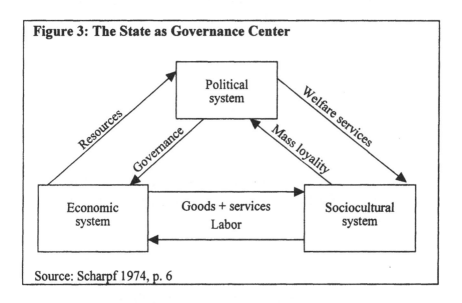

Figure 3: The State as Governance Center

Source: Scharpf 1974, p. 6

It seemed as if the process of rationalization described by Max Weber for Western states and societies could be resolutely pushed on with. "Political planning" and "rationalization of politics" were core terms of this discussion, marked as it was by an almost hermetic optimism and boundless trust in the possibilities available for the democratic state to shape society.[8] It is not by chance that the idea of organization of society by a rationally planning state calls to mind the hierarchical governance of big Fordist corporations by corporate headquarters.

The optimistic view of the possibilities open to the democratic state overlooked both from the ambiguity of the concept of rationality developed by Max Weber and Weber's equivocal description of the development of large-scale modern organizations. The rational exercise of power by modern bureaucracies, Weber noted, supplants the arbitrariness and dilettantism of earlier forms of rule. A state bureaucracy operating fully in accordance with the principle of formal rationality tends, however, in the direction of a continuous bureaucratization of society that stifles any initiative and undermines the creativity of individuals. As much as Weber admired the organizational achievements of modern bureaucracies - whose rationality can unfold only through detachment from value-neutral attitudes and particularist interests and a depersonalization of the relations between administrative organizations and their clientele - he at the same time shuddered at the thought of the inherent dynamics of the bureaucracies that are thus set in motion and can give rise to *"rationally functioning machines"* and *"an iron cage of bondage"* (Weber 1956, pp. 1040 ff.). Weber perceived and described the danger proceeding from a state authority that was becoming ever further removed from society and its principles, was never purely cognitive-instrumental and always at the same time normatively structured, an agency that in the end threatens to stifle the dynamics of the civil society and its individuals - a fact not acknowledged by the planning optimists at the beginning of the 1970s.

2.2.3   Limitations of Regulative Policy and Initial Approaches Seeking Solutions in the Project of *"Rationalist Statism"*[9]

The experience made with *"rationalist statism"* has shown that the vision of the all-powerful planning state has foundered. Despite, and indeed even because of, all of the successes met with in building social security systems, the limitations facing the hierarchical state in shaping social conditions have become more and more clear in the course of the attempts made at implementing the project of "planned capitalism".

Ernst-Hasso Ritter pointed out that the notion of the democratic constitutional state as a hierarchical agency of governance rested on implicit assumptions that have proven to be unrealistic. The classical understanding of the constitutional state sees state action as bound by the rule of law; administration is subject to clearly defined decision-making chains marked by command and obedience; the powers of state are separated; state and society are distinct from one another; essentially, the state appears to the citizen as a sovereign agent issuing directives. Planning and policy-making rationality of a constitutional state so defined would be conceivable only under specific conditions:

-   *"The state is faced by an environment characterized by relatively simple structures. For it is only when the complexity of the environment can be reduced and abstracted down to the level of relatively few universally valid constituent elements that the abstract law becomes applicable in the first place as a principle instrument of sovereign action.*

-   *The governance effects intended by the state operate basically via straightforward and simply structured chains of action. For the state's unilaterally-sovereign means permit it only direct access to the agents whose behavior it wishes to influence. (...)*

-   *The state is in possession of all relevant information. For its unified-sovereign powers must at least bear within themselves the presumption of correctness, since they demand obedience of those to whom they are applied, and the procurement of information can thus not be made directly conditional on the responses of those affected. This presumption is in turn justified only when the use of these powers is based on all relevant information.*

-   *The goals aimed at by state action must be implemented without demanding any commitment, initiative, and identification with these goals on the part of those affected"* (Ritter 1987, pp. 338 f.).

Willke argues in a similar vein; he points to three fundamental (albeit for the most part implicit) assumptions of the paradigm of rational planning, which, in view of the complexity of social reality, can by no means be regarded as proven:

"(1) ... the notion of clear, distinctly ordered goals, clear, identifiable means, and clear-cut causality;
(2) the notion of clear criteria for reaching goals, criteria such as profitability, effectiveness, and efficiency; and
(3) the central premise that the variety of individually rational single actions will aggregate completely to form a rational and optimal overall outcome" (Willke 1992, p. 114).

In the phase of planning optimism there was hardly any doubt as to the realism of the premises noted by Ritter and Willke. Basically, Ritter and Willke emphasize the problem of the high level of complexity of societies, which makes it difficult to analyze and prognosticate causalities and thus hampers state-level interventions.

The problematic addressed by Ritter or Willke also gradually impressed itself on the planning theorists as a consequence of the empirically observable limitations faced by the problem-solving capacities of the welfare state. The debate that got underway on the pitfalls of regulative policy supplanted the "feasibility illusions". In Germany this discussion included above all those who felt committed to the project of "taming capitalism" but at the same time emphasized the myopia of any exaggerated planning optimism, and subsequently went on to an attempt to fathom realistically the scopes open to effective state action.

Renate Mayntz distinguishes four causal complexes that can be responsible for the failure of regulative policy (Mayntz 1987, pp. 96 ff.). Political planning can fail when policy programs are not implementable, either because the responsible state institutions are unable to implement them (**implementation problem**) or because those for whom such programs are devised refuse to abide by them (**motivation problem**). These first two problems thus affect the effectiveness and enforcement capacities of the agent of governance (state) and the responses of the social actors concerned. Even when these problems can be solved, i.e. when it proves possible to successfully influence the behavior of those concerned, it is still possible that the initial problem will not be solved or that undesired secondary effects will turn up. The responsibility for this may lie in a lack of knowledge on the part of the legislative and the responsible state institutions as regards effective contexts relevant to governance (**knowledge problem**) or the impossibility of intervening selectively in given system processes with the instruments available to the central governance authority (**governance capacity problem**). The last two problems thus result both from the characteristic features of the object of governance and the complexity of social structures.

This problem analysis goes far beyond the problem consciousness of pluralism theories and the euphoric discussion on the planning state. The discussion of these four problem dimensions addresses issues that had until then been largely disregarded:

-    It addresses (knowledge and implementation problem) the internal conditions required for any effectiveness on the part of the state (institutional structures, patterns of organization and management).

-    The reflections on the institutional presuppositions of state effectiveness and governance capacity are on the one hand closely connected with the growing complexity of the social subsystems to be governed, i.e. the objects of governance (governance capacity problem); on the other hand it becomes clear that democratic elections and decision-making processes based on them do not per se solve the problem posed by the legitimation of state action, and thus at them same time the problem posed by the relationship between state and society (motivation problem).

The thrust of the approaches devised to deal with this problem constellation and the weighting assigned to the causes chiefly responsible for the limited scope of political governance have shifted over the course of time. In Germany, but also in other industrialized Western societies, both the debate in the social sciences and efforts aimed at actual reforms first (in the 1960s and 1970s) centered on **knowledge problems.** The establishment of planning elites, planing procedures, and information systems, it was hoped, would serve to make the "state apparatus more intelligent", thus enhancing its capacity to act. The information deficits that were diagnosed were to be overcome by developing the right planning methods, i.e. via a "technical" modernization of the state. The core problem was thus seen as associated more with the agent of governance than with the structure of the object of governance.

In keeping with this understanding of planning as a purely technical procedure, a variety of instruments were developed that were to be used to prognosticate society's future paths with a sufficient degree of exactitude and to reliably calculate optimal paths. Planning-programming-budgeting systems, lookout institutions, complex simulation models, cost-benefit analyses, economic models, and input-output matrices appeared to offer the right methods of rational planning and policy preparation. These approaches still operated tacitly under the premise that the state could basically be conceived as sovereign in its actions.

The course of the second half of the 1970s saw the publication of a number of studies dealing with **problems of implementation and motivation**. The experience that even a well-planned reform policy can fail to achieve its goals led to a shift of the focus of problem diagnosis from the knowledge problem to the implementation problem. Thus, for instance, the then government of the Federal Republic of Germany noted a lagging implementation of its environmental reform programs. "Executive deficits" stemming from inefficient structures in government institutions were suspected as being responsible for this reform blockade, and expertises were commissioned. Implementation research focused on the way in which reform programs were put into practice and noted that the state agent of governance is in fact a tiered system of actors in which the lower-level authorities not only function as neutral institutions in charge of implementing governance measures, but that they at the same time intervene in the governance process both within their own scopes of competence and in violation of given behavioral norms. Administration has considerable weight of its own and also has potentials to influence the legislative process that are not provided for in the classical theory of the constitutional state. *"The implementation process itself"*, Renate Mayntz notes in summarizing her studies on implementation problems, *"... must become an object of governance in the interest of an efficient pursuit of goals"*.[10]

Mayntz warns against any strategy aimed at merely instrumentalizing the executive authorities, because this provokes motivation problems that can lead to situations in which important know-how incorporated in the administrative apparatuses is blocked. Her policy recommendations aim in the direction of decentralization and delegation of responsibilities to the lower-level executive agencies as a means of better harnessing their expert knowledge, thus defusing the knowledge problem and at the same time encouraging a more effective implementation of policy. This view points to the limitations of the concept of hierarchical governance that proceeded on the premise of complete state autonomy (which as a rule meant government; often this separation was not made explicit, as though "the political", "the state" constituted a monolithic entity). In solving the implementation problem, but also the knowledge problem, a democratically legitimated government is also forced agree to cede some of its governance authority and to decentralize some of its policy-shaping potentials to lower-level executive authorities. In Mayntz "the state" thus takes on a more complex structure than it does in the approaches outlined above. Yet it is first of all only the internal organization of the state that is affected by strategic considerations on reform; its relationship to the addressee of policy (social actors) remains unchanged.

Implementation research furthermore unearthed two dimensions of the **motivation problem** that affect the effectiveness of regulative policy. What was first noted was a resistance on the part of the addressees to restrictive state-imposed behavioral norms that grew as regulation density increased. In the second place, it became clear that regulative norms often tend to obstruct behavioral attitudes on the part of social actors oriented toward self-initiative, innovation, and positive engagement. The consequence drawn from these observations tended more in the direction of positive and negative financial incentives than restrictive norms and seemed to call for the initiation of programs of information and persuasion, i.e. tended in the direction of altering the forms of governance.[11] In other words, the focus shifts to the role played by the social actors in the success of regulative policy, even though their active participation is not called for.

At the beginning of the 1970s Fritz W. Scharpf presented a further-reaching approach that thematized *"complexity as a barrier to political planning"* (Scharpf 1972). He criticized the technocratic illusion that proceeded on the premise that all that is needed to enhance the innova-tiveness of a political system is improved decision-making and plan-ning technologies. Scharpf's critique centers on the notion that, apart from the **knowledge problem** - i.e. the question as to how the infor-mation level of state governance authorities can be increased - what has to be focused on is above all the **problem of governance capacity**, i.e. questions bound up with the increasing differentiation of the socioeco-nomic structures to be influenced by political intervention and the great variety of interdependency relations between social subsystems. For Scharpf the core problem of political planning lay in the fact that *"although politics, in its information and decision-making system, at-tains a level of differentiation of its own internal structures corre-sponding to its environment, it has until now nevertheless proven ex-traordinarily difficult, and possible only to a limited extent, to repro-duce as well the actual interdependencies of the problem contexts in the socioeconomic environment by appropriately patterning the link-ages between ways in which problems are processed at the political-administrative level"* (Scharpf 1972, p. 169). The reason why attempts at political planning were frustrated is that interdependent socioeco-nomic structures were confronted by state decision-making structures and procedures tending toward separation.

In Scharpf's view, the problem is as follows (Scharpf 1972, pp. 172 ff.): to solve an information problem, the administrative structures are fur-ther differentiated (*polity* dimension). The price paid for the institu-tionalization of specialized units sensitive to and qualified for their tasks is that these units have a selective perception of social problem areas. Their attention is restricted to their own area of responsibility, problems beyond its boundaries are scarcely perceived, and therefore regarded as less important. This "Taylorization of politics" gives rise to two problems. First, due to segmented problem perception, interde-pendent problem contexts involving several scopes of responsibility are less reliably perceived. The political system tends to perceive and act on these adjacent partial problems. Second, the actual interdependencies between social subsectors make it probable that political interventions based on segmented problem perception will entail unintended effects in other areas if no coordinating mechanisms intervene. In the current discussion this problem constellation is referred to as "policy coherence".

Any simple centralization of problem-solving processes in turn tends to radically simplify problem contexts, and thus doomed to founder on the complexity of socioeconomic structures. Centralized decision structures are capable of successfully dealing only with rountinized or simple problems entailing a low level of information. There is therefore no alternative to decentralization and further differentiation of state institutions.

Scharpf distinguishes two forms of political coordination which can be understood as instruments to be used in dealing with the weaknesses of fragmented decision-making systems. First, it is theoretically conceivable to solve the interdependence problem by means of forms of simultaneous problem processing for cross-sectoral problem contexts; Scharpf refers to this as **positive coordination**. The conditions for this would, however, be *"analysis of the entire factual problem context, control over the entire action space, i.e. over all of the action alternatives related to the problem contexts, and this on the basis of the whole of the problem- and action-related knowledge of the specialized units responsible for the individual subsectors"*.[12]

This large-scale form of integrating coordination between departments of ministries, or indeed between ministries themselves, are, however, Scharpf notes, very rare in practice. It should be noted here that at this point Scharpf himself seems to be falling victim to a "technocratic illusion". He furthermore fails to consider interest and power structures that can block comprehensive reform strategies. For Scharpf, the problematic of governance capacity remains a technical problem of coordination and knowledge.

Scharpf refers to the usual pattern of processing problem interdependencies as **negative coordination**. The main feature of this is that problem-processing proceeds from a specialized unit and is restricted to its scope of duties. Above and beyond the modus operandi of a fully decentralized decision-making system, however, coordination processes involving other departments, ministries, states, etc. are involved in the course of program development. The essential advantage of this form of coordination is its ability to radically reduce coordination costs and to simplify complex problem contexts in such a way as to make possible information processing and consensus formation between a larger number of state units in the first place.

As a rule the issue involved in negative coordination is to rule out in given areas possible negative effects of interventions for other subsegments. This process may be able to reduce unintended secondary effects, though the issue is often apt to be to target policy patterns that do not affect divergent interests of adjacent units that have to be consulted. Negative coordination thus implies the weakness of always having to seek solutions at the level of lowest possible common denominator, which leads to a pronounced tendency in the direction of incrementalism. Incrementalism and a policy consisting of small steps and half measures can have a counterproductive impact on the overall system when partial social problems aggregate to form crisis situations that can be avoided only by means of comprehensive strategies of change that encompass the individual subsectors concerned.

Policy planning is thus faced with a dilemma: it can either restrict planning fields so narrowly that positive coordination is possible, though in doing so it segments interdependent problem contexts; or it can expand planning fields in such a way as to take actually existing interdependencies into account, though it is then forced to look to reductionist coordination techniques that likewise entail negative impacts for policy quality. For Scharpf, there is *"no satisfactory way out of this dilemma"*. In political practice it is therefore necessary to develop *"pragmatic simplification strategies"* as a means of mastering the complexity problem (Scharpf 1972, pp. 175 f.). This might, for example, mean dispensing with any problematization of current policy programs and deciding instead in favor of limited political innovations in strategic core areas yet to be defined (*"core planning"*, priority planning).

The Positions of Mayntz and Scharpf in the Context of the Planning-governance-discussion

Any attempt to define the positions of the studies by Mayntz and Scharpf in the discussion context outlined thus far makes it clear that they on the one hand develop views on the limitations of state-level regulation that critically reflect the premises of pluralism theories and the optimistic planning theorists and extend beyond their reductionist analytical matrices, while on the other hand their reflections nevertheless remain within the framework of traditional theory of the state.

While the pluralism theorists saw the solution of the state's legitimation problem in democratic elections and the realization of civil rights, Renate Mayntz, in her references to the motivation and implementation problem, shows that the legitimacy of state action is not secured per se in democratic societies either, and that in addition a lack of acceptance of policies on the part of those affected by them restricts the scope of state interventions. This means raising again the issue of the - always precarious - relationship between state and society that pluralism theorists regarded as solved in principle. Mayntz' advice for state actors is to engage in permanent persuasion-oriented work as well as to launch an offensive information policy aimed at plausibly explaining state action.

Scharpf demonstrates that, regardless of how perfect they may be, the planning methods and political good will from which planning optimists anticipated a "rationalization of politics" can founder on the complementarity of the environment to be governed. Attempts to transfer into the "administrative world" the task of further differentiation of sectors of society that are set to be changed by political intervention prove to be ambivalent strategies for solving problems of knowledge and governance capacity, since increases of complexity within the state institutional structure themselves give rise to new problems. On the whole, the studies by Scharpf and Mayntz relativize the feasibility and planning illusions very widespread at the beginning of the 1970s by thematizing the problem posed by the limits and pitfalls of state regulation; these they ultimately localize in the complexity of the environment to be shaped as well as in effective contexts that are becoming more and more difficult to read. However, the patterns of solution suggested by these authors are too one-sidedly bound up with the internal structure of the state. Organizational reforms that at the same time acknowledge the limits of political regulation are expected to heighten the state's efficiency and increase its degree of planning rationality. These approaches thus remain within the state-centered paradigm.

2.3 From the Planning Illusion to the Issue of the State's Governance Capacity: The First Relativization of the Modern Understanding of the State

The term "planning" implied the notion that all social subsystems could by and large be structured by a state sovereign both externally and internally. In the course of the disappointment of the planning illusion and the deepening discussion over the pitfalls and limitations of regulative policy, the state's comprehensive claim to governance has been successively reduced. Instead of the term *planning* we more and more often encounter in the literature the term *governance*, which, first of all, expresses a new modesty as regards the scope of policymaking.[13]

In spite of the inflationary use the term governance has experiences since the middle of the 1980s, it is often not precisely defined. The term "governance" stems from control theory and cybernetics (originally Greek: the art of steering a ship).[14] In the discussion in the social sciences the concept of governance was understood as the capacity of political authorities to shape the social environment with an eye to conceptual considerations; and thus the term "political authorities" was understood to mean primarily state institutions. The further course of the debate led to a more and more diffuse understanding of the term. With reference to Luhmann and Parsons, who defined money as a generalized medium of governance, "the market" was introduced into the discussion in German- and English-speaking countries as a form of governance seen as an alternative to political governance. Moreover, the terms "community" and "solidarity" turned up in the literature beside state and market as a third variant of governance (Hegner 1986, Ouchi 1980). This definition of terms, growing ever broader and less precise, ended up in a situation in which governance came to be seen as a synonym for "social order" or "coordination of action". Thus, for instance, Kaufmann speaks of *social governance* and means any form of *"successful coordination of action"*. Market, hierarchy, solidarity, or even electoral systems, become, in this perspective, *"pure types of social governance"* (Kaufmann 1985).

It is evident that the concept governance is losing its analytical substance when it is generally identified with action coordination and social order. Thus it is that governance is sometimes described as a type of action, then as a process, or even a system function. In what follows, on the other hand, the concept of governance is linked to the actor perspective and thus understood in the framework of action theory. *"Political governance as the chance for a goal-oriented self-change of the polity cannot be conceived without recourse to subjects of political action"* (Scharpf 1989b, p. 19). Governance accordingly presupposes, **in the first place**, a subject of governance (**governance actor**), who, **in the second place**, uses selective influence to conduct a system (**governance object**) *"from one place or state to another"* (Mayntz 1987, p. 93). The traditional notion stating that the subject of governance could be only the state or its institutions is abandoned in the transition from the planning discussion to the governance discussion and in this way implicitly dissociated from modern theories of the state. Political governance can also be effected by the synergy of state and private actors, who intervene selectively in politics, the economy, and other functional systems by means of different patterns of action coordination, and do so with the aim of changing them in a sense defined by their own goals (**goal of governance**). Seen from this perspective, both actors and constellations of actors can be subjects of governance, while "the market" or "solidarity", if they are employed selectively for purposes of governance, are **governance instruments.** The emergence of markets or communities would thus be specific forms of action coordination, but not governance in the sense defined here. Governance-related action is thus as a rule not restricted to one-time acts or interventions, and must instead be understood to mean a learning and search process of social actors; and thus the analysis must focus on **governance processes** as its object.

Whether the goals aimed at by the actors of governance are in fact reached or whether unintended consequences are involved is not at issue here. Indeed, from the actor perspective we can speak of attempts at governance even in the limiting case that in acting subjects of governance attain no effects at all - i.e. when from the system perspective no governance materializes. This means that it is essential to differentiate systematically between governance-related action and the effects of governance. Any undifferentiated use of the term governance for these two states of affairs simply masks linguistically the central problem, which must always be sought in the precarious relationship between action and effect.

2.4   The Neocorporatist Discourse on Patterns of Social Organization: Governance of Society via Networking between State and Large-scale Organizations: The Second Relativization of the Modern Understanding of the State - The Discovery of the Governance Potentials of Society

During the course of the 1970s the pluralism-oriented views that had until then dominated the discussion in the German- and English-speaking worlds were confronted by the concept of neocorporatism. The debate, shaped above all by the American political scientist Schmitter (see Schmitter 1974, 1981; Streeck/Schmitter 1985) and the German social scientist Lehmbruch (see Lehmbruch 1977, 1979; Lehmbruch/Schmitter 1979), centers on the thesis that the countries in which a greater measure of political stability, social compromise, and social integration are those in which large-scale organizations or federations (business federations, labour unions) not only articulate their own interests and exert pressure on the political system but also are involved in formulating and implementing policy. The concept neocorporatism addresses a specific type of relationship between the state and federations: Neocorporatism *"... refers to institutionalized, voluntary participation of federations in the formulation and implementation of state policy - above all in industrial, agricultural, and welfare issues"* (Czada/Schmidt 1993, p. 12). The one-sided process that sees the state influenced by pressure groups is replaced by cooperation between the state and the (large-scale) federations, the goal being to seek joint solutions to problems. Neocorporatist coordination of interests aims in particular at a consensual internalization of the costs of policies geared to social interests.

Neocorporatism, understood as a regulative (*ordnungspolitisches*) Model, thus questions both the clear-cut functional separation between state and social groups and the one-dimensional logic of competition between the latter. It is precisely in the mutual influence exercised between state and federations and in the state's negotiations with large social groups that liberal political theory sees the Original Sin of corporatist systems (e.g. Eschenburg 1955, Lowi 1969, and Olson 1992).

The term neocorporatism is in need of explanation inasmuch as it awakens associations with fascist theorems. The most ancient root of corporatism, though, is the corporative constitution of society in the Middle Ages. Antipluralist theories that begin here aim to replace the power of "naked numbers" in political liberalism with a representation of quasi-corporative groups (professional groups, groups of interests, classes) in order in this way to prevent the atomization of society, the seeds of which are seen in liberalism. As a rule such patterns of argumentation tend toward the notion that *"organic communities"* can be reconstituted; various traces of them can be found in the social teachings of the Catholic Church, in cooperative theory, but also in fascist concepts of society.

Neocorporatism disassociates itself from these sources insofar as it sees itself not as a counterconcept to liberal pluralism but rather as a further development of it. Schmitter speaks of *"social corporatism"*, and delimits this from forms of *"authoritarian state corporatism"* (e.g. in Latin American dictatorships in the 1970s, the Franco regime in Spain, etc.) (Schmitter 1974). Lehmbruch distinguishes between "liberal" and "authoritarian" corporatism: *"Unlike the romantic-reactionary program of a 'corporative order', liberal corporatism rests not on more or less rigid attributions of status of the type characteristic of preindustrial social structures but on the conflictual differentiation of interests of a capitalist industrial society characterized by relatively high social mobility ... In contrast to authoritarian-corporative experiments, liberal corporatism develops on the basis of the freedom of association and the autonomy of federations, and adheres to this principle"* (Lehmbruch 1979, p. 53).

Schmitter distinguishes neocorporatism (he himself speaks for the most part of corporatism) from pluralism in the following way: *Pluralism*, he argues, *can be defined as a system of interest mediation whose essential components are organized in an open number of different, voluntary, competitive, nonhierarchical, and autonomous ... groups.* It exerts influence on politics via lobbyism and pressure-group behavior: *"Corporatism,* he goes on, *can be defined as a system of mediations of interests the essential components of which are organized in a <u>limited</u> number of singular nonvoluntary federations that do not compete with one another, have a hierarchical structures, and are delimited from each other by functional aspects. They are,* he notes, *recognized or licensed by the state, if they were not founded on state initiative in the first place. And they are expressly granted a <u>monopoly over representation</u> in the sectors for which they are responsible"* (Schmitter 1974, pp. 94 f.).

Neocorporatist decision-making structures based on coordination between state and large-scale social organizations are understood by Schmitter and Streeck as a new *intermediary form of governance* superior to purely pluralist patterns of politics (Schmitter/Streeck 1985). In contrast to pluralism theories, which emphasize the distance of interest groups to the political system, the neocorporatists' interest groups are seen as actors largely integrated in the political process, who are therefore endowed with political corresponsibility. In functional terms, the shift of problem-solving from parliamentary interest-mediation systems into corporatist systems is interpreted as an attempt on the part of the state to secure its governance capacity while at the same time avoiding legitimation problems.

For Schmitter and other proponents of the concept, neocorporatist forms of interest mediation make sense in particular as instruments used to coordinate economic policy. The neocorporatist approach can thus be understood as the governance-related complement to the Keynesian economic policy dominant at the beginning of the 1970s. The empirical studies thus primarily center on the trilateral patterns of bargaining between state, trade unions, and industrial federations. From the state's perspective, so the argument goes, cooperation with the large-scale federations is an important means of avoiding external effects in the field of economic policy and solving implementation problems. External effects may, for instance, occur when wage agreements directly affect prices and employment levels; and economists oriented in terms of Keynesian economic policy may for this reason find it preferable to coordinate state policy aimed at flattening out the economic cycle and encourage activities on the part of industrial federations and trade unions that can influence the macroeconomic variables.

Corporatism theorists have made out implementation problems **first** where state goals cannot be achieve by means of direct state activities. They refer here, for instance, to the fact that the contribution of state "incomes policy" toward a Keynesian global management of overall economic demand can achieve its effects only when state policies are at the same time flanked by parallel wage agreements. **Second**, implementation problems tend to occur where the control-related effort required to implement state policies would be high and thus costly (e.g. industrial safety, control of emissions in factories); and, **third**, in sectors in which it is not possible to formulate or implement policies without the direct cooperation of the persons effected (e.g. in the dual system of vocational training, development of eco-audit programs). Neocorporatist arrangements are thus seen as patterns of problem-solving for the marginal areas of state regulation. They thus serve to disburden the state.

It is striking that the theorists of corporatism as a rule acknowledge only a few actors: "the state" and "the large-scale federations", i.e. the representatives of capital and labor, form the triad that, through cooperation, is expected to bring about a coordination of divergent interests and to contribute to reducing conflicts as a means of shaping society in a goal-oriented fashion. The neocorporatists proceed on the assumption of *centralization tendencies* in more or less pluralistic societies, or at least regard these tendencies as desirable. Thus it is, for instance, that Katzenstein states that stable economic policy depends on *centralization of the state* (Katzenstein 1978, p. 134; Atkinson/Colemen 1985 argue along similar lines) and the ability of state, labor unions, and industrial federations to jointly compromise their interests. Organization of the important social pressure groups in large-scale federations, and the capacity of these federations to reach overall social compromises under the auspices of the state, are the concept's central figures of thought.

In the literature there is a discussion over the issue of whether neocorporatist arrangements are to be seen as a sign of strength or of weakness on the part of the state. On the one hand, it is pointed out that the "neocorporatist state" does not face social groups merely as a helpless addressee of pressure groups, and that it actively intervenes in the mediation of conflicts of interest between the major groups and thus can clearly be described as having a position "above society"; moreover, it is argued, the neocorporatist project of harnessing the federations to the goal of shaping society strengthens the state's governance capacity. On the other hand, the delegation of governance potentials to interest groups and the growing constraint faced by the state to negotiate with federations in order to implement its policies are interpreted as indicators of the state's weakness and overstrained condition as well as a loss of its autonomy of action.

Both views contain a kernel that is correct: the neocorporatist studies concede that the state, in particular in the field of economic policy, is in a position to intervene effectively only in close coordination with the major federations. This is tantamount to an abandonment of the state's absolute autonomy of action; in this sense one might speak of a weakness on the part of the state. In fact, however, neocorporatist organizational patterns have emerged only where the state was in a position to integrate the central groups of actors within the national formulation of policy. Neocorporatist patterns of politics work in the northern European countries, Germany, and several other EU countries. In the UK or the US, on the other hand, the traditional liberal separation of state and society has retained its cogency; state regulative capacity has been too weak to integrate the major federations in corporative strategies. These instead have operated as classical lobbyist organizations geared to pushing through the interests of their members. Neocorporatism is thus a model that reduces the demands of central planning and governance. But at the same time political decisions continue to be made at the central level. The negotiating state remains the center and peak of society in which centralization tendencies are working.

As a guiding normative principle, corporatism theories go back to the idea of the commonweal. This implies that organizations integrated within neocorporatist arrangements cannot only be oriented toward their own interest, but must at the same time take account of the overall utility of society. This can, for instance, be the case when labor unions moderate, in the overall economic interest, the demands of their members for higher incomes, in this way proving themselves to be reliable partners of cooperation who bear overall social responsibility, at the same time ensuring their continues participation in the political decision-making process. If a federation is to be able to decide whether, in a concrete case, to seek its orientation in the ad hoc interests of its members, in the interest of the federation (continued participation in the political decision-making process), or in an imaginary overall social interest, or indeed in a mixed constellation of such interests, it must have relative autonomy to act vis-à-vis its members. In contrast to the liberal pluralism theories, which expect that a compromise of social interests will result from the political competition between a great variety of interests, the neocorporatists see a *"restrained particularism"* (Mayntz 1992, p. 18) on the part of the federations as essential to avoiding obstructions in the political process and preventing any one-sided realization of particularly well-organized interests. The problem that remains is how the federations are to handle this tightrope act between representing member interests and participating in the process of formulating overriding policies. Neocorporatist theory has little to say on this problematic area.

Many studies cast light on the proximity of neocorporatist theorists to social-democratic notions of the welfare state. Neocorporatist organizational patterns are understood as concepts beyond any untrammeled capitalism. By integrating labor unions and industrial federations into the process of economic policy, capitalism is to be given a shape more compatible with the public interest. A number of studies understand neocorporatism as a third approach between capitalism and socialism (Winkler 1976), sometimes even as a postcapitalist arrangement of society (Lawson 1986). Chiefly, however, neocorporatism is described as *"the highest stage of social partnership"* (Czada 1983, p. 435; also: Jessop 1979, Panitsch 1977).

We can summarize the contributions made by the neocorporatism discussion to the debate on governance theory as follows: the picture outlined above of a society marked by neocorporatist forms of organization turns out to be somewhat simplistic. The triad consisting of state (as the central agency regulating conflicts), labor unions, and industrial federations - as the most important organizations representing the organized interests of society - guide overall social development by means of consensus-oriented decision-making mechanisms. The theorists of neocorporatism thus detect in industrialized countries primarily centralizing, centripetal forces. The formulation of policy centers on redistribution issues, which is demonstrated clearly enough by their orientation in terms of the economic model of Keynesian global management.

The assumption that neocorporatist patterns of organization constitute a structure embracing all social subsystems cannot be upheld in view of the diversity of interests that are organized in industrialized or industrializing societies beyond the neocorporatist triad as well as the variety of policy fields below the macrolevel of policy analyzed by the neocorporatists (sectoral policies, regional and local policies, etc.). Neocorporatist organizational structures constitute only one partial segment of political governance in societies. Apart from the centripetal forces that find expression in modern societies in the existence of large-scale federations, the neocorporatists overlook the great variety of centrifugal forces that limit the scope of neocorporatist governance.

Central questions remain open against this background: Does the close neocorporatist network consisting of state, industrial federations, and labor unions coexist with the forms of political competition between the highly divergent interests described above, or are these completely covered over? How do neocorporatist regimes interact with the functional mechanisms of parliamentarism, or how might the latter be modified? And what are the limitations of neocorporatist policy-making structures themselves? The claim of neocorporatists to have worked out the underlying functional mechanisms of highly developed pluralist societies is much exaggerated.

It can be noted here that the neocorporatist concept on the one hand goes beyond the state-centered pattern of argumentation, focusing attention on social groups and federations as actors of governance, and in this way possibly casting overboard the classical liberal vision of a clear separation of state and society. While, for instance, Scharpf, in the studies he published in the 1970s on problems of political governance, essentially points to the need for reform within state institutions, the neocorporatists show that at least part of the governance problems - in particular the implementation problem - can be tackled through cooperation with the persons addressed by policy. Political governance is discussed not only as a state-level problem area but as a social one as well. This the actually innovative contribution to the governance debate that neocorporatism theory has to offer. On the other hand, the neocorporatist studies lag far behind the differentiated analyses of political governance problems of the type published by Scharpf and Mayntz as early as the 1970s. While the latter address in particular the problem constituted by the growing differentiation of societies and increasingly complex effective contexts (centrifugal forces), this core problem is as good as absent in neocorporatist studies. The neocorporatist nexus of state, labor unions and business federations plays the role of a substitute of what Marx referred to as the *"ideal generic capitalist"*; and it takes the place of the governance optimists' "omnipotent planning state".

CHAPTER 3   **Neoconservative and (Neo)liberal Discourses on the Crisis of the State: From the "Ungovernability Debates" to the "End of the Governance Illusion"**

Not unlike the discussion on economic-policy (from Keynesianism to neoliberalism), the social sciences experienced a reorientation in the course of the 1970s. What is diagnosed is the *"overburdened state"* (Matz 1977), *"the limits of government"* (Lehner 1979), *"ungovernability"* (Hennis et al. 1977) of highly differentiated-pluralistic societies, overregulation, the "colonization of society by the state", or "the state by society", and this leads to a growing significance of reflections on a *"minimal state"* (Nozick 1974) as a solution to the problem posed by the *"failure of the state"* (Arnim 1987).

In general terms, two approaches can be distinguished in the initial phase of the discussion: on the one hand, concepts of a liberal hue that call for a reduction of state activity and the retreat of the state from society and economy, expecting this to lead to a strengthening of the efficiency of the free market, and demands that the power of the federations be restricted and the state be reduced to its original core functions (monopoly of domestic power, minimum social standards, preservation of external peace), anticipating from this a greater measure of individual freedom and economic dynamism; on the other hand, ground has been gained by conservative patterns of interpretation that see the increasing entanglement of state and society as the core problem and - proceeding from the classical theory of the state and a neoconservative critique of the tendencies in pluralist societies working in the direction of a corrosion of state and society - demand that the state's decision- and policy-making monopoly be strengthened vis-à-vis particularist social interests.

Both directions will be illustrated in the following section with an eye to working out their entirely justified critiques of the multifarious planning illusions of the Keynesian era, to work out the core shared by their concepts - in spite of their entirely different approaches - and, finally, to demonstrate the unrealistic nature of the approaches to the problem of governance which they present.

3.1 The Antipluralist Core of the Neoconservative Critique of the Modern State: An Attempt to Revitalize the Leviathan's Absolute Sovereignty

The underlying theme of neoconservative authors is the growth of particularist interests; it, so they argue, leads to a loss of the state's internal sovereignty, which makes it increasingly difficult for the state to take binding decisions, and they alone are *"able to establish reliable order"*.[15] In 1971 Forsthoff noted that in view of the overwhelming power of particularist interests the state is no longer able to fulfill the *"tasks that are most peculiarly its own"*, i.e. as an authority superior to the actors of society, a regulative power capable of enforcing its will (Forsthoff 1971, p. 121).

The critique aims at pluralism theories no less than theories of neocorporatism, and in some cases it addresses important problems that have been neglected by them. Thus, for instance, Kielmannsegg discerns three dangers that stem from the growing strength of organizations representing social interests and cast a cloud over the harmonious worldview of pluralism and neocorporatism (Kielmannsegg 1979, pp. 144 ff.): first, the instrumentalization of state institutions, e.g. by lobbying activities of powerful federations; second, the obstruction of state institutions through the refusal of important particularist interest groups to cooperate and participate in the implementation of policy; and third, the exercise of autonomous governance power, e.g. by the parties to collective bargaining, who - beyond the reach of the state - make decisions essential to society.

The state's scope of action is growing more narrow, its problem-solving capacity remains dependent on the cooperation of the most important particularist interest groups. These dangers read like the reverse side of the successes of the neocorporatist approach to policy formulation. It would be possible to find empirical material in support of both the neo-corporatist interpretation and the view critical of federations. The decisive questions would thus be: Under what conditions is the interaction of the state with interest groups strengthened and under what conditions is it undermined. This issue is, however, not pursued by the neoconservatives. Rather, the neoconservative interest in some real dangers to highly differentiated societies leads into antipluralist and anti-enlightenment patterns of problem-solving that are unable to come to adequate terms with the complexity of modern societies and are in the end based on predemocratic concepts. The neoconservative attempt to resuscitate a state that recalls the regulative ideas of the state as a *"spiritual entity"* in Hegel and totalitarian notions of the state in Carl Schmitt. Hennis, for instance (Hennis 1977, p. 17), pleads for a state with *"the power to create unity"*, one that embodies *"what was never denied to it in the tradition:* (the role of) *protector, guardian, promoter of morality, ... guarantor of moral standards"*. The point of departure here is premodern societies, and what is presented is an understanding of the state directed against plurality and diversity of interests, *"as it was ... understood by classical philosophy: the state writ large"* (Hennis 1977, p. 16). This, it is argued, is conceivable only if it proves possible to *"emancipate ourselves from the premises of modern political thinking"* (Matz 1977, p. 102) (i.e. liberal-pluralist ideas, D.M.), which culminate in the destruction of transcendence, religion, and the moral foundations of every social order.

This discourse represents a futile attempt to rescue the unity of society, the absolute sovereignty of the state, and the pre-Enlightenment authority of ultimate certainties (such as those offered by religion). True, the neoconservatives' warning against endowing strong, particularist interest groups with any superior power rings true, but their picture of society is obsolete: on the one hand, there is no retreat from the high level of differentiation of social interests and society's ability to articulate them - and it is in this phenomenon of pluralization and organizational capacity on the part of society that the neoconservative localize the core of "ungovernability"; on the other hand, heroic governance optimism (which recalls the action-theoretical voluntarism of the planning optimists discussed above) projected by the neoconservative on to their "strong state" overlooks the complexity of effective social contexts that irreversibly restrict the state's autonomy of action.

The neoconservative pattern of analysis is unsuitable to describing the complexities that actually exist and thus offers no constructive points of departure for the theoretical debate on governance. In the field of politics the neoconservative discourse has nevertheless gained in influence as an ideological lever to be used to criticize the pluralist welfare state. It is not seldom that neoliberal economic-policy projects of the type familiar from the USA under Reagan or Chile under Pinochet were provided flanking support by inflated neoconservative views of the state. These projects cannot remain viable in the long run, since it is precisely economic liberalism that advances tendencies leading to individualization and accelerates the dynamics inherent in the market, and this in turn successively undermines the state's scope of action. Any recourse to the myth of the strong state soon reveals itself to be an ideological construct standing on feet of clay.

3.2   (Neo)liberal Models for Restructuring the Relationship between State and Society

3.2.1   Nozick: The Concept of the Minimal State

In 1974 Nozick presented an especially pronounced and widely discussed critique of the "active state". In his concept of the *"minimal state"* he seeks to demonstrate that the only true and just function of the state is to protect individuals from violence and fraud and to ensure that contracts are enforced. Nozick's interest centers on the need to protect the rights of the individual. He maintains that, **first**, the only rights that are conceivable are individual rights and that, **second**, the state possesses no right that would infringe the rights of any individual

(Nozick 1974, p. 113). There is only one exception to this general rule: the state has the right to exert physical force in a given territory to protect the rights of the persons inhabiting it.

However, Nozick's interesting question concerning the minimal tasks of the state misses its point inasmuch as he neglects to address the problem posed by the highly differentiated structures of modern societies. Nozick outline a society whose sole actors are the *"minimal state"* and the individual. His minimal state, whose sole functions consist in safeguarding the collective legal goods of "protection from violence" and "security of contract", is unable to do justice to the demands and realities of a highly differentiated society. In modern industrial societies goods such as health, education, provision for individual needs become collective goods for the individual, since in many cases they are not secured through private, individual, or family activities. If we think of the findings of recent theories of economic competitiveness, the provision of collective goods - such as efficient educational, training, and research systems - must be ensured if economic development is to be strengthened. The idea of the radical-liberal minimal state makes sense only in a "minimal society" far from reality, one in which there are no intermediary instances between the individual and the state.

In modern industrial societies it is possible to secure a diversity individual rights only when the state or organizations representing group interests create and safeguard collective goods and rights. This can be explained in three ways (see Willke 1992, pp. 101 ff.): **In material terms**, the increasing differentiation of society and economy entail a variety of unintended, difficult-to-forecast secondary consequences and long-range effects. Gases emitted by industries or individual consumers are leading to a thinning out of the ozone layer; investment decisions in East Asia can entail severe and lasting effects for the competitive situation of other economies. Often secondary effects or combined effects threaten the rights of individuals (e.g. to health), although these effects affect them not directly and individually but indirectly and collectively. The sequence from the CFC hairspray via the ozone hole to death from cancer cannot be individualized, yet the effects are very real. Another example: international competition places entire industrial locations under adjustment pressure, individual firms are eliminated. A firm's competitiveness, however, depends on a variety of environmental factors that make it appear advisable to view not only individual actors and their rights, but to consider collective actors and groups of actors and, accordingly, collective goods as well.

In social terms, the emergence of collective goods can be traced back to risks and hazards connected with the increasing density, size, and complexity of social systems. If, for instance, a limited number of cars operate in a small area, no problems will result. But if the number of cars grows immensely, the result is a variety of effects and secondary consequences (diseases, accidents, changes to the environment due to road-building, etc.) for **all** persons concerned. The same is true by extension for industrial developments and their potential health-relevant or social impacts. In other words, highly differentiated societies give rise to hazards that come about collectively and can no longer be dealt with adequately by rights protective of the individual.

The significance of the **time dimension** has become clear in connection with problems of environmental degradation. The core of the problem is the short-term and myopic nature of a market geared to individual goods. This entails a tendency toward underproduction of goods that require medium- to long-term rationales or promise gain only over the medium- or long-term (e.g. investment in education/training, infrastructure). On the other hand, new technologies can give rise to medium- and long-term hazards or even detrimental effects on future generations (e.g. nuclear energy), and the market is unable to include these effects in its rationale. It is from these potential hazards that collective rights can be derived as protective measures for collective goods.

Against the background of this line of argument it is impossible to uphold Nozick's restriction of the tasks of the minimal state to the protection of individual rights. What we find instead is that in many cases it is hardly possible distinguish clearly between individual and collective rights. It thus makes little sense to limit the activities of the state along lines based on these criteria.

3.2.2   Olson: The "Decline of Nations" as a Result of the Organization of Social Interests

"I don't know any more society, I know only individuals."
M. Thatcher, cited after Brunkhorst (1994)

The studies of Mancur Olson play a major role in the critiques of the "excessive power of federations" and forms of institutional sclerosis as causes of economic stagnation. Like other political scientists (e.g. Arnim 1987, Eschenburg 1963, McConnel 1966) or economists (Lindblom 1977), Olson argues that the emergence of social interest groups as well as patterns of cooperation and arrangements between state and social groups prevents that state from addressing the "public interest". As he sees it, there is a causal link between *"strong societies and weak states"* (Migdal 1988). His view of the functional logic of modern societies, which is anchored in neoliberal economic theories and had a strong influence on the **market-orthodox** *mainstream* of the 1980s, contrasts sharply with the planning and corporatism concepts of the "social-democratic era" and will for that reason be presented at some length.

As early as 1968 Olson, in his book *"The Logic of Collective Action"*, questioned, with reference to the *"free-rider* problem", the premise of pluralism theories that it is possible to organize all social interests in a balanced fashion. Olson argues that it is not only the state but every interest organization that provides collective goods. The labor unions produce, among other things, the collective good "binding wage agreements", a citizens' initiative proposing a new playground will, if it is successful, secure the provision of the facilities required, etc. Now, collective action is in principle faced with the problem that the positive effects of such action (the use of the collective goods provided) often at the same time benefit those who were not involved in the provision of the collective good. In contrast to private goods, one feature of collective goods is of course that they rule out the principle of exclusion.

This problem, Olson argues, is all the more weighty, the more universal the interest is, i.e. the larger the group concerned, and the more "collective" the result of the collective action. The free-rider phenomenon in large groups results from the fact that the individual contribution to the production of a given collective good is as good as impossible to quantify and there is thus little incentive for individuals to participate. Rationally acting individuals will therefore tend shy away from paying their share of the costs of providing collective goods if they can in any case not be excluded from enjoying them.

Small groups accordingly have an organizational advantage in that here, on the one hand, the individual contribution to the provision or procurement of a collective good remains tangible for the group in its effects and any free-rider strategy would lead to perceptibly poorer results in achieving the groups interests. On the other hand, in small groups there are social control mechanisms in effect that in large organizations cannot as a rule be replaced even by institutionalized control. *"The logic of collective action"* thus favors the emergence of a variety of small interest groups. Particularist interests are easier to organize than relatively general interests, e.g. those of unemployed or poor persons.

Olson convincingly explains that, in contrast to the assumption of pluralism theorists, there cannot be any balanced, symmetrical structure of organized interests in pluralist societies. This implies that the harmonistic equilibrium thesis of pluralism theories that sees competition between individual social interests as giving rise, almost automatically, to aggregated public welfare proceeds from false premises and it thus not tenable.

He furthermore presents good reasons for the circumstance that there are at work in modern societies centrifugal forces conducive to the emergence of more and more small interest groups that make it difficult for the state to gear its activities to general social interests. This line of argument presents strong objections to the assumption of corporatist theorists, who see a increasing organization of society in large-scale federations. Olson agrees with the corporatism theorists on the point that large organizations representing broad interests are better able to integrate general social interests than smaller organizations whose aim is to achieve particularist interests. Since, however, the organizational advantages are on the side of the small groups, large organizations - i.e. the "great hope" of the neocorporatists - are for Olson more or less relicts of the past.

Olson pursed his thoughts on the rationality of collective action and collective actors in another, much-discussed book entitled *"Rise and Decline of Nations"*. In this study he notes an increasing *"institutional sclerosis"* of modern democracies that, he argues, leads inevitably into economic stagnation (Olson 1982). The study's main impulse fell on fertile soil, especially in consideration of the fact that from the end of the 1970s on neoliberal economists were pointing emphatically to the obstruction of market forces due to the expansion of the state sector and the strength of the labor unions.

Olson's core thesis is that the longer political and social stability is guaranteed in a democratic state, the more organizations with a particularist bent will emerge that more and more impede economic growth. Over the course of time social and political stability encourage the emergence of purely redistributional coalitions, and these, through their interest policies, produce *"social rigidities"* which lead to *"institutional sclerosis"*. For Olson the decelerating rates of economic growth to be observed in the major industrialized countries since the second half of the 1970s is linked (mono)causally with the process entailing the growing organization of interests. *"Distributional coalitions slow down a society's capacity to adopt new technologies and to reallocate resources in response to changing conditions, and thereby reduce the rate of economic growth"*.[16]

Olson introduces the thoughts he developed in the *"Logic of Collective Action"* into this larger context. The restrictive impacts of organized interests on economic dynamics are explained with reference to the fact that growth is a collective good and that not all social actors contribute equally to advancing it. The social differentiation of modern societies implies a growing segmentation of interests and the way they are organized. In the face of longer-term political stability, this trend translates out into a reassessment of particularist interests within the political-administrative system vis-à-vis general interests. The complexity and contradictoriness of regulative state policy increases.

According to Olson's logic, small, segmented interest groups have no reason to contribute to economic growth, since their members would receive any a small share of the overall yield. They therefore devote themselves to free-rider strategies and concentrate on the strict pursuit of their own particularist interests. It is in this way that redistributional coalitions arise which, for instance, attempt to restrict the market access of competitors or to push through special tariffs and subsidies and to externalize the costs of this policy. The decisive question here is not whether these strategies always meet with success; the significant factor is that there are, in Olson's logic, more and more interest groups of this type "beleaguering" the state, while contributions to the collective good "economic growth" are steadily declining. These organizational and behavioral patterns give rise to innovation blockades and barriers to growth (Olson 1982, pp. 47 ff.). It is only in (exceptional) cases in which the members of an organization are the main victims of a policy on the whole unconducive to growth, or there are not longer any scope of economic action for clientelist distributive policies, that an incentive emerges for small groups as well to contribute to increasing overall economic growth.

The behavior to be expected, in Olson's eyes, of small, particularist interest groups is not necessarily applicable for larger organizations ("encompassing interest organizations"). For them there are incentives to take overall economic efficiency into account in their cost-benefit rationales, since they, as large groups, will, ex definitione, profit more by the collective goods concerned. On the other hand, at least segments of their memberships are affected by the negative consequences of any inefficient particularist policy. To illustrate this with an example: a given labor union will, in a crisis, first attempt, often together with the employers' federation concerned, to seek solutions that externalize the costs, burdening the whole of society (protectionism, subsidies, etc.). If the industrial organizations are imbedded in overall economic structures (umbrella union, industry-wide employers' federation), this would mean that the costs of these particularist strategies accruing to other parts of the overall organization would be addressed. It is thus more likely that large organizations will develop policies that can be used to largely internalize such costs and, for reasons of self-interest, more clearly gear their activities to overall economic interests. In a nutshell, Olson's résumé is that larger organizations will, for egoistic motives, pursue an interest policy more compatible with society than that of small segmented organizations.

Olson's studies address problems of state governance that (may) result in particular from the growing differentiation of society and the interaction between state and social interest organizations: empirical evidence for his line of argument is easy to find in any society - which is not sufficient proof to justify the manner in which he generalizes his thesis. The problem involved in the restriction of the scopes of action open to the state that are imposed by powerful interest organizations and their influence on the state was not addressed by the pluralist theorists. The concepts of corporatism reductionalistically abbreviates the interaction between the state and federations to productive alliances between state, labor unions, and business federations; the demonstration that there are such productive alliances is, however, itself an argument against the generalizability of Olson's sclerotization thesis. Olson's argumentation at any rate constitutes an important enlargement of the governance debate:

-    The centrifugal forces within modern societies that Olson describes and explained with the aid of his *"Logic of Collective Action"*, point to the real problem of how, from the angle of the state and society as a whole, it is possible to harness the dynamics of social segmentation and the emergence of various interest organizations with an eye to avoiding social **disintegration** and prevent the "colonization" of the state by particularist interests. Neither the pluralism theorists' trust in the invisible hand of the political market nor the hopes placed by the neocorporatists in a harmonious integration of social interests via coordination processes on the part of the triad of state, labor unions, and business federations has proven very convincing as regards this problematic.

- Olson's line of argument addresses an important paradox of modern societies: while, in the view of theories of pluralism and corporatism, the growing organizational capacity of social actors almost automatically gives rise to a greater measure of social rationality, Olson emphasizes the **paralyzing divergencies of interests** stemming from the articulation capacities of a large variety of interrests. Olson has on his side empirical evidence that indicates that increased capacities for self-organization and action on the part of social actors at the same time open up a variety of free-rider options for particularist interest groups, and that these (can) contribute to obstructing the state's governance capacity. Based on Olson's argumentation, however, it is not possible to explain the forms of productive cooperation between state and social actors that are also empirically demonstrable.

- The existence of distributional coalitions which achieve their particularist interests by externalizing costs can hardly be disputed. One example of this in the European Union is the massive state support provided for agriculture by means of subsidies and protectionism at the expense of the European consumers and taxpayers and the producers in developing countries.

- It is also correct that societies (may) give rise over time to **institutional rigidities**, encrusted structures, and rigidifying distributional coalitions which work to conserve structures and slow down or even obstruct the process of social change.

In other words, Olson addresses problem areas that are important for the issue of governance capacity and that are addresses neither by the state-centered regulationists nor by the neocorporatists. Some present-day governance theorists do indeed, as is discussed below, take account of these "Olson phenomena". Their studies center on the question of what normative action orientations on the part of actors, what institutional framework conditions and specific organizational patterns encourage or cause the blockade mechanisms in pluralist societies outlined by Olson.

The theoretical and political conclusions drawn by Olson are undercomplex, completely remote from reality, and incompatible with democratic structures. He first calls for market forces to be strengthened (e.g. abolition of tariffs, free trade, improvement of factor mobility), seeking his orientation here in standard neoliberal concepts (Olson 1982, pp. 59 ff.). In these passages, Olson gives up any claim to draw social institutions out of their shadowy existence as data from the framework corona of the economy. Olson develops schematically the "vision" of a political system in which interests are mediated without federations and other intermediary institutions, one that is completely unrealistic for modern societies. His arguments switch back and forth between the radical-liberal hope for an absolutely unrestrained play of free forces (of firms, but also individuals) in an *"unconstrained market"* and the fiction of a complete statist regulation (of society) by a state which, in fulfilling its governance tasks, is neither reliant on cooperation with social actors nor checked by them in its omnipotence. What emerges is a social vision which includes only the market, the individuals, and the free-floating state, detached from social interests and capable of implementing *"coherent programs"* (Olson 1982, p. 237). In this Olson falls, in normative terms, behind the democracy-oriented pluralism theorists and decouples his vision from the irreversible structural characteristics of actually existing, highly differentiated societies. In terms of his confidence in the autonomous governance performance of the state (once it is "rid" of interest groups), he finds common ground with the conservative theorists of the state.

Problematical are also the conclusions that he draws from his observation that the long-term effects of political and social stability tend to diminish growth. His hypothesis *"that countries that have had democratic freedom of organization without upheaval or invasion the longest will suffer most from growth repressing organizations and combinations"* (Olson 1982, p. 77) reads like a justification for potentates à la Pinochet. And in fact Olson contends that occupation powers or totalitarian governments are best suited to effectively break up interest organizations that obstruct growth. Olson's theoretical analysis leads him into political reflections that he summarizes with a refrain from Jefferson: *Sometimes the tree of progress must be watered with the blood of patriots.*[17]

This view is untenable not only for normative reasons. Theoretically interesting is Olson's naive confidence in the authoritarian state, which need "only" be rid of particularist social interests to be able to purse overall social interests disinterestedly. Any consistent application of his *"logic of collective action"* to the action orientations of an uncontrolled state apparatus would, in contrast, lead to a different picture: more likely than a public-welfare orientation on the part of authoritarian regimes is free-rider behavior on the part of the state actors, and with it the emergence of a self-enriching state class.

What is instructive in Olson's analysis is his coupling of free market economy and authoritarian state. Olson fails to realize that the *"logic of collective action"* worked out and regarded by him as cogent a priori - and consisting in the free-rider behavior of particularist interest groups and leading into an institutional sclerosis - emerges from an action orientation that is regarded by rational-choice theorists as the essential characteristic and the motor of free market economies: namely the action orientation of the "utility-maximizing individual", which is in a position to represent only its own interests. It is, in other words, the action logic of the *homo oeconomicus*, raised as it were to an ethical norm in neoliberal theory, that, transferred to the level of interest organizations, leads to the paralyzing phenomenon of the generalized lobbyism outlined by Olson.

Olson is here caught up in one of the core contradictions of neoliberal theory: the egoistical individualism propagated (as a contrast to Etzioni's idea of an "individualism compatible with the public interest") becomes - as a norm underlying human behavior - a problem for the development of society as a whole. Olson finds no way out of this dilemma. He propagates on the one hand the untrammeled market economy which, in accordance with his assumption of an individual exclusively dedicated to maximizing its egoistic utility, sets free and gives scope to precisely the particularist forces which he in the last analysis regards as self-destructive; on the other hand, he recommends the concept of the authoritarian state as a means of restraining particularist interests. The question raised here concerning the action orientations of the actors involved and their effects on different governance concepts (hierarchical governance by the state, governance by networks) will be taken up again in the course of this study.

It may be noted by way of summary that both Olson's analysis of the causes of governance blockades in modern societies and his proposals for overcoming them fail to do justice to the complexity of highly differentiated social formations. The formation of social organizations and intermediary structures is an expression of modernization processes that are irreversible. Neither the all-powerful state nor the unfettered market, nor for that matter Olson's combination of a completely sovereign state with a largely untrammeled market economy, is in a position to meet the complex demands posed by social integration or economic development. This is also demonstrated by recent studies on competitiveness. Aside from distributional coalitions, there are a number of examples that indicate that the activities of federations and interest organizations can contribute to disburdening the state, that nonstate organizations can, in cooperation with the state, develop and implement problem-solving strategies, and that it is often highly efficient interest organizations that make state regulatory activities possible in the first place. Federations are accordingly not only disruptive factors for the market mechanism, they also fulfill important tasks associated with articulating and aggregating social interests and controlling state power. They are thus a part of complex webs of social relations whose problem-solving capacities - if one looks at the cases of various countries - tend to differ greatly. The central question is accordingly what normative and institutional conditions make it possible to mobilize the productive potential of a great variety of efficient social actors and limit any fragmentation or particularization of society. No answers are to be found in Olson's theory. He remains bound up in the logic of action theory, which knows only individual or collective actors oriented solely in terms of their egoistic self-interests. Against this background it is not possible to explain why it is that in reality, in spite of all, both distributional and "productivity-minded and problem-solving coalitions" are possible.

Even a superficial comparison of patterns of social organization, e.g. in the US, western Europe, and Japan, should have cast any all too rash generalizations concerning the allegedly unstoppable trend toward *"institutional sclerosis"* in a questionable light. Here it quickly becomes evident that, in the first place, sharply divergent organizational patterns have developed and that these, in the second place, obviously differ considerably in their efficiency and performance. Olson on the other hand is not impressed by this empirical diversity and claims for his theory, wholly in the tradition of neoclassical economics, a temporally and spatially unlimited validity.

Aside from this fundamental point of criticism, two further objections to Olson's view must be mentioned here in the name of completeness: first, Olson's study raises methodological doubts inasmuch as he, based on highly aggregated data, a limited number of influencing variables, and quantitative econometric analyses generalizable for only a few North American regions, arrives at propositions on social development per se. Even the operationalization of his central variables raise doubts as to the validity of his results. This objection applies both for his definition of "interest groups or their activities" as independent variables and for their negative consequences for macroeconomic aggregates such as "economic growth" as dependent variables. One point that is also questionable is his independent variable "age of democracy", which serves as an indicator for political stability and the duration of the influence of interest groups. According to Olson, the latter correlates positively with the level of institutional sclerosis and significantly negatively with economic growth. The empirical material on which Olson's far-reaching hypotheses are based is, in other words, weak (Abramovitz 1983, Keller 1990).

Second, a more differentiated approach is needed to assess the role played by small- and large-scale federations in social decision-making processes. Large-scale interest organizations have the political power to pass on the costs of realizing their interests disproportionately to other groups or to society as a whole. This means that the incentives for an organization to work for an economic policy efficient for the overall economy depend not only on their size but also on the articulation capacity of other social groups and organizations. The greater their scope of and claim to participation, the smaller the possibilities large organizations have to pass their costs on to others. If the political power of large-scale organizations is taken into account, the small-scale interest groups can also be seen as representing a control potential vis-à-vis these power-based structures. All in all, we see that Olson's analytical matrix is from the outset too narrow to capture these complex arrangements of society.

3.3   Résumé

Willke points correctly to a fundamental problem facing both modern and modernizing societies. This consists in the simultaneous intensification of two seemingly contrary developments: *"... on the one hand the split between state and society due to a process of functional differentiation that is growing more and more complex and on the other hand the confusion of state and society (the mutual interpenetration of society and state, D.M.) due to the ubiquity of the problem of organized complexity"* (Willke 1992a, p. 51).

The linkage between democracy and market economy in the industrialized Western countries and especially the considerable success of the project of the welfare state in western and northern Europe (dynamization of the differentiation of state and society, heightened social mobility of citizens, democratization) is accelerating this development dynamic and undermining the state's sovereignty and governance capacity in the course of the process. On the one hand, the democratic, constitutional and welfare state is expected to constitute the hierarchical peak and the center of society so as to counter the centrifugal dynamics of the great variety of existing particularist social interests and rationalities. On the other hand, it is expected (thus the normative claim), by improving equal opportunity and social mobility and opening up opportunities for its citizens, to successively relinquish its definitive control and the decision-making authority it enjoys as the peak of society so as to strengthen the autonomy and self-organization of an emancipated and self-confident society.

These development trends are in part disregarded by the dominant theories concerned with the governance of society. The liberal theorists of the state and the modern theory of the state insist on a clear-cut separation of state and society and persist in their assumption of a state sovereign both internally and externally. The theorists of pluralism do not question this basic position, supplementing it instead with their mechanistic and harmonistic notions on the mediation and translation of social interests into state policy. The "planning optimists" of the 1960s and 1970s proceed unquestioningly from this theoretical tradition, though they at the same time demand of the state more and more governance potential.

It was only in the course of the 1970s that **governance problems** were perceived. **Three distinct problem dimensions** are here culled from the approaches discussed above (see Overview 2):

- **Complexity problems**: state sovereignty and the state's action potentials are being undermined by increasingly complex effective contexts stemming from the increasing differentiation of society and economy as well as from ubiquitous globalization trends.

- **Power-related problems**: the growing organizational capacity of social actors leads to the emergence of influential particularist, distribution-oriented interest groups (lobbyist federations) that "beleaguer" the state, restricting its decision-making latitudes. Society's organizational capacity threatens to turn into a blockade of political governance geared to overall social demands.

- **Motivational problems**: diagnosed trends toward individualization, fragmentation, and desolidarization are leading to a breakdown of civic commitment accompanied by a decline of the willingness of citizens to follow the state's lead as well as to an erosion of the moral-normative resources on which the public-welfare orientation of private and state actors is based. This can result in tendencies toward social disintegration.

In his studies from the 1970s presented above, *Fritz W. Scharpf* points in particular to the problematic of complexity. *Renate Mayntz* supplements this diagnosis with references to power-structure problems and motivational problems; the implementation of state policies often fails because of unwillingness on the part of citizens to follow the state's lead and cooperate in implementation. *Neocorporatist approaches* likewise emphasize complexity problems, though for them these are manageable; problems associated with power structures and motivation are disregarded. The *neoconservative authors* insist in particular on the problems related to power structures and motivation; they infer from them the risk of a breakdown of state sovereignty. *Radical-liberals* like Nozick address the problematic of power structures less as an expression of the "colonization of the state" by lobbyist groups than, conversely, as a siege of society by the ubiquitous state. *Olson*, finally, like the neoconservatives, points to problems of power structures and (less clearly) motivation, yet without sharing their skepticism toward market-liberal ideologies.

Interestingly, **the regulative (*ordnungspolitische*) responses** to the governance problems diagnosed from case to case remain within the framework of the classical "market-state logic". Scharpf and Mayntz relativize their governance optimism and the demands they place on the state, noting instead that the apparatus of state should be modernized. The neocorporatists see as sound the political governance capacity of modern societies based on close cooperation between the state, in their view still the dominant agent, and the large-scale employer and employee federations. Counter to all objective trends working toward a restriction of the state's scopes of action, neoconservative authors plead for a reactivation of the sovereign state as the clearly defined center of society. Radical-liberal authors like Nozick place their confidence in the inherent dynamics of an unregulated market economy and insist on a far-reaching reduction of state interventions. Finally, Olson's vision (not unlike Nozick's) boils down to a largely unregimented market

Overview 2: Governance Problems from the Perspective of Different Authors and Theories

	Complexity problems (loss of state sovereignty due to increasingly complex effective contexts, globalization, etc.)	Power problems ("colonization" of the state by particularist interests)	Motivational problems (individualization tendencies, social fragmentation, de-solidarization)	Conclusions
Pluralism theory	0	0	0	Governance problems not addressed
"Planning optimists"	0	0	0	Great governance competence on the part of the state (voluntarism)
F.W. Scharpf (1) ("positive and negative coordination")	++	0	0	Relativization of governance optimism;
R. Mayntz (2) (causal complexes of governance problems)	++	+	+	Modernization of internal structure of the state
Neocorporatism theory	++	0	0	Relative loss of state governance autonomy compensated for by triad of state, business federations, and labor unions
Neoconservative "ungovernability debate"	0	++	++	Emphasize "rule of federations" and decline of values; plead for reactivation of the "sovereign leviathan"
The "minimal state" - Nozick	0	++	0	Notes obstruction of society by all-powerful state; pushes for radical reduction of state regulation and "Free Market Economy"
"Institutional sclerosis" - M. Olson	0	++	+	Loss of state governance capacity due to particularist interests; reestablishment of social governance capacity by market and authoritarian state

(1) F.W. Scharpf, Planung als politischer Prozeß, in: Die Verwaltung, No. 4, 1970; -, Komplexität als Schranke politischer Planung, in.: Politische Vierteljahresschrift, No. 4, 1972

(2) R. Mayntz, Politische Steuerung und gesellschaftliche Steuerungsprobleme, in: T. Ellwein / J.J. Hesse (eds.), Jahrbuch für Staats- und Verwaltungswissenschaft, Baden-Baden 1987

++ = very important　+ = important　0 = not addressed

economy, but one that is complemented by a powerful (authoritarian) state whose task is to contain the organization of particularist interests.

One striking aspect is that none of these approaches is geared to reforming the relationship between society and state; the solutions they propose to the governance problems they note entail strengthening the market and/or state. Yet all three dimensions of the governance problem result from the fact that the social dimension between the state on the one hand and the market on the other has become enormously differentiated in the last decade. This structuring of social space is either regarded as negligible, which entails continued recourse to a given regulative (*ordnungspolitisches*) design and its two pillars, "market" and "state", or perceived as a stumbling block that needs to be pushed aside by a strong "State".

The following chapters will illustrate that this strand of the discussion, localized as it is within the classical "market-state framework", is not an adequate basis on which to discuss fruitfully the problematic of governance. The problem of the erosion of state sovereignty gives rise to the question of social governance capacity. But we will start out by looking into Luhmann's systems-theoretical "general offensive" against the "governance illusion"; it marks a turning point in the governance discussion.

CHAPTER 4   The Systems-theoretical General Offensive against the Idea of any Governance Capacity of Societies

4.1   Luhmann's View of the Problem of Social Governance

"During the governance process ... millions of other things are happening at the same time which, because they are simultaneous, can neither be known nor causally influenced."
N. Luhmann (1989), p. 7

"That governance is necessary is not to say that is feasible."
H. Willke (1992), p. 111

The discussion on "ungovernability" and the neoliberal and neoconservative theoretical critique of the *"feasibility utopia"* which was dominant up to the mid-1970s and banked on the *"scientific state"* as the central agency has been radicalized by Luhmann-style systems theory. Luhmann uses the concept of governance in a purely pejorative sense. While until then the debate centered on the issue of the degree of governance capacity of state and society - along a continuum extending from *"minimal state"* to *"welfare state"* - without questioning the traditional understanding of the state (the state as the hierarchical center of society, and thus clearly separate from it), Luhmann's studies have set their sights on presenting the discussion on the state and governance conducted to date as irrelevant. Luhmann began a debate with Scharpf with the following provocation: *"With an eye to societies or political systems, economic systems or other complex entities, it makes little sense to pose the question of governability. The question, put in this way, will certainly have to be answered in the negative"* (Luhmann 1989, p. 12).

Even though Luhmann is always confronted with the suspicion that his autopoietic view of the world tends toward overgeneralization, is unsuited to any real analysis of social processes, and has, *"with an extravagant display of terminology"*, immunized itself against any model designed to shape and change social relations (Müller 1992, p. 361), his studies at first contributed strongly to disconcerting governance theorists representing other views, and then led to a substantial advance in the debate. The reason for this can only be that Luhmann formulates questions to the governance theorists that in fact reveal weaknesses in the traditional approaches.

Luhmann takes leave of the notion of both any cybernetic governance of society and of the concept of rationality - *"from Weber to Habermas"* (Luhmann) - which proceeded on the assumption that knowledge, learning, and communication give rise to actor knowledge that makes it possible to forecast the future and thus to shape society.[18] He instead describes the *"self-generation"* and *"self-production"* of closed subsystems, which, at the level of their *"own operations, cannot maintain any contact with their environment. Nor can they, not even one little bit, operate in their environment, i.e. not extend their internal operations into the environment"* (Luhmann 1992, p. 213). Thus it is that, from its functionally specific logic, no one subsystem is capable of purposively governing other subsystems or providing a generally valid perspective for society as a whole.

The assumption of an operatively closed self-reproduction of functionally highly differentiated subsystems applies for the political system as well. According to Luhmann, the latter has, in the first place, developed into one subsystem among others, i.e. it can no longer represent the peak of society, and, in the second place - like all other subsystems - is self-referential in its actions, geared to its own communicative context and thus unable to govern other functional areas or assume responsibility for society as a whole. *"The political system can ... govern only itself. ... That and how this happens no doubt has powerful repercussions for society. ... But this effect is no longer governance, and is not governable either"* (Luhmann 1988, p. 337). Luhmann goes on to note: *"Every functional system is geared to its own distinctions, i.e. to it own constructions of reality. ... No attempt at governance can abrogate, or even bridge, this difference"*. It would accordingly be naive to assume *"that what the economy is unable to achieve ... in terms of self-*

governance should be accomplished by politics" (Luhmann 1988, pp. 346 and 325).

According to Luhmann, the core problem and governance dilemma facing modern societies consists in the fact that two evolutionary principles pose mutual problems to one another: on the one hand, the principle of **growing functional differentiation** in subsystems such as economics, politics, science, education, etc., which leads to increasing specialization and thematic constriction of the subsystems that extend their **interdependencies**. Each subsystem is capable of reproduction only in combination with other functional domains. On the other hand, as internal complexity increases, the principle of **operative closure** gains prevalence because the subsystems form autonomous functional principles (Luhmann speaks of *codes*) which, in the process of social evolution, are decoupled from general social communication and become increasingly self-referential. The increasing interdependence of the subsystems, marked at the same time by the impossibility of any goal-directed exchange (**independence**) between the *"internally directed subsystems"* (*"mutually independent self-reference"*) (Bendel 1993, p. 263) leads to a *"structural rationality deficit"* (Luhmann 1984, p. 69).

Increasing differentiation thus implies both an efficiency-boosting autonomization of specialized subsystems and an *"increase of the diversity of options"* (Willke 1989, p. 61) and, at the same time, the growing risk that the modes of action of the subsystems will no longer be (able to be) geared to overall social rationality, which poses a danger to social integration. In Luhmann's view politics that retains its claim to exercise governance functions is bound to fail of these structural and functional principles characteristic of modern societies. Since the development dynamics of a system is never fully predictable and at the same time millions of new events take place whenever attempts are made to influence a system by means of control and planning, ungoverned effects will always occur no matter how ambitious the attempts at governance may be.

Luhmann in no way interprets the - thus diagnosed - impossibility of overall social coordination as a crisis of modern societies. Until then sociology had been concerned with the issue of the mechanisms that might be able to integrate the partial rationalities of subsystems in order to ensure the survival capacity of society as a whole. Parsons (1968) localized a potential of this type in the binding effects of institutional norms; Durkheim (1988) saw this potential in a morality with the power to institute solidarity; and Habermas (1981) sees it in the structures of understanding-oriented communication. Luhmann, on the other hand, views the increasing differentiation of society as *the* condition for the success of modernity, viewing the self-referentiality of subsystems as the actual identity formula of modern societies. He is here not concerned with whether or not the world is in order or evolving toward order. State governance is, in his view, to be had only at the price of dedifferentiation, and thus of social regression.

Luhmann's concept of autopoietic stability has a distinct ring of the neoclassical concept of the invisible hand guiding the market and - like it - rids itself of any empirical or indeed normative questions as to the direction that social development might take or what might result from the autonomization of social subsystems. Social evolution is in principle contingent, the only question that arises for Luhmann concerning the development of autopoietic systems is thus the question of existence itself: *"To be or not to be .... They continue or discontinue their autopoiesis like living systems or die. There is no third possibility"* (Luhmann 1986, pp. 184 and 176).

From a perspective as nihilistic as this it is no longer possible to thematize the need for social regulation or the issue of specific organizational patterns. Any attempts to identify patterns of regulation of different societies and to learn from successful cases become pointless, any reflections on civilizing social evolution, or at least on rectifying the pathologies of governance, are thus null and void. Luhmann's attempt to comprehend social complexity is far removed from concrete analyses, loses any openness toward knowledge, description and explanation of variations and different types of social organization and patterns of state regulation, is therefore unable to develop any action orientation, and ends up in a phenomenological reductionism that Luhmann himself tersely formulates as follows: *"For the survival* (of systems, D.M.) *evolution is sufficient"* (Luhmann 1984, p. 645).

Here there is no scope for action strategies on the part of actors. Willke, who himself comes from the school of systems theory, though in his writings - in the field of systems theory - he distances himself critically from Luhmann's orthodoxy, rightly criticizes the fact that Luhmann's rigorous theory formation ends up in the last analysis with the abdication of politics.

Luhmann is also criticized in a similar vein by Hans Jonas (1979), who demands that responsibility be assumed for the consequences brought about by technical or any other types of individual action. This appeal - argues Luhmann -, assuming that it has been noted in the first place, is certainly well meant, though it seeks recourse in a helpless ethics. For *"if he who brings about effects (he, in other words, who dares to act) does not know and cannot know what effects he is bringing about, and if he is permitted to state this, the dilemma is obvious: either nonaction (but who then assumes the responsibility for the effects of such nonaction), or a leap in the dark"* (Luhmann 1992, p. 182). What remains is the *"autopoietic contemplation of society"* (Müller 1992, p. 358) along the lines of the maxim 'order is a citizen's first duty' for: *"... how is one to make one's action plausible to others by explaining that one does not know what its outcome will be"* (Luhmann 1992, p. 186).

The great interest experienced by Luhmann's studies is presumable fed by three sources. **First**, in a period in which a general crisis of large-scale theories has been perceived, Luhmann proposes a "great theory". While, in tendency, science is breaking down into an increasingly large number of disciplines and special fields and the hopes placed on achieving scientific breakthroughs through interdisciplinary research have long since drastically diminished and given way to general modesty as far as the scope of scientific research is concerned, Luhmann offers an integrative, all-encompassing, macrotheoretical road of access to society. The claim to be able to explain "everything" with one approach is very attractive in view of the discontent experienced in the face of the "new obscurity" (*neue Unübersichtlichkeit*) identified in the end of the 1980s by Habermas. The high price to be paid from Luhmann for the attempt to thematize "the totality of the whole" is the constraint to reduce all social phenomena to "evolution" - a process of scientific "dedifferentiation".

Second, - and this is more significant in our context - any study of Luhmann forces the reader to address the conditions under which governance and political intervention take place in the first place and can lead to success, and to do so more precisely than the governance theories presented until now have done. Luhmann's questions are more interesting than his answers. We see just how radical Luhmann's questions are when we realize that even a few years ago it was regarded as feasible for the hierarchically organized state to engage in comprehensive social planning on the basis of extensive information systems; this was basically and in the last analysis seen as a technocratic problem. At the latest it was Luhmann's more precise and emphatic insistence on the complex repercussions of social evolution that led to an effective disconcertedness among the governance optimists of the past.

Third, Luhmann's descriptions underline the growing fragmentation of modern societies, disintegration tendencies, and the helplessness of state institutions and other groups of actors in even understanding diverse, often global crisis phenomena, to say nothing of responding adequately to them. The risk potentials inherent in modern societies were not discovered by Luhmann. One need only think of Habermas's *"New Obscurity"* (*Neue Unübersichtlichkeit*), the *"ungovernability discussion"* conducted by neoconservative thinkers, Beck's *"Risk Society"*, or any number of other studies on the ecological endangerment of the world. But while all other approaches pursued by the social sciences continue to search for development perspectives, and these efforts again and again lead to complex considerations on the limitations, risks, and chances of attempting to influence social dynamics, Luhmann's bombastic fireworks display finally ends up in simplistic formulas on the course of the world.

Luhmann's core concepts that challenge governance theories are the following: growing differentiation of society into subsystems and the increasing lack of transparency implied by it; growing internal complexity in the subsystems and the resultant self-referentiality of these subsystems; the political system as one of many subsystems, one that is in principle unable to brings its effects to bear selectively and successfully on other subsystems, thereby influencing the direction and dynamics of their development. The emphasis placed on the centrifugal dynamics of the increasing functional differentiation of societies radically questions the hierarchical principle of order of traditional theories of the state and points to heterarchical, polycentric, and decentral arrangements as basic patterns of social organization. This reduces the explanatory power of concepts that interpret the state as the hierarchical peak of society, which itself is, in its fundamental domains (firms, parties, etc.), organized along hierarchical-bureaucratic lines. In particular in his central reference to phenomena of an at the same time growing interdependence between subsystems themselves and independence of the subsectors from their environment, Luhmann has without any doubt contributed to the *"demysification of the state"* (Willke 1987). The simultaneity of interdependence and independence could prove to be the decisive motor behind the complexity problems pointed to by the theories analyzed above, though they were not able to specify the functional logic behind them.

Two decisive issue complexes may be induced here:

1. May we cogently infer from the growing differentiation of overall societies and the increasing internal complexity of their subsystems the impossibility of governance assumed by Luhmann? Or are intersystemic forms of governance and coordination as well as patterns of social organization conceivable which, despite their high level of complexity, lack of transparency, and the indisputable danger posed by the self-referentiality of subsystems (independence and interdependence), are nevertheless able to permit targeted governance and with it a minimal measure of rational self-reproduction of highly differentiated societies - even if this should be localized beyond the omniscience fancies of the planning theorists of the past? This issue complex points the

need to reconciliate systems-theoretical insights with action-theoretical approaches.

2. Are modern societies still able, despite the increasing internal differentiation and external intertwinement of political systems, to integrate the dynamics of centrifugal partial rationalities to form a viable overall context, and what resources might they make use of to do so? Or is, as Luhmann thinks, the only question left to answer whether or not evolution will succeed or fail?

The governance-theoretical approaches outlined thus far have been unable to respond adequately to the disconcertedness provoked by Luhmann. They

- either proceed on the assumption of the fundamental possibility that governance can succeed on the basis of relative trivial transmission mechanisms between politics and society (pluralism theorists, planning theorists, even neocorporatists) and give inadequate attention to the pitfalls of governance, or

- emphasize social complexity as an essential problem for governance (like Mayntz and Scharpf), but then offer as a core solution no more than a "perfection of the state", which - following Luhmann - first of all boils down to an increasing differentiation of the state apparatus, thus additionally exacerbating the complexity problem, or

- argue against the background of an extremely reductionist, (neo)liberal understanding of society (as do Nozick or Olson), characterized by the existence of the market, the framework-defining state, and the individual, which, in optimizing their specific utility functions, generate states of equilibrium.

It was the above-mentioned core issues raised by Luhmann that have constituted the center of governance theories since the end of the 1980s. Luhmann no doubt has the merit of having contributed to a sensitization for the intractability and the narrowness of functionally specific communication systems. The traditional understanding of society, i.e. as an agency sharing *one* governance center with the state, is being successively modified by new governance theories. The analytical matrix is also expanding at the same time. The subject that interests governance theorists is no longer merely the state and public policies, it is the complex architecture of modern societies, and it can no longer be reduced to market, state, and tripartite coordinations of interests. Luhmann has contributed toward bringing a social-theory orientation into governance theories, which until then had in essence concentrated on the state. This makes the issue of the governance capacity of modern societies more complicated, but not, as Luhmann thinks, pointless.

4.1.1   Objections to Luhmann's Orthodoxy

"The necessity to decide extends further than the capacity to know."
Immanuel Kant

Before we go into more recent theories of governance, some fundamental objections to Luhmann's orthodoxy will be pointed out that will prepare the terrain on which more complex governance-theoretical studies operate. Six lines of argumentation are essential.

1. Actors must act. The preliminary theoretical decision to replace action with communication causes Luhmann to abstract explicitly from empirically observable actors, in this way closing himself off from theoretical approaches oriented to institutions, actors, and action. A first argument important to the study of governance theories and the actions of actors, actor groups, and the political system is that, despite all imponderables, they are forced to act in reality and have decided in favor of action. In view of the great variety of crises and economic, social, and ecological challenges that exist, there is also apparently a need for social governance and regulation - and there are options open.

Autopoietic systems theory is not very helpful here in that it only permits statements on non-goal-directed evolution. Governance-theoretical approaches, on the other hand, have to make action-theoretical statements, though without being able to claim that they are informed of all conditions that determine and influence action. In view of the complexity of causal relations, any naive action theory that aggregates the actions of individual actors in linear fashion to come up with overall trends is bound to fail. Political governance takes place in a complex field of tension. On the one hand, specific functional logics are active in the subsystems (competitive mechanisms include the "logic of money" in the economy, etc.); on the other hand, individual and collective actor interests collide, and unintended consequences of actions are conceivable. The actors are unable to annul the inherent necessities that emerge as a result of system logics or power structures, and yet through their actions they change the structures in which they move. Structural configurations stamp the actions of individuals and collective actors, though they themselves are at the same time changed by actions. In this force-field of structure and dynamics, action and system emerge as restrictions on and chances for governance. Social development must thus not be misunderstood as a linear process but should be seen as a result of an overlapping of inherent systemic dynamics and attempts at governance induced by different actors.

The "feasibility illusion" of the past is no longer possible against this background. Governance actors must consider that efforts aimed at governance are always based on uncertain data and imperfect information, though they for the most part derive from proven methods and concrete experience. Statements on social development trends, the necessities and possibilities of governance, cannot be understood as ultimate truths but must always be seen only as preliminary results. A proceduralist approach of this sort is regarded by systems theorists as a simple legend, though it is unavoidable in any science open to practice and application. The medical man gives instructions based on imperfect information and uncertain data, and yet the life expectancy of the population nevertheless rises. The knowledge available on the origins of and possible therapies for cancer are limited, and yet action is taken, and know-how is accumulated in the process of acting that later permits the development of more precise therapeutic methods.

The matter is similar in the field of politics. In view of the complexity of societies, there can be no governance on the basis of perfect information on determinant factors and the great variety of effects to which actions may give rise. If it is necessary to act, there is no alternative to a governance theory that attempts to combine insights based on both systems and action theory and takes into account the system logics and action rationalities of actors or groups of actors, in this way contributing to the process of shaping society. Seen in this way, governance must be understood as a permanent learning process on the part of actors. Any such view systematically recognizes (in contrast to autopoietic systems theory) the potentials, options, and chances of governance and (in contrast to naive action theories) the restrictions faced by governance. It is in this way possible to overcome Luhmann-style "restriction theories" that see political action as impossible and at the same time avoid the approaches widespread in the political sciences which, in voluntaristic fashion and ex ante, regard everything as possible and, in the ex post perspective, invariably categorize, on the basis of functionalist argumentations, developments that have been completed as consequential and unavoidable.

2. Luhmann overrates the mutual intransparency and closure of subsystems and underrates the communication, coordination, and integration potential of individuals, groups of actors, and institutions. Luhmann rightly points out that a function-specific *code* first structures reality in its own language system, that, in other words, the language of law first of all speaks of reality as a legal nexus and the language of politics operates in the conceptual world and interpretive matrices of the political. But the question is what this means in practical terms. It is often that case that individuals and organizations belong to more than one functional system at the same time; for instance, research institutions of business firms; it is not only their own scientific codes but at the same time the logic of the industrial firm for which they are active that constitute their relevant framework of action. Organizations and other actor systems can simply not afford to speak only one functional language and to close themselves off from others. They have to build intersystemic communicative competence and, depending on situation, be able to switch or combine functional logics. It is for this reason that large scale corporations have law departments, research labs, and marketing divisions that follow their own functional logics so as to achieve success **and** at the same time to be able to recognize and understand the languages and logics of other departments and fields, in this way reproducing themselves as an overall organization.

This is not to rule out in highly complex organizations the possibility that activities may take on an autonomous nature, that selective perception and narrow self-referential outlooks may develop in functionally subdivided units. In corporate research departments it will always be difficult to get across the need for economic calculations; financial departments are apt at times to have little understanding for the resources and time needed by research departments, and so on. But action systems and organizations would hardly be able to stabilize and reproduce themselves if they were systematically unable to develop efficient mechanisms that make possible interfunctional communication and coordination. This is all the more the case in the framework of the new production paradigm: the competitive advantages of networked firms and clusters vis-à-vis centrally managed big corporations are based precisely on their intersystemic communication skills. In clusters the logic of increasing independence between the participating firms and organizations is combined at the same time with the logic of growing interdependence (since what is produced is a collective output); the self-referentiality of subsystems predicted by Luhmann thus fails to materialize. That this need not succeed, i.e. that complex patterns of the division of labor are fragile, was already pointed out in the 1960s by Karl Deutsch. He pointed out that subsystems may have a tendency to close themselves off from their environment (i.e. to be self-referential in Luhmann's sense of the word) and that this can lead to pathologies and risks to the existence of the systems concerned (Deutsch 1963). He detected the causes for this tendency in exaggerated routinization, the dominance of the present over the future, and the circular closure of decision-making structures, and he recommended the establishment of a variety of (redundancy-generating) control and rectification mechanisms.

3. Luhmann underrates the capacity of the political system to intervene successfully in other functional systems. If one follows Luhmann in his assumption that law and money are the basic governance media employed by the state, the consequence is that state governance has repercussions in all areas and in particular on formal organizations that are reliant on law and money. This, for instance, is true of educational and health-care systems, of the field of culture, or of the economic system. State promotion of environmental technologies or the establishment of environmental standards will, to be sure, not invalidate economic rationales (i.e. permanently violate the code of the subsystem economy), though it can determine the direction in which solutions are sought. Or, contrary to the interests of the automobile and oil industries, fuel prices are increased or catalyzers required as a means of increasing the environmental compatibility of motorized transportation. If, in spite of all, the intended governance effects are not reached, this will often not be the fault of the self-referential logic of the addressees but will be the result of resistance, power and interest structures, that are always encountered by policy when it seeks to bring about change and shape society, in this way shifting the interrelations of forces in society.

One can of course also imagine attempts at governance that are doomed to failure, attempts that are either not "understood" by the targeted subsystems, violate their functional logic, or are easily dodged by the addressees. An example for the first case would be attempts in the field of population policy aimed at lowering the birth rate by distributing contraceptives, while the cause of population growth is in fact to be sought in the function of old-age security for parents, and on top of that religious beliefs may be undermining the acceptance of birth control. An example for the second case would be environmental legislation that overburdens industry and jeopardizes its existence. The third case would be, for instance, that of a government that attempts to push through speed limits against the articulated will of the populace, and without initiating the controls required.

These considerations show that the crucial problematic is not Luhmann's question a general capacity or incapacity for governance but

rather the - to be sure - complicated question of the specific scope of
political interventions. Many examples presented by Luhmann in his
studies show that he has primarily attempts at governance in mind that
completely annul the constitutive modes of operation of subsystems
(e.g. rigid state industrial planning contrary to the imperatives of the
world market). As a rule, however, state policy is today concerned with
gaining scopes of action against the background of the acceptance of
relatively autonomous chief orientation of subsystems.

**4. Tendencies toward growing differentiation and the emergence of
effective actors can either strengthen or weaken the governance
capacity in a sector.** The increasing differentiation of functional systems and their internal organization lead, according to Luhmann, to
self-referentiality and make impossible any goal-directed governance.
This interpretation is one-sided. The more scopes of action, and thus
self-governance capacity, actors gain, the more they **are able** to relieve
politics of governance tasks or to take on governance functions in cooperation with the state. It at the same time becomes increasingly difficult for the state to push through its own governance intentions against
the interests of well-organized actors. The objects of governance in this
way become veto-bearing partners in negotiation systems. Intersystemic governance (of the economy by politics, the influence that scientific research gains on firms, and so on) is thus possible, though its
success is by no means assured. Instead, like Luhmann, of speaking of
the impossibility of governance, it make more sense to operate on the
assumption of unsecured governance capacity.

**5. In empirical reality there are obviously ways of improving the
integrative and coordinative competence of social actors** (including
those from different subsystems) which differ in terms of efficiency;
Luhmann shows no interest in them since he does not acknowledge the
"theoretical qualification of actor systems", although they are of great
significance for any action-oriented theory of governance. In the course
of the 1950s and 1960s the countries of western Europe were able to
implement forms of social organization and patterns of regulation that
permitted them to make up for the enormous edge in productivity enjoyed by the US economy. In the 1980s Japan's patterns of organization

and governance and its specific network structures linking economy and state proved superior to those of the other industrialized nations. This implies on the one hand that there are no patterns of social organization that possess timeless efficiency. Instead, techno-organizational upheavals and innovation pushes as well as economic and political globalization trends exercise changing constraints acting in the direction of adjustment in patterns of organization and governance aimed at gaining the ability to come to terms with new challenges. On the other hand, it is becoming clear that it is essential for any action- and policy-oriented governance theory to determine which patterns of organization and interaction are suited to boost the coordination and integration capacity of actor networks or organizations in specific historical situations.

6. The "independence-interdependence phenomenon" does not necessarily lead to self-referentiality and incapacity for governance; independence and interdependence are, rather, linked together in a tense relationship that, depending on the concrete shape it is given, can develop productively (in the sense of an increase of problem-solving capacities) or pathologically. In Luhmann's view the growing differentiation of society leads to increasing interdependencies, while at the same time the social subsystems are more and more concerned with themselves and are thus incapable of intersystemic interaction. This results in the assumption of the impossibility of governance in complex societies. This view is one-dimensional, and thus insufficient, in that as differentiation increases it is not only that the autonomy (independence) of the subsystems grows; also, and at the same time, the conditions for their reproduction become more and more dependent on their exchange with neighboring subsystems or on their ability to consciously zero in on their environmental conditions as the object of their decision-making processes (interdependence). Thus, for instance, a democratically legitimated government could ignore over the long term problems like unemployment and environmental degradation only at the risk of its own decline. And larger-scale corporations are forced - much more intensively today than in earlier times - to observe and to respond to changes in the fields of politics, law, science, and training, these having either restrictive or conducive impacts on corporate decisions, while at the same time gearing their activities to economic efficiency and innovation, i.e. to an orientation of their business policy to the functional logic of economic subsystem closest to them. It is exactly the high degree of differentiation of society that has led to a situation in which, for instance, the competitive power of firms no longer depends only on internal factors, but is at the same time reliant on external factors such as the quality of the training systems, the capacity of economic policy to provide for stable macroeconomic framework conditions, and the material, physical and nonphysical infrastructure developed by private and public actors. A further example is the environmental problematic: in a democratic society no firm can today afford to completely disregard the environmental problematic in planning or realizing major investment projects. Subsystems must thus (in Luhmann's language) learn to perceive the codes of the other subsystems and to engage in intersystemic communication.

As the complexity of society increases, the densifying links between the subsystems are - even in their own eyes - more and more in need of intersystemic exchange and coordination. High levels of differentiation in societies, developing in the process more and more subsystem autonomy **and** "structurally coupling" these subsystems with the environment by means of growing intersystemic communication and coordination, do not necessarily constitute antagonisms, they can also represent complementary relationships.

While the subsystems gain autonomy on the one side by developing specific functional logics and communication codes, the same development dynamics increases their dependence on external contexts. Subsystems, or better: actors in subsystems, that are able to develop communicative and coordinative competence in interaction with adjacent subsystems will be more successful, even in terms of increasing their own internal rationality, than subsystems that fail to develop modes of intersystemic exchange, that, in other words, behave autopoietically in Luhmann's sense of the term.

4.1.2   The Complex and Fragile Relationship between Social Interdependence and the Self-referentiality of Sub-systems

This line of argumentation leads to a governance logic that differs fundamentally from planning-oriented governance theories. Differentiation processes and the growing level of social division of labor no doubt reduce the governance capacity of higher-level agencies, while the self-governance potentials in the subsystems is on the increase. The need for horizontal and vertical coordination between the growing number of subsystems increases. Governance in this way becomes a process marked by efforts aimed at horizontally and vertically networked communication, coordination and integration of actor groups. Due to the increased autonomy of many social subsectors, one-sided hierarchical governance by the state is as good as impossible. Many subsystems are at the same time reliant on interaction with the political system and other social sectors, and conversely: firms depend on efficient technological and research landscapes, political stability, and many other factors that they cannot themselves create; the political system in turn must be geared to interaction and cooperation with actors within the subsystems that are to be governed (e.g. the economy), since without their know-how or help in implementation the state can become overburdened or even incapacitated.

This line of argument leads (in contrast to Luhmann's logic) to the important consideration that subsystems are not even able to follow their own particularist interests, functional logics, and codes. Because of their dependence on functioning communication and coordination mechanisms linking them with other system areas, *"it is entirely possible, and in tendency even rather probable, that even aspects of overall social rationality will link them to the narrow rationality of system-specific self-reproduction"* (Bendel 1993, p. 275). In Luhmann's terminology, one might thus state that the logic and interdependence (at least potentially) "traps" the dynamics of the subsystems working in the direction of self-referential independence.

High levels of differentiation, division of labor, the emergence of decentral structures impede and prevent hierarchical governance in many social subsectors, though they can at the same time entail gains in overall social reflection potentials if intersystemic communication and coordination succeed. In the model of hierarchical governance, central agencies (the state, a ministry, corporate management) constitute the active actors, and the subsystems to be governed, or the actors active in them, adjust to them. In social reality, characterized as it is by high levels of complexity, division of labor, differentiation, autonomization, and interdependence, many subsectors, and the actors active in them, elude this governance pattern. At the same time they in this way bear a large measure of responsibility for their own reproduction and are forced to observe the environment and society and to develop mechanism of communication, interaction, and coordination that can secure the reproduction of their subsystem with an eye to the conditions of reproduction of neighboring subsectors. Paradoxically, it is the contexts constituted by simultaneously increasing independence (of the subsystems) and interdependence (between the subsystems) that, despite increasing complexity, represent a strong trend counter to the risk, not to be denied, of a self-referentiality of social groups of actors.

The fundamental impossibility of governance maintained by Luhmann thus does not apply per se, though it certainly holds true for specific constellations: if traditional governance mechanisms continue to exist in spite of altered patterns of social organization (high levels of differentiation, division of labor), successes in governance are unlikely. This is the reason for the crisis of the "planning state", but also for that of the Fordist mass-production firms, which are characterized by a growing internal division of labor, increasing differentiation of subsectors, complex supplier relations, and a top-level corporate management that, using one-dimensional, hierarchical governance mechanisms, helplessly attempts to steer these heterarchical organizational structures and in doing so gives rise to growing coordination, control and transaction costs. Any one-sidedly hierarchical governance undermines the innovative and creative potentials that emerge precisely from the autonomy of the subsystems (independence). As far as the political governance of societies (including the governance of complex corporations) is concerned, the challenge is to gain influence on the development of the subsystems (e.g. environmentally compatible operation instead of absolute "self-referentiality" of the economy), to target development corridors, and to pay particular interest to the growing interdependence between the subsystems. Scharpf had pointed out that state institutions have as a rule developed in parallel to, and as a mirror image of, the process of growing social differentiation in society, which made it possible for actually existing social interdependencies simply to reproduce themselves. The argumentation now presented would suggest giving some thought to patterns of organization and governance that would make it possible - in dealing with interdependence phenomena - to engage in interface management. Governance institutions should accordingly not be not be responsible only for specific social subsystems, but should at times even stand counter to interdependent social fields.

It can be noted by way of summary that in Luhmann's studies the emphasis on social complexity coincides with ultimately one-dimensional interpretive schemas. Luhmann has emphatically opened our eyes to the fact that exaggerated planning demands automatically entail disappointments. Luhmann makes it plain that the notion that efficiency in governance and planning can be augmented by means of constant differentiation, increasing division of labor, plus hierarchical governance (this was the vision of the Fordist project, and it held sway in the business world no less than in the world of politics) is a fiction. His conclusion that the unstoppable growing differentiation of society ultimately renders it impossible to govern social subsectors is not shared by this study. Still, critical analysis of Luhmann's approach has entailed important gains in knowledge that were left out of consideration even by the most differentiated governance theorists (such as Scharpf or Mayntz).

In the **first** place, theories of governance must divorce themselves from the traditional theory of the state, the conceptual frame of reference of the approaches discussed thus far. The notion of an absolute sovereignty of the state vis-à-vis society is obsolete. The increasing differentiation of social subsystems leads to a situation in which sovereignty and governance competences and potentials "seep" into society. The single-minded functional logics in social subsystems - from science to training, research, and media up to the overall social system - elude traditional state-level governance mechanisms, though they at the same time generate a variety of subsequent effects that affect society as a whole. In the **second** place, the heightening of rationality in the subsystems (the *"active society"*) may be causally linked with an increasing measure of irrationality and a loss of governance at the level of society as a whole (*"blocked society"*). In the **third** place, the state's loss of autonomy does not, however, simply imply that other social subsystems will gain in autonomy. The proper functioning of the other subsystems as well is tied up with interaction with specific environments (e.g. dependence of the economy on efficient technological landscapes and the stability of the political system). A high level of functional differentiation likewise (but not in equal measure) generates gains and losses of autonomy, independence and interdependencies. Thus state is, in other words, not replaced by a different, dominant subsystem that represents the peak of society; instead, what develops is a complex system of divided sovereignties, *"co-sovereignties"* (Meyer 1994, p. 43). In the **fourth** place, one-sidedly hierarchical governance concepts cannot do justice to these social structures and functional logics, in that they proceed from the autonomy of the central agency (state, corporate headquarters) vis-à-vis the subsystems to be governed. Governance by the centralist state governance of detailed developments in the fields of technology, training, and research is, seen against the background of the current state of the division of labor, only conceivable at the prices of a paralysis of the internal problem-solving and creativity potentials of the subsystems. More complex patterns of social organization call for more complex forms of governance. This raises the question of autonomy-compatible possibilities of intervention in the subsystems as well as of mechanisms of an "interface management" between the subsystems as a means of preventing tendencies toward social disintegration. In the **fifth** place, there is also the possibility of distinguishing clearly between the actors and the addressees of governance. The relative loss of autonomy of the political system as compared with the social subsystems, the structural pattern of divided sovereignties, in many cases calls for an interplay between the political system and the actors whose behavior is to be influenced. Governance theories can therefore not continue to argue from the standpoint of a one-sidedly centralist state. They are confronted with the complicated theoretical question of the logics of the interplay between state and society in the development process.

This problematic can be adequately discussed neither with the instruments of the governance-theoretical discussion offered by pluralism theories or neocorporatist approaches nor on the basis of the romantic revival of the leviathan by neoconservative authors or Olson's vision of a market economy flanked by an authoritarian, though welfare-oriented, state. The process in which state and society gradually dovetail, both the interdependence between and independence of social subsystems increase, and centralization and decentralization tendencies in society are on the increase calls for patterns of interpretation imbedded in both governance theory and social theory that point beyond the approaches dominant prior to Luhmann. The question is not whether *more* or *less* state intervention in economy and society is called for, the concern is that the development dynamics of modern societies are undermining the traditional forms of state governance and social integration, giving rise to forms of organization and governance whose modus operandi is only inadequately grasped in all of the patterns of interpretation discussed thus far, as important as some of them may still be (in theory and in practice).

CHAPTER 5   Initial Responses to the "Demystification of the State"[19]

5.1   The New Modesty in the Discussion on Governance Theory Following the Ungovernability Debates and the Insecurities Generated by Luhmann

"The history of political thought in the 20th century can be written as a history of growing modesty with regard to the claims to governance capacity placed on the state."
K. v. Beyme (1991), p. 32

Before new responses to the *"demystification of the state"* (Willke) sketched there are worked out, the state of the debate up to the mid-1980s will be briefly summarized in six points. The aim is to synthesize the problems and questions concerning and the dimensions of the crisis of state-level governance capacity with which current governance theories are forced to come to terms.

Compared with the 1960s and 1970s, the **first** thing that can be noted about the result of the discussion on governance theory up to the mid-1980s is its generally more skeptical attitude toward the possibilities of modern societies to act upon themselves by means of rational state planning and intervention. In retrospect the pluralism-theoretical notions of a self-stabilizing political state of equilibrium (political invisible hand) based on uncomplicated patterns of interaction between state and society seem overly simplified. The same is true of governance optimism and the hopes of a rationalistic and democratically restrained statism raised by the theories geared to planning and the welfare state as well as of the neocorporatist vision of a society governed by the triad of state and the top-level organizations of labor and capital.

Second, a variety of the objections advanced by authors skeptical toward governance, like Olson, neoconservative theorists, or Luhmann against the notion of the all-powerful state is worthy of consideration. The studies critical toward governance can in general terms be reduced to two fundamental directions. On the one hand there are those - in particular e.g. neoliberal authors like Olson - who criticize any **over-regulation** of society and economy by the state, seeing here the spreading danger of institutional sclerosis. In other words, the issue in this context is a state that is too strong or at least overly present. On the other hand various observers note an **overburdening of the state**. They point to the problem posed by an incapacitated state or one too weak to respond adequately to social challenges:

Summarizing the up to now presented argumentation, the state is confronted by

-   growing governance-related requirements (globalization of problems, environmental issues, unemployment, and so on) accompanied by declining governance capacities and potentials;

-   a variety of governance problems (Mayntz speaks of problems involved with motivation, implementation, information, and complexity) that result from the growing complexity and inherent dynamics of the social sectors to be influenced;

-   the challenge of safeguarding social integration from globalization trends and tendencies toward internal fragmentation.

These needs can overtax the state. Phenomena like the following have been noted:

-   the colonization of the state by well-organized, powerful particularist interests;

-   a slowdown, or indeed even obstruction, of political decision-making processes due to the increasing level of organization and growing claims to participation on the part of social groups of actors;

-   centrifugal forces active in society that trigger tendencies toward social disintegration and are as good as inaccessible to the state;

-   loss of shared values on the part of social actors and - consequently - difficulties in coordinating processes between state and organized groups in arriving at a general-welfare orientation based on consensus and compromise.

Third, these demands placed on the state and the problems observed conceal processes of change in society that overburden the traditional forms of state-level governance; the "state's reach" is limited. The growing differentiation of society, globalization trends, and the increasing complexity of social processes that are associated with them and are marked by inherent dynamics in social sectors which are difficult both to understand and to govern are on the one hand an expression of social modernization, though, on the other hand, they imply a growing need for coordination, the risk of social disintegration, and scarcely governable social dynamics with uncertain outcomes.

The processes of change and the increasing complexity found in modern and modernizing societies are characterized by two important tendencies: on the one hand, increasing interdependencies between social subsectors (economic sectors, state institutions, the environment, etc.); on the other hand, the declining capacity of large-scale, hierarchically integrated organizations and firms, both private and public (themselves "products" and "motors" of the modernization process), to manage effectively and efficiently the complexity problems present in their own spheres of activity. The tendencies toward fragmentation and decentralization resulting from them, however, are not automatically translated into independence between organizations and social subsectors. Instead, a variety of forms of cooperation can be observed between organizations both in the political system and in the private sector: policy networks, neocorporatist systems of negotiation, the allocation of new roles between state- and nonstate actors in politics, profit centers in large corporations, subcontracting, just-in-time production, joint ventures, strategic alliances on the level of the global economy. *"... we seem to live in a world in which both the number of separate actors and the degree of interdependence between their choices are simultaneously increasing"* (Scharpf 1991b, pp. 279 f.).

Fourth, the responses of the governance pessimists to the problems worked out by them are highly unsatisfactory. They boil down to attempts on the part of neoconservative authors to restore the traditional strength of the leviathan, which, in view of the irreversible process of increasing social differentiation, amounts to a hopeless project. On the other hand, they propose deregulation projects that place their bets on a strengthening of the market and the self-governance capacity of modern societies, largely abandoning any claims to governance. This project can not provide an answer to the question how the great variety of risks, social, ecological, economic, and political problems resulting precisely from the inherent dynamics of modern societies and the globalized economy might be contained or solved. In other words, in their debate with the planning optimists the neoconservative and neoliberal sides again trot out, in its full sterility, the classical, dichotomous controversy of state versus market.

It is not seldom that the two lines of argumentation are synthetically intertwined (as they are in the theoretical concepts presented by Olson, but also in political practice): neoliberal economic policies and deregulation projects are supposed to provide a response to overregulation and the overburdening of the state, and these are flanked with conservative social policies that emphasize the authority of the state, the unity of the nation, the state as the pinnacle of society, and traditional values as a means of halting the breakup of society feared in these quarters. One could name as examples for this style of politics nearly all ruling conservative alliances in the Western industrialized countries during the 1980s, and not least the Pinochet regime. The crucial weakness of this project is that any forced strengthening of market forces (accelerating social fragmentation and differentiation, the breakdown of traditional structures, and the weakening of the state) permanently undermines the outlined goals of conservative policy and their vision of a strong, hierarchical state.

Fifth, responses to the *"demystification of the state"* that want to avoid the pitfalls of the simplistic market-versus-state discussion would have to accept the twofold challenge consisting on the one hand in the tendency toward overregulation and on the other in the real danger that the state might be overburdened by processes of increasing social differentiation. Both tendencies give rise to different demands:

-     Institutional encrustations and overregulation, which can hardly be
      denied, call for deregulation. The question in need of clarification
      is the areas in which state efforts aimed at governance can be gi-
      ven back to society.

-     Yet the fact that the state is overburdened in view of the complexi-
      ty with which it has to cope by no means renders regulation and
      governance superfluous, though it does cast doubt on the tradition-
      al forms of governance and calls for altered patterns of social or-
      ganization and governance.

The governance pessimists discussed, with their simplistic state-market
approaches, offer no orientations adequate to the twofold challenge
posed by governance concepts in modern societies.

Sixth, it has become clear against this background that the premise underlying traditional theory of the state, i.e. the state's internal and external sovereignty, which constitute the ultimate foundation on which
the governance-theoretical discussion is based, can no longer be upheld
in view of the structural changes in modern societies. The state is no
longer interpreted as the leviathan enthroned above society.

Modernizing societies appear to be affected by centrifugal forces
working in the direction of a reversal, or at least a relativization, of a
development tendency that was seen for centuries as an iron-clad law
in the process of civilization: the trend toward territorial centralization
and the enforcement of a state monopoly of power against secular or
ecclesiastical powers (see esp. Elias 1974, vol. 2). What is unmistakable is a dispersion of competences and social governance potentials,
which has caused some authors to speak of *"refeudalization tendencies"* (see Held 1991; Marks 1991) which are marked by the emergence
of uncontrolled and uncontrollable *"private governments"* (see Ronge
1980; Streeck/Schmitter 1985). It can at the same time hardly be
imagined how the great variety of economic, social, and ecological
challenges at the global and national levels are to be tackled without
any agency of social governance competent for, or at least committed
to, *"overall responsibility"* (see Offe 1987).

This field of tensions make it plain that the question of national governance capacity can no longer be discussed merely with an eye to the effectiveness of the state. Governance capacity must be thematized within the context of patterns of organization, communication, and interaction between the state and other social actors. But this means a loss for the state of the clear-cut contours that are attributed to it by pluralism theories and neoconservative theories of the state alike. The space between "market and state" is gaining in significance. At the same time the boundaries between state and nonstate tasks and organizations in *"polycentric societies"* (Rosewitz/Schimank 1988, p. 304) are beginning to blur. The de-limitation of the state emerging from the *"cosovereignty"* (see Eschenburg 1989) of social actors and the converse *"division of the sovereignty"* (Tocqueville 1959, p. 187) of the state is interpreted by the one side as a *"socialization of the state"* and by the other as a *"'statification' (*Verstaatlichung*) of society"*. These conceptualizations make it clear that the old issue of the state's governance capacity (the "active state") leads into the question as to the organizational and governance capacity of societies (the *"active society"* - Etzioni 1968). The dichotomization of self-governance and state intervention that has often dominated the discussion on *Ordnungspolitik* is in this way blurred.

What follows will work out three strands of the discussion in which responses are sought to the *"demystification of the state"* that make possible a minimal measure of governance capacity even under the outlined conditions of an increasing complexity of societies.

5.2 Policy Research in the Political and Administrative Sciences in Search of a Realistic Discussion on the State: Empirical Search Processes

5.2.1 From the Leviathan to the "Cooperative State"[20]

Under the lee of the one-sided deregulation concepts which were dominant in the 1980s, marking the political agenda of nearly all industrialized countries and determining the fundamental orientation of the two major international financial institutions, World Bank and International Monetary Fund, there developed in the social sciences differentiated views of the problem field of "political governance". This process can be compared with developments in the economic sciences. The new theories of competitiveness also emerged in the decade of neoliberal hegemony in the 1980s, and in doing so drew the line between themselves and the Keynesian economic policy approaches.

The discussion on the state and on the chances and limitations of governance of societies that was resumed in the mid-1980s and opened paradigmatically with the publication of the study *"Bringing the State back in"* (Evans et. al. 1985), constitutes not a return to the traditional concepts but an attempt to work out realistic concepts concerning the problematic of governance. The general offensive launched against the theory of the state which was dominant until the end of the 1970s and on which the relevant planning-policy approaches were based explicitly or implicitly led to a far-reaching correction of the course of administrative and policy research in Germany.

In 1987 Hesse wrote in the *"Jahrbuch für Staats- und Verwaltungswissenschaft"*, which was then in the process of redefining its position, that what was at issue was an expanded discussion that was not restricted only to the constitutive ideal, normative, and conceptual foundations of the state; the real issue, the argument went, was a reorientation dedicated in particular to a *"definition of state action derived from actual empirical analysis"* (Hesse 1987, p. 56). The reorientation centers on a questioning of the fundamental premises of the classical theory of the state as to the state's unity and sovereignty. What is noted is the *"observable finding"* that *"the functions of the state are becoming more and more manifold and differentiated"*. What, however, is more important is that *"the boundary between state, private agents, and 'intermediaries' [grows] more diffuse when more and more state functions are assumed in part by private agents, more and more intermediaries replace state services, and the private agents delegate more and more tasks to the state"* (Fürst 1987, pp. 261 f.). The state as the clearly defined center of governance is being replaced in the public sector by *"multicentric action centers"* (Fürst 1987, pp. 263 f.), while at the same time increasing intertwinements are emerging in the relationship between state and social actors. This process is experiencing change both in action and decision-making constellations and in the modes of problem-solving, procedural sequences, and their normative governance.

The hierarchically governing state is supplanted by the *"cooperative state"* (see Hartwich 1987; Ritter 1979) which either supplements or indeed replaces centralist directives with decentral coordination and expands traditional regulative systems based on *Ordungspolitik* by a variety of forms of cooperation and participation on the part of social actors in the process of governance. This has led to a situation in which the traditional dualism between society and state, between governance agency (state) and addressees of governance have become blurred and imprecise.

The discussion over governance capacity in modern and modernizing societies is therefore forced, as Fürst rightly notes, to leave the beaten path: *"The discussion over the state's share, the growth of the state, the delimitation of the state sector from the private sector, the age-old question of the relationship between collective and individual governance in a society then evidently encounter only framework conditions, though they also become more unspecific the greater the mixed zone, the gray zone, becomes in which state and private, collective and individual governance processes and issues are linked with one another"* (Fürst 1987, p. 268).

In this discussion policy researchers recognize that the change in the structures and processes of the way in which political-administrative problems are dealt with and the development of new forms of governance, involving in many different ways nonstate institutions and interest groups, must be conceived as a function of social change. It is the modernization of society itself (increasing levels of organization of society, claims to participation on the part of the population, permeation of life-spheres by science, etc.) that is undermining the state's traditional sovereignty. The autonomous state is overburdened in many policy fields when it comes to assessing the relevance of problems, formulating adequate solutions to them, implementing these solutions, evaluating the results, and inferring from them needs for change. This puts an end to the heroic premise of the state acting independently of society. The "overburdening of the state" consists above all in the felt need to encounter more and more complex needs with the means of traditional forms of governance.

5.2.2   A Differentiated View of Governance Activities

An overview developed by Geile, Schubert, and Lehnert (Lehnert/ Geile/Schubert 1983) illustrates how increasing social complexity is translated into increasingly differentiated demands on state-level governance activities.

Overview 3: Demands on State-level Governance			
Effective contexts		Goal	
	Clear/consesus		Unclear/conflict
Clear	I. Codification; Authoritative determination of standards	II.	Conflict regulation; Negotiation of goal systems
Unclear	III. Information-processing; Pulling together know-how; search for and bargaining over solutions to problems	IV.	Accommodation of goal conflicts and information conflicts; Negotiation of goal systems and solutions to problems
Source: after Schubert (1989), p. 35			

Type I corresponds to a situation in which a state-level governance activity consists in realizing, in clear and precise legal regulations, socially acknowledged and accepted values on the basis of well-founded knowledge about effective contexts in a policy field. What is at issue is the **codification**, the translation of governance objectives into norms formulated in a legally unobjectionable manner. In these cases authoritative decisions by the proper state institutions will as a rule suffice. Pluralism theories started out from this constellation. Even though the "planning optimists" of the 1960s and 1970s regarded the definition of the goals of policy as at times conflictual, they nonetheless presupposed a sufficient level of know-how on effective contexts in specific policy fields or assumed that it was in principle possible to rapidly develop such know-how. Accordingly, they too regarded this constellation as typical.

Type II corresponds to a situation in which the contexts in a policy field are sufficiently clear, though there exist no objectives capable of consensus. The crucial governance activity here would first be to **regulate conflicts of interest and to come to terms on objectives capable of consensus**. A constellation of this type is realistic in, for instance, phases of crisis or upheaval in which, often, consensus has already emerged on the causes of the crisis (e.g. at the end of the 1980s in Latin America on the crisis and the failure of import substitution or in the mid-1990s in the newly unified Germany on the causes of the government debt), even though, as yet, the thrust and final shape of policies is conflictual, since at this stage the issue is the distribution of costs and the redistribution of power resources. State-level conflict-settlement mechanisms are essential in democratic societies with well-organized interest groups if situations are to be prevented in which the activities of functioning interest groups with "disruptive potential" can obstruct political decisions or the best-organized forces can quickly succeed in achieving their interests. The theorists of neocorporatism thematize the "power of intervention" of social groups and see in corporatist coordination procedures the possibility to minimize any such conflict potentials. Neoconservative authors, but Olson as well, see the state's scope of action in this area dwindling in view of the dominance of well-organized particularist interests.

Type III corresponds to a situation in which, even though the goals are acknowledged, there is nevertheless uncertainty as to the effective regulative contexts. Initially the most important governance activity here is to **digest and assess information** and to **accumulate applicable knowledge**. A constellation of this type is likely in more complex policy fields (e.g. environment, labor-market policy, locational policy) in which it is unlikely that specific and adequate policies will be able to be formulated if use is not made of the know-how of the actors involved. The "rational statists" thought that this problem could be managed by developing comprehensive information systems. The theorists of corporatism were convinced that the information problem could be solved on the basis of the tripartite bargaining structures favored by them.

Type IV corresponds to a situation that frequently occurs in social reality. There are abstract objectives (e.g. a clean environment, job creation, strengthening of competitiveness), but concrete goals and the ways and means of attaining them are unclear in material terms, because effective contexts pose problems of understanding or appear more or less inaccessible to influence. Since knowledge on governance-relevant factors is for the most part broadly dispersed across various social actors (e.g. in the case of labor-market policy: firms, science, labor unions, specialized state institutions/labor departments) and organized groups of social actors (e.g. labor unions, industrial federations, chambers of industry and commerce) can contribute to the success or failure of policies, the state is forced to **negotiate goal systems and solutions to problems**. This case, "typical" of complex societies, was not addressed by the governance optimists.

The governance theories had until then understood governance basically as the codification of norms and rule systems and regarded the process leading to it as a technical problem. The extended view of the phenomenon of governance outlined here problematizes the process from problem detection to policy implementation and specifies important governance activities such as, for instance, the successful working out of consensuses as a condition for the acceptance and implementability of policies, which had previously - as a result of the premises of the state's sovereignty vis-à-vis social actors and pluralism theory's thoughts on legitimation - not been taken into account.

What emerges clearly is a palette of governance tasks and activities that had hardly been perceived by the planning optimists. It also becomes clear that the state must become an agency of negotiation and cooperation if it is to come to grips with its tasks. This means that the question as to the patterns of negotiation and forms of problem-processing engaged in between state and social actors has been posed, but as yet by no means answered. Policy research opens up a broad field of study by thematizing the complexity of social structures, the resultant complexity of the governance tasks to be dealt with, the difficult relationship between the state and social actors, which likewise needs to be rethought, and the broad palette of the forms of governance that are available in the first place. A look back at the discussions of the 1960s and 1970s showed that these issues had previously received wholly inadequate attention.

5.2.3   Partial Loss of State Sovereignty or the State as *Primus Inter Pares*?

It can be noted by way of summary that the policy-oriented German discussion in the fields of political and administrative sciences has, since the mid-1980s, developed a distinctly modified understanding of the state that has expanded the traditional definitory element of the legal concept of the state (possession of unilateral-sovereign powers vis-à-vis social actors) and in part replaced it with the *principle of bilaterality or cooperation*. As a result of the requirements regarded as necessary to shape society, the talk now is of *"cooperative pluralism"*, a concept attained by delimitation from the pluralism theories based on a clear-cut separation of state and society and the idea of the *"political market"* (see e.g. Hartwich 1987). Agreement is to be found on the view that the state is, at least in part and in many policy fields, particularly in economic policy, no longer in possession of the power of definition over the problem area and the solutions relevant and adequate to it. That has spelled the end of the picture of the hierarchy as the (only) principle of order in society.

What remains controversial is whether this process is a question of *"deinstitutionalization"* (Lerman 1985) in consequence of which the state is *"no longer the central governance agency but only a coplayer in a network of actors"* (Fürst 1987, p. 266). It can, with good reasons, be argued against this thesis of the complete decline of structures of state sovereignty that, in spite of its manifold intertwinements with groups of social actors, the state remains the agency that defines binding regulatory systems and laws, possess a monopoly of power, and enforces compliance with existing legal principles. Below this level, in the policy process (problem detection, assessment of problem relevance, analysis of governance-relevant effective contexts, elaboration of patterns of solution, policy formulation, policy implementation, control of policy impacts), one might imagine a great variety of different cooperation and coordination mechanisms between state and groups of social actors that work to undermine the ideal of the classical leviathan. The concept of *"split sovereignty"* (Hartwich 1987, p. 17) can be useful to express this **partial loss of sovereignty** and a side-by-side of different regulative logics and forms of governance. Hierarchical governance by the state here gives way to a state that is not completely and unreservedly responsible for governing society and that merely assumes leadership tasks. In dealing with problems, the state makes use of mechanisms of cooperation, coordination, and moderation, takes on orientation, organization, and mediation functions, and monitors compliance with the systems of state regulations.

5.2.4 The Discovery of the "Third Sector" by the Theory of the State

Now that the classical political and administrative sciences have taken leave of the hierarchically active, fully sovereign state, empirical studies are contributing to a "discovery" of the confusing diversity of forms of organization and governance on which governance activities in modern societies are based. Only since the *"demystification of the state"* by systems theory has it been possible to catch a glance of the diversity of state governance aids and social self-governance potentials, such as: the creation of parastatal institutions; the delegation of state tasks to social groups; state action in accordance with the principle of subsidiarity, making state action necessary only when self-governance fails in social subsectors; active governance by means of liberal corporatism; loose concertation; and so on.

This organizational diversity corresponds to a picture of society beyond traditional statism and Luhmann's world of autopoietically closed subsystems. The newly "discovered" forms of organization and governance are geared precisely to management of the interdependencies and communication between various social subsectors in order in this way to render compatible self-governance in social subsectors and goal-directed and politically intended governance. The term used in the discussion in the social sciences is the "Third Sector" that assumes the intermediary functions between state and market.

There is on this dimension between market and state a wealth of literature, chiefly empirically oriented, that cannot be discussed here (see Ronge 1988, Levitt 1973, Anheier/Seibel 1989, Schuppert 1989). What is important is that the term "Third Sector" may conceal a variety of highly different organizations, institutions, and actor groups that assume divergent governance functions in specific policy fields. Some authors (see Levitt 1973), Anheier/Seibel 1989) underline the aspect of voluntariness (sometimes also the motive of self help) as the characteristic functional principle of the Third Sector and distinguish it from the functional logics of uncoordinated competition (market) and hierarchical control (state). Streeck and Schmitter have taken over this distinction and speak of the regulative models *"community, market and state"*.[21] The concept *community* includes the self-help and self-organizational potential of society.

The heterogeneity of the Third Sector can, however, not be described by means of this characterization. Streeck and Schmitter have proposed adding to the three models of social order the *"world of the federations"*, in which collective interests are organized. In contrast to the narrow view of the neocorporatists, it might be more appropriate to understand here the totality of established interest organizations at various social levels (from the national business federations and labor unions to regionally or locally organized sectoral industrial federations, welfare associations, and so on), i.e. not only the triad consisting of the state and the top organizations of capital and labor. In the literature this extended view of corporatist problem-solving alliances is designated by the concept "mesocorporatism" (see Cawson 1985/1986, Katzenstein 1984, Kleinfeld 1987). This strand of the literature is concerned with patterns of cooperation between state and groups of social actors at the sectoral or regional and local level and thematizes a great variety of different problem areas (e.g. health policy, industrial policy, etc.), i.e. it goes far beyond any concentration on the problematic of redistribution.

It is here necessary to differentiate further in order to complete the panorama of actor groups that are able to assume governance functions. Apart from

- **state-level institutions** which have the immediate function of taking universally binding decisions (legislative) and implementing these decisions (executive),

- **interest organizations/federations** that represent the interests of their members, which have at the same time, in many areas, become important partners of state-level institutions in detecting problems at an early point of time, developing adequate policies, and implementing these policies, and

- **self-help groups, citizens' initiatives and non-governmental organizations**, or other temporary voluntary associations consisting of members of civil society and geared to a limited number of goals, other institutions have gained in significance which

- first of all differ from the other groups in that they neither make generally binding decisions nor represent particularist group or member interests. These are private, semi-public or public **functional institutions**. In specific social sectors they take on governance-relevant tasks such as the procurement and processing of information, scientific consulting of state institutions and federations, and additional services that contribute to increasing the effectiveness of the actors in the various sectors (e.g. through advan-

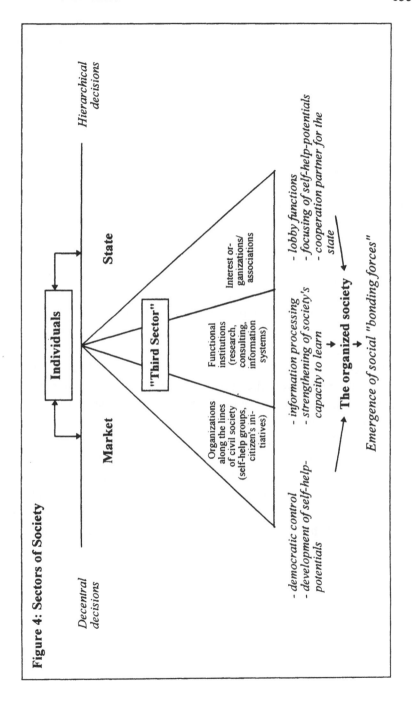

Figure 4: Sectors of Society

ced training of decision-makers) or mediating between actors (e.g. by preparing and moderating regional or sectoral conferences that facilitate, or indeed even force, the process of exchange between actors). This group includes, for instance, scientific institutions (research, advanced training, and advisory agencies, technology institutions, etc.) or advisory boards.

The "functional institutions" are growing in significance as agencies that are still capable of grasping and dealing with social complexity. Karl Deutsch had already pointed out that the effectiveness and the cohesion of societies can be measured in terms of *"their capacity to transmit information with more or less small losses of information"* (Deutsch 1969, p. 21). Beside the interest organizations, which are likewise in possession of governance-relevant information, though they use it chiefly for particularist interests, the primary task of "functional institutions" is to strengthen society's learning capacity. Karl Deutsch noted that social learning is based, at a first level, on the capacity of social actors to continuously assimilate new information and correct traditional knowledge and to illuminate, on the basis of new information, new possibilities of action and to advance their realization. At the second, structural level, the task is to create information channels capable of feedback and to improve the storage and processing of information (Deutsch 1977, pp. 280 ff.). The traditional exercise of power - the use of force to regulate social processes - is losing in significance to the extent that is it is no longer capable of meeting the governance needs of modern societies. What is becoming more important is the settlement of group conflicts and communication within the overall social system, which must be conceived of as an intermeshed rule system capable of learning and innovation. The "functional institutions" provide an important contribution to coming to terms with these fundamental tasks. The increasing significance of the "functional institutions" reflects the fact that, beside power, money, and law, knowledge is becoming a crucial governance medium in the development of modern societies.

The existence of the Third Sector is not at all a new phenomenon. What is new is the governance-theoretical view of the dimension be-

tween state and market. Whereas in state-centered governance theories
the state was the only legitimate governance actor and social individuals and actor groups were the addressees of governance, who were occasionally consulted or were able to represent their interests as lobbies,
governance theories are now centered on the cooperation of state and
social groups in the policy process. The question is no longer how the
state governs society, it is how highly differentiated societies are able
to act selectively on themselves. In other words, in this extended view
nongovernmental actor groups in the Third Sector can also take on
governance tasks with very different functions (after Fürst 1987, p.
264):

First, nongovernmental organizations may be active in problem areas
with which the state has either been insufficiently capable or fully unable to deal (e.g. organizations concerned with job-creation measures,
environmental organizations). **Second**, nongovernmental organizations
can be established as a means of keeping the state out of given problem
areas (e.g. self-administration in the health-care system). **Third**, the
state can delegate public tasks to nongovernmental organizations
(disburdening the state) and restrict itself to monitoring results (e.g.
job-creation measures conducted by church etc. organizations; institutions measuring standards, testing, and quality, technical control tasks).
Fourth, the addressees of state policy can, in cooperation with state
institutions, actively participate in dealing with problems and shaping
society at the state level. This can be useful as a means of boosting the
acceptance of reforms (implementation problem) and concentrating the
required knowledge of private and public actors (information and
complexity problem), which can be necessary to secure the effectiveness of governance measures (e.g. industrial and technology policy).
Fifth, nongovernmental organizations can take on monitoring and rectification functions vis-à-vis state level governance requirements and
measures (e.g. environmental organizations, federations).

5.2.5   Institutional and Organizational Pluralism Instead of Market Versus State

The discussion over governance in the field of tension described by overregulation and overburdening of the state links the question of the governance capacity of societies to the question of the patterns of organization and governance that can disburden the state; these, seen until now as alternative concepts and patterns of problem-solving, are becoming components of an **institutional and organizational pluralism**:

The delegation of tasks to nongovernmental institutions (limited deregulation), close cooperation between state and intermediary institutions (neocorporatist approaches to problem-solving), the retreat of the state from traditional spheres of activity and the strengthening of market forces (deregulation and market), the formation of groups of social actors and institutions that strengthen society's self-organizational and governance capacities and exercise control functions vis-à-vis the state and other powerful actors groups (strengthening of civil society) are understood as complementary concepts geared to disburdening the state and at the same time as a condition of the maintenance of its governance functions in core sectors. The question as to the governance capacity of societies thus goes far beyond the question of the state's efficiency. Simple deregulation concepts prove at the same time to be reductionistic. Governance capacity emerges by means of a mix consisting of the state's capacity to act, self-organization in social sectors, and various forms of cooperation and interaction, at various levels, between the state and nongovernmental actors. The question as to how these organizational patterns complement and overlay one another and work together has, however, largely been left open by the political and administrative scientists who are in search of their subject.

5.2.6   The Palette of Governance Media

Against this background we are confronted with the question of governance media. In studies by authors who attempt to describe the structure of society with reference to the triad of market, state, and Third Sector, the regulative structures as a rule correspond to the governance principles of competition (market), hierarchy and directive (state), and normative obligation via solidarity (Third Sector). This perception, based on clear-cut separations, is, **first**, overly narrow in that, for instance, the more recent theories of competitiveness have shown that firms active in the market are forced to combine competition and cooperation in order to strengthen their competitiveness. It is, **second**, too limited in that the Third Sector consists not only of institutions that rely on the action resource of solidarity. The latter applies unreservedly only for the organizations of civil society (see Figure 4), certainly not for functional, intermediary institutions. Interest organizations (labor unions, business federations) are, it is true, pledged internally to the principle of solidarity and geared to concentrating the self-help potentials of their members; outwardly, however, their basic function as solidarity-based organizations is to represent and push through particularist interests vis-à-vis other interest groups and the state. Moreover, federations often act as cooperation partners of the state in preparing and implementing policy. This dual function (lobby on the one hand, cooperation partner of the state on the other) gives rise to a situation to which the theoretical studies discussed here have paid too little attention. **Third**, it is not particularly helpful to reduce the broad field of state-level governance to the concepts hierarchy and directive.

The dominant governance media available to the state are without doubt the codification of law and the use of money. In addition, due to the growing significance of cooperation between state and nongovernmental organizations in solving problems, there are procedural governance mechanisms like persuasion, the flow of information, and bargaining. The following can be said of the governance media against the background of empirical studies (see e.g. Offe 1975, Ritter 1979, Ronge 1980, Powell 1987):

1. The palette of governance media is broad and can be modeled on a continuum ending in the points hard and soft governance (see Figure 5). What is meant by hard governance are administrative acts for which a sovereign administration is responsible. Soft governance includes bargaining and cooperative processes, discursive procedures aiming at coordination between the state and other social actors that pursue the goal of moving development in a policy field into directions as yet to be defined. The state can, for instance, stimulate or oblige the actors concerned to search for solutions for problems either under its control or without any state participation (e.g. sectoral working groups on technology policy with participation of firms, labor unions, and industry). Furthermore, optimizing the flow of information between relevant actors (e.g. by developing information systems, bringing together different actors) can increase the transparency and enhance the governance capacity of social subsectors. Procedural governance mechanisms take into consideration the fact that the shaping of complex structures with high levels of nontransparency, variability, and dynamism is possible only as a continuous learning process geared to the necessity of coming to terms with current tasks of change and adjustment. Herbert Simon discussed this state of affairs under the heading *"procedural rationality"*.[22]

2. It can generally be observed that regulations increasingly focus on the **formulation of framework conditions** and that the tendency of the political sphere to "govern into" different social sectors ("fine governance") is on the decline. This means, first of all, that the dynamics inherent in specific subsystems is respected. True, it is possible to define development corridors by changing framework parameters, but the way in which they are finally formulated is left up to the actors concerned, or to their competence and creativity. State-level governance and self-organization are combined. Examples of this would be, in environmental policy, the definition of emission values instead of any state-level specification of technological solutions; in youth policy the provision of funds for the support of free youth groups and nongovernmental groups involved in youth work instead of regimented and fully organized youth centers; in technology policy continuous improvement of research and training institutions in cooperation with

firms, science, and labor unions instead of subsidizing individual firms or specific process technologies.

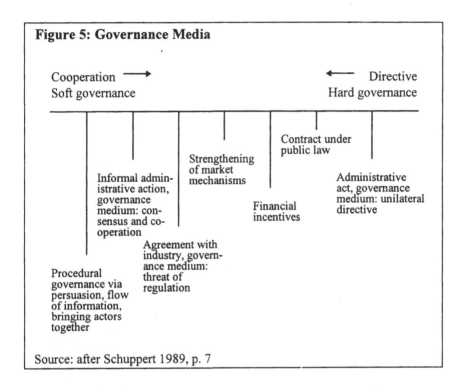

Figure 5: Governance Media

Cooperation ⟶   ⟵ Directive
Soft governance   Hard governance

Contract under public law

Strengthening of market mechanisms

Informal administrative action, governance medium: consensus and cooperation

Financial incentives

Administrative act, governance medium: unilateral directive

Agreement with industry, governance medium: threat of regulation

Procedural governance via persuasion, flow of information, bringing actors together

Source: after Schuppert 1989, p. 7

3. If the policy process is broken down into its phases (problem detection, assessment of problem relevance, analysis of governance-relevant effective contexts, development of patterns of problem-solving, definition of policies, implementation, evaluation of the impacts of policies, corrections), it might generally be said that at the beginning of the policy process, the phase in which decisions are prepared, soft governance mechanisms are particularly important as a means of accumulating know-how in combination with participating actors who have strategic knowledge, illuminating alternative forms of dealing with problems, and building acceptance for the deployment of policies. Depending on the problem situation in question, it is then possible to use either hard of soft governance instruments to solve concrete problems.

Overview 4: Phases of the Policy Process
Problem identification Assessment of problem relevance Analysis of effective governance-relevant contexts Development of approaches to solutions Definition of policies Implementation Evaluation of policy impacts Corrections

4. The growth of the significance of soft governance media and the character of procedural rationality confront the state with altered functions that were not provided for in the concept of the hierarchical, sovereign state. The state assumes

-   **tasks of coordination, organization, and moderation** in order, for instance, to get on with the solution of problems in combination with other social actors;

-   **moderation functions** between conflicting parties in order, for instance, to strengthen the self-organizational capacity present in social subsectors that are in danger of being obstructed by particularist interests, or in order to contribute to defining common goals and heightening acceptance;

-   **control tasks** that emerge, for instance, when public tasks are delegated to nongovernmental institutions whose success or lack of success must be monitored;

-   **initiator and orientation functions** in order, for instance, ensure future interests against present interests and to "carry" problem areas into social subsectors (e.g. industry) that tend gear their activities exclusively and self-referentially to their own rationality criteria (e.g. growth, profit) and ignore external effects (e.g. environmental problems);

- **correction functions**, for instance, in that the state strengthens the self-organization capacity of weak social actors by providing them with financial or institutional incentives that enable them to build up their own power and control potentials.

5. Which forms of governance are appropriate depends on the **characteristics of the policy field**, the **structure of the actor system involved**, and the concrete **problem** to be solved. But the main concern here is that the relative significance of soft forms of governance is on the increase.

6. We can diagnose as a trend overlapping patterns of governance, **combinations of governance modes**, that as good as rule out any patterns of regulation in terms of the basic classical coordination mechanisms (more market, more state, more self-administration) or in terms of the market (interventions on the supply or demand side) or in terms of incentive mechanisms (administrative steering versus market-like governance). Thus, for instance, we observe in Germany's economic policy since the mid-1970s deregulation processes (more market), new self-governance mechanisms (e.g. voluntary obligation of firms from the chemical industry to report on environmental matters), new control and regulatory functions (more stringent health and environmental regulations), close and innovative forms of cooperation between firms, science, and state (e.g. regional conferences as an instrument of technology policy), and a strong tendency toward a more scientific approach to economic policy in state, firms, and federations.

5.2.7 Results of the Reorientation in the Administrative and Political Sciences

The more recent discussion in the administrative and political sciences has tended to break with the core premises (separation of state and society; internal and external sovereignty of the state) of the traditional theory of the state and the narrow statist view of the debate on governance. The studies, basically empirical in approach, show that the ac-

tually observable forms of organization and governance of modern societies go beyond both the underlying patterns of planning, pluralism,
and corporatism theories and the notions of social theory held by neoconservative and neoliberal authors.

The primary concern of the policy-research studies discussed was their
search for their subject. Accordingly, we are now more clear on the
facets of the "research project of governance". What is elaborated here
is: the **complexity of the governance process** (from problem detection
to policy implementation and evaluation of the impacts of policy), the
great diversity of potential **governance actors**, the significance of interaction and **coordination between state, market, and intermediary
groups and institutions** of the Third Sector, the **presence and side-
by-side existence of different patterns of organization** (hierarchical
state-level governance, neocorporatist regimes, self-organization, and
so on), different **functions** and tasks that can be assumed by the **Third
Sector**, the range of possible **governance activities** (encouragement of
consensus, accommodation of information, etc.), **functions of the state**
(standardization of law, supplemented by functions in the areas of coordination, organization, moderation, control and orientation) and **governance media** (the continuum extending from hard to soft governance
media), the significance of various patterns of organization and governance, depending on **problem situation and sector**.

Against this panorama we can now define more precisely what claims
and demands governance systems must be able to meet in modern societies:

First, the growing fragmentation of social problem-processing procedures gives rise to an **need for internalization** to counter growing external effects. **Second**, the growing division of labor and differentiation
of society increases the **need for cooperation and coordination** between actor groups, institutions, and social subsectors. **Third**, the trend
toward growing social differentiation and division of labor at the same
time calls for a higher level of autonomy of the subsystems vis-à-vis
the state as a means of mobilizing subsystem creativity potentials and
compensating for the loss of state-level governance capacity by en-

couraging self-organization and self-governance. **Fourth**, the complexity of problem contexts implies a **need for collective definitions**. **Fifth**, the pluralization of shared values gives rise to a growing **need for consensus**. **Sixth**, the time dimension of governance (e.g. development of energy or training systems) gives rise to a need for **medium- and long-term perspectives and visions** that can be used as orientation by the social actors concerned. **Seventh**, the task of providing for future generations and the scope of, e.g., technological development (e.g. nuclear energy, genetic engineering) give rise to a **need for risk minimization**.

The empirical studies published by administrative scientists describe social learning processes and "governance innovations". It appears that linking the governance potentials of the Third Sector with modified forms of governance at the state level can generate organizational patterns that can be used to deal with the complexity problematic addressed in particular by Luhmann. The empirically demonstrated, increasing differentiation of governance media, the redefinition of the state's tasks, the interlinkages between the state and the Third Sector, and the overlapping of various governance logics (market, hierarchical governance/directives, horizontal coordination, and bargaining) are geared to "processing" the phenomena of growing interdependence and independence of social subsystems and increasing complexity and coming to terms with the losses of state-level governance capacity caused by them. These findings are significant inasmuch as they distantiate any fundamental governance pessimism à la Luhmann, or indeed even Olson. The empirical descriptions provided by political scientists do, however, open up a difficult theoretical field. After all, when one goes beyond traditional theory of the state, one leaves behind an enormous theoretical vacuum. The chapters that follow will discuss attempts to fill in this vacuum.

What we have attempted to show here is the inadequacies of the current one-sided theories:

Olson rightly points to asymmetric structures of the representation of interests and social stagnation that result from mutual obstruction brought about by clashes between social interest groups: Yet his concept hardly permits any clarification of the question how any functioning synergy between the state and Third-Sector actors is possible in the first place. If, in other words, obstruction and synergy effects may arise from the cooperation between state and social actors, what are then the conditions for the one and the other variant?

Luhmann in turn can serve very well to explain governance problems, though he is far less able to work out the conditions of successful forms of "intersystemic management" between social subsectors (e.g. science-industry, politics-industry). This is particularly regrettable insofar as the innovative patterns of organization and governance described point toward social learning processes that can be used at least to process, if not to solve, the complexity problematic emphasized by Luhmann (but also Mayntz and Scharpf). It is precisely economies and societies that develop the forms of organization and governance that are regarded as improbable by Luhmann and which are capable of fully exploiting the modernization effects brought about by growing differentiation and, by systematically linking the - no longer autopoietic - social subsystems, of organizing synergy effects and steering overall social and/or economic development.

The **neocorporatists** rightly point to the virtues of the tripartite bargaining system, especially for solving distributive conflicts, though in doing so they occlude the great variety of forms of social organization and governance and underrate the centrifugal forces that are set free in connection with the process of social differentiation and lead to the above-sketched needs for social governance, which the neocorporatists do not overlook.

Due to their fixation on the modern concept of the state, the **neoconservative authors** are more or less blind to the fact that nonhierarchical forms of governance need not necessarily be interpreted as symptoms of decline, even though the risks posed by social disintegration are not to be dismissed lightly. It is precisely increasing differentiation and intertwinement that can entail an increase of social coordination and problem-solving capacities.

Part III The Network Society: Further Development of Theories of Social Governance Capacity

CHAPTER 1 Network Theories: An Innovative Look at Altered Organizational Patterns in Societies Marked by a High Level of Division of Labor

What follows will discuss recent approaches dealing with network and bargaining theory that attempt, in going beyond taking stock of and breaking down the hierarchical structures of state and society and the *"vanishing of the boundaries of the state"* (Grande 1993), to penetrate at the theoretical level the significance of the upheavals in the patterns of organization and governance of modern societies for their development dynamics.

The intention is to show that the changes underway in the social sphere are nearly as far-reaching and go as far toward modifying the functional mechanisms of modern societies as is the case at the economic level. While, however, numerous studies have appeared in the field of economics on the emergence and the contours of a New Production Paradigm, the changes that are taking place in the political-social sphere have not even nearly been illuminated in their entire range.

The reconstruction of the governance debate showed that political governance occurs under turbulent conditions and is subject to limits that were, until far into the 1970s, almost completely disregarded in scholarship (and in political practice). The problems and limitations of governance capacity result from the growing differentiation of social division of labor, advances in science and technology, the globalization of the economy, and the high mobility of capital, goods, information, and persons. Under these conditions Luhmann regards even the notion of the possibility of political governance as obsolete, the conservative leviathan theorists following in the footsteps of Carl Schmitt see in the pluralist structures of modern societies the seeds leading to the decline of the polity. On the whole, modern sociology provides more plausible grounds for the unlikelihood, or indeed the impossibility, of any communication, coordination, and governance beyond the boundaries of social systems than for chances of intentional performative coordination. Political science is also investing more intensive efforts in describing the erosion of state-level governance activities than in work that might contribute to understanding the logic of societies characterized by pluralist forms or organization and governance. Fritz Scharpf thus rightly notes: *"In view of the present state of theory, it appears that it is less the increasing disorder everywhere to be observed that is in need of explanation than the measure of intra- and interorganizational, intra- and intersectoral ... coordination and reciprocal certainty of expectations that continues to exist in spite of all. Beyond pure market, hierarchical state, and control-free discourses, there are evidently more and more effective coordination mechanisms in internally differentiated and internationally integrated modern society than scholarship has until now established empirically and comprehended theoretically"* (Scharpf 1993a, p. 57).

1.1   Network Phenomena in Economy and Society as a Reaction to Processes of Social Transformation and a "Response" to Luhmann's Complexity Problematic

Recent governance-theoretical concepts have centered on the observation that in many areas modern societies are characterized by network-like forms of organization and that problem-solving is increasingly based on *"horizontal policy coordination"* in *"joint decision systems"* or *"pluralist policy networks"*.[1] These network-like forms of organization and the governance based on them can be interpreted as a response to phenomena of increasing social, political, and economic differentiation, specialization, and interdepence. Network concepts differ in many respects, though they do converge in one important point: the coordination between political and economic actors and the forms of problem-solving based on it in network-like forms of governance differ from the three standard forms of social coordination in modern societies, and do so in the following respects: the **price mechanism** that coordinates the behavior of firms and consumers in anonymous markets, the **hierarchical-majoritarian mode of politics** in which a parliamentary majority legitimated in democratic elections, or the executive supported by this majority brings about and implements, on the basis of its legislative and governance competence, decisions binding on the polity, and the higher-level authority (within government institutions, nongovernmental organizations, firms) makes decisions binding on the lower-level units (**hierarchical decision-making and problem-solving mechanisms**). (Scharpf 1992b)

The concept "network" underlines the self-organization and/or self-coordination between de facto autonomous actors aimed at achieving a joint result. Kenis/Schneider even see in network approaches a new paradigm for understanding the *"architecture of complexity"* (Kenis/Schneider 1991, p. 25); this paradigm could, in terms of its significance, prove to be comparable to the otherwise dominant concept of hierarchy as the instrument for reducing complexity in societies marked by ever increasing processes of differentiation. One interesting aspect is that we can observe in the discussion in economics and the social sciences developments that run parallel in economy and society and are dealt with under the headings *"beyond market and state"* and *"neither market nor hierarchy"*: patterns of organization, coordination, and governance have emerged in economy and society that are located beyond the three standard models and are termed, here and there, *"network phenomena"*.

Since the end of the 1980s the study of policy networks has become a metaphor for inquiry into the patterns of social organization and forms of political governance that cannot be thematized with the means available to traditional approaches based on the theory of the state. Network theorists have noted social transformation processes behind which is concealed a *"major shift ... in societal governance from hierarchical control to horizontal coordination"* (Kenis/Schneider 1991, p. 36).

This transformation process is being encouraged by the overlap of the following phenomena:

1. A trend toward **organized society** is obvious. The number of collective actors (like parties, federations, interest organizations, clubs, non-governmental organizations, and associations) and their significance for social development is on the increase. Collective actors have influence, financial resources, know-how, and organizational capacities and are thus in a position to influence political decision-making processes and to play a strong role in shaping society.

2. It is obvious that there is an increasing **sectoralization** underway **in economy and society**. Increases in social complexity, growing interdependencies between a variety of actors, i.e. processes of **functional differentiation**, are heightening the significance of social subsystems in society as a whole. Be it in science, politics, economy, at the level of intermediary institutions or publicity and the media, specialization and sectoralization are everywhere gaining in significance. This process is rapidly advancing the internal differentiation of social subsystems. Luhmann's picture of the complete self-referentiality of social subsectors is exaggerated, though the trend toward the development of separate arenas of policy or science (genetic policy, technology policy, development policy) is undeniable.

3. Sectoralization and the increasing degree of organization of social interests lead to participation of a growing number of groups private and state actors in the process of policy formulation and can substantially boost the level of intervention in a great variety of social sectors. Jordan and Richardson coined the term *"overcrowded policy-making"* (Jordan/Richardson 1983) for this development trend.

4. The organizational and political capacity of social sectors and the new governance needs resulting from the differentiation of society (e.g. environmental policy, risk potentials of new technologies, unclear or intricate relations of interdependence between policy fields) have led, stimulated even further by the planning optimism of the 1960s to mid-1970s, to a **process of "policy growth"** (Heclo 1978). The growing

measure of state-level intervention is, however, at first scarcely accompanied by innovative new forms of governance (e.g. delegation of governance tasks to intermediary institutions). Instead, we can observe a variety of different attempts to accompany a process of growing differentiation of society accompanied by a parallel expansion of the state apparatus. In the last analysis these attempts overburden the state.

5. The policy-growth process is translated into a **process in which the state is increasingly decentralized and fragmented**. While it was long customary to view the state as a monolithic structure, it has now become more common to view the dynamics inherent in the state's subsectors in more differentiated terms and to pay more attention to the great variety forms of intervention and policy-making activities open to the state, and to do so in terms of policy field, industrial sector, and policy level (local, regional, multilateral). It is important in this context to point out that it is not only for the last two decades that the state has constituted a heterogeneous nexus - even though it is no doubt true that the trend toward increasing differentiation has accelerated sharply. Theories of the state long remained bound up in the classical understanding of the state, proceeding on the assumption of the "unity" of the state; they were, with their analytical matrix, unable to perceive adequately the heterogenization of state and society, and thus departed further and further from the realities of social change.

6. Decentralization of the state and a great variety of forms of cooperation between the state and groups of private actors has lead to a **blurring of the distinction between "public" and "private"**. Forms of soft governance are "discovered", "informal administrative action" or forms of "state-sponsored self-regulation" detected (see Hanf 1982, Hucke 1982).

7. A number of studies have demonstrated that in many policy fields the state is for all practical purposes unable to realize its governance and policy-making functions without the aid of the know-how or indeed the implementation capacities of nonstate actors. The **state's loss of autonomy** does not, however, imply any automatic gains in autonomy for other social actors, since their effectiveness is likewise de-

pendent on interaction and cooperation with others (see the comments in this study on systemic competitiveness and the phenomenon of collective efficiency).

8. The *"cooperative state"* (Ritter 1979) or the *"bargaining state"* (Scharpf 1993d) learns to delegate tasks and supports the development of capacities for social self-organization (e.g. by promoting federations or establishing forums in which social conflicts can be dealt with and a search can - with or without state institutions assuming a moderator function - be initiated for problem-solving patterns). Offe discusses such strategies under the heading *"state policy of disburdening the state"* (Offe 1987, p. 315).

9. The interplay among these trends gives rise to an *"active society"* (see Etzioni 1968); it, and the policy arena developing within it (health policy, university policy, industrial-sector policy), experiences an increase of the significance of *"systemic interaction"* (Etzioni) between the relevant actor groups as a response to deepening interdependencies. Specific sectors develop a variety of relationships of coordination and exchange beyond pure market allocation and hierarchical control by the state. At the same time the demands placed on intersystemic communication and coordination capacity increase as a means of avoiding both the external effects of decisions made in individual sectors for all of society and beggar-my-neighbor policies. Etzioni describes these structural principles and comes to the result that **collective knowledge,** and with it the effectiveness of social actors and their capacity and willingness to exchange information (access to information), turn out to be a **governance resources** just as important as power and money. In addition, this development promotes a *"scientification of politics"*.[2]

10. Finally, the **globalization** of the economy and the integration of nation states in supranational institutions imply a loss of autonomy on the part of nation states. The governance. capacity of nation states accordingly relies not only on the efficiency of new forms of "internal" organization and cooperation but is also modified by the delegation of action potentials to the international level (for instance in the framework of, e.g., the EU or MERCOSUR) or indeed even by the loss of

scopes of action resulting from the globalization of the economy (e.g. interest-rate policy). (Messner/Nuscheler 1996)

The effects of these overlapping transformation processes is that in many areas governments are no longer in autonomous possession of the governance resources required to formulate policy. Governments are forced to rely on cooperation and coordination of their activities with groups of actors that are not immediately subject to their control. It would be wrong to interpret this process as a one-sided loss of autonomy on the part of state or government. Social actors are themselves forced to rely on cooperation with public institutions in many areas, as, for instance, research on the systemic character of competitiveness has shown. This mutual loss of autonomy and the interdependencies resulting from it lead to a situation in which politics is increasingly at home in *"informal political infrastructures outside conventional channels such as legislative, executive and administrative organizations"* (Kenis/Schneider 1991, p. 27).

1.2 Network Phenomena and the Limits of Hierarchical Governance

We can note at a higher level of abstraction that the functional presuppositions for the success of hierarchical coordination depend on the solution of two fundamental problems - which at the same time indicate the limits faced by hierarchical governance. Hierarchical governance holds out promise for success and is normatively acceptable only if, first, solutions can be found for the complexity problematic resulting from the tendencies toward growing differentiation in modern societies and, second, it may be assumed that the governance actors gear their activities to the overriding public interests. These latter two pitfalls of hierarchical governance are discussed in the following section.

1.2.1   The Complexity Trap as a Core Problem of Hierarchical Coordination

The development dynamics of societies toward increasing complexity entails a problem fundamental to central decision-making authorities, viz. that of acquiring sufficient information on the conditions of problems and the possibilities of solving them.[3] Even if this problem is successfully solved, the question is whether the knowledge accumulated will be able to be effectively processed and utilized in the decision-making center. This problem, central to current governance theory, is not at all new, though it does intensify as societies continue on in the process of differentiation. Authors as different as Hayek, Deutsch, Simon, and Polanyi (see Hayek 1945, Deutsch 1969, Simon 1973, Polanyi 1978) were early to point out that the centralization of decision-making often leads either to extreme scarcity of information or information overloads and that these problems grow as the size of the system to be governed increases. For these authors, the broad dispersion of the economically and socially relevant knowledge across a variety of actors constituted the core problem facing social coordination. They emphasize that economically and socially relevant knowledge is often of an idiosyncratic character, is therefore difficult to articulate verbally, graphically, or in writing, and can thus not be properly processed by central decision-making centers.

Karl Deutsch points to the significance that efficient information structures have in societies if governance is to succeed. As is well known, Hayek infers from his reflections the absolute primacy of decentral, market based coordination (in society and economy).[4] Herbert A. Simon doesn't follow Hayek's radical rejection of any form of targeted governance beyond decentral coordination, though he does show that successful hierarchical coordination presupposes the "near decomposability" of problem contexts. Hierarchical coordination accordingly holds out promise of success only in the presence of a pattern of interaction in which the interaction between actors subject to one superior or one common hierarchical authority is far more important and occurs more frequently than horizontal interactions with members of other units. The primary task of organizational development is accordingly the creation of a modular order of this sort (Simon 1973).

However, with an increasing interdependence of the problems to be dealt with between both policy fields and social subsystems, it becomes more and more difficult to create any such modular organization. The interaction *between* fields of activity grows in significance. Where the horizontal interaction between fields of activities becomes more important, frequent, and variable, hierarchical organizations and decision centers find themselves faced with an unattractive choice: they can either maintain the hierarchical division of competences in spite of all or they can reduce their claim to central coordination and rely instead on horizontal self-coordination between the subunits. The first case entails the risk of ignoring interdependencies of tasks between organizational units at the same level. The coordination problems that occur are shifted upward to the next-highest shared level or the next hierarchical level above. The result is that advantages stemming from decentralization and selective interaction are not perceived and the higher management level, and in particular its information-processing capacity, is overburdened. Where this takes place the conditions of efficient hierarchical coordination are systematically undermined and what occurs are the well-known phenomena of overcentralization and overburdening of the central decision-making authority. In the second case the information-processing capacity of the decentral units is utilized, interdependencies of tasks are easier to thematize, and the problem-processing capacity of the overall organization can be enhanced. Nonetheless, a fundamental problem remains in the model of horizontal self-coordination: mechanisms must be developed to compensate for the advantages of hierarchy, which consist of ensuring coordination, integration, and fine-tuning between the subunits.

1.2.2 The State as the Agency of Social Integration? Remarks on the Demanding Normative Foundations of Hierarchical Governance

Beside the "technical-institutional" difficulties involved in solving the complexity problem, the question of the action orientations of the governance actors - i.e. first of all of "the government" - move into the foreground. The traditional concepts of planning and governance proceeded on the assumption that the state is the guardian of the public interest, though they seldom addressed the issue of the action orientation of the governance actors. The current discussion ranks the controversy over the action orientations of the social actors on the same level as the debate on institutional-organizational innovations geared to solving the complexity problem.

What follows first deals with the discussion of the action orientation of social actors as the basis hierarchical or majoritarian-democratic decision structures. The discussion is later taken up again in the context of the analysis of the significance of the action orientation of actors in policy networks.

The point of departure is the consideration that the hierarchical state and majoritarian democracy are acceptable normatively and in terms of efficiency only when it is assumed that *"governing and democratic majorities are on principle both willing and able to engage in activities oriented toward the public interest"* (Scharpf 1991, p. 625). It is, however, precisely this that is fundamentally cast into doubt by the mainstream of public-choice theory.[5] The public-choice theorists proceed on the assumption of the isolated, utility-maximizing individual: *"The community is a fictitious body, composed of ... individual persons"*.[6] The actors of public-choice theory are incapable of any public-interest-oriented behavior, orientation in terms of criteria or objectives beyond their own interests: *"... the rational thing to do is to try to gain as much value as I can while giving up as little value as I can"* (Dyke 1981, p. 29). Ehrenberg and Smith note on the interaction between firms and employees or between rulers and the ruled: *"... however, as in any transaction, each side will try to get the most while giving as little as it must"* (Ehrenberg/Smith 1982, p. 32). The notion that a government or public administration could prioritize the provision of "public goods" is, from this perspective, completely naive. Anne O. Krueger, one of the World Bank's most influential economists during the 1980s, also argues in this direction: *"... competition for entry into government service is ... a competition for rents"* (Krueger 1973, p. 293).

Against the background of this basic structure of societies, public-choice authors, in their pessimistic variants, insinuate not only egoism and self-interest but also opportunism and lust for power (*"self-interest seeking with guile"* - Williamson/Ouchi 1981, p. 351) as the basic action orientation of those in power (and other social actors). Frey summarizes this state of affairs precisely: *"Opportunistic behavior, i.e. the exploitation of any opportunity to the maximum of one's own advantage, has been a center piece of much work in modern economics"* (Frey 1994, p. 137).

On the basis of this egoistic action orientation the "ideal state", and majoritarian democracy as well, are conceivable only as exceptional cases in the form of a well-meaning dictatorship in which the state functionaries are oriented exclusively toward the aggregate utility of the overall polity and not toward their own interests. From the perspective of the mainstream public-choice approaches, the normal case of hierarchical coordination would have to be assumed to be more on the order of predatory rule, whereas democratic majority decisions would imply the subjugation of minorities (Scharpf 1991, p. 625).

What is inferred from this action orientation of state decision-making authorities, and assumed to be the natural course of events, is the failure of the state, and this leads to the conclusion that it is only through orientation in terms of a concept of the *"minimal state"* (see Nozick 1974) that the damage can be contained that necessarily emerges in the public sector as a result of a great variety of forms of self-enrichment and exploitation: as a result of interest groups that enrich themselves at the expense of consumers and taxpayers; as a result of political parties and bureaucracies that are basically concerned only with maximizing their budgets and privileges; as a result of governments that arrange for the preservation of their own power at the expense of the public interest.[7]

The skepticism of the mainstream of public-choice approaches as regards the state, justified as it is with the assumption of systematically opportunistic behavior on the part of actors, correspond to the extraordinarily naive belief in the operational and subsistence capacity of societies, which are stamped fundamentally by the market and morally indifferent individuals oriented purely in terms of their own advantage: *"They hold that if prices are correctly set, society is best served if individuals go ahead maximizing their own, unrestricted utility and that there simply does not exist any moral issue"*.[8]

Public-choice theory is, however, full of contradictions. If one were forced to assume opportunism as a *general* action orientation, the constitutional-institutional safeguards against opportunistic behavior recommended by the *"constitutional political economics"* variant of public-choice theory[9] would prove fully ineffectual. In view of the general edge on information and competence enjoyed by politicians, bureaucrats, and functionaries, there is no reliable incentive and control structure that could not be dodged by clever and self-interested actors - and even the attempt to set up any such control system would destroy all the anticipated efficiency advantages of hierarchical or majoritarian decisions.

If we follow this line of argument, every political theory is, for reasons of internal consistency, forced to assume that human behavior is *in principle* - albeit imperfectly - oriented to norms that at the same time make possible nonegoistical, nonopportunistic behavior. This is the direction in which Etzioni argues. While public-choice theory centers on the utility-maximizing individual, Etzioni emphasizes the integration of individuals in *"social collectivities"* and the normative setting of egoistical-rational action orientations - the existence of which is not at all denied, though it is relativized - in values shared by groups, organizations, and societies. He underlines the *"internalization of the social context, the partial overlap between the I's and the commons ... people have at least some significant involvement in the community, a sense of shared identity, and commitment to values, a sense that 'We are members of one another'.*"[10] In other words, what is rejected is the uncritical application of economic models to the behavior of actors in organizations and in politics, which is (also) regulated by other norms. And this critique has a double thrust: **First**, it rejects the reductionist assumptions on the determinants of the behavior of individuals, i.e. in reality human beings behave differently. This is essentially a critique of the liberal theory of the action orientations of humans. **Second**, it rejects the thesis that societies develop optimally when their members behave strictly as utility-maximizing beings. The absolute behavioral rules postulated by public-choice theory in the name of value neutrality are, instead, criticized in terms of their (at times) destructive impacts on society (e.g. disintegration, power of the stronger). This is basically a critique of the effects of liberal vale preferences on social practice.

Elster (1991, p. 120) argues in this direction: *"While there is always a risk of self-serving behavior, the extent to which it is actually present varies widely. Much of the public choice - literature with its assumption of universally opportunistic behavior, simply seems out of touch with the real world, in which there is a great deal of honesty and sense of duty. If people were always engaged in opportunistic behavior when they could get away with it, civilization as we know it would not exist. "*

The views of Etzioni, Elster, and others presented here proceed from the tradition of Locke and Montesquieu and recall distinctly Elias' core thesis that modern societies, marked by the dissolution of traditional milieus, growing division of labor, and increasing differentiation, can prove able to survive only if their members have internalized shared values, principles of action, and rules, and - as a rule - behave in accordance with them. Etzioni, Elster and Scharpf show that public-choice theory, with its premises borrowed from neoclassical economics, overrates the realism of its basic assumptions on the *homo oeconomicus*. The underlying figure of the public-choice approach, viz. the "context-free", utility-maximizing individual (the *"rational idiot"* - Sen 1981) fails to recognize that even in modern societies individuals are integrated within social and cultural lifeworlds and are *at the same time* oriented in terms of their own self-interests as well as in terms of values, ideas, arguments, and institutional habits shared in groups, organizations, and societies.

A similar argument is advanced by Michael Walzer, who, as far as both overall social development and the functioning of the market are concerned, points to the significance and in particular the actual existence of *"institutions, rules, customs, and habitual practices"* to which actors gear their activities (Walzer 1992, p. 50). A convergence is emerging in the debate in the US between the progressive wing of the communitarians (to which Walzer belongs; he sees the communitarian discourse not as a counterproject but as a corrective to a one-sidedly individualistic-market-oriented liberalism, which is, for that very reason, self-destructive) and liberals (along the lines of John Rawls, who clearly reject the neoliberal reduction of liberalism to positions of the *"free-trader vulgaris"* (Karl Marx)). This debate is concerned with the significance of moral resources and values for the "viability and reproduction capacity" of modern societies. This convergence is to be sought in the assumption that modern societies must, to a certain extent, be tied to a community of overriding values, i.e. are in need of a shared cultural community or life-form.[11] This means that the dichotomy has been broken up that dominated the initial phase of the discussion between the liberals (along the lines of Rawls), emphasizing the primacy of individual rights and universal values, and the communitarians, who represented the primacy of collective and - in essence - particularist value concepts.

An issue that has remained open in this discussion is *what* shared values may be seen as a necessary presupposition for the reproduction and integration capacity of modern societies. Conservative authors refer primarily to traditional values such as patriotism, nation, etc., while the liberals point to the significance of internalizing values such as tolerance, fairness, reciprocity, and solidarity. But the line of demarcation does not separate only liberals and conservatives, it above all divides *"atomists"* and *"holists"*.[12] *"Atomists"*, here understood as liberals who, on the basis of their ontological premises, derive the structure of society from the behavior of utility maximizing individuals, can restrict themselves primarily to institutional procedures needed to create a viable order. The *"holists"*, be they of a conservative or a progressive hue, do not see society as an aggregated substrate of individual acts, but emphasize the social, collective character of social development dynamics; they will have to look more deeply than the *"atomists"* into the issue of what binding values are needed among the members of society to integrate modern societies. No doubt both conservative and progressive "holists" will arrive at different value concepts, but what unites them - as opposed to the "atomists" - is the need to establish propositions on the mechanisms of social integration.

This interesting discussion, which must be understood as a "counter-movement" to the hegemony of neoliberal concepts in the economic sciences and public-choice theory in the social sciences in the 1980s, cannot be presented here in a more differentiated fashion.[13] But what is significant is the emerging concurrence among the different partici-pants in the debate on the **common problematic** (significance of moral resources, action orientation, value contexts for the viability of modern societies). As the discussion got underway, most liberals (thus, for in-stance, Rawls) regarded the question of binding values as relatively unimportant. They pointed to the crucial significance of institutional procedures for the creation of a just and viable social order. It is now becoming clear that both issues are relevant. This result is also reached by the liberal Ralf Dahrendorf, who points to the importance of *"ligatures, ties, and deep structures"* that provide orientation for indi-viduals and without the existence of which modern market societies would be threatened with disintegration (Dahrendorf 1992, p. 41).

Marwell and Ames (1981) conducted a free-rider experiment in the US to test the underlying premises of public-choice theory. In eleven of twelve experiments the great majority of participants failed to make use of free-rider opportunities (i.e. chances for opportunistic behavior). The participants used 40 - 60 % of the resources allocated to them to provide public goods. They did not utilize the opportunity that the ex-periment gave them to consume the resources wholly for themselves without any control or chance of being discovered, and instead pro-vided the public goods to the other participants. The same experiment was conducted with a number of groups composed of students of economics from "neoliberal faculties". Here a majority made use of the free-rider opportunities, and only 20 % of the resources available were used to proved public goods. The internalized value concepts and the action orientations stemming from them were underlined by the answer given to the question what is to be understood as "fair behavior". The economics students refused to define the concept or declared that a small or no amount for the provision of public goods was "fair". The other groups articulated a quite unified understanding of fairness. Over 75 % of the participants saw individual involvement in the provision of public goods, including a share for themselves of some 50 % of the resources available, as "fair" and termed any systematic exploitation of free-rider opportunities as "unfair".

The results of Marwell and Ames on the significance of free-rider behavior permit three conclusion important in our context. **First**, they demonstrate that the behavior of individuals is dependent on the cultural and social contexts in which these individuals act. **Second**, the action orientation of the great majority of the persons participating in the experiment is based on the pursuit of egotistical *and* common interests as well as on the attempt to find a compromise between these poles. **Third**, is has become clear that the internalization of neoclassical assumptions on the behavior of individuals can give rise to self-fulfilling prophecy phenomena.

Theories that completely ignore the normative base of action orientations and the *"logic of appropriateness"* worked out by March and Olson (March/Olson 1989) are accordingly deficient in terms of their explanatory power. Working out the significance of socially anchored norms by no means implies the irrelevance of self-interests. The views presented by Etzione, March and Olson, Scharpf, and others differs from public-choice approaches in particular in terms of a different relationship between rule and exception. Instead of assuming opportunistic behavior **as a rule**, it is assumed **in principle** that persons in power, functionaries, and citizens pursue the public interest and collective interests in dealing with public affairs, and that these interests many also conflict with self-interests. As opposed to the anthropological optimism of, for instance, Rousseau, however, this view takes into account imperfection, human weakness, and the possibility of opportunistic behavior and seeks mechanisms to strengthen public-interest orientations with the aid of institutional structures and to restrict the temptation to abuse hierarchical authority.

In other words, there are points of contact between public-choice theory and the line of argumentation advanced by Etzioni and the other authors named. Still, the difference is a fundamental one: institutions, controls, sanctions, incentives can be sufficient for social actors who are in principle loyal to norms, though fallible; they are, however, completely helpless in the face of consistently opportunistic actors. Elias speaks in this connection of the significance of *"we-identities"* (in groups, organizations, the political community from the local to the national level). The stronger the normative moorings of *"we-identities"* in *"I-identities"*, the more likely it is that acts serving the public interest will materialize voluntarily and decisions will be accepted even when they are contrary to immediate or short-term self-interests (Elias 1987, pp. 207 ff.). Without the existence of *"we-identities"*, the effort involved in controlling and sanctioning effective collective action in modern societies would be prohibitive.

From this perspective the public-choice analyses might be interpreted as warnings against a "worst-case" development; they point to the **fragility of the architecture of modern societies**. Public-choice theories, do, however, not offer a model for explaining the normal working of democratic constitutional states. Against the background of the Marwell/Ames study, we might even ask whether or not public-choice theories obstruct any analytical access to an understanding and regulation of problems of political order under normal conditions.

In the context of the argumentations presented here, there is, for the time being, thus no reason to question per se the effectiveness of state-level action and hierarchical coordination. There is much that indicates a need to search for institutional forms whose incentive structures can bring about the greatest possible measure of complementarity between **personal** and **internal organizational** self-interests and **normative duties**. This consideration corresponds to an institutionalization of

checks and balances, political competition, freedom of opinion, association, and assembly, i.e. the fundamental principles of the democratic
constitutional state and - the network theorists are dedicated to this
problem - the embeddedness of hierarchical coordination in horizontal
negotiation systems.

1.3   Social Integration in Societies Marked by Division of Labor: A Problem Rediscovered, not a New Problem

The controversy between public-choice approaches and authors like
Scharpf, Etzioni, March and Olson, or Walzer is not at all new. Rather,
it thematizes a basic problematic of modern social sciences: the question of the integration mechanisms in modern societies in the process
of growing differentiation. It was as early as in Durkheim's (1858 -
1917) debate with Spencer (1820 - 1906) that the terrain surrounding
this still topical core conflict was demarcated. In looking for integration mechanisms in modern societies, Spencer came across the market
mechanism (Spencer 1972 - first published 1893).The market, Spencer
noted, is able to integrate society "spontaneously". Instead of action
orientations brought about by moral rules, he stated, the functional
nexus of the market permits an unconscious adaptation of individual
acts tailored to egotistical utility rationales. The social context emerges
here via the nonnormative market mechanism and finds its expression
in a *"gigantic system of private contracts"*. With this view, Spencer is
squarely in the individualist-utilitarian tradition of Adam Smith and
can at the same time be seen as a forerunner of today's public-choice
approaches.

In Durkheim's view, primitive, archaic societies are integrated through
a collective consciousness and via a fundamental normative understanding that leaves no room for the development of individual identities. Durkheim's term for this integration mechanism is *"mechanical
solidarity"* (Durkheim 1977, first published 1893, Book One, Chapter
2). *"Mechanical solidarity"* breaks down in modern societies stamped
by division of labor. Social integration is now achieved via mecha-

nisms of *"organic solidarity"*. Group solidarity and the immediate constraint of primitive societies are replaced by the legal system and contractual law. The reciprocal dependence of the autonomous exchange partners, sanctioned by the legal system, is supplanted by the development of a system of collective values in societies marked by division of labor. This new collective consciousness or *"organic solidarity"* develops out of the increasing *"material density"* of the interactions between individuals and subsectors or modern society, and in the course of this process a greater *"moral density"* and a new *"collective consciousness"* emerge. In other words, division of labor in this way becomes the main source of *"organic solidarity"* (Durkheim 1977, Book One, Chapters 3-7). Durkheim constructs a causal chain leading from division of labor, interdependence of relationships, increasing contacts, cooperation, and - as the concentrated impact of these variables - organic solidarity.

The central difference between Spence and Durkheim is to be found in their assessment of what Durkheim terms *"collective consciousness"*. For Spencer the emergence of a *"collective consciousness"* is insignificant in view of the integrative power of the market assumed by him. Durkheim, on the other hand, regards as unrealistic any notion of a differentiated society integrated solely via market mechanisms: *"Is that really the character of the society whose unity comes from the division of labor? If that were the case, one could really doubt its stability. For even though (the market) approximates the interest of individuals, it does so only for moments; where ... interest rules alone, every ego, since there is nothing to curb the opposing egoisms, is at war with every other one ..."* (Durkheim 1977, p. 243).

The *"organic form of social solidarity"* must therefore also be sanctioned via values and norms: *"It is thus incorrect to oppose the society that comes from the community of belief to the society that rests on cooperation by according moral character only to the former and seeing in the latter only an economic group. In reality cooperation likewise has a morality of its own"* (Durkheim 1977, p. 268). Durkheim speaks in this connection of the increasing significance of *"noncontractual elements"* of contracts. Spencer's *"gigantic system of private contracts"*, it is argued, could produce social integration in societies stamped by division of labor only if the members of society in fact adhered to contracts and obligations. It is precisely societies marked by division of labor that are reliant on a great measure of voluntary moral concurrence by the members of society, i.e. interactive value principles. Societies characterized by division of labor, in which these forms of *"organic solidarity"* do not emerge, drift - Durkheim contends - toward a state of anarchy. Habermas rightly points out that this force-field between successful social integration and anomie problematized by Durkheim corresponds *"in a certain way to Weber's paradox of social rationalization"* (Habermas 1988, p. 178).

Anomie comes about when, in the process of increasing division of labor, a gap opens up between the development of the social structure, the collectively binding and obliging rules (solidarity), and the social bands (morality). Anomie is accordingly a sign of advancing functional differentiation in the face of underdeveloped rules.

It is Durkheim's merit to have worked out that it is not only market relations based on the existence of noneconomic norms and laws, but social division of labor, or in more modern terms: functionally highly differentiated societies, that are practically inconceivable as long as they are not imbedded in a matrix of norms and rules. There are, however, still some fundamental open questions that need to be answered to explain the connection between division of labor or functional differentiation, organic solidarity, and social integration; and these questions can be answered more precisely by more recent authors, as is demonstrated below in the discussion of the action orientation of actors in networks.

It is interesting to note that this classical controversy, which can only be adumbrated here, long went unnoticed in the course of the discussion over the state and governance. The dichotomist discussions of the state presented above "overlooked" the complex problem of "social integration" which conceals the fragile relationship between the individual, social subsystems, society, and the state in societies in the process of growing differentiation. The governance and state optimists of every hue have regarded the integration of society via the state as a matter of course. The liberal critics of the state, on the other hand, regarded social integration as jeopardized precisely by the activities of the state and pointed to the market as an efficient center for the coordination and integration of modern societies. The "systems-theoretical general offensive" was instrumental in unjamming this sterile discussion, though without itself being able to provide any convincing answers to the problematic questions surrounding governance and social integration. The great merits of systems theory in Luhmann's manner is, however, that it brought the complexity of social development dynamics back into the discussion. The current debate on governance potentials in polycentric societies is once again returning to this classical discussion on mechanisms of social integration now that it has become clear that patterns of organization and governance in societies characterized by division of labor are in many areas reducible neither to the state as an "integration mechanism" not to the coordinative and integrative impulses provided by the invisible hand of the market.

CHAPTER 2   Analytical Network Theories as a New Perspective on the Problem Posed by Social Governance

There is one issue that links network theories: network concepts attempt to grasp complex relations and interactions between a great variety of actors in policy fields and to gain an idea of how policy outcomes emerge in this process. They thematize the limitations of one-sided market- and/or hierarchy-oriented organizational concepts. The majority of authors furthermore describe policy networks as *"policy-making arrangements characterized by the predominance of informal, decentralized and horizontal relations between policy actors"* (Marin/ Mayntz 1991, p. 15). Beyond this shared conviction we find a great variety of approaches concealed behind the term network theory. What follows will first outline the empirically oriented approaches and then work out the conceptual core of network theory that yields results interesting for the discussion on governance.

2.1 The Limited Contributions Provided by Descriptive Approaches to Networks

One important group of researchers understands network analysis primarily as a method for determining relationships of units or actors in a networked system.[14] The goal is to produce structural descriptions of networks. In describing the interactive relations between actors and/or organizations, these studies contribute to the task of recognizing differentiated relationship patterns and avoiding simplifications ("the state", "the firm" as actors). They do, however, not go beyond this descriptive level.

The term "network" also occurs in neocorporatist studies, as a rule to characterize relationships between the public and private sectors in the process of policy implementation. Katzenstein (1978) or Rhodes (1990) use the term network especially at the mesolevel to depict the interactions between public institutions and firms in a given industrial sector. Lehmbruch (1984) also occasionally speaks of networks, though he does so to thematize forms of cooperation between the national top-level organizations of firms, labor unions, and the state, i.e. he moves more at the macrolevel. In these studies too the term "network" basically has a descriptive character.

Heclo goes a step further (Heclo 1978). He coins the term "issue network", characterizing with it specific relationships between the public and private sectors. Heclo observes that, in a variety of policy fields, there are a great number of actors (e.g. scientists, citizens' initiatives, interest organizations, expert journalists) involved in the policy process. On the basic of these observations Heclo criticizes the neocorporatists, who narrow down their analyses to the "iron triangle" (of state, firms, labor unions), thus registering only one section of reality. As opposed to the closed "iron triangles" based on formalized relationships, the *"issue networks"* are characterized by informal, open, unstable webs of relationships between a great number of actors who work together in a policy field. Heclo points out that *"issue networks"* mark a type of political governance that is characterized by the absence of any clear-cut hierarchical structure. Instead of the theories dominant since the mid-1970s that proceeded on the assumption of an increasing centralization of society and hierarchical governance patterns, he points to horizontal self-governance mechanisms and the growing number of actors involved in the policy process.

Laumann and Knoke likewise point to the growing number of actors involved in the policy process referred to by Heclo. They argue that this tends to blur the traditional distinction between the state (as an autonomous governance actor) and society, and they conclude that, in the last analysis, the distinction between state and society has become obsolete. The state presents itself to them as *"a complex system of governmental and nongovernmental organizations that struggle for power and legitimacy in the making of public policies ..."* (Laumann/Knoke 1987; see also Waarden 1992). This manner of grasping complexity by radically reducing complexity (fusing complicated network structures consisting of private and public actors to form the "state") obstructs our view of the different functions of private, state, and semi-state actors in network-like bargaining systems, as well as of the specific forms of cooperation and the important question of the role played by the state in polycentric societies. Artificially subsuming under the concept state all activities of private and public actors who contribute to formulating public policy merely deflects our attention from the fact that in societies marked by a high level of division of labor there are not only more public institutions (the state) but also private actors involved - in specific ways - in the making of public policy. The semantic abrogation of the tense relationship dominant in (many) policy networks between public and private actors, state and society involved in the category "the state" thus constitutes an inadmissible oversimplification.

A number of studies typologize network phenomena with an eye to various criteria. Atkinson and Coleman (1989) investigate at the sector level the relations between state and industry and distinguish various network types, defined in terms of the broadly dispersed or centralized scopes of competence enjoyed by state-level or private organizations and in terms of the capacity of employers' federations to mobilize their members. They here go beyond the neocorporatists' narrow network concept and present arguments more differentiated than those of Laumann and Knoke. Their typology indicates the existence of a variety of organizational patterns, though these are, too simply, reduced to a limited number of structural factors.[15]

This variety of approaches to networks offers, not unlike the studies presented by administrative scientists, a wealth of interesting empirical material. The studies show that political governance capacity is not merely a question of the strong, effective, and active state, but that it depends on the effectiveness of a great number of social actors. But what have we gained by describing networks as complex social structures or as *"complex arrays of relationships"* (Johanson/Mattson 1989) between social actors? It makes little sense to position networks, as *"hybrid phenomena"*, along a sliding scale extending from market to hierarchy, contract to organization (*"something between market and organization"*; Thorelli 1986). It remains unsatisfactory that many empirically oriented studies fail to grasp the relative significance of the forms of organization described for the development dynamics of modern societies. The studies document formal changes in the policy process that provide a picture similar to the studies of the political and administrative scientists discussed above. The new complexity is designated with a new term - "network structure". The descriptive approaches to networks fail to take into account the social dynamics behind these surface phenomena.

2.2 Strengthening Social Governance Potentials by Developing Network Structures - (Partial) Answers to New Demands on Society and the (Partial) Loss of State Governance Autonomy

2.2.1 Networks as Organizational Patterns for Dealing with Reciprocal Dependence

In spite of the differences between them, the network studies revolve around one central point: political decision-making structures are increasingly characterized by the dominance of informal, decentral, and horizontal interorganizational relationships. In the analytically oriented approaches, a **new view of political governance** is gaining currency; it is characterized as follows by Kenis and Schneider (Kenis/Schneider 1991, pp. 26 f.):

"... the network perspective implies a new perception of causal relations in social processes.... The core of this perspective is a decentralized concept of social organization and governance: society is no longer exclusively controlled by a central intelligence (e.g. the State); rather, controlling devices are dispersed and intelligence is distributed among a multiplicity of action (or processing) units. The coordination of these action units is no longer the result of 'central steering' or some kind of 'prestabilized harmony' but emerges through the purposeful interactions of individual actors (what is meant here are collective actors, organizations, D.M.), *who themselves are enabled for parallel action by exchanging information and other relevant resources".*

Seen from this perspective, the network phenomena are more than a different way of looking at an essentially unaltered social reality. Renate Mayntz concludes from the empirical studies available that the *"notion of a clear-cut separation of state and society and the idea of the state as the supreme social control center"* can no longer be sustained. She notes far-reaching changes in political decision-making structures that point to changes to the basic structures of society: *"instead of being created by a central authority, policy today often comes about in a process in which a multiplicity of both public and private actors are involved"* (Mayntz 1993, p. 40).

As the analysis of the theories of competitiveness at the company level has already shown, *"tacit knowledge"* is gaining in importance in the policy process as well. Kenneth Arrow (1994, p. 16) argues in this direction: *"It seems to me that there is in fact no knowledge that can be fully codified and transferred at the level of consciousness. Even a formal thing like doing mathematics depends to some extend on tact, feel and intuitive understanding, on things you cannot put down. Ways of doing this types of things are transferred by teachers to students, by doing things together and by working through examples. There is a certain element of tacit knowledge in every knowledge"*. The significance of noncodified knowledge has changed the form of learning processes. Noncodified knowledge cannot be purchased and traded in markets; imitative learning is limited in scope inasmuch as noncodified knowledge cannot be grasped by it; state-level efforts, e.g. to build technological know-how with an eye to developing an effective technology policy are relativized in view of the relevance of tacit knowledge. In detecting problem areas, working out viable and adapted solutions, and implementing policies, state institutions are therefore forced to rely on actor knowledge in given policy fields that is difficult to transfer and often not codified. This is true, as is shown by the empirical network studies, of health policy no less than in environmental or industrial policy. Networks are organizational patterns which, by focusing the knowledge of different actors and the learning processes they have gone through together, are more apt to be in a position to convey "tacit knowledge" than are market mechanisms and hierarchical decision-making systems.

Kenis and Schneider are the authors who have worked out this **crucial dimension of networks** most clearly: *"Policy networks are mechanisms of political resource mobilization in situations where the capacity for decision making, program formulation and implementation is widely distributed or dispersed among private and public actors ... In situations where policy resources are dispersed and context (or actor)* *dependent, a network is the only mechanism to mobilize and pool resources"* (Kenis/Schneider 1991, pp. 41 f.).

The cooperation of actors and organizations in networks can thus be explained by the fact that the individual actors do not have all the resources needed to realize the output aimed for, inasmuch as these resources are dispersed among different actors. It is precisely this state of affairs that is defined in resource dependence theory as *"interdependence"* (see Aldrich 1975, Benson 1975, Mandell 1988). The interorganizational structure of a network aims to draw together the array of different resources important for the collective output so as to achieve a joint result that cannot be attained individually. Networks are accordingly forms of organization that, in view of the limitations of hierarchical coordination and central political governance, have emerged to deal with the complexity problem outlined above and the interdependence phenomenon, with its governance logic, that is associated with it.

Networks in which formal autonomous organizations work together do justice on the one hand to the trend toward differentiation, to the **independence** and relative autonomy of subsystems and organizations; i.e. they abandon the claim to govern highly differentiated systems centrally ("from the top down"). On the other hand, they are based on the capacity for intersystemic communication and coordination among the organizations involved; i.e. they process the actual **interdependence relationships** that emerge because actors, in pursuing their tasks, are more and more often confronted with problems *"that tend to cut across the boundaries of the several jurisdictions and specializations"* (Hanf/ O'Toole 1992, p. 166; see also Mayer 1994).

Networks are accordingly a type of organization and governance capable of articulating the phenomena of simultaneously increasing independence and interdependence emphasized especially by Luhmann. The networked organization counteracts the self-referentiality of individual subsystems (organizations) that Luhmann regards as inevitable. What emerges is a qualitatively new mode of governance.

Network approaches permit a theoretically more precise understanding of formal changes in the underlying structures of society which were closed to understanding within the framework of traditional theories of the state. The discussion on the *"socialized state"* and the *"statified' (*verstaatlichte*) society"* point clearly to the aporia into which governance theory had maneuvered itself in the mid-1980s. From a statist perspective, the state's autonomy of action was threatened by the omnipresence of social organizations (the "socialized state"). A more critical view of the state perceived the same matter in exactly the opposite way: the term "'statified' society" pointed to the circumstance that in modern societies hardly any sector of society remains "free of the state". Both terms show that the discussion on governance theory had great difficulties in freeing itself from its statist traditions.

On the other hand, the network studies show that the **reciprocal dependence** of public and private actors has increased. The tendency analyzed by Luhmann toward simultaneously increasing the independence and interdependence of social subsystems and organizations undermines the action autonomy of all social actors (though not to the same degree); it is the source of the spread of mutual dependencies. This dynamic casts doubt on the classical notion that there are either private matters for which individuals, specific organizations, or firms are responsible or public affairs that are regulated by the state (as a state under the rule of law, legitimated by elections). It appears as though, aside from the spheres in which solely private actors deal with their private affairs and the fields in which the state autonomously handles public problems, there is emerging a growing mixed segment in which there is a need for "collective governance" that can be dealt with effectively neither by private nor by state-level actors on their own.

State-level policy formulation is often possible only in the form of interlinkages between state and private actors - i.e. as "socialized policy-making". This is the reason for the phenomenon of the "socialized state". At the same time the private actors (e.g. firms) are reliant on stable framework conditions, long-term action orientations, and efficient public institutions in order to settle their private affairs. This is the basis of the phenomenon of the *"'statified' society"*. While, however, the two pairs of terms describe the occupation of the state by society and vice versa as a pathological syndrome, analytical network theories point to the need for close interaction between private and public actors in sustaining political governance capacity and the ability to shape society. Policy networks are needed in policy fields in which there are complex political, economic, or technical tasks to be mastered and the governance resources are distributed over a larger number of actors. In a situation of this sort the traditional interventionist state is hamstrung. In the context of classical theories of the state it was at first impossible to perceive the social innovation implied by networks (or, as is shown by the discussion over the *"socialized state"* and the *"'statified' society"*, possible to perceive it only as a series of decadent symptoms of decline) insofar as it contradicted the existing habits of thought.

2.2.2   Networks: Emergent Patterns of Organization and Governance beyond Markets and Hierarchies, or Hybrid Forms?

One issue controversial in the theoretical discussion is whether network structures must be understood as a new type of social action or merely as a hybrid form somewhere between market and hierarchy, contract and organization. We will here represent the thesis that network structures must be understood as qualitatively new (in the sense of "distinguishable") patterns of organization and governance *"beyond markets and policy hierarchies"*[16] in polycentric societies. Network structures can be understood as emergent phenomena in the sense that they are, as a whole, more than the sum of their parts.

It is important to distinguish between different types of social action, characterized by specific forms of coordination and governance mechanisms, if the complexity of social governance is to be adequately addressed and understood in the first place. Thus, for instance, Laumann and Knoke see a breakdown of social coordination and governance mechanisms into a great variety of unclear and intricate interaction relationships between public and private actors that are then also defined as "the state"; this proves to be undercomplex and generally not very useful. The view presented by transaction-costs economists is likewise unsatisfactory. From this perspective, actors assess institutional arrangements in terms of cost-benefit aspects with an eye to reducing transaction costs. The level of the transaction costs calculated for given cases determines whether or not actors will sign a contract or join an organization (a corporation). There is in principle no difference between contract and organization: organizations are interpreted as the sum of contractual arrangements. The studies published by Williamson differentiate at least gradually in terms of the intensity of the linkage between the actors involved. Markets are accordingly characterized by the fact that there are between the actors involved no structural linkages, whereas hierarchical linkages are marked by fixed links; networks, per definitionem characterized by loose interlinkages, accordingly take up an intermediate position.[17]

However, an analysis of this type, which dissolves social phenomena into hypothetical contracts, fails to recognize the autonomy of and the fundamental difference between the specific types of social action involved and the organizational structures on which they are based. In contrast to simple interactions between actors, organizations are characterized by membership, norms and rules binding for members within the organization, and the "standardization" of the sum of individual action in the shape of the decisions and actions taken by the organization as a whole. In other words, contracts are essentially concerned with exchange relationships, organizations with relationships based on cooperation.

Networks are not located in a gray zone between market and state or between contract and organization, they have a specific action logic of their own. They are phenomena whose point of departure is constituted by the limitations of state and market, i.e. failures on the part of state and organizations. Grabher (1994) or Teubner (1992) discuss networks with reference to the always precarious relationship between redundancy and variety. Purely market-mediated contractual relationships have a high degree of variety and low levels of redundancy. Market-based relationships are flexible, open to rapid change, innovative - but they seldom evince a long-term orientation, coherence, and accumulated experience. Organizations can solve theses problems entailed by a lack of redundancy, but only at the expense of variety. Rigidity, bureaucratization, motivational problems, lack of innovativeness, high information costs prove to be problems affecting organizations (and not only public institutions, but also, for instance, large-scale private corporations). By way of contrast, the modus operandi of networks can be seen as a **combination** of these two logics. The Japanese economists Imai and Itami describe this state of affairs by pointing to the example of corporate networks: *"Market principles penetrate into the firms' resources allocation and organization principles creep into the market allocation. Interpenetration occurs to remedy the failure of pure principles either in the market or in the organization"* (Imai/Itami 1984, p. 285).

In other words, in networks the problem of variety and redundancy is restructured by interlinking the logic of social exchange (contracts) with the logic of relations based on social cooperation (that has until now been assigned to relationships in organizations). This linking of logics that have until now been assigned to divergent types of social action can be detected both in networks between firms and in policy networks. Between parent firms and their strategic suppliers there exist contractual relationships (exchange orientation; high redundancy) as a means of avoiding the organizational disadvantages of integrated organizations (too little redundancy, too much complexity). Above and beyond the market-mediated relationships, there develop at the same time (as was demonstrated with reference to Italian industrial districts and clusters of firms) a variety of social, reciprocal, cooperative relationships (exchange of engineers and information, development of new corporate models, stable supplier relations). The emerging firms networks differ in terms of these dual logics (redundancy and variety; competition and reciprocal relationships) both from firms active solely in the marketplace and from integrated large-scale corporations. Applied to policy networks, the picture that emerges is similar. In the "competition-oriented" pluralism model, organizations (as lobbies) represent their own interests. Their attitudes toward other organizations are either indifferent or geared to competition. The various actors in policy networks are forced to represent their own interests (exchange logic) and at the same time to aim for results reached jointly with other parties concerned. Exchange- and cooperation-based orientations overlap here as well. That is to say, networks are not intermediate forms in the sense of "not more market, but not integrated organization, either", but a special type of social action, in that they refer **at the same time** to contractual and organizational relationships, i.e. cannot be assigned a position on a continuum **between** market and contract or hierarchy and organization.

2.2.3   Social Modernization as the Motor behind the Formation and the Universalization of Networks

Renate Mayntz shows that networks do not constitute isolated phenomena but can be interpreted as a central expression of social modernization (Mayntz 1991, 1993). Policy networks emerge as a consequence of the gradually developed significance of formal organizations in almost all social sectors and the fragmentation of power associated with them, as a result of the distribution of important governance resources over a variety of actors, and, finally, because of the loss of action autonomy on the part of the state in many policy fields. Networks are to this extent of theoretical relevance for any understanding of basic social structures.

The usual practice is to "measure" a society's development level in terms of a package of aggregated indicators such as degree of literacy, number of doctors and teachers per capita of population, energy consumption, per capita income, and sometimes even more qualitative indicators like political participation of the population. One problem with these indicators of modernization, however, is that they ignore **structural features** of societies. The universal characteristic of modernizing societies is, in structural terms, functional differentiation in the sense of the formation of social subsystems. Mayntz demonstrates that functional differentiation in societies with millions of members is conceivable only in terms of a process entailing the emergence of organizations, i.e. collective actors. It is the existence of organizations that coordinate and concentrate the actions of many individuals which leads to a capacity for collective action and the formation of social subsystems. Perrow describes societies in the process of modernization, differentiation in this sense, as *"societies of organizations"* (Perrow 1989).

If the concept of system is to be taken seriously, functional subsystems are characterized by boundaries to other subsystems and a minimum of identity and subsystem autonomy. The emergence of *"formal organizations is thus not merely one of many structural characteristics of modern* (and modernizing, D.M.) *societies; without formal organizations the social subsystems would not have the degree of relative autonomy that normally characterizes functional subsystems such as the state, the economy, the system of science, health care ..."* (Mayntz 1993, p. 42).

We can also learn from the collapse of the former socialist countries that the sheer existence of organizations constitutes only a necessary, but not a sufficient, condition for the modernization process. Only when the growth of organizations is linked with a minimum of action autonomy and independence of organizations as well as a (relative) autonomy of the subsystems (freedom from political or religious control), is it possible for a functional differentiation of society to take place. The socialist countries were not at all marked by a degree of organization similar to (or higher than) that in Western market economies. The fundamental difference was basically the lower degree of functional differentiation stemming from the lack of autonomy of their subsystems. The absolute hegemony of the state parties in all social sectors and the complete subsumption of existing organizations under the power of the state party led to total centralization and, in the end, to the absolute incapacitation of the state.

The preponderance of the Party has often, for instance in connection with theories of totalitarianism theories, been interpreted exclusively in the sense of political repression. Convergence theorists inferred from the existence of *"institutionally rich societies"*[18] in East and West a convergence of the two systems. When we look back, it become clear that one-party rule obstructed the functional differentiation of society despite the formal existence of a variety of organizations and that this structure turned out to have negative repercussions on modernization. The erosion of the socialist states can thus be interpreted more as a result of obstructed innovation, a lack of flexibility and responsiveness of the social system - i.e. a lack of or at least obstructed modernization - than as the result of a goal-directed revolt against political repression.

Networks are social innovations, institutional inventions for solving complex problems in view of which both market-like allocation (due to the production of negative externalities, a lack of long-term orientation, insufficient redundancy relations) and hierarchical forms of decision-making (due to rigidity, a lack of flexibility, imperfect information, a lack of variety) prove dysfunctional. The **functional logic of networks** is characterized by a combination of elements of the two fundamental patterns of order (market and hierarchy) and, in this sense, constitutes a qualitatively higher type of action. Networks are characterized by

-   the existence and action logic of autonomous, decentrally organized actors typical for market-based governance and

-   an action strategy geared to defining medium- and long-term goals and the means adequate to attaining these goals and contributing, through goal-directed action in a network, to shaping the structures in a social subsystem; this collective goal-directed action strategy is typical for hierarchical governance concepts (see Mayntz 1991, p. 12).

The discussion dominant in the 1980s over "market versus state" over-looked both these innovative forms of shaping social structures and the fact that networks overlap market mechanisms, hierarchical state governance, and horizontal self-coordination. The logic of networks can unfold, as reflections on the erosion of the socialist countries show, only against the background of specific patterns of social organization and the action rationalities of actors or organizations associated with them.

2.2.4 The "Art of Separation" and the "Art of Connection" - Reflections on the Organizational Patterns Underlying "Network Societies"

Actors integrated within interorganizational networks (i.e. neocorporatist systems, sectoral network structures in which firms, research institutions, and labor unions work together) must first of all have a **minimum of action autonomy**. The capacity to shape without constraint a specific sphere of responsibility (firm, department, labor union, research institution) makes it possible, easier, and, as it were, unavoidable to engage in autonomous learning processes, to mobilize tacit knowledge, to accumulate selective knowledge, and to formulate organizational strategies. It is only a minimum of action autonomy that encourages responsible behavior in the sense of the organization in question. What is meant are learning processes that cannot develop in structures that are strictly hierarchically governed, in which decentral decision-making competences in organizations and social subsystems are substituted for by centralized decisions. The action autonomy of organizations is thus an essential condition for their ability to optimize their performance.

The problem-solving strategies in networks are marked by collective decision-making. This requires two things of the actors: first, they must be able to precisely define and represent their own interests and to contribute, from their perspective, to working out a relatively complete analysis of existing problems and to elaborate solutions to them based on this analysis. It is precisely the pooling of the know-how scattered over a problem area that constitutes an institutional advantage over hierarchical decision-making authorities, whose knowledge is necessarily deficient. Second, the actors must be capable of strategic interaction and compromising.

Actors of organizations working together in networks act along three complementary logics. First, they, on their own responsibility, optimize their organizations (**inward orientation**). Second, they define their interests and represent them vis-à-vis the state and other social actors (**representation of interests**). Third, they shape their specific environment through cooperation and networking with public and private organizations (**cooperative competition**). In other words, increasing social organizational capacity **and** concentrating and channeling of social creativity potentials can be complementary processes.

Luhmann sees the articulation of these three logics in networks as plainly and simply impossible. In contrast to his assumption of self-referentiality, networks link together logics, codes, from different sub-systems. Organizations, firms, a political system are obviously capable of purposive interaction. The more current theories of society have thus far distinguished as functioning actors only individuals, organizations (as collective actors in which parallel interests are brought together), and the state. The network has entailed the emergence of a collective actor, or better: a constellation of actors, that does not articulate a unified interest (of the individual, the organization, the state), but acts along the three logics named above. It is this ability of networks to articulate their own as well as divergent and common interests of actors that makes of networks a new type of social order in which a new type of "collective responsibility" emerges. In the classical theories the state bears collective responsibility, in the sense of a uniform overall responsibility. Organizations bear collective responsibility, but for actors with homogeneous goals. Networks develop action orientations along the individualistic, conflictual, and common interests of those participating in them. In performing this articulation of different logics, networks reflect and process the growing interdependencies and independencies found in differentiated societies.

The formation of actor action orientations in networks presupposes a **pattern of social organization** that is outlined by Michael Walzer along the continuum marked by the terms *"art of separation"* and *"art of connection"* (Walzer 1992, pp. 46 and 78). The first concern is to secure the autonomy of organizations and social subsystems against influence exercised by the state. It is only the *"intactness of institutions"* that makes it possible to develop self-responsibility and unlock social creativity potentials (**"art of separation"**). In this point liberal authors are right who warn against the fusion of political, social, and economic power under the aegis of parties, state and federations - but this, and here lies the problem, is often where their analysis ends.

The success of this separation, curbing the state, does, however, entail further threats to the autonomy and capacity to act of social organizations and thus to the efficiency of societies. The autonomy of organizations is threatened not only by the state but by the inherent dynamics of the market as well (which can, for instance, lead to concentrations of power that are difficult to control) and the emergence of powerful, private, privileged organizations (*"private governments"* [Streeck/ Schmitter 1995]).

It is the task of the state to control tendencies toward concentration of power that threaten democracy and the capacity to act of social organizations and subsystems by creating the required regulations and frameworks. That is, *"just as once the institutions of civil society had to be protected by the power of the state, the state* (and it should be added: and society, D.M.) *now must be protected from the new power that is emerging within civil society"*. Only in this way is it possible to sustain the "separations" in society (i.e. the functional differentiations). If the state is to fulfill these functions, it must be protected not only externally against *"excess"* concentrations of power but also against a *"takeover of power from within"*. This difficult and fragile balance between the inherent dynamics of social subsystems, the protection of this autonomy, and the necessary control over the eventuality that any uncurbed internal dynamics of an organization and/or a subsystem may undermine, or indeed even block, the action autonomy of other organizations is described by Walzer under the heading *"the art of separation"*.

It is only on the basis of clear-cut institutional separations between state, economy, and social actors that functioning network structures, i.e. **inter**-organizational patterns of organization, can emerge which link the strengths of decentral organization and decision-making with the advantages of a governance geared to joint problem-solving (e.g. in a policy field). The **"art of connection"** is based on the **"art of separation"**. The one presupposes the other, i.e. does not aim at any complete integration of the actors engaged in a subsystem. Rather, the concern is the articulation, the compatibility, between actor groups that continue to be autonomous; this is characterized more by loose linkages (weak ties) than by overly strong ones (strong ties). Granovetter, one of the "fathers" of network-theory, argues: *"Those to whom we are weakly tied are more likely to move in circles different from our ones and will thus have access to information different from that which we receive... this means that whatever is to be diffused can reach a larger number of people, and traverse greater social distances ..., when passed through weak ties rather than strong"* (Granovetter 1973, pp. 1371, 1366).

The formation of these patterns of organization is the result of the development process of market-oriented, democratic societies; its dynamics can be summarily described - at the level of society, firms, and the state - as follows: the rise of formal organizations at first destroys unstructured social "quasi-groups" and replaces them with formal hierarchies. In the end, the growing number and the increasing size of organizations undermine the efficiency and capacity to act of the hierarchies, in this way again giving rise to decentralization tendencies. This decentralization does, however, not restore the originally "unstructured state of society", but instead gives rise to networks which combine the elements of the organizational models hierarchy and market.

Parallel developments can be observed in the economy. The emergence of internationally operating large-scale corporations and the formation of oligopolistic structures are leading to the disappearance of small- and medium-sized forms and a transformation of formerly atomistic markets. The "Fordist mode of production" is characterized by the dominance of large-scale corporations. The increasing size of corporations and the growing complexity of production trigger in the markets new decentralization tendencies and various forms of division of labor between firms, but without restoring the classical form of fully atomistic markets. Instead of the in-house production aimed at during the period of Fordism, large-scale corporations are radically reducing their vertical integration and building complex supplier structures. Corporate networks or clusters emerge. At the same time the firms start to decentralize internally and to break up traditional hierarchies as a means of mastering in-company complexity. Instead of continuing with the Fordist-Taylorist organization of labor, which entails on the one hand workforce demotivation and on the other implies more and more control by the decision-making center over a "firm system" that continues to differentiate, i.e. that intensifies bureaucratization and inflexibilities, responsibilities are now being shifted downward (as a means of solving the motivation problem and mobilizing the know-how present at the shopfloor level and in different corporate departments).

In the Fordist model the interaction between corporate departments (e.g. production, research and development, and marketing) was governed by corporate headquarters. The action autonomy of the subunits grew as a result of the limited information on the dynamics inherent in these subunits, or departments, available to headquarters. The subunits tended to pursue their own interests without taking systematic account of the interfaces with other departments (Luhmann's "self-referentiality"), since the networking functions were part of headquarters' responsibility. In increasingly large corporations this hierarchical type of organization was finally no longer able to mobilize the potentials of the various departments and to orient them toward a common corporate goal. The hierarchical pattern of organization is supplemented by forms of horizontal communication and network-like coordination between the departments. Headquarters no longer governs the total process of interaction between departments, restricting itself instead to monitoring tasks.

Analysis of the state confirms the operation of this development logic: the development of the modern state is first characterized by the emergence of a monopoly on power and the centralization of political power with the state. As it expands, the state begins to differentiate internally and becomes a complex system consisting of many corporative actors who no longer form a single, integrated hierarchy. Externally, we see the successive emergence of policy networks specialized in specific policy fields; in them public and private actors work hand in hand.

This view of the existence of networks makes it clear that networks can be seen as an essential indicator of social modernization. The development of network-like structures is accompanied by the formation of qualitatively new forms of governance and integration characterized by highly dense communications between formally autonomous organizations and subsystems as well as horizontal coordination.

Network structures accordingly carry the seeds of problem-solving **potentials** that can blur, or at least reduce, the boundaries between market and hierarchy. In terms of their form and organizational structure, networks offer **possibilities** of coordination and governance that, in particular, are more adequate to the complexity problem than one-sidedly hierarchical decision-making structures. However, and in contrast to the optimism of many network theorists, this is not to say a priori that policy networks will operate efficiently. The existence of formal organizations capable of strategic action is no guarantee that these, in networks, will prove able to work out system-rational, innovative, and viable solutions. Within networks organizations can be just as opportunistic and short-sighted as are individuals and the state. This poses the crucial question as to the specific **"action logic"** (Mayntz 1993, p. 45) and the **"decision styles"** on the basis of which networks become operational. This crucial problematic is discussed systematically only by a very limited number of authors. Before we look into this problem area, we will attempt to derive from the discussion conducted thus far elements for a definition of policy networks.

2.3   Elements of a Definition of the Network Phenomenon

We can note the following characteristics of networks:

1. The **structure of networks** is characterized by three basic elements: a) the lines defining the relations between actors in a policy field are of a more horizontal than hierarchical nature; b) these are accordingly **"interorganizational"** webs of relationships, while traditional policy research focused on individual organizations; c) the interactions be-

tween actors in networks are more marked by loose relationships (weak ties).

2. Networks **are phenomena in polycentric societies** in which, in many social sectors, *"there is and can no longer be any a priori assumption of a crucial, central, hegemonic actor, which is ultimately determinant or only significant or even simply present in all kinds of networks"* (Marin/Scharpf 1991, p. 17). In contrast, the classical theory of the state was based on the ideal model of the centripetal, monistic society in which the state represented the clear-cut peak of the polity.

3. The existence of networks, characterized as they are by interorganizational relationship structures and the declining significance of actors with an a priori central role, reflects the relationships of **reciprocal dependence between the actors involved**. The latter are unable to derive all the resources they need to handle their tasks "from themselves" and therefore work together in a network with other actors who are in possession of different resources important to their collective output.

4. Policy networks are characterized by their function of formulating and implementing policy. This functional description is a criterion for **specifying the boundaries of individual networks**. Actors in no way involved in the collective decision-making process aimed at elaborating policies are thus not part of the network.

5. Policy networks consist of autonomous actors with different but reciprocally dependent interests. **"The theme of [their] interaction"** (Héritier 1993, p. 433) is the attainment of a common goal.

6. The network structure can contribute to **achieving common goals and solutions** in cases in which the governance resources are distributed over several actors, and do so **by means of the following functions**: pooling of decision-relevant know-how; ongoing exchange of experience, which makes it possible to selectively correct, complement, and broaden knowledge and at the same time encourages learning processes on the part of the actors involved; the development of struc-

tures of consensus and compromise by creating transparency as regards common and divergent interests; the development of a common problem-solving orientation reached through compromise of interests and the emergence of trust in stable network structures.

7. The relationships in networks are as a rule not of equal import; **power structures** are involved. An actor's influence and centrality increases in relation to the importance of the resources controlled by him (e.g. information, financial resources, legal resources) for the other actors. Positions of power are not necessarily determined by "organization size" or "financial clout". Even smaller, financially more weak organizations or actors with strategic resources (e.g. scientists with specific know-how; groups with "blockade or veto power") can play a significant role in networks.

8. The way in which actors work together in a networks ("**decision styles**") is not the same thing as harmonious or symbiotic cooperation. Since the actors have their own specific interests and may on occasion also pursue both divergent and common interests, competition and cooperation alike have a role to play. Some authors speak of *"cooperative competition"* (see e.g. Esser et al. 1993), others of *"antagonistic cooperation"* (Marin 1990); empirically, it is possible to distinguish various policy styles (see the empirical studies in Marin/Mayntz 1991).

9. **Different network types** can be distinguished in terms of the number of actors involved, the internal structure of the organizations involved (capable in terms of strategy, action, and mobilization versus low-powered), the degree of network stability, the character of the interorganizational relationships (that can be "measured" along a continuum of "weak to strong ties"), the specific policy field concerned, and "policy styles" or dominant action orientations, or indeed rules to which the actors are oriented.

10. A network's "social innovation", its **logic of interaction**, consists in the combination of elements derived from the underlying organizational pattern of "market" and "hierarchy": on the one hand, the existence, characteristic for markets, of a variety of autonomous actors; on

the other hand, the capacity (or at least function), typical of hierarchies, of approaching goals by means of coordinated action. In this sense the network appears to be an organizational form that is capable of disarming the "**Luhmann paradox**" (growing functional differentiation - increasing interdependence of the subsystems; at the same time: increasing closure of the subsystems toward one another - independence - self-referentiality). Independence (existence of independent actors and organizations) and interdependence (interorganizational cooperation) themselves become characteristics of network governance. Properly functioning network structures prove that functionally highly developed subsystems in fact grow more and more difficult to govern by means of traditional hierarchies, though the horizontal self-coordination between the subsystems (e.g. between production, research and development, and marketing in a large-scale corporation) can give rise to governance potentials. In contrast to the assumption of an uncheckable trend toward self-referentiality on the part of the subsystems, communication, coordination, and joint efforts aimed at solving problems across functional sectors prove to be entirely possible. The "Luhmann phenomenon" of simultaneously increasing independence and interdependence is "processed" in networks.

11. Networks are a **phenomenon of modern societies**. They presuppose an institutional separation between state, economy, and social actors and thus the **autonomy of social organizations**. At the same time, this in turn calls for protection of society from "imperialist" tendencies on the part of the state and protection of state and society from "private governments" (Walzer's *"art of separation"*). It is only on this basis of a growing functional differentiation that actors can work together productively in networks (Walzer's *"art of connection"*).

12. The functioning of networks presupposes a **capacity on the part of the actors involved for self-organization, efficiency, and action**. In other words, networks do not substitute for the action of individual organizations. It is only seldom that efficient networks will emerge from cooperation between weak individual organizations.

**CHAPTER 3   Network Failure: The Problem Dimensions
of the Organization of Networks**

The notion that the governance problems of societies can be solved a
priori and in principle by building network structures proves premature
on closer analysis. The literature on **"market failure"**[19] broadly docu-
ments the fact that without the governance instrument of the "market"
complex societies and economies, in particular on the world scale, are
not viable, though market allocation is nonetheless not a panacea, either. The same is true for the state, though it no doubt has important
governance tasks to meet; there are nevertheless cases of **"failure of
state"**. Network-like patterns of organization are in this sense no exception. Beside the strengths and functions of networks worked out
above, it is also possible to describe forms of **"network failure"**. The
literature on this complex is, however, quite limited in scope. What
follows will first work out the pitfalls of network governance in seven
central problem dimensions, then analyze the interaction between networks (which gives rise to an eighth problem dimension), and, in the
chapter concerned with this dimension, present various instruments and
mechanisms that - bearing in mind the limitations of network organization - can contribute to enhancing their efficiency and functional effectiveness. It should be pointed out here in order to avoid any misunder-
standings that similar core problems of network organization crop up in
several of the problem dimensions to be discussed. That a problem is
specified in a number of ways should not be confused with redundancy
in that several core problems are triggered by different functional
logics in the individual problem dimensions. It is only an exact understanding of what causes certain problem constellations of network governance that makes it possible to think systematically about strategies
that can be employed to avoid or diminish them.

3.1   The Problem of Numbers

The first problem area is trivial and is nonetheless often disregarded.
The problems bound up with negotiated coordination in networks grow

as the number of actors involved and their interdependent options of action increase. Scharpf points out that the theory of cooperative games offers concepts for solving problems of multilateral negotiation and coordination, although they are of a mathematical complexity that makes them unproductive for actual applications.

In principle we can discern for bargaining processes in networks three coordination problems based on different types of interdependence relations (Thomson 1967, pp. 45 ff.). The first case is concerned with reaching understanding on common standards (*"coordination by standards"*) as a basis of orientation for individual behavior in cases in which, in Thompson's terminology, we are dealing with *"pooled interdependence"* among the actors involved. Examples would include technical standardization procedures, the definition of quality standards or industrial safety criteria. These cases can very easily entail conflicts over the choice between competing standards. Once, however, binding standards, "routines or rules", have been defined and accepted, the actors are free to shape the options still open to them in any way they see fit. In this situation the problem of numbers is only of limited relevance, and it can be solved without undue complications.

The second case is concerned with *"sequential interdependence"*, for instance when firms or organizations define priorities or are forced to coordinate processes in terms of time. In such cases it is possible, through *"coordination by plan"*, to reduce complexity before policies or corporate strategies are implemented. In this case, too, the actors can retain their autonomy on the basis of coordinated sequences, *"decision schedules"*. The problem of number remains manageable. In other words, wherever "coordination by standardization" or "coordination by plan" are concerned, interactive coordination activities are needed only in an initial phase.

The third case is concerned with *"reciprocal interdependence"*. Here the decision potentials of the actors involved depend on the specific behavior of the others, because *"the outputs of each become inputs for the others"* (Thompson 1967, p. 55). As compared with the two coordination patterns already described, reciprocal interdependence relations are possible only via *"coordination by mutual adjustment"*, i.e. they place great demands on the actors involved. This is the case, for instance, in or between firms which need - via standardization and establishment of priorities - to closely coordinate activities between departments and develop them successively, and in which the joint outcome is reliant on continuous processes of coordination. A further example would be policy networks in which the governance resources (e.g. know-how, implementation capacities) are distributed over several actors and solutions can be reached only on the basis of joint decision-making processes and/or collective efforts geared to solving problems. Here it is not enough to agree on common rules (*coordination by standardization*) or to coordinate action sequences (*coordination by plan*); rather, what is needed are continuous processes of coordination. Individual actors possess substantial **veto and blockade potentials** in constellations of this type, marked by mutual dependence. It is above all these cases that, as a result of the social development dynamics sketched above, are constantly gaining in significance which pose the problem of numbers.

Analysis of this problematic leads to two important conclusions:

First, there are, both in a growing number of policy fields and in the economy, challenges that - as a result of their complexity and the distribution of governance-relevant resources over different actors - pose for hierarchical-centralist decision-making structures problems that they are more or less at a loss to solve; and hierarchical-centralist decision-making structures lead to suboptimal results. Interorganizational, horizontal ways of coordinating action have greater problem-solving capacities in these cases, as Scharpf (1993c, p. 141) demonstrates: *"... of course, the advantage of hierarchical coordination are lost in a world that is characterized by increasing dense, extended and rapidly changing patterns of reciprocal interdependence, and by increasingly frequent, but ephemeral, interactions across all types of preestablished boundaries, intra- and interorganizational, intra- and intersectoral, intra- and international. Under such conditions, forms of horizontal self-coordination, whatever their comparative disadvantage, may be the only type that works ..."*. But: if prohibitive demands on information-processing and conflict-settlement capacities in networks are to be avoided, the goal must be to limit as far as possible the number of actors involved whose task interdependence must be dealt with by means bargaining coordination. This applies in particular for the case of "reciprocal interdependence".

This shows, **second**, that skepticism is called for in the face of approaches that propose, on the basis of critics on one-sidedly centralist coordination and decision structures, high levels of decentralization or division of labor in firms, organizations, or indeed in regions and countries as an organizational model suited *a priori* to boosting efficiency. Studies of this hue often disregard (among other things) the trivial "problem of numbers". It should be noted that these are problems that result in particular in networks intended to process forms of *"reciprocal interdependence"*. Of course there is no reason not to pool the know-how of as many actors as possible, for instance in order to raise the level of information in private and public enterprises or in an entire sector. Difficulties arise, however, when a large number of actors are forced to work out an overall outcome that depends on the decisions and actions of all (or many). These considerations do not rule out the possibility that a procedure of this type may, in exceptional cases, make sense as a decision-making strategy (for instance, to legitimatize a fundamental decision).

The problem of numbers can at least be reduced in scope and rendered manageable by an action orientation on the part of the actors involved that is geared to finding joint solutions to problems as well as by combinations of hierarchical and horizontal forms of coordination.

3.2   The Time Dimension of Decisions

In the dimension of time, every pattern of organization and governance is faced with the crucial question whether the institutional conditions under which the decision-making process takes place can guarantee that policy decisions will not follow short-term impulses but can be geared to the development and implementation of solutions viable over the long term. In view of this problem, **hierarchical decision-making systems** have, in purely theoretical terms, the largest scopes of action. If they are able to operate independently of other social actors, it is possible to conceive of both decisions geared to long-term perspectives and viable solutions of problems and short-term policies keyed, for instance, to the self-interests of the decision-makers. In principle, however, hierarchical decision-making systems are able to implement future-oriented interests against interests geared to the present and structurally important decisions against power-based particularist interests. At the same time, it is true, hierarchical decision-making systems not subject to any control mechanisms are particularly susceptible to opportunistic behavior and rent-seeking strategies on the part of the decision-makers.

In **majoritarian decision-making systems** we can sometimes observe a tendency, bound up with the pressure of elections and uncertain majorities, to give preference to short-term orientations and to put off to a future date decisions that are necessary but painful in the short term. In **networks** the actors are to some extent unaffected by the party competition dominant in majoritarian systems and thus not subject to the pressure to generate quick decisions that find the approval of external actors or voters. The actors in networks work above all to find solutions to problems that concern them directly. One thing that characterizes networks is of course the fact that in them the roles of decision-maker and person directly concerned largely converge. Against this background there is no immediate incentive to work for a maximization of utility geared to the short-term.

Still, we do encounter three problem constellations. **First**, situations are conceivable in which the **individual utility** of the actors or organizations involved in networks is calculated for the short term, whereas the implementation of "**system interests**" affecting the overall network calls for a longer-term orientation. This can, for instance, be the case when, in objective terms, the "system benefits" are to be found at a level different from that of the decision-relevant benefits of the individuals involved. An example: in a regional network in the field of technology or industrial policy that brings together employers (federations), ministries, labor unions, and scientists to lay the groundwork for structural decisions aimed at strengthening regional competitiveness, the "system utility" might consist of a process of radical, innovation-friendly structural change. At least part of the actors, above all those who would be threatened by structural change, would in this case gear its activities to safeguarding its domain. In this case the pursuit of individual utilities therefore constitutes a foundation not secure enough to elaborate an optimal solution to the problems facing the overall system (in this case an economic region). Accordingly, a **structurally conservative tendency** is built into the bargaining system.

Second, actors in networks may be interested in the temporal **stability** of a specific bargaining structure which has yet to be created, since we are dealing here for the most part with voluntary forms of cooperation and coordination ("weak ties"). Interest in stable cooperation results from the interdependence of the action-related resources held by the other actors involved and from the high transaction costs that come about as a result of the complex bargaining process. Continuous cooperation is the condition for safeguarding the expectations of all actors involved. This constellation keyed to safeguarding stability gives rise to a **tendency toward conflict avoidance and incremental change**. Discussions and problem-solving efforts within the network, including more fundamental reorientations that could negatively affect the interests of important network actors will tend to be put off. What is conceivable here are status quo orientations that are based on agreements and compromises found in the past and are less reflective of present, or indeed future, interests.

Third, once a network is successfully stabilized, the high level of **social cohesion** thus attained can favor solutions that correspond more to a *"parametric"* than a *"strategic rationality"*. What is meant by *"parametric rationality"* is a pronounced preference for decisions that keeps close to the traditional development path (Grabher 1994, p. 79). The development of a "consensus culture" and symbiotic relationships between the network actors set on incremental change can lead to *"collec-*

tive conservatism" (Kuran 1988) and slow down and obstruct required structural change.

Networks are thus most efficient when they are concerned with shaping structures within an established and dynamic development corridor. Here we would for the most part find positive-sum games. Networks are, however, faced with major difficulties stemming from the above-noted tendencies toward conservative decisions and incremental change when they are forced to come to terms with structural crises entailing the emergence of upheavals and the need to manage them.

In other words, one might also say that networks in policy fields marked by the mutual dependence of the actors on the governance re-sources of others (e.g. industrial and technology policy) will be highly efficient when the task facing them involves making progress in shap-ing structures on the basis of an established development path and pre-sent interests. Networks are confronted with major challenges when they are called on to push through future interests against established present interests. The question of how these problems inherent in the phenomenon of networks can be diminished will be discussed below.

3.3 Institutional Consolidation of Networks: Condition of and Problem Facing their Operation

The mutual dependence of the actors involved in a network on the gov-ernance resources of others implies a tendency toward continuity in actor relationships and thus a minimum of institutional consolidation - in the cases relevant here, below the threshold of constituting a formal organization, which would mean abandoning the network structure it-self. Relatively stable cooperative relations characterized by a specific pattern of mutually accepted organizational identities, competences, and spheres of interest, i.e. a minimal basic institutional consensus, make it easier to find compromises to settle conflicts of interest be-tween network actors.

The pressure to stabilize a network and find compromises increases in relation to the reliance on the governance resources of other network actors and the duration of the cooperative relationships involved, both of which lead to specific transaction costs that constantly rise over time. The accumulating *"costs of exit"* (Scharpf 1991b, p. 288) make it more and more unattractive to abandon network cooperation.

As a rule, consolidation and continuity of the relationships between network actors are accordingly an essential condition for the functioning of networks. If stabilization fails to materialize, loosely linked networks are threatened with disintegration. The transition from the "weak ties" characteristic of the precarious relationship structures of emerging networks to "stronger ties" can, however, at the same time serve to illuminate potential weaknesses of network structures. Networks act in a field marked on the one hand by disintegration, adjustment risks, and "endless disagreement" between the actors involved and on the other hand by functional and cognitive obstruction stemming from a surplus of social cohesion. We can discern in this field four problem dimensions that are in part also intensified by the "time dimension of decisions", and this gives rise to particularly clear-cut problem trends.

The potentially retardative function of the compromise logic effective in networks: First of all, closer relationship structures in networks and the need to seek compromise entail the problem that it is difficult to redistribute, against the will of the actors, the power and other resources (e.g. money, market entry or access to information, social status) between the actors who might be instrumental if the overall network is to achieve a given goal. While in hierarchically structured decision systems the central authority is generally able to push through it interests, and majoritarian systems are faced with the possibility (and the danger) of realizing their interests at the expense of minorities, as a rule networks are reliant on consensual decisions. True, this constellation is faced with a strong inherent conservative tendency: *"...unanimous decisions permit each party to defend the existing pattern of distribution, while majoritarian and hierarchical decision rules create the possibility of involuntary redistribution ..."* (Scharpf 1991a, p. 60).

Functional obstructions or the "joint decision trap": Since the costs entailed by the breakdown of negotiations are often high (high "exit costs"; risk of "endless disagreement"), it is likely that - to avoid conflicts - solutions that negatively affect the interests of established and strategically important actors will fail to materialize and that strategies will be sought within the framework of the existing development corridor. Scharpf coined for this constellation the term *"joint decision trap"*: networks *"with high internal consensus requirements will find it difficult to exploit new opportunities that are attractive on balance, but not for each member individually, and they will encounter similar difficulties when it would be rational to cut their losses in response to worsening conditions"* (Scharpf 1991b, p. 285).

Cognitive blockades: These functional barriers to innovation can be overlapped by cognitive blockades. Long-term relationships between network actors favor the development of joint orientations, views, bargaining styles, and even prejudices. In the course of this process there emerges a social cohesion that is the sine qua non of any cooperation founded in trust. The reverse side of social cohesion as a resource productive for the functioning of networks can be seen in cognitive blind spots resulting from an exaggerated standardization of views and overly symbiotic relationships between network actors. This entails a growing risk that alternatives, new development paths, proposed solutions and strategies beyond rountinized options will not be perceived. Thinking and acting in a network threaten to become exaggeratedly path-dependent and structurally conservative. It is important to emphasize that functional and cognitive blockades in networks tend to materialize particularly when it is necessary to depart from accustomed development paths, i.e. when incremental social, political, and economic solutions are no longer sufficient to overcome a problem complex that a network is particularly well suited to deal with as a result of its interactive functions, keyed as they are to focusing know-how and shaping structures.

Grabher cites as an example functional and cognitive blockades in traditional industrial regions (like e.g. the German Ruhr district) in which, in spite of persistent crisis, networks have been used: *"as the disease worsens, merely to increase the dose of the old medicine instead of trying out a new one"* (Grabher 1994, p. 79). Other prominent examples of the *"high degree of inertia"* (Scharpf 1991b, p. 285) due to functional and cognitive blockades that can creep into policy networks and obstruct intended change are - to cite additional examples from Germany - the strong resistance of elements of the health-care system against attempts to reform it or the inability of the university system to reform itself. The institutional consolidation of networks and the logic of compromise are thus conditions for preventing decision blockades in collective bargaining systems, for ensuring that compromises are found for divergent interests, and for diminishing tendencies toward disintegration, although they do not automatically guarantee that "system-rational" solutions will emerge and gain the day.

The ingroup-outgroup logic of networks, or the "Luhmann trap": The inward stabilization of networks is linked with the formation of joint rules, conventions, and routine acts. It is only in an action context of this type that trust and the ability to anticipate the behaviors of other actors can develop. The emergence of such "ingroup" structures is based on the constitution of *"ingroup-outgroup boundaries"*. A number of studies have shown that *"trust among insiders ... could arise from common distrust of outsiders"* (Scharpf 1991b, p. 296). Mayntz and Neidhardt have investigated this mechanism with reference to German parliamentarians. They found strong solidarity norms within the political factions, ritualized "animosities" between the government and opposition factions, and typical "ingroup behavior" on the part of parliamentarians as an overall group, e.g. in representing their own interests as the "political class" vis-à-vis the media (Mayntz/Neidhardt 1989). Scharpf makes reference to a study by Edward Banfield, who discovered in southern Italian towns and villages relationship structures which he referred to as "amoral familism": *"Trust and cooperation within the family coexisted with complete distrust and morally unrestrained cheating among individuals not belonging to the same family"* (Scharpf 1991b; Banfield 1958). Further examples would be relationship patterns between the insider and outsider world of organized crime, in international politics, between athletic teams, corporate groups, or even networks in the field of science. Formulated more generally, a certain "hostile orientation" toward the environment seems to favor the consolidation of ingroups - i.e. in our case, networks - and the development of trust-based ingroup relationships. Max Weber already addressed this phenomenon under the heading of *"social closure"* (Weber 1960, p. 35).

The development of functioning networks on the basis of ingroup-outgroup boundaries can lead to segmentation tendencies between the subsystems with an inclination to insulate themselves and refrain from communication. Any such tendency is extremely dangerous in highly interdependent societies. It favors two divergent types of externalization:

-   active strategies on the part of networks with a one-sidedly ingroup orientation and a tendency to respond with "hostility" to their environment (*"boundaries of distrust"* [Scharpf 1991b, p. 297]) aimed at consciously shifting negative externalities to third parties (*opportunism with guile*);

-   Activities of narrow-minded networks that, as a result of a lack of coordination with other subsystems or networks, lead to effects that are uncontrollable because they are not taken into account (**unintended effects**). This second type of externalization is likely to occur more frequently than the first one, since the relationship between networks stabilized by ingroup mechanisms and their environment are as a rule marked less by antagonisms (in the sense of "opportunism with guile") than by actor indifference to the negative externalities they cause in the pursuit of their interests (*"boundaries of irrelevance"* [Scharpf 1991b, p. 298; see also Willke 1992]).

Both types of externalization are based on the fact that the ingroup mechanisms geared to stabilizing networks *"may segregate systems of communications, but they do not have the power to interrupt chains of real interdependence among functional subsystems"* (Scharpf 1991a, p. 299).

The externalization and segmentation problematic worked out here corresponds to Luhmann's thesis of the increasing self-referentiality of subsystems in modern societies and the impossibility of *"intersystemic discourses"*. This **"Luhmann trap"** can accordingly, as Lindberg rightly points out, be triggered not only by "opportunism with guile" between actors or groups of actors but also by "strong solidarity among insiders" based on distrust of outsiders (Lindberg 1988, p. 43). It is important to point out that the "Luhmann trap" refers not primarily to pitfalls *in* networks but to problems that can crop up as a result of the interaction between networks and their environment (i.e. affecting overall social governance). True, networks are forms of organization in which, in contrast to Luhmann's restrictive assumptions, cooperating organizations overcome their exclusive self-referentiality; but this does not mean that the danger of "self-referentiality" is thus eliminated at the next-highest level, i.e. that of the network.

It must be noted at the same time that the "Luhmann trap" represents a real possibility (risk), but not the rule. Modern and modernizing societies would be unable to function and survive under the condition of generalized distrust between actors from different networks. When functional differentiation turns into structural and generalized segmentation, the outcome that threatens is disintegration. Aside from the "ingroup-outgroup logic" and the possibility that groups of social actors and networks may *"play side-by-side according to their own specific logic"* (Scharpf 1991b, p. 298) - as a field of productivity and creativity resources in highly differentiated societies - there are evidently mechanisms which - above and beyond the emerging and necessary boundaries between networks and subsystems - make intersystemic communication possible, thus making allowance for real interdependencies. Scharpf speaks of *"mechanisms that are able to connect as well as to separate"* (Scharpf 1991b, p. 299) in order to characterize this force-field.

3.4   The Coordination Problem

Network theorists often assume a priori higher rationality for network
coordination as opposed to decision-making systems constituted along
hierarchical or market lines. This is often justified with reference to the
Coase theorem, which states that gains in welfare that could be reached
by ideal hierarchical coordination can also be attained by voluntary
agreements between autonomous, purely egoistical-rational actors.[20]
The problem dimensions already discussed illustrate that such blanket
statements can easily obscure the possibilities of network failure.
Moreover, Scharpf has demonstrated that not only market and hierarchy but also voluntary, negotiated solutions in networks pose their
specific coordination problems and that the presuppositions for the
functioning of coordination in network-like bargaining systems are
complex.[21] Scharpf uses the Pareto optimum and the Kaldor criterion as
indicators for measuring the efficiency of coordination activities. As is
known, the Pareto optimum, the welfare-theoretical yardstick of economy, defines the allocation of scarce resources to competing possible
uses as efficient when no changes are conceivable that would increase
the utility of at least one person concerned without worsening the position of another person. This theoretical indicator consciously disregards aspects of distributive justice and the possibility of a redistribution of existing assets. The Kaldor criterion, a measure of welfare more
interesting in political terms, rates as positive all measures whose utility is great enough for those favored to be able to fully compensate all
persons disadvantaged by the measure (Kaldor 1939).

At first glance the democratic nation state, bound to the public interest
and internally and externally sovereign - i.e. a hierarchical decision-
making authority - seems best suited to do justice to the demanding
Kaldor criterion. The state can disregard the objections of individuals
who would be affected and is theoretically in a position to act in the
interest of the public welfare. But a second glance demonstrates the
limits of the concept of the hierarchical state: the state has lost much of
its internal and external sovereignty, the state's public-welfare orientation cannot simply be presupposed in a voluntarist manner, and the

state is, in many policy fields, forced to rely on the cooperation of other groups of social actors.

And what is the situation of the coordinative and decision-making capacity of networks as regards their potential welfare-related effects? Scharpf starts out by exemplifying the coordination problems of two actors (see figure). He proceeds from two egoistically rational actors (X and Y), who have utility vectors independent from one another and a number of action options (A; B; C; D; E). The status quo is designated by the origin of the coordinate system. If we now assume that the two actors can realize their action option in taking one-sided decisions, what will be acceptable for X will be restricted to projects to the right of the Y-axis, whereas Y will be able to accept only projects located above the X-axis. Accordingly, (X) would ignore projects (D) and (E) and have a clear-cut preference for (A); (Y) would be unable to accept (A) and (E) and would prefer solution (D).

A welfare-theoretical evaluation of the unilaterally preferred solutions under the Pareto optimum comes to the result that both are unacceptable, because in each case an improvement of the status quo would worsen the position of the other side. If the Kaldor indicator is taken as a base, the result is different. The difference becomes entirely clear when both projects - i.e. (A) and (D) - are appraised from the perspective of a hierarchical coordinator - e.g. a corporate headquarters with two departments. Based on one utility function (Uc=Ux plus Uy), it is evident that no project at all below the northwest-southeast diagonals would be acceptable. Projects would become the more attractive the further to the northeast of the diagonal they were located. Accordingly, the hierarchical coordinator would block the project (A) preferred by (X) but approve the project (D) supported by (Y), although this would go against (X)'s interests, and would do so because the overall utility is higher than (X)'s losses.

What would happen if coordination had to be achieved by bargaining between (X) and (Y) beyond hierarchy? Let us proceed on the assumption of a compulsory bargaining system (in which, in other words, the two one-sided actions already discussed were ruled out) entailing clearly definable projects that, for the time being, rule out any compensation payments. Under these conditions, (X) would reject all solutions to the left of the (Y)-axis and (Y) would decline any solutions below the (X)-axis. Accordingly, only Pareto-superior options in the northeast quadrant would come into question. Among the possible solutions given, (X) would prefer project (B) and (Y) project (C). For neither of the two would there be any reasonable grounds to accede to the wishes of the other.

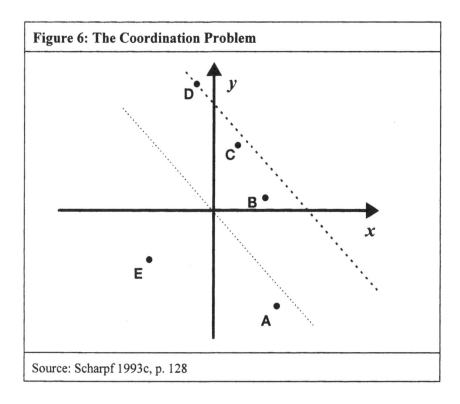

Figure 6: The Coordination Problem

Source: Scharpf 1993c, p. 128

In other words, the attempt to coordinate by means of bargaining runs up against three specific problems:

- Solutions that maximize aggregate welfare are systematically ignored if they do not at the same time imply for each of the network actors an improvement over the status quo (i.e. are not located in the northeast quadrant).

- The case that under these conditions more than a Pareto-superior solution should be possible would also entail the risk that the negotiations might be blocked by a dispute over the choice between the possible solutions.

- What this means is that networks are able to reach the Kaldor optimum only when they are not guided by competitive, or indeed hostile, action orientations vis-à-vis other network participants (in the sense of "getting the best of the others").

These problem dimensions grow as the number of participants increases, since it is only in this case that veto positions can begin to accumulate (see the discussion above on the "problem of numbers").

If the conditions are now changed in such a way as to make it possible to compensate both the winners and the losers, and if this possibility is used as an instrument, one could - disregarding the transaction costs - well imagine solutions to the problematic outlined above. If voluntary negotiations are to come about in networks, the actor who stands to lose from a given project would have to compensate those who are interested in it if they are to relinquish their position. In a compulsory bargaining system (e.g. when property rights are legally protected against negative externalities), the compensation payments would have to flow in the opposite direction.

In both cases the negotiations between the egoistic-rational actors would maximize the aggregate welfare of those involved. To illustrate this with reference to the figure: in realizing project (A), (Y) would stand to lose more than (X) could gain. In a voluntary bargaining system he would accordingly prevent the project by making compensation payments. Conversely, (Y) would stand to gain more with project (D) than (X) would lose; in a compulsory bargaining system he would therefore buy off the former's potential veto. Accordingly, under both conditions (and disregarding transaction costs), the only projects realized would be those above the diagonal, and the actors would agree on solutions located in the isoquantile furthest to the northeast, thus maximizing the aggregate welfare of those involved.

The inclusion of two other factors, however, aggravates the coordination problem. First, as already noted, the growing number of parties involved increases the transaction costs. What is more serious is, second, that any considerations on the issue of indemnification are based on the availability of clearly definable solutions and the possibility of monetary compensation. Both are plausible assumptions in economic contexts in which money functions as a universal equivalent. In these cases compensation payments or shadow prices may open up the way to coordination between firms or semi-autonomous departments within a firms or, in many cases, even in the public sector or between public and private actors. In many political constellations, however, solutions cannot actually be expressed in terms of monetary values. In addition, compensation payments may also be unacceptable for moral reasons.

Scharpf points out that even under these conditions approximations to the Coase theorem are conceivable if it possible to bundle together bargaining packages containing separate projects with complementary cost-benefit balances that would make possible a more or less acceptable balance of interests. Studies by Benz and Zintl on the problem field show that the main problem in these cases consists in the need to build a common understanding of a balance of interests and distributive justice (Benz 1992, Zintl 1991). The working of networks is accordingly highly dependent on the action orientation of the actors involved and their ability to define their own interests as well as conflictual and common interests and to reach compromises. It is only in this way that the bargaining blockades sketched above can be broken up.

Since there are more and more cases in which the gains and losses to be distributed are either difficult or impossible to monetarize, while at the same time hierarchical decision-making mechanisms that could solve these problems by *"diktat"* are overburdened in many policy fields, it is not surprising that theories of distributive justice have experienced a heyday in the past ten years.[22]

In the **1970s** this issue seemed, at least in Western Europe in the heyday of the welfare state, to be obsolete, or, as it were, to have been settled. Issues of justice and the implementation of policies geared to securing and improving life-chances and distributive justice were delegated to the state. In the **1980s,** the decade of the hegemony of neoliberalism, it seemed possible, and above all desirable, to monetarize all (or nearly all) relations between human beings. The question of social justice was privatized and reduced to the problem of the "productivity and efficiency of the individual". Neoliberal theory was concerned with the question of distributive justice only in the sense of allocative efficiency seen in terms of the Pareto-optimum; welfare-theoretical considerations of the type addressed by Kaldor were strictly rejected. In the **1990s** a new paradigm shift is emerging in view of the increasing significance of networks in governing economy and society. Social actors and groups alike are forced to develop common notions of justice if they are to create the conditions under which their networked relationships are to function. This task, previously assigned to the state and then to the individual, must now be dealt with in interactive communication processes. This challenge is particularly difficult, and ambivalent in its overall social consequences, inasmuch as network-specific notions of justice and distribution tend to intensify tendencies working in the direction of social segmentation. This is the case when the rules of justice valid in one network are incompatible with those of other networks with which they share real interdependencies. We will be returning to this question.

3.5   The Bargaining Dilemma

The discussion of the coordination problem will have made it plain that the *"motivational requirements"*[23] - i.e. the action orientation of the actors involved - are of key significance for the efficiency of networks. Coordination in networks and the maximization of aggregate utility succeed as a rule only when the actors are able to reach agreement on the distribution of the costs and gains that accrue. The condition for this is open communication, trust-based cooperation, fairness, viz. a bargaining style keyed to finding joint solutions to problems.

The following dilemma emerges: on the one hand, successful coordination is likely only on the basis of trust-based and cooperative orientations on the part of the actors involved. On the other hand, the course of the negotiations and the determination of the solution will entail conflict over the distribution of the costs and gains as well as over fairness criteria. While it is impossible to reach a result without a cooperative bargaining style on the part of the actors involved, it is likely that the process of negotiation will entail strategic action, manipulation of information, and bluffing or threats. The constructive action orientation appropriate to the overall outcome can, since it is bound up with joint solutions, easily be exploited during the bargaining process. Conversely, effective bargaining strategies such as successful tactical maneuvers and manipulation of information - imperfect information under the usual conditions - can mean bargaining edges, and at the same time finally prevent the parties involved from solving common problems and maximizing the cooperation-based gains that would, on the whole, otherwise be attainable. It is thus not unlikely that above all actors open to supporting reaching the "Kaldor optimum" by means of cooperative strategies will run the risk of being cheated in the matter of distribution. It is in this constellation that the *bargaining dilemma* is at home.

3.6   Power in Network Relationships

"The phenomenon of power is simple and universal, but the concept of power is multifarious and difficult to lay hold of."
Michel Crozier/Erhard Friedberg, *Macht und Illusion*, Königstein 1979, p. 39

Power phenomena are just about systematically disregarded in network analyses geared to governance theory. Network structures often appear as a smoothly functioning interplay between actors aimed at reaching a common goal. There is initially one wholly plausible argument for disregarding power relations in network approaches, though it is seldom made explicit. As a rule networks come about because the governance resources that need to be mobilized to solve a given problem are distributed over a variety of actors. In networks there exist, in other words, **reciprocal interdependencies** between the actors involved, so that the classical definitions of power and rule provided by Max Weber, which are in essence based on the notion of clearly identifiable "power centers", and which still serve the social sciences as terms of reference, are, all in all, hardly applicable to networks.

Weber writes: *"**Power** means every chance to assert one's will even against resistance, regardless of what this chance is based upon. By sovereign authority (Herrschaft) is meant the chance to find obedience among specifiable persons for a command of a given content"*. **Sovereign authority**, thus Weber, *"is based on discipline and mass obedience, whereas **discipline** means the chance to find, by dint of practiced attitudes, prompt, automatic, and schematic obedience for a command among a specifiable multitude of persons"* (Weber 1960, Weber's italics).

This understanding of power and sovereign authority cannot simply be applied to networks, since here governance resources, and this means power resources, are distributed over a number of different actors. The enforcement of power, "even against the resistance" of others, is difficult in a network system characterized by structures of mutual dependence; whereas the exercise of sovereign authority via command and automatic obedience is conceivable in hierarchical decision-making structures, it is a hopeless undertaking in networks. This is demonstrated by a great number of empirical studies in wholly different policy fields in which network-like structures have developed. Decisions are often difficult or indeed impossible to push through "against resistance" on the part of the persons concerned. If decision centers are forced to rely on cooperation, e.g. willingness or readiness of those concerned to help in the process of implementation, it is extraordinarily difficult to enforce power in Weber's sense of the term. In many cases the enforcement of decisions thus depends on the concurrence, or at least acceptance, of the persons concerned. Attempts to enforce sovereign authority via "obedience" and "discipline" - in Weber's sense of the terms - would be even less likely to succeed.[24]

The same studies, however, illustrate that there are also, as might be expected, imbalances in networks, that the action options of the actors may be more or less large, that, in other words, some actors have more (albeit far from absolute) power than others. Organizational sociologists Crozier and Friedberg are right, as was Weber before them, when they emphasize that the phenomenon of power often seems close enough to grasp, and nevertheless remains difficult enough to conceptualize, or indeed to "measure" empirically (Crozier/Friedberg 1979, pp. 39 ff.; Weber 1969, pp. 42 ff.).

In view of the complex situation in networks, characterized as it is by power balances and reciprocal dependencies between the actors, and lacking as it is in power and sovereign authority in the classical sense of which Max Weber spoke, one might be tempted to adopt Hannah Arendt's notion of a *no-man's-power*. The attributability of power - and thus also of powerlessness - in networks is, in principle, complex, whereas it is relatively trivial in hierarchical diction-making structures.

One way out of this unclear situation, or at least some points of orientation, are to be found in Crozier and Friedberg. They point out that *"power [is] a reciprocal, though imbalanced, relationship"* (Crozier/ Friedberg 1979, p. 40). This view modifies Weber's absolute concept of power and permits it to be applied to interactive relationships in networks. Crozier and Friedberg describe power as a exchange relationship based on reciprocity, but one in which the conditions of exchange favor one (or more) of the actors involved: *"It is an interrelation of forces from which the one can derive more than the other, but in which, at the same time, the one is never fully at the mercy of the other".*[25]

The basis of power is the **disposal over resources**. It is possible to distinguish (aside from repression and violence) four significant sources of power, i.e. power

-    that is based on the mastery of specific expert knowledge,

- that stems from control over information and communication resources,

- that can be derived from the presence of universal organizational rules or value patterns, and

- that rests on the disposal over financial resources that can be used to influence the first- and the second-named factors.

If power resources in networks are distributed within a field of forces of this kind, and there is, then, also a *"power of the weak"* (Crozier/ Friedberg 1979, p. 42), how are these interrelations of forces and asymmetries determined in a specific field of forces? Crozier and Friedberg speak of the *"degree of relevance of resources"* (Crozier/Friedberg 1979, p. 46), without defining more precisely the term relevance. It is, instead, reasonable to distinguish between **strategically significant** and **strategically less insignificant resources**. Strategically significant are resources that cannot simply be substituted; strategically less significant are resources that can be substituted.

In a policy network, for instance, in which state institutions in charge of implementing a program are forced to rely on the assistance of intermediary institutions, this would mean: If the policy program is generally regarded as important and the social actors concerned are forced to rely on the state to finance the project, it is the state that is in possession of the strategically significant resources. If there were only one intermediary institution that could provide assistance in implementation, then it, too, would be in possession of strategically significant power resources. If there are several institutions between which the state can choose, the power resources of these institutions are of less significance, even though the state, being dependent on cooperation with others, has no more than limited autonomy. If, in the second case, the state decides in favor of cooperation with one institution, the latter's power resources would increase over the course of time inasmuch as this institution would accumulate learning effects that would make it unattractive for the state to switch its cooperation partner (transaction-costs argument).

The example makes it clear that it is entirely possible to think systematically about power structures in networks. The idea, at times implicitly, at time explicitly prevalent, that social relationship structures for which it is not possible to localize a clearly identifiable center are dominated by communications not based on power or relationships free of domination is, accordingly, naive. Power asymmetries in networks imply **on the one hand** that network governance also knows winners and losers, and that for the simple reason that the relatively powerful are in specific situations able to realize their interests against those of the relatively weak, even though there can be no doubt that networks - as opposed to structures in which one actor holds all the relevant governance resources - enhance the "power of the weak".

The phenomenon of power structures in nonhierarchical bargaining systems conceals, **on the other hand**, a more relevant problem that may affect the working of networks. What is defined in a network as relevant problems, adequate solutions and instruments, and reasonable goal systems certainly depends on the network's efficiency and creativity, i.e. its "cognitive potentials", although it depends just as much on the "**definitional power**" of specific actors. These actors are likely to be concerned primarily with realizing their own interests. Thus, for instance, chemical companies in a policy network concerned with formulating suitable sectoral policies will rarely be willing to accept voluntarily environmental arguments that might increase their production costs or at least force them to think about innovations.

In spite of their interactive character, networks thus do not stand per se for "greater intelligence". This circumstance was discussed above in the context of the possible social, political, and cognitive blockades facing networks. Any discussion of power structures in networks leads to a further problem facet: the "definitional power" of strategically important actors in networks may lead to situations in which relevant problem dimensions are disregarded or marginalized. The same is of course also true of the relations between networks and their environment. Networks that develop into power cartels are in a position to block or slow down solution-oriented social learning and search processes and to burden their environment with costs stemming from adjustment needs.[26]

Karl Deutsch particularly underlined this problem context in his definition of power. He circumscribed *"power"* as *"the ability to afford not to learn"* (Deutsch 1963, p. 21). In his understanding of power, Deutsch succeeded in expressing its ambivalent character. **On the one hand**, power dispenses its holder from the need to learn inasmuch as the holder of power is not subject to pressure to adjust exercised by other actors. Those who possess power in this sense are thus, at least initially, in an extremely comfortable situation, one that permits them, as was pointed out above, to burden third parties (weaker, less powerful actors) or the future with their costs. **On the other hand**, positions of power in Deutsch's sense of the term, are always precarious, in particular in social development sequences in which "learning" is one of the most important assets and disposal over "information" (i.e. the results of learning processes) constitutes an important power resource (see e.g. Arrow 1994). If positions of power can lead actors not to learn and adjust to changing conditions, then the seeds of its erosion already lie dormant in the foundations of power. That the nonpowerful are forced to learn poses a constant threat to established positions of power.

Contrary to the hopes of many network theorists, the search for mechanisms to develop solution patterns geared to problems and not one-sidedly to (particularist) interests is thus not at an end with the emergency of the social innovation of networks. Networks and the relations between networks and their environment are subject to a never-ending process that might, to quote Axel Honneth, be described as a *"struggle (of actors) for recognition"* (Honneth 1992, Honneth 1989, pp. 384 ff.) of their identity, their arguments, their right of participation. In this *"struggle for recognition"*, it is entirely possible for "definitional power" to be redistributed, as is demonstrated, for instance, by the success of the ecological movements, which managed within two decades to change what was until then a marginal issue into a central one. The fact that once-achieved "recognition" can again be eroded is shown by the same policy field: in the economic crisis of the mid-

1990s, and in spite of the UNCED conference in Rio, the environmental issue is losing relevance in political practice. Power resources, definitional power are again being reshuffled, short-term "necessities" gaining the day over long-term system imperatives.

3.7   The Tense Relationship between Conflict and Cooperation

As was noted in the discussion of the "Institutional consolidation of networks: condition of and problem facing their operation", networks, if they are to be stabilized, must develop a "culture of cooperation", consensus, and coherence. "Cooperation" is a key concept of network theories. It serves to integrate networks, and it counteracts the virulent forces of disintegration, fragmentation, and the *"culture of separation"* (Dubiel 1992, p. 134) active in modern societies and contributes to strengthening common interests in networks.

This view is derived from the correct assessment that functioning network structures are unable to build on purely competitive, or indeed hostile, relationships between the actors involved. But this discourse often turns into a one-sidedly harmonistic and thus naive interpretation of the way modern societies function. This is true, for instance, of a number of studies on the "industrial districts" in northern Italy. Local and regional networks designed to contribute to developing *"collective efficiency"* and competitiveness are not seldom idealized as practically idyllic countermodels to a roughshod, liberal market economy, those who sing their praises do so with reference to forces of social integration active in stable identity and value patterns and homogeneous social structures in the districts. In the charged atmosphere of today's global village we can observe the growth of a yearning for clear-cut contexts and solution patterns as harmonious as possible. This is also the actual thrust of the appeals made by conservative communitarians. Against the conflictual nature of secularized societies they set the homogeneity of communities that are integrated by means of concurrent notions of the *"good life"* and *"patterns of community values"*.[27]

It has already been pointed out in connection with thoughts on the effects of the institutional consolidation of networks that too close cooperative relationships in networks can lead to social, cognitive, and functional blockades. In interactive processes, "cooperation" can thus prove to be highly productive as a motor of development, although it can also turn out to be a blockade mechanism. This field of forces should not be overlooked.

Interestingly, the social sciences are conducting, in parallel to the cooperation-focused discussions, a debate aiming in just about the opposite direction. In his search for institutions and action orientations that might contribute toward the integration of modern societies, Dubiel comes up with a *"culture of conflict"*. While conflicts are generally regarded as destructive, and attempts are made to contain them with the aid of a sense of solidarity, Dubiel argues that ties and cohesion in modern societies are practically generated by social conflicts.[28]

The debate centers on the thesis that, in modern, democratic societies, conflict is an essential socialization factor and an eminently significant mechanism for creating coherence and integration. Conflicts produce the "social capital" needed to master conflicts and hold societies together. In contrast to the Marxist discussion up to the 1970s, which interpreted conflicts as antagonistic crises that in the end break up capitalist societies, conflicts are now being discovered as the real pillars of society.

Habermas' notion of *"constitutional patriotism"*, intended to commit citizens to the legitimacy of democratic procedures and their outcomes, is taken a step further by Dubiel, who sees in the peaceful settlement of social conflicts the primary motor of solidarity and social integration. The train of thought is supported by the argument that the vitality and innovativeness of pluralist and market-oriented societies consists in their ability to renew themselves with their own resources. Society generates a continuous current of conflicts that its members have to learn to confront and deal with. The result is that permanent social learning and search processes are stimulated. Albert O. Hirschman point out that the cause for *the decline and the loss of viability of the communist-governed societies lies in the "success" that was met with in suppressing open social conflicts* (Hirschman 1994, p. 300).

In his *"Open Society"* Karl Popper also pointed to the link between conflict and cooperation and harmony, always precarious and yet constitutive for modern societies. He noted that open societies are always in danger of developing into *"abstract, depersonalized societies"* in which growing conflicts between social actors, anonymity, and isolation endanger individuals as social beings (Popper 1980, vol. 1, p. 235). Due to this latent danger posed by phenomena of decline and dissolution - Popper argues - people overburdened by the *"Open Society"* tend to revert back to the *"closed society"* in the hope of being able to redevelop there, on the basis of collective and binding values, an *"organic, harmonious whole"* (Popper 1980, vol. 1, pp. 232 ff.).

Any such turn of the tide back to a closed order of society would destroy the personal freedom, responsibility, and creativity of the individuals making it up, thus undermining the development potentials of the *"Open Society"*. At the same time, as Popper rightly emphasizes, the hope of encountering the risks posed by the *"Open Society"* by harmonizing and overcoming conflicts is illusory - since it leads in the end to social stagnation.[29] The *"Open Society"*, Popper argues, must assert itself against both these risks - social disintegration in the conflict-dominated *"abstract society"* and reversion to holistic harmony and closed collectives in the *"organic society"*.

These arguments advanced by Dubiel, Hirschman, and Popper should be taken very seriously by network theorists leaning toward exaggeratedly cooperation- and harmony-related orientations. In both overall societies and in networks, the elimination of any and all conflict potential undermines social, political, or economic innovativeness and responsiveness. Aside from this quasi "innovation-theoretical" argument, there is one more essential point: the frequency and omnipresence of conflicts is evidently a central characteristic of pluralist and market-oriented societies. Societies constituted along the lines of democracy and market economy necessarily and endlessly generate conflicts, and thus any notion of a permanent order and harmony is untenable. The hope that conflicts will prove able to be neutralized by cooperation is thus an illusion bound to run aground in reality.

The function of networks can accordingly not be to "neutralize" conflicts and aim for perfect social cohesion based on the largest possible measure of cooperation, but to make them manageable. Hirschman rightly emphasizes that, as a result of the generally conflictual and charged structures of modern societies, the mode of problem-solving that might be termed "muddling through" can prove extraordinarily successful.[30] This is true as well of network structures, which may even be particularly suitable to this end.

Hirschman, however, also points out that the conflicts in societies should be seen less as *"cement"* than as solvents, or indeed as *"dynamite"*, that dissolve or break up social relationships (Hirschman 1994, p. 294). That is to say, first, that the issue to be looked into would the social conditions under which conflicts develop their effects in given directions, and what these directions are. It is no doubt impossible to find a universal answer here.[31] Second, and this is the crucial point in the context of the issue under discussion, all the arguments against the one-sidedly cooperation- and harmony-oriented view of decision-making and problem-solving mechanisms also apply for an exaggerated glorification of the productive potential of conflicts.

In highly differentiated societies in general and in networks in particular, there exists a tense relationship between conflict and cooperation and between individual liberty and creativity and group responsibility and security.

Fred Hirsch, too, rightly pointed out that it is precisely in market economies based on competition that a substantial measure of **cooperation and trust** between the social actors constitutes the **condition required for functioning competition in economy and politics** (Hirsch 1977). The minimal and at the same time most basic form of cooperation between people, the abstention from mutual injury, is without doubt an essential condition for any potentially fruitful competition and conflict between actors in economy, politics, and society.

It could be precisely the network, as opposed to the market, that constitutes an organizational pattern the strength of which is to be found in the chance to link productively together the logics of "conflict and cooperation". This question will have to be discussed in more depth. What is certain is that the efficiency of networks is threatened both by one-sided conflicts and exaggeratedly harmonistic action orientations.

3.8   Instead of a Résumé: The Five Core Problems of Network Governance

The overview on "Problem dimensions and pitfalls in networks" again summarizes the problem dimensions in networks worked out above and the pitfalls of network governance resulting from them. This overview makes it plain that the "pitfalls" that arise in the various problem dimensions are in part the same ones. What develops in this way is a trend toward functional and cognitive blockades in networks in connection with both the "time dimension of decisions" and in the process of institutional consolidation. Knowledge of the various sources of undesirable developments is essential to any considerations on adequate mechanisms aimed to eliminate or diminish these problems - which is the topic of the following chapters.

Overview 5: Problem Dimensions and Pitfalls in Networks

Problem dimension	Potential pitfalls of networks
(1) **Problem of numbers** Number of actors involved in a network may be large.	(1) - The greater the number of actors, the higher the risk of veto positions that may block a network.
(2) **The time dimension of decisions** Networks are faced with the challenge of establishing long-term interests against short-term interests. Mechanisms: - conflict avoidance - cooperation - development of social cohesion	(2) These mechanisms can contribute to - conservative and structurally conservative tendencies, - trends toward agreement on the "smallest common denominator", and - collective conservatism
(3) **Institutional consolidation** The institutional consolidation of networks is a condition for their functioning. Mechanisms: - stabilization of cooperative relationships by developing common identities - development of "weak ties" into "strong ties"	(3) These mechanisms can trigger the following: - the retardative function of the logic of compromise in networks, - cognitive, social, and political blockades, - path-dependent action, - "internal" consolidation, "hostile" or "indifferent" attitude vis-à-vis network environment: tendency to consciously externalize costs and produce unintended effects.
(4) **Coordination problems** Networks have the possibility, important to many policy fields, of working out horizontal coordination between a large number of reciprocally dependent actors.	(4) The coordination problem is that - the Kaldor optimum is difficult to achieve and - a common actor understanding on the criteria for the distribution of "profit and loss" as concerns product-solution options is needed as a condition for preventing bargaining blockades ("endless disagreement").

Overview 5 (continued)	
Problem dimension	**Potential pitfalls of networks**
(5) <u>Bargaining dilemmas</u> Development of trust-based relationships between network actors is the condition for the functioning of networks.	(5) The dilemma is that trust-based relationships between actors are the condition for successful coordination, but at the same time - especially trustworthy actors may easily be cheated in the bargaining process, - strategically oriented bargaining patterns (e.g. including manipulation of information) may prove successful over the short term, but they undermine trust-based relationships and prevent any approximation to the Kaldor optimum.
(6) <u>Power</u> In networks the governance resources are distributed across a great number of actors. There are no clearly identifiable power centers.	(6) - In networks, too, there exist asymmetric relationships between actors who possess resources of varying strategic significance; - networks are not a priori "democratic" und "hierarchy-free"; - "power" in networks and between networks and their environment can lead actors "not to have to learn". Then the "systemic intelligence" of networks is threatened with erosion.
(7) <u>Tensions between conflict and</u> <u>cooperation</u> Cooperation in networks permits cumulative, goal-directed search and learning processes on the part of the actors involved.	(7) The following applies for the relationship between conflict and cooperation: - in networks there are as a rule both cooperation and conflict; - exaggerated harmony orientation can hamper efforts aimed at innovation; - conflicts are a potential productive force; - cooperation and conflict can operate in networks as a "bond and a solvent".

The following overview summarizes the list of potential pitfalls to form five core problems of network governance. This figure is a synthesis of the discussion on phenomena of network failure.

Overview 6: The Five Core Problems of Network Governance	
Core problems	**Problem dimensions in which core problems emerge**
(1) Decision-making blockade due to buildup of veto positions	(1) - Problem of numbers - Power in network relationships
(2) Structurally conservative action orientation; trend toward agreement on the "smallest common denominator"; functional and cognitive blockade; collective conservatism	(2) - Time dimension of decisions - Institutional consolidation of networks - Power in network relationships - Tense relationship between conflict and cooperation
(3) Networks are always active in field of tension of disintegration (into "weak ties") and too dense relationships that reduce innovative power (see. Point (2))	(3) - Time dimension of decisions - Institutional consolidation of networks - Power in network relationships - Tense relationships between conflict and cooperation
(4) Risk of obstructed bargaining in deciding on alternative solutions; problem in defining distributive criteria	(4) - Coordination problem
(5) Twofold externalization problematic: - intended externalization of costs at the expense of the network environment, - unintended effects due to exaggerated inward orientation of network actors	(5) - Time dimension of decisions - Institutional consolidation of networks - Power in network relationships

3.9 Governance Problems Resulting from the Interaction between Networks

Aside from the pitfalls that can develop in networks, the existence of networks and the interaction between them pose governance problems for society as a whole. This point was addressed in the context of the discussion on the consequences of the institutional consolidation of networks. Networks may develop an ingroup-outgroup logic and tend in the direction of closure toward their environment. I referred to this phenomenon as the *"Luhmann trap"*. For "network societies", this risk of developing subsystems that disregard the effects of their activities on their environment represents a core problem, the dimensions of which will be discussed systematically in what follows. The first issue to be looked into will be self-coordination between networks, i.e. social "coordination without hierarchy".

Five of the seven problem dimensions of significance for the internal functioning of networks also play an important part for the interaction between networks: the problem of numbers, the coordination problem, the bargaining dilemma, and the tense relationship between conflict and cooperation. What dynamics result from these problem dimensions for societies in which networks represent a constitutive dimension?

The further the process of differentiation has advanced in societies, and the more networks that have constituted themselves (**problem of numbers**), the stronger will be the **fragmentation and segmentation tendencies** in society as a whole. Networks unfold social-integrative effects inasmuch as they give the field of activity which they shape an inward direction and optimize the creativity potentials within the network. In view of the complexity of the tasks to be mastered that face social subsystems, any such inward-looking "organizational work" could not be performed by external or upper-level agencies (i.e. by the state of other hierarchical authorities). Networks at the same time tend to close themselves off from their environment, in this way releasing disintegrative effects.

Here, in the interplay between networks, two phenomena are of significance: on the one hand, effects negative for other networks or society as a whole may result from a network's activities (intended or unintended by the actors). A successfully operating network aimed at strengthening the export sector may have consequences detrimental to the environment or burden other parties with its costs (e.g. export subsidies for which the taxpayer is responsible). On the other hand, activities of networks may also develop countereffects. It would be conceivable that a corporate network might intensify its research endeavors, thus providing a contribution to strengthening an industrial location, while the state is in this way able to cut is spending in the research and training sector - or vice versa. While in the model of hierarchical governance the state (corporate headquarters) is solely responsible for shaping specific policy sectors (corporate sectors), the **coordinative efforts** required to attain governance goals may rise in network societies. This state of affairs can be observed both within networks and between them.

The negative and contravening effects can of course be ignored, e.g. with the argument that it is up to specific groups of social actors, subsystems, and networks to respond adequately to emerging requirements (that may stem from the activities of other groups of actors). The negative and contravening effects would thus be referred back to the social subsectors to be processed there. If the externalities stemming from the conscious or "blind" interaction between networks are to be avoided or at least minimized, two additional coordination mechanisms to which Scharpf pointed in the 1970s might be conceivable: *"positive and negative coordination"*. What, in other words, is the situation of the forces of horizontal self-organization, bearing these two coordination mechanisms in mind?

Positive coordination is concerned with coping with the interdependence problem, i.e. overriding problem contexts, by dealing with problems simultaneously. This presupposes an analysis of the entire factual problem context, and this in turn implies focusing problem- and action-related knowledge for the units specialized in particular subareas. Any such strategy of positive coordination between networks would in the end mean constituting a new network in which the actor groups that have until then worked independently of one another attempt jointly manage the interdependencies between their specific action spheres. In this case all the problem dimensions of network organization already discussed must be looked into in terms of the possible limitations and pitfalls of such solutions.

Positive coordination between networks, i.e. coming to terms with interdependence problems and negative externalities by forming new networks, is likely to be envisaged by social actors only when *"reciprocal interdependencies"* (Thompson) have developed between networks and no solutions to specific problems can be found without joint efforts. This might be the case between two economic regions that have until then competed for locational advantages (by tax dumping, etc.) and then determine that "positive coordination" prevents ruinous competition and, for example, collective efforts aimed at improving shared infrastructure can mean advantages for both regions. Positive coordination between two actor groups or networks that have been operating independently of one another and now set their sights on diminishing negative effects, i.e. the outcomes of one-sidedly self-referential network activities, can, however, just as well be stimulated or even forced by the state. The German laws covering collective bargaining and code-termination, or even the involuntary membership of firms in the chambers of commerce and industry and legally stipulated joint responsibility of the social partners for shaping and advancing the German system of vocational training are examples of a state-regulated delegation of problem-solving tasks to groups of social actors in areas in which the actors were not always willing to work together.

Negative coordination implies that the task of coming to terms with problems remains inside separate subsystems and networks, while consultative coordination processes going beyond the decentralized decision-making system are used to link up networks so as to prevent or limit possible negative effects of activities within an action system for other such systems. Negative coordination aimed at avoiding external effects thus implies coordination processes below the threshold of joint problem-solving efforts. Negative coordination can be initiated by the networks themselves or by external institutions. The success of coordination between networks is, however, by no means a matter of course. Indeed, **coordination pitfalls** are entirely conceivable. Three problem constellations can be distinguished here:

1. Networks are likely to have a self-motivated interest in coordination processes with other networks whose activities impair their own efficiency. This logic poses a threat from the angle of society insofar as **chains of real interdependencies** may be disregarded by the actors involved, in that damage and **dependencies** may develop and some of the **effects** that occur are **not reciprocal** ones, which can mean that some of the actors will not be interested in coordinating their activities with others so as to reduce external effects. An example: a successful network promotes the development of an industrial cluster; this process leads to uncontrolled development of a region, which in turn entails various types of ecological damage. From the perspective of affected actors organized in a network concerned with uncontrolled development and environmental problems (i.e. with negative effects of the industrial network) it would be very important to coordinate the three policy and problem fields of economy, housing, and the environment. The industrial network, however, is threatened by the negative effects stemming from adjacent policy fields and shows no interest in coordination. Or: the industrial network attempts to evade coordination with other networks as a means of getting around the necessity to internalize the costs it is causing. In other words, real interdependencies are not dealt with if there are no reciprocal dependencies between network fields and actors and their activities are self-referential (Luhmann). A case of this type would disappoint the confidence placed in the "robustness" of the forces of horizontal self-organization in network societies.

2. Network societies are marked by interests organized more or less strongly, networks that are more or less powerful, i.e. **asymmetries of power**. Here, in discussing the phenomenon of "power" and its effects on social development dynamics, we must bear in mind all the considerations developed above, in the chapter on "Power in network relationships", with regard, for instance, to the erosion of centers of absolute power and the - albeit imbalanced - distribution of power resources

in society. One other point is, however, of considerable importance: as regards the significance of power within networks, it was pointed out that, owing to the reciprocal dependence of network actors on the governance resources of others, even weaker actors are able to mobilize power resources, since they are in possession of a minimum of strategically important governance resources. Actors within a network are (as a rule) reliant on cooperation. These reciprocal dependencies are (as a rule) not given in the interaction between networks, and thus stronger networks are in a position to refuse to coordinate their activities with other networks and groups of social actors whose resources are not essential to them. The power of well-organized networks can thus lead to situations in which some social subsystems dominate others; this would present a danger to the *"art of separation"* emphasized by Walzer. Here, too, a governance concept relying wholly on horizontal self-coordination between networks proves to be undercomplex. It must be combined with hierarchical and democratic mechanisms of control and governance. It should, however, be noted that - as a trend running counter to the dynamic described here - interdependencies and reciprocal dependencies generally increase between networks, and that the relationships of dependence now tend more to be perceived than in the past (e.g. the relationship between industry and the environment). This increases the chances of efforts aimed at coordination, though it at the same time steps up the complexity in the political process that has to be dealt with by networks.

3. Societies are always faced with interests that are more or less easy to organize. Future interests, ecological interests, or the interests of the unemployed are difficult to organize. This state of affairs leads into an **indifference phenomenon**. Willke (1992) pointed out that the attitude of social subsystems to one another is not hostility but indifference. This form of indifference toward the effects of one's own actions is highly likely when the actors concerned (e.g. unemployed persons) and the subsystem affected (e.g. the environment) are unable to articulate their interests.

Analysis of all three problem dimensions shows that coordination processes between networks that are necessary from the perspective of society as a whole - as a means of preventing external effects - come about only when reciprocal dependencies are involved, i.e. when the functioning and the efficiency of specific networks depend on coordination with other networks. This constellation demonstrates that there is a need for governance involving higher-level instances.

It must also be noted that when negative, or indeed positive, coordination between networks functions, this gives rise to a pronounced tendency toward incrementalism. Making allowance for a variety of (theoretically: global) different outcomes can lead to an accumulation of veto positions and impede the development dynamics that emerge in networks and subsystems precisely because of their independence and autonomy. Incrementalism may on the one hand prove counterproductive for the overall system; structurally conservative, path-dependent action orientations could result from successful positive or negative coordination between networks. On the other hand, it is only coordination processes that can restrain the egoism of the subsystems - Habermas (1992) speaks of *"subsystem paternalism"* - and inject a minimum of overall social orientation into the action logic of networks. Coordination between networks and social subsystems is a *conditio sine qua non* for counteracting fragmentation and disintegration tendencies in differentiated societies.

When coordination processes occur between networks, the potential blockade mechanisms discussed in the chapter on the "**Bargaining dilemma**" may pose problems. As regards the **tense relationship between conflict and cooperation** discussed above for networks, the following points, which go beyond the remarks made on the fundamental significance of this relationship for social development dynamics, must be made here: It was noted that if networks are to function properly, both conflict *and* cooperation are essential to ensure a balanced relationship between a joint problem-solving orientation and conflictual elements aimed at reducing functional and cognitive blockades. The matter must be weighted somewhat differently when we consider the interaction between networks. Networks are not seldom indifferent toward one another, their relations are often marked by asymmetries of power and one-sided dependencies - which means that there is no lack of conflict potentials. These relationship patterns can obstruct processes of coordination and fine-tuning between them. If these blockade potentials are to be reduced, networks have to develop a certain measure of cooperativeness vis-à-vis their environment. Networks that are per se unable to develop this cooperativeness, i.e. exclusively inward looking and potentially opportunistic networks, accelerate social disintegration tendencies.

CHAPTER 4   **Dimensions of the New Pattern of Organization and Governance Designed to Mobilize the Governance Potential in Network Societies**

Network structures gives rise to synergy effects, though they can also lead into segmentation, fragmentation, and blockades. It is difficult for the scientific observer to make prognoses on the development dynamics of existing networks, since they lack any linear development logic. The task at hand is therefore to uncover the in part counteractive development trends, potentials, and obstructive aspects inherent in network structures.

The last chapters made it clear that, in the **first** place, the overall outcome of networks in which, in their interaction, the actors look only to their own specific interests is no more than an unintended side-effect, comparable to unintended secondary effects of market processes. This implies the risks of disintegration facing networks and the danger that costs will be externalized to their environment (see core problems (3) and (5) of Overview 6). In the **second** place, networks tend toward functional and cognitive blockades when they reach a too great measure of internal cohesion (see core problems (2) of Overview 6), and power-based relationships and the participation of a great number of actors in a network can give rise to decision blockades resulting from the development of veto positions (see core problem (1) of Overview 6). In the **third** place, negotiations run the risk of being obstructed unless common evaluation and distribution criteria can be defined for the potential costs and losses of alternative solution-related options (see core problem (4) of Overview 6). The pitfalls discussed above need not necessarily lead a priori to failure of network governance. Network governance is, however, as is the case with market governance and governance by the state, bound up with normative and institutional conditions that will be discussed in what follows. It will furthermore be noted that the social functional logic of networks is endowed with an inherent dynamic that can undermine the efficiency of network governance over the course of time. In the "network cycle" the strengths of this type of social organization can turn into potential development blockades. It is only knowledge of the strengths and weaknesses of network organization that makes it possible to optimally harness governance potentials.

4.1 Interest Constellations, Action Orientations, Value Patterns, and Decision Styles in Network Structures

The analysis of the limits facing hierarchical governance has shown that any proper functioning of state governance is inextricably bound up with the value patterns and action strategies held by social actors. It was also shown that hierarchical governance can only work if we can assume, in contrast to public-choice theory, which assumes that those actors will **as a rule** behave opportunistically, that government officials, functionaries, and citizens are **in principle** able and willing to bear the public interest in mind when they are concerned with public matters. Network actors are forced to rely on joint decision-making mechanisms. On the one hand, this governance structure is in many respects superior to hierarchical governance, though, on the other hand, it is constantly faced with the danger of drifting into structurally conservative incrementalism, cognitive and functional obstructions (core problem 2), endless disagreement and inability to reach decisions (core problem 4) and/or finding solutions at the expense of third parties - i.e. by externalizing costs by burdening the network's environment with them (core problem 5). The key factor in the occurrence or avoidance of these core problems is (among other aspects) the action orientation of the actors involved.

What follows will differentiate interest constellations typical for networks and work out the significance of the action orientations of actors for the problem-solving capacity of networks. The discussion will focus on "real-world" interest constellations that frequently occur in networks that confront their actors with dilemma situations. It will be shown that in many cases the capacity to act of networks and network actors depends on whether the persons involved are able to develop a common problem-solving orientation that goes beyond individualist-egoistic rationales on the part of individual actors.

In public-choice theory, in contrast, the analysis of interest constellation is dominated by a dichotomist view: it differentiates, ideal types of "symbiotic" or "competitive" relationships. On the assumption that individuals will base their rational choices on the alternatives most amenable or profitable to them, symbiotic relationship patterns turn into positive-sum games, whereas competitive relationship patterns take on the shape of negative-sum games. This analytical framework is unfamiliar with distinguishable normative orientations on the part of actors: actor decisions result from individualistic rationales.

Scharpf has pointed out that in the "real world" purely symbiotic and purely competitive interest constellations and relationship patterns between actors are, in the **first** place, relatively rare, the rule being what he terms "mixed motive games" that are characterized by the fact that actors pursue both common interests and their own private interests, which can also be directed against one another.[32] In the **second** place, he shows that both symbiotic and competitive relationship patterns need not necessarily turn automatically into "stable" positive- or zero-sum games. Instead, this often depends on the action orientation of the actors involved and, in the end, on their underlying normative position, which is systematically neglected by public-choice theory.[33]

Thus, for instance, a positive-sum constellation can turn into a prisoner's dilemma when one of the actors fears free-rider behavior on the part of one or the other of the actors involved; this can also take on the character of a "battle of the sexes" (see Overview 7) if the gains to be distributed are difficult or impossible to monetarize and conflicts materialize over a common understanding of distributive justice. Even

---

Overview 7: Interest Constellations Relevant in Networks

The following is a typical **prisoner's dilemma** situation: let us take two firms, both of which have the possibility to bribe a government official to secure an order. If firm A decides to bribe and firm B does not, firm A will - under the condition of universal corruption - receive the order. If both decide to pay bribes, they are working against one another and will drive up the price. The optimal solution for A and B would be to take action against corruption, a situation in which neither firms would bribe the official. In this case the price for the order will be lower (in that the bribe will not have to be added to it), and the firm with the most favorable price-to-performance ration will get the order. The dilemma is that both A and B are forced to place their trust in the integrity of the other firm. The first one that cheats, breaks the agreement, and bribes the official, while the other holds its end of the agreement, will get the order.

The standard situation of the **chicken game** is a car race in which two cars approach each other at high speed. The first to veer off so as to avoid the crash is "chicken". There are at first three possible solutions: joint disaster; equal cowardice, a victory of one. Real-world situations would, for instance, be: the arms race, polarization/escalation between firms and striking workers whose communication channels have broken down.

The following example is seen as the typical **battle-of-the-sexes** constellation: A couple would like to spend the evening together. The husband would prefer to attend a football game, the wife opts for a concert. So the actors have (as in the case of the prisoner's dilemma) both common and opposed interests. In contrast to the prisoner's dilemma, however, here there is initially no solution that could satisfy the interests of both actors. They are forced to decide between two solutions that differ completely and have no common denominator (such, for instance, as the equivalent "money") that would render them comparable in a simple fashion. Such situations are easy to imagine, e.g. in the relationship between firms that plan a joint venture and have to decide between two alternative investment projects, in bargaining between firms and labor unions, in cases of termination talks, in interministerial coordination processes, or policy networks, e.g. when very different options that are difficult to compare have to be weighed one against the other.

relationship constellations initially purely competitive in nature, e.g. those between employers and employees disputing over the distribution of a "surplus value", can turn into mixed-motive games. If the actors develop a common interest in not harming one anothers' interests, zero-sum games can take on the shape of "chicken games", which, at least theoretically, are open to solution (see Overview 7).

The mixed-motive constellations are central to the network discussion since they entail as a rule relationship patterns between actors that are characterized by common, self-oriented, and even sometimes competitive interests. Game theory distinguishes in particular between the three mixed-motive constellations already mentioned (chicken game, prisoner's dilemma, battle of sexes). Conventional game theory, though, concentrates primarily on noncooperative games. What is presupposed here is that the interaction between the actors involved no communication between them and binding agreements are impossible. On the basis of these restrictive assumptions, the mixed-motive game situations that often occur in the "real world", and in particular in networks, lead for both actors to unstable and/or suboptimal outcomes (see Shubik 1978, pp. 240 ff.; see the standard situation in Overview 8).

4.1.1   Conditions for Mastering the Dilemma Posed by Typical Interest Constellations: The Simple Cases (Prisoner's Dilemma and Chicken Game)

Scharpf shows that if these assumptions are relaxed two of the three mixed-motive constellation (the prisoner's dilemma and the chicken game) can be transformed into trivial coordination events with positive effects for the actors involved (see Scharpf 1991a, p. 64). In networks it is not unrealistic to assume the existence of **communication** between the actors and a chance to reach **binding agreements**. Under these conditions the prisoner's dilemma can turn into a positive-sum game for the actors involved. This is also true of a chicken-game constellation in which escalations and possible collisions result precisely from the fact that communication and binding agreements are impossible. If, in contrast, we proceed on the assumption that communication and binding agreements are possible, the standard outcome provided for in conventional game theory (*"joint disaster, equal cowardice, a victory of one"* - Shubik 1987, p. 395) can be averted.

The condition for transforming dilemma situations into constellations beneficial to all parties concerned is that agreements that are based on communication and make communication possible between the actors are honored, i.e. that the cooperation of the one side is not exploited by opportunistic behavior ("defection") on the other side: *"Once the possibility of exploitation is eliminated, there is no doubt that both parties will prefer the outcome obtained by mutual cooperation over that which is expected in the case of mutual defection"* (Scharpf 1991a, p. 64). That is to say, an agreement between network actors in the relationship constellations named above is unproblematical and trivial as soon as binding agreements are possible.

The conditions guaranteeing that binding agreements are honored can, however, not be assumed as given in all societies or subsystems of societies (like networks). The simplest solution (provided such relationships are enforceable under the law) is to be found in societies that guarantee (as a rule, from which there are exceptions) **legal and contractual security**. If this is the case prisoner's-dilemma and chicken-game constellations can be regulated by legally binding contracts. In other words, in these cases "cooperative solutions" presuppose no more than communication between actors oriented exclusively to their own interests and a fulfillment of binding contracts guaranteed by a state under the rule of law.

But preventing the possibility, on the basis of legal and contractual security, that the cooperativeness of the one side will not be exploited by destructive behavior on the part of the other (defection) is anything but trivial in a number of societies. In many countries social relations are marred by corruption. Where this is the case, "generalized distrust" develops, with the consequence that the dilemma situations outlined above will as a rule end up in confrontation, obstruction, and/or suboptimal solutions. In societies in which this is the case, political governance (geared to the Kaldor optimum) will prove to be a very difficult undertaking both in hierarchical decision-making systems and - above all - in network-like organizational structures.

Apart from the aspect of legal security, a second (sometimes substitutive, sometimes supportive) factor contributes to making binding agreements possible: the **existence of trust** between actors. Trust between actors involves a great number of presuppositions - particularly in situations in which the prisoner's dilemma or the chicken-game situation, both marked in their points of departure by mutual distrust, must be solved. While in societies in which there is a relatively high degree of legal security trust can serve to support the development of binding agreements, countries without sufficient legal security are faced with a situation in which the existence of a minimum of trust between actors forced to rely on interaction is of crucial significance for any successful joint decision-making. Here interpersonal relationships based on trust are often the substitute for regulative state functions and thus constitute an essential foundation for the efficiency and proper functioning of such societies.

But the significance of trust for finding solutions to the dilemma situations discussed above also increases in countries in which legal and contractual security is given, the reason being that governance activities performed by networks gain more and more importance in highly differentiated societies. As opposed to actor relationships based on conventional contracts, networks often rest on noncodified arrangements and agreements. And in this way there emerge in modern, highly differentiated societies ever larger governance-relevant sectors and policy fields beyond the immediate scope of the constitutional state as the traditional agency responsible for safeguarding legal and contractual security.

The capacity to act in these segments of society will always remain precarious also in democratic societies under the rule of law, if they lack the general *milieu* that creates trust between actors, even if the constitutional state is not able to safeguard globally "trust from above" with the aid of sanction mechanisms. One realizes how crucial a minimum of trust between network actors is when one considers that decisions have, in general, to be taken under the condition of imperfect information on the preferences and perceptions of other actors even when communication between the actors is assured and serious attempts are made to break up dilemma situations on this basis. Since the actors are in the end not able to predict with certainty the anticipated actions and reactions of the other actors, a slight measure of risk aversion is enough to cast exaggerated caution in the role of the behavioral rule most appropriate in such situations. This might mean refraining from cooperative action and thus blocking negotiations or encouraging suboptimal outcomes for fear that one's own cooperative behavior might be exploited. Once faced internally with generalized distrust, networks lose their capacity to act.

In other words, it can be stated generally that, when the prisoner's dilemma or the chicken game are involved, **communication between actors**, a **minimum of trust**, and the **existence of legal and contractual security** are sufficient to arrive at satisfactory coordination-based solutions. This successful coordination will also come about when the actor constellation is dominated by an **egoistic-rational action orientation**. The ideal type of the individual as seen by public-choice theory would accordingly remain capable of action and cooperation even without having to revert to value orientations beyond the category defined by methodological individualism (if we may for the moment leave aside "trust" as a normative orientation not addressed by public-choice theory). This, however, is not the case for the third mixed-motive game, the battle-of-the-sexes constellation.

4.1.2 Conditions under which Complex Conflicts of Interest can be Mastered in Networks: The Difficult Case (Battle of the Sexes)

The core problem in the "battle of sexes"-constellation is that actors are forced to choose between outcomes (in the standard model: visiting a football game versus a concert) that differ so significantly from one another that no simple compromise solution along the lines of the distributional principle of "a little of both" is possible, i.e. the actors are confronted by an "either-or" decision situation. Hierarchical decision-making systems are not troubled by the battle-of-the-sexes problem. When different outcomes are possible, the central unit responsible makes the decision. The battle-of-the-sexes constellation is very frequent in network structures inasmuch as they are less homogeneous than, for instance, hierarchically structured organizations, and this makes it more likely that different actors will envisage different solutions. The battle constellation, on the other hand, confronts networks with difficult problems in that they are forced to reach *joint* decisions: firms engaged in a joint venture and forced to decide between alternative investment strategies, firms within a cluster that prefer specifically different solutions to problems and innovation strategies, or policy networks forced to set priorities and decide between alternative solutions.

Actor constellations faced with the battle-of-the-sexes constellation are invariably faced with the same problem: *"While important benefits are dependent upon the ability to cooperate, cooperation is seriously threatened by conflict over the choice of one of the cooperative solutions (or over the distribution of costs and benefits of cooperation)"* (Scharpf 1991a, pp. 65 f.). Interestingly, this constellation-of-interest conflict, which often occurs in reality, has found little attention in the literature, e.g. compared with the wealth of material on the prisoner's dilemma.

The specific element of the battle-of-the-sexes constellation is the co-existence of cooperative interests (in the standard situation: spend the evening together; or: common investment interest; common interest in formulating policy in an interdependent policy field, etc.) and competitive actor motives and interests that are difficult to compare and reduce to a common denominator (in the standard situation: football game versus concert; or: choice between the alternatives of building roads or rail networks; construction of a technology center versus investment allowance). Even under the condition that it is possible to reach a binding agreement and all those concerned are seriously interested in doing so,

this constellation of interests will often end up in conflicts over distribution and evaluation as regards the preferable solution (and the costs
and benefits) and agreement on which of the solutions is the one acceptable and in the end just for both sides concerned. If these processes
aimed at reaching agreement fail, there are no ways out of the dilemma,
despite common interests.[34]

This situation differs fundamentally from the prisoner's dilemma and
the chicken-game constellation, which - assuming legal and contractual
security - rely above all on confidence-building strategies on the part of
the actors if a positive outcome is to be reached. The battle of sexes-
problematic is, in contrast, marked less by the danger that cooperative
behavior may be exploited by noncooperative actors than by the factual
reality that this situation involves solutions only one of which can be
chosen. In other words, if the battle constellation is to reach a viable
solution, what is required, above and beyond mutual trust, is a common
understanding of criteria of evaluation and justice. It is only in this way
that agreement can be reached between fundamentally different solutions.

This makes it clear that, **first**, the battle-style conflicts of interest,
which occur frequently in the real world, are more difficult and can be
solved only under presuppositions more complex than those of the
prisoner's dilemma and the chicken game. **Second**, battle conflicts frequently occur in networks (interdependent structures, dependence on
cooperation with others, thus common interests, but potentially different and incompatible proposed solutions). Hierarchical or majoritarian
decision-making systems would have little trouble coping with battle
constellations inasmuch as here the dominant agency of decision would
be able to push through the solution it preferred. But in network structures in which the actors are forced to rely on joint decision-making
processes, the battle constellation turns out to be a serious problem.

From the perspective of public-choice theory, the action orientation of
the actors is derived from the basic premises of neoliberal macroeco-
nomics; individuals are at efforts to maximize their own utility. Where
does this action orientation lead us in the case of the battle problem-

atic? In the standard situation the actors are interested in spending an evening together, but each of them will attempt to achieve his own solutions. Proceeding from a purely individualist action orientation, there is no reason for the one actors to give in to the other. Accordingly, the situation leads to endless disagreement. That is, on the basis of public-choice theory networks would be hamstrung in battle constellations. This finding is all the more important as in more and more policy fields and economic sectors both hierarchical and majoritarian decision-making systems can generate only suboptimal outcomes, and cooperation of actors in a network promises, theoretically, better results.

4.1.3   Three Decision Styles and their Effects on the Governance Behavior of Networks

In other words, what we are looking for is a solution beyond the precincts of conventional public-choice theory. Proceeding from thoughts developed by authors such as March and Simon, Scharpf, or Etzioni, it is possible to contrast three fundamental action orientations that are based on distinguishable cognitive and normative actor dispositions (see March/Simon 1958, Scharpf 1988a and 1991a, Etzioni 1961 and 1994). The actors assume individually definable styles of decision-making. Etzioni distinguishes *"utilitarian, coercive and normative"* action orientations. March/Simon and Scharpf, whose terminology is used for the following discussion, distinguish between *"bargaining, confrontational and problem solving"* orientations:

-   The **bargaining orientation** describes the typical, egoistical perspective of the "public-choice individual", who is guided by the rationale of his individual interests.

-   The **confrontational orientation** implies that one's individual utility is measured in terms of benefits gained over others. The issue here is thus not utility maximization, as in the case of the bargaining orientation, but the desire to "vanquish" other parties, to exert one's advantage over others.

- A **problem-solving orientation** on the part of actors implies that they are geared to seeking an anticipated **common utility**.

What happens in the battle constellation when the three distinguishable normative and cognitive action orientations are fully conjugated? It was already demonstrated that an **individualist bargaining orientation** on the part of actors leads into bargaining blockades and endless disagreement. This finding is important in that both public-choice theory and, often, network theory wrongly assume that the individualist-egoistic action orientation is the only conceivable one and at the same time the one that is most promising for the actors involved.[35] A **confrontational actor orientation** is geared to either winning or losing. While the individualist action orientation is apt to lead to "endless" disagreement inasmuch as both sides are interested in a common solution, but are unable to agree for fear of giving up their egoistic interests and thus "get in each other's way", the confrontationally oriented actors will prefer in the standard situation to spend the evening alone and to reject on principle any alternative solutions proposed by others. Networks in which confrontational action orientations prevail have no prospects of successfully solving problems.

A **problem-solving orientation** on the part of the actors can, in contrast, contribute toward breaking up the battle constellation and increasing collective welfare (in the sense of the Kaldor optimum). Only when actors able and willing to cooperate are geared to achieving a solution not necessarily their own but as optimal as possible for the network will there be a way open out of confrontation and endless disagreement.

This finding is extraordinarily important in that it shows, **first**, that, bearing in mind the different cognitive and normative actor orientations systematically disregarded by public-choice theory, the development dynamics of the battle constellation that are often found in the reality of networks can differ in very large measure. **Second**, it is clear that a solution as optimal as possible for the overall system can be imagined only on the basis of an action orientation that is not provided for in the world of individual utility maximization of public-choice theory, indeed is not even regarded as possible: an action strategy geared to a **joint solution of problems**.

But a joint problem-solving orientation on the part of the actors, i.e. the existence of a phenomenon that might be termed "cooperative individualism", is only a necessary, not a sufficient condition for successful decision-making in battle constellations. This would means that actors oriented to solving problems would first agree on procedural rules and time hierarchies that are in line with the interests of all the actors concerned. This would imply, for instance: the football game this week, the concert the week after. If, however, stable solutions of this sort are to be possible, it is important to reduce, and indeed, in the ideal case, eliminate, the risk that the cooperative behavior of one actor might be exploited by others. Here two presuppositions play a role that were referred to in the discussion on the prisoner's dilemma and the chicken game: **first**, legal and contractual security (in cases in which legally binding contracts are involved; see the discussion above) and, **second**, a minimum of trust between the actors, which would serve to diminish the "fear of exploitation". The conditions under which trust is built have already been discussed; it being so important, this point will be taken up again below. A common-**problem-solving orientation, trust** - wherever possible (in the sense of: enforceable) **legal and contractual security**, and the willingness to accept alternative solutions over the course of time (**establishment of time hierarchies**) thus make it possible, in the standard situation (and comparable constellations), to develop stable negotiated solutions that enhance collective welfare.

In the group of battle-of-the-sexes conflicts, there is, however, a large subgroup, presumably significant in the real world, in which the alternative solutions are less standardized and it is complicated, if not impossible, to establish time hierarchies. Examples would be bargaining in networks to decide on different, alternative investments or types of solution and attempts to define a time hierarchy are of no use (e.g. construction of a superhighway versus construction of a railroad line versus construction of kindergartens; policy-level decisions on whether to promote future-oriented technologies or support mature industries).

4.1.4 The Problem of Justice in Network Structures: Reflections against the Background of the Studies of Rawls, Walzer, and Honneth

In battle constellations, a joint problem-solving-orientation thus makes it possible to at least initiate a promising discussion on possible alternative solutions, and this would be ruled out per se under the conditions of a confrontational or bargaining orientation on the part of the actors concerned. The success of negotiations will, however, in many cases depend on the actors' ability to define evaluation criteria on the basis of which alternative solutions that are not immediately comparable can be weighed one against the other. Since as a rule the choice in battle constellations is not between projects per se reasonable or unreasonable but between entirely specific alternative variants and action preferences, which entails an assessment of possible gains or losses of welfare, the evaluation criteria involved will for the most part be criteria of justice.[36]

A very important issue, and one that has until now been seriously neglected in the context of the discussion on the conditions for the efficiency of networks is (first) how **criteria of justice** come about, how (second) they are to be justified, what **concepts of justice** are (third) available in the first place, and what institutional structures (fourth) are favorable to **discourses on justice**. Without going into any detail on the extremely differentiated debate in the social sciences and philosophy on the issue of justice, a few relevant lines of orientation will be developed here regarding this problematic.

4.1.4.1 How Can Universally Accepted Principles of Justice be Grounded and Developed? - Thoughts on Rawls' Theory

The fundamental studies published by Rawls are a good starting point for a look at the problem area of theories of justice.[37] What is interesting about Rawls is that he is concerned with how individuals can find justice, and do so in the context of a *"well-ordered society"*. For Rawls justice is - in contrast to radical liberals like Hayek - not simply an outcome of market processes and individual achievements but a question of fundamental social order. Rawls is concerned primarily with the problem, which is extremely relevant to our problem as well, of how (in principle) notions of justice come about at all in a complex society and what principles of justice can (in principle) be shared by all.

Rawls does not argue along the lines of anthropology and natural law, using a fictive "nature of man", but reverts to the instrument of contractualist theories. His basic idea for deriving binding principles of justice is simple, but at the same time ingenious and, as will be shown, interesting for network theory. Rawls proceeds from rationally deciding individuals who, in a fictive and fair *'original position'*, are to take decisions on just basic structures and organizational principles of the society in which they live. In this original position the individuals are covered by a *"veil of ignorance"*. Their future position in society, their disposal over power, law, and money, their strengths and weaknesses, their talents, and their gender are unknown to them. Justice is, in this sense, understood by Rawls as "fairness". In complex modern societies in which principles of justice cannot be derived solely from higher insights, principles of justice can be legitimated only by defining them in terms of a fair original position.

Since in this original position no individual can rule out that he will be among the disadvantaged in a future society, individuals will, Rawls argues, agree on the following two fundamental principles of justice:

The first principle refers to legal-political justice:

1.   Everyone will have an equal right to the most comprehensive system of equal basic rights that is compatible with the same system for all others.

The second is a principle of socioeconomic justice that permits inequalities, but only under very specific conditions:

2. Social and economic inequalities can be accepted only when (a) policies are defined and implemented that - with the proviso of the principle of just savings - entail the greatest possible benefit for the least well-off, and social inequalities must (b) be corrected and controlled via offices and positions that are open to all in the sense of fair and equal opportunity.[38]

The normative core of Rawls' conception of justice thus consists in linking the goal of the greatest possible liberties (1st principle) with the imperative of socioeconomic justice (2d principle), which, however, entails accepting inequality under specific conditions (2nd principle: (a) and (b); Rawls speaks here of the *"principle of difference"*). The distribution of goods, Rawls states, must proceed on principles that are known to all and acceptable to all concerned.[39]

Rawls' approach is interesting for our problem for two reasons:

First, network actors who have to cope with battle constellations are faced with the problem of **how** they are to arrive at justifiable, common principles of justice, since these principles cannot be "inferred" deductively from any theory or worldview. Rawls' core idea of proceeding from a fictive, fair original position could also provide a fair instrument, a method for developing principles of justice in networks.

Second, the two basic principles of justice "inferred" from the original position are largely compatible with the functional logic of networks. The first principle of legal-political justice could doubtless provide a reasonable rule for bargaining processes in networks in which the actors are dependent on one another. What is behind the first principle of justice is, basically, the rule of reciprocity; and it, as will be demonstrated below, constitutes the essential functional principle in networks. The second part (b) of the second principle of justice amounts to a fair system of "checks and balances" and can, as a structural principle, easily be applied to networks. What is not immediately applicable is the first part (a) of the second principle. The question whether decisions always and in every individual case should (or can) be shaped in such as way as to entail the greatest possible benefits for the least advantaged involves a normative principle entirely current in the context of social policy (which is what Rawls mainly had in mind), though it is not applicable in every decision-making situation. It is also important to add that, as far as the realization of the last-named principle of justice is concerned, Rawls had in mind society as a whole and thus mechanisms of overall social balance. Any infraction of this principle of justice in a social subsystem (e.g. closure of an unprofitable state-owned enterprise, which would be certain to disadvantage most those who are worst off - e.g. the least qualified) can be compensated for (e.g. by qualification measures, etc.). Any application of the first part of the second principle to the tiniest unit of decision within society would mean accepting a situation that might be termed gridlock, since social and economic change and modernization entail replacing weak structures with more efficient ones (e.g. closure of a run-down state-run factories, promotion of efficient firms). Rawls does not rule these processes out, although they would have to be corrected by ex post measures in favor of the least well-off.

It is furthermore interesting that Rawls, in his remarks on his principles of justice, underlines the ability of social actors to cooperate as a precondition essential to the working of complex societies. He understands his notions of justice generally as the basis for anchoring cooperative relationships in societies. His core thought reads like a description of the fragility of networks, definitively dependent as they are on cooperative interaction-based relationships: *"The intuitive notion is that everyone's welfare depends on cooperation, without which no one would have a satisfactory life, and that therefore the distribution of goods should make the less well-off more inclined to cooperative willingly"* (Rawls 1994, p. 147).

Accordingly, when we consult Rawls' theory of justice, we see that, with reference to the idea of the "original position", there is a justifiable, fair principle that can be employed as a method for reflecting on common criteria of justice and distribution in networks as well. Rawls' achievement in the debate on justice is to be seen above all in this contribution to a justification of a procedure that can, in a world in which values and rules can no longer be "inferred" from a priori grounds or posited by authorities, lead to the emergence of common principles of justice.

Rawls' views leave open **three problem dimensions** that are essential in our context:

First, Rawls, in his principles of justice, basically thematizes dimensions of justice in which monetarizable problem constellations (e.g. welfare transfers aimed at compensating for social imbalances) or legally negotiable issues (e.g. laws against discrimination) have to be solved. Networks, however, often center on bargaining that cannot be cast in contracts, that, in other words, cannot be solved by litigation. In addition, it is often necessary to resolve problems of justice that are concerned not with social justice or monetary compensation but with, for instance, a just compensation for risks taken (e.g. policy networks concerned with the issues of whether a second nuclear power plant should be built in the same region or somewhere else) is necessary or whether it is necessary to weigh up the advantages and disadvantages of different options of formulation in a given policy field (e.g. in locational policy, promotion of small and medium-sized industry versus strengthening the hand of large-scale enterprises). The **principles of justice** would accordingly have to be **expanded**. What follows will argue that criteria of justice specific to different social sectors may exist and that Rawls' search for *the* two universal principles underlying justice is not comprehensive enough.

Second, there is another question that Rawls largely disregards: How can universal principles of justice in specific conflict and bargaining situations be translated into **concrete criteria of justice**? **Third**, for Rawls the state is the decisive agency responsible for intervening to bring about distributive justice. This is achieved on the one hand with the aid of ex ante policies as a means of bringing about equal opportunity (e.g. by means of specific educational or training policies). On the other hand, the state intervenes ex post in order to rectify undesirable developments that run counter to Rawls' basic principles. Rawls justifies the **role of the state as the "agency of justice"** by stating that the citizens of complex societies are unable to create justice or bring about agreement on principles of justice. In many respects this is correct. There is no doubt that state-level rules and prohibitions are needed to relieve citizens of the insoluble task of bargaining out "just" solutions in every new situation requiring a decision. In networks, however, the actors rely on their ability to work out common criteria of justice in specific interest constellations (e.g. in the battle-of-the-sexes situation) in order to retain their ability to act. The state and other central decision-making authorities (hierarchical governance) are overburdened here. And here we are faced with the question: What conditions must be given if actors are to be enabled to solve this difficult problem?

4.1.4.2   Context-bound and Network-specific Principles of Justice - Reflections with Reference to Walzer

"Every human society is universal because it is human, and it is particular because it is a society."
M. Walzer (1994), p. 8

In his study, *"Spheres of Justice"*, which - beside Rawls' standard work - is one of the most important contributions to the discussion of the issue of justice, Walzer develops ideas that can provide at least partial answers to the questions posed in connection with Rawls (Walzer 1992a/1983). Walzer explicitly understands his conception of justice as a countermodel to Rawls' theory. What follows will attempt to distill, as briefly as possible, the thoughts relevant to our problem from Walzer's edifice and, in order to avoid the reproach of indulging in untenable eclecticism, demonstrate the compatibility of Walzer's line of argument with the structures underlying Rawls' thinking.

Walzer's core idea is that in modern societies justice cannot be reduced to one universal principle. He develops a theory of *"complex equality"* that demonstrates that there exist in different spheres of social action (*"Spheres of Justice"*) autonomous, specific principles of justice and rules of distribution.[40] His convincing argument is that specific spheres of action are dominated by particular action logics that lead to "sphere-specific" rules of justice. While, for instance, the economic sphere is concerned with transparency and fair competition, but not at all with an equal distribution of resources, other rules of justice apply in the family, between parents and children: here one would certainly expect "just parents" to distribute affection and love for their children as optimally as possible. It might be added, going beyond Walzer, that notions of justice change in the course of history and thus have procedural character: How, for instance, do we define precisely a "just" division of labor between men and women; how are environmental risks and costs to be distributed "justly"; how are we to imagine social justice between countries in the world society? These are questions that must answered in historical contexts.

Walzer opens up scopes for a discussion of justice that offers points of contact that can be used to look into the question, not settled in Rawls' studies, of how his two principles of justice can be concretized in different social subsectors, an issue of some significance for network theory. It is important to note here that Walzer has been accused by a number of critics of having generally abandoned any attempt to discuss fundamental principles of justice and of having drifted off into particularist-arbitrary notions of justice, and that the present study finds these objections, in their overgeneralization, untenable. The attempt to reduce Walzer's thoughts to the smallest common denominator and look for ways of linking them up with Rawls' theory leads to two of the three universal principles posited by Rawls. Walzer's view is immediately compatible with Rawls' first principle of justice, which is concerned with legal-political equality (*Everyone should have an equal right to the most extensive system of equal basic liberties that is compatible with the same system for all others*). The second part of the second principle of justice likewise poses no problem; it states that social and economic inequalities (should) *be controlled via offices and positions that are open to all in accordance with fair equal opportunity*. We can note agreement between Walzer and Rawls in these two points, which center on basic democratic rights and institutionalized checks and balances.

What is controversial is the first part of Rawls' second principle of justice; in it Rawls designates as a criterion for socioeconomic justice that social inequalities can only be accepted when *policies are pursued that - with the proviso of the principle of just savings - entail the greatest possible benefit for the least well-off.* With this statement, Rawls had in mind the problem of social inequality in capitalist societies. Walzer, for his part, looks for criteria of justice in different social subsectors can cannot, in all cases, be concerned a priori with bettering the lot of the "least advantaged". One might, for instance, think here of industrial policies in regions in economic crisis: applying Rawls' logic to this field (which Rawls would not do, since the issue that concerns him is social policies and social balance in the overall social context) would lead to a situation in which industrial policies would be concentrated on the least competitive firms with the lowest innovation potential, possibly even at the expense of the strongest firms. In this "sphere" Walzer would certainly plead for a different "just solution", one that might entail strengthening the strong firms and concentrating on industries with a future instead of on crisis-ridden ones, though a solution of this sort would certainly have to be accompanied by appropriate social policies. Rawls fails to pose this question as to context-bound justice above and beyond the problematic of monetary distribution. In this question, he (entirely in the liberal tradition) would presumably plead for market solutions, in order then (in contrast to liberalist economic positions) to demand, in keeping with point one of his second principle of justice, redistribution in favor of those who are most disadvantaged.

The key difference between Walzer and Rawls is accordingly that the former shifts his theoretical focus from the level at which he justifies universal principles of justice to the level of issues concerning context-bound application; the first level, with which Walzer hardly concerns himself, is the level containing Rawls' pioneering idea of the "original position", a concept that has yet to be surpassed. This step is made possible by the discussion of action logics specific to the "spheres". By looking into the "spheres" of society, Walzer comes up with the observation that there are, first, specifically sphere-dependent criteria of justice and that, second, these often cannot be monetarized. In many areas, justice can, accordingly, not be simply established via compensatory payments; the issue is the just distribution of risks (e.g. in environmental policy), love and affection (e.g. in the family), equal opportunity, free exchange, both social and otherwise (in the economy), the distribution of chances of advancement (e.g. in administration), or political power (in the political sphere). In this Walzer goes beyond Rawls, for whom justice is based on the political-legal equality of citizens and a financial equalization on the principle of a prioritary betterment of the position of those who are worst off.

It is precisely this search direction of Walzer's that is, for two reasons, extremely interesting for the network discussion. First, the discussion of the battle constellation showed that bargaining blockades in networks are likely precisely in situations in which decisions have to be made on alternative solutions, and the advantages and disadvantages of these solutions can (often) not be expressed simply in terms of money, i.e. situations in which compensatory payments do not represent a way out of the dilemma and from which, therefore, nonmonetary criteria of distribution and justice must be sought. Second, the picture painted by Walzer of modern societies (as polycentric systems) is more realistic that the notions presented by Rawls, who, basically, remains within the ambit of the traditional theory of the state.

Walzer makes great efforts to point out clearly that the problem of justice must be dealt with in and by society, and that it cannot be reduced to constitutional-democratic framework conditions and mechanisms of social balance mediated via the state. Rawls' efforts are on the one hand directed against a radical liberalism that fails to address justice as a social problem and on the other hand against antiliberal and antipluralist ideas that aim, via the authoritarian state or other hierarchical agencies (churches, parties), to anchor even in modern societies notions of the "good state" binding for all citizens. Rawls' formulation of universal principles of justice leaves individuals broad scopes for their different ideas of "the good life". In Rawls' conception, the liberty of individuals can be restricted only by the state geared to these universal principles.

Rawls' discourse must accordingly be understood as a bulwark against radical-liberal approaches (à la Hayek) and premodern, antipluralist theories. The actors in which Rawls is interested are the individuals and the state. Walzer's thoughts do justice to the fact that complex societies have collective or network-like organizational structures aside from the state and the individual and state regulation and the market as governance mechanisms. These structures may be corporate networks, working groups in firms concerned with horizontal sectoral coordination, or federations, research and consulting institutions and other intermediary institutions that operate in policy networks. The network structures are all characterized by the fact that the mutually dependent actors active in them are forced to develop solution-oriented bargaining styles and shared, "just" principles of evaluation if they are to remain capable of acting (see the battle problematic). In Rawls these network-like decision-making processes and structures are, as it were, not provided for. For him the question of any concrete formulation of justice going beyond the universal principles he sketches poses itself only for the individuals. To pose, against the background of the structural complex of modern societies that Rawls has in mind, the question of concrete criteria of justice would mean dictating values to individuals and curtailing their liberties.

By way of contrast, Walzer's approach reflects more the picture of network societies in which the problem of justice "seeps" into the social subsystems and networks, to be jointly processed there by the actors concerned, to the extent that these actors (networks) work together with the aim of finding solutions to collective tasks. Proceeding from this structural model, it makes sense to think about concrete, "sphere-specific" principles of justice. Justice can no longer be discussed at the level of corrective measures taken by the state, general frameworks, and individuals. Walzer thus comes closer to the reality of network societies than Rawls.

Walzer emphasizes that his theory does not aim to single out one criterion of distribution. He names three principles as fundamental points of orientation for evaluating different criteria of justice in the specific spheres: "free exchange", "need", and "desert".[41] While other theories of justice emphasize one or the other of these criteria, Walzer refers to the field of force linking the three principles. He argues that a specific mix is possible in individual spheres, depending on the actors involved: *All three criteria have their real force of validity, but none of them has this force across all distributional spheres. They are part of the story to be told, but they are not the whole story* (Walzer 1992, p. 51).

Walzer's concept of justice is nowhere arbitrary. Against the background of the different spheres and the field of tension constituted by "free exchange", "need", and "desert", Walzer formulates **two principles basic to his theory of "complex equality"**:

First, he emphasizes that justice does not require a strictly equal distribution of all goods, but that solutions must be found in the field of force linking "free exchange", "need", and "desert", solutions that depend on the concrete conditions and demands found in the spheres and based on equal exchange between the actors involved. While in the economic sphere the criterion of desert is for the most part of greater significance, the criterion of need is decisive, for instance, in the spheres of family, education and training, and security and welfare. Walzer presents the grid of a playing field in which principles of justice come about in the course of social conflicts: *If the members of a society are at odds over the importance of social goods, if their ideas are controversial, then the society must, to be just, come to terms with these differences by creating on the one hand institutional forces for their articulation and on the other hand adjudicative techniques and alternative forms of distribution* (Walzer 1992, p. 441). This proceduralist view (whose more exact contours will be outlined below) comes very close to the real world of networks. While in Rawls criteria of justice have to be justified on the basis of a fair original position, Walzer points to the significance of fair bargaining procedures in defining concrete principles of justice.

Second, Walzer restricts the initially rather high measure of contingency by introducing a reference measure for justice. It is essential to rule out tradeoffs between different distributional positions, thus precluding any dominance of one sphere over others, or indeed all others.

This means, for instance, that it is in Walzer's eyes in principle unjust and intolerable when less well-off citizens have no access to political office, education and training, etc.

The "imperialistic" sphere, which, in Walzer's eyes, massively threatens the scopes of action on the other spheres, and thus falls under his tradeoff criterion, is the sphere of money: *"This means that the capitalists will always be tyrants when possession and wealth are not checked and neutralized by a strong state. Political power and possession must control and check one another"* (Walzer 1992, p. 446).

This focused normative expression of the concept of justice is relevant to the network discussion. Walzer's thoughts can be applied to the "power problem" in and between networks discussed in the last chapter. Walzer insists that proceduralist attempts to unify criteria of justice among the actors involved, dependent as they are on reaching understandings, can be sustained only if the structures of dominance addressed in his tradeoff argument can always be controlled and restricted. This rule should be kept in mind in networks that are forced to rely on negotiations over criteria of justice and distributions.

4.1.4.3 Institutional Conditions for a Solution of the Problematic of Justice

The problem is now under what **institutional conditions** principles of justice come about in the individual spheres and in society as a whole. Applied to the network problematic, this would mean asking under what conditions the actors might succeed in developing common notions of justice in order to find a way out of the bargaining blockade defined by the battle constellation. The view that Walzer has developed on this problem offers a point of departure for the network discussion. While Walzer, as regards the question of concrete criteria of justice, insists on a high degree of contingency - in the triangle defined by "desert", "free exchange", and "need" and the concrete action logics in the individual spheres - the institutional demands on societies that wish to come to terms with the problem of justice in Walzer's sense of the term are formulated quite concretely and are of a very high level.

Walzer works out six essential complexes of factors that make up the institutional contours of a society able to come close to "complex equality" (Walzer 1992a, pp. 26-64):

1. The development of "complex equality" presupposes in the individual action spheres **persons who regard themselves as equal in terms of their value and their rights**.

2. It is only on the basis of the first condition that ties can develop between persons which enable them, in an act of self-determination, to join forces to form political communities, associations, and polities (one could just as well add: networks). For this Walzer coins the term **membership**.

3. The individual associations of social actors must be more or less able to ban free-rider behavior if they are to create cooperative and trust-based relations between the members.[42] Only if it proves possible to **ward off egoistic exploitation and individualistic impoverishment of associative structures**, can action orientations and principles of justice geared to the public interest prevail.

4. "Complex equality" can, however, not reproduce itself on the basis of institutional conditions. It needs a **minimum of stabilization stemming from the convictions of justice held by individuals**, affective ties, and experience of joint action. I.e. the principles of justice must be anchored in the moral convictions of social actors.

5. Walzer by no means rules out the possibility of interest-driven conflicts over the social significance of specific goods and disagreement over concrete distributive criteria in the "spheres" and in the community. Against this background, he pleads for principles of **tolerance, dialogic practice**, and **democratic public opinion** as foundations of a society that is engaged in the task, always incomplete, never concluded, of establishing "complex equality". This **proceduralist understanding of justice** comes close to the

reality of networks that are forced to bargain continuously over common principles of justice.

6.   Finally, in terms of institutional conditions the **state** has three tasks fundamental to a just society. It must first **watch over the boundaries between the spheres** ("art of separation") so as to safeguard their autonomy against any infringements by other action spheres. Second, it has the task of **defining rules for the fragile interplay between the spheres**, rules keyed to the two fundamental criteria used to evaluate his theorem of "complex equality", and of ensuring that they are observed ("art of connection"). Third, the state must assumes a **supervisor function** vis-à-vis the spheres, which are otherwise largely autonomous, in order to prevent powerful actors from violating fundamental principles of justice in the individual action spheres.

If one follows Walzer's thought, it become clear that the demands on a society and the actors in social subsectors that are willing to face the problem of "complex equality" are extraordinarily high. These demands can be transferred to the network problematic. The development of common criteria of justice, and the task of observing and stabilizing them, call for a) individuals with a specific **value orientation** (points 1 and 4: mutual acknowledgment of persons as individuals having equal value and equal rights; defense against free-rider behaviors); b) **self-organizational capacity and a public-interest orientation** on the part of the social actors (in associations, networks, etc.) (points 2 and 3); c) a **state** with the control, policy-formulation, and intervention functions outlined above (point 6) and d) a **democratic pattern of organization** that safeguards tolerance, dialogue, and democratic public opinion (point 5).

4.1.4.4   Mutual Social Recognition among Individuals as a Condition of Discourses on Justice - Reflections with Reference to Honneth

According to Walzer, the functioning of discourses on justice depends in the end on individuals who must recognize each other's equal value and equal rights. Principles of justice can find recognition only when they are anchored in the moral principles and notions of justice held by citizens. Against this background, we become aware of the reductionism of conventional public-choice theory, which reduces the entire problem of justice to the basic assumption of the utility-maximizing individual.

In this section we will discuss some studies by Axel Honneth as a means of expanding and enlarging the insights gained from Walzer's thoughts on the motivational demands placed on individuals who, in order to stabilize their interpersonal relationships in organizations, associations, and networks, are compelled to engage in discourses on justice. Based on his analysis of a great quantity of historical and sociological research, Honneth distills the conditions that makes it possible for individuals to develop, internalize, and acknowledge principles of justice and, on this basis, to heed public-welfare interests along with their own private interests (see above all Honneth 1992). In essence, his finding is that the normative core of (often intuitive) notions of justice and moral principles is linked with experiences and expectations *"that are bound up with respect for one's own dignity, honor, or integrity"* (Honneth 1994a, p. 86). His studies lead Honneth to conclude that the normative precondition of all communicative action, and thus of the capacity for public-interest orientations and conflicts with others over common criteria of justice, consists in the possibility to **acquire social recognition**: *"Subjects encounter one another against the horizon of the mutual expectation of finding recognition both as moral persons and for their social achievements"*.[43]

In the absence of this experience, feelings of **neglect** result that, in the long run, obstruct any communication on an equal footing. Honneth's argumentation incorporates the model of recognition developed by

George H. Mead, who argues that subjects are capable of communication only when they are able to place themselves mutually in the position of the other (see Mead 1980 and 1983).

These sociopsychological considerations serve to illustrate the high demands placed on individuals as well as the institutional framework conditions in social formations in which actors, in many social spheres, e.g. networks, are forced by the broad dispersion of governance-relevant resources, **first**, to engage in permanent communication and contribute to joint governance efforts that have until now been the preserve of hierarchical decision-making centers (corporate headquarters, union leadership, government) and, **second**, to agree, even in specific situations (e.g. in "battle" conflicts , on common criteria of justice, because formal contractual and legal security and the majoritarian decision-making principles customary in Western democracies are by no means sufficient to ensure the governance capacity of social subsystems, such, above all, as networks, and society as a whole.

4.1.4.5 Orientational Framework for the Problem of Justice in Network Societies

Combining the thoughts of Rawls, Walzer, and Honneth on the network problematic and the battle constellation, which actors are forced to solve by developing common notions of justice, we find ourselves faced with an extraordinarily complex state of affairs. We can here derive a five-stage frame of reference and orientation:

1. **Grounding of principles of justice**: With reference to Rawls' "original position", it is possible to answer the question how, in polycentric societies, generally accepted principles of justice can be grounded at all.

2. **Legal-political principles of justice**: Rawls' basic principles of legal-political justice discussed above are shared by Walzer. These principles state that, first, *everyone has equal rights to the most compre-*

hensive system of equal basic freedoms that is compatible with the same system for others (Rawls) and, second, inequalities and injustices must be rectifiable via offices and positions that are open too all *in terms of fair equal opportunity* (Rawls).

3. Context dependence of principles of justice and the procedural character of justice: First, we can argue with Walzer that there exist context-dependent, i.e. network-specific, principles of justice that cannot be reduced to *one* universal principle. Walzer in this way opens up a path for discussing even distributional conflicts that cannot be monetarized, and this makes it possible to move from the level of universal criteria of justice and fairness to concrete dimensions of justice in different spheres of society. Second, Walzer describes how criteria of justice arise in a social and conflictual process in the field of tension defined by "free exchange", "desert", and "need", and in close relation to the functional logics of specific action spaces (economy, administration, politics, family, etc.).

4. High demands on the institutional design of societies: This procedural understanding of justice, "adapted" to the network discussion, places, as Walzer demonstrates, high demands on the basic political-organizational patterns and the institutional framework conditions of societies. Walzer's studies cast a light on the structural picture of an active society in which the problem of justice can no longer be discussed and dismissed on page one with reference to the state, which watches over the observance of universal rules, and the free and autonomous individuals, who act in accordance with their preferences and notions of "the good life". Discourses on justice interpenetrate all of society, and network actors as well as other collective actors are forced to engage in processes of communication on common principles of justice and evaluation in order to sustain their capacity to act.

5. The normative and psychosocial dimension: Walzer and, in particular, Honneth show that the functioning of discourses on justice depend in the last analysis on mutual recognition of individuals as persons endowed with equal values and equal rights as well as on an anchoring of value patterns compatible with both the public interest and individualism in the day-to-day practice of citizens.

This demanding frame of reference does not constitute the minimal requirements for the general governance capacity of societies. The potentials of network governance can, however, best be exhausted when societies or subsystems of societies succeed in gearing their efforts to the catalogue of requirements outlined above. Wherever this is not possible, networks in politics and society in which the actors are mutually dependent on their governance resources will lose their ability to act in the frequently encountered battle situations is which the crucial concern is to develop common criteria of justice and evaluation. It thus becomes clear that network governance is anything but trivial. Overview 8 illustrates that the discussion over justice, individualism, and solidarity is in need of a new concept of society and state. Individual interests cannot simply be played off against orientations geared to public interest and community. If social problem-solving capacities are to be strengthened, it is necessary to mobilize both individual and community resources instead of structuring social problems, along one-dimensional and reflex-like lines, in keeping with the traditional patterns (statist concept versus market traditionalism).

4.1.5 Résumé: Action Orientations and Decision Styles Capable of Overcoming the Pitfalls of Network Governance

Three of the prominent core problems of network governance (Overview 6) can be defused with the aid of specific action orientations on the part of actors and the decision-making styles based on them. The action strategy pointed out as a means of solving these problems differs sharply from the one-sidedly egoistic action orientations presupposed in public-choice theories; indeed, the latter are in many cases more apt to end up in obstruction of action.

The trend toward structurally conservative incrementalism and functional and cognitive blockades (**core problem 2**) arises primarily when network actors agree basically on the smallest common denominator, thus giving rise to collective conservatism. This trend can, as was shown, be attenuated by the capacity of network actors to develop a common problem-solving orientation geared to the demands facing the network as an overall system and not simply to the aggregate individual interests (and at times privileges) of network actors. Action orientations geared to joint solution of problems can make it possible to realize future interests against present interests.

Even the network problem involved in passing on the costs of joint action to third parties (**core problem 5**) can be diminished by a problem-solving orientation on the part of the actors concerned. Central to this is an action orientation that takes systematic account of the consequences of network action for both the internal world and the environment of the network.

The constellations of interests underlying these two core problems are marked by the existence of both individual and common interests (mixed-motive games). If the actors pursue one-sidedly individualist action orientations, it is impossible for a common problem-solving orientation to gain ground in networks; the likelihood that in this case the above-named core problems (two and five) will become virulent is high. It is, however, difficult to develop a common problem-solving orientation and cooperative behavior in that there exists a real danger, or at least the possibility, that cooperative behavior may be exploited by others (see chicken game-constellation, prisoner's dilemma).

What would contribute to overcoming this bargaining dilemma (prisoner's dilemma or chicken-game constellation), which on the one hand makes it difficult to develop a common problem-solving orientation and on the other hand cannot be solved without it, is **communication** between the actors concerned, the existence of **contractual and legal security** and a **minimum of trust** between actors, a factor important in that networks often depend on informal agreements that are beyond the power of a state ruled by law to impose sanctions.

Overview 8: The Problem Field of "Justice" in a Developing Market			
Phases Characteristics	Preindustrial societies	Early industrialization	Fordism
Value context	Traditional, community-based and particularist notions of morality and justice	Dissolution of traditional value contexts; development of universalist notions of morality and justice and class-struggle-oriented disputes over implementation	Dominance of universalist notions of justice; curbed capitalism/social partnership; dissolution of class milieus/beginning individualization
Economic regime	Local economy, agrarian society	Market economy	Keynesianism
Power and sovereignty structures	Paternalist-authoritarian power structures at local and higher levels	Authoritarian state; strengthening industrial bourgeoisie; class struggle	Welfare state; neo-corporatist inter-linkage between state - business federations - labor unions
Mechanisms and instruments for creating social justice	Family-based social security systems	"Top-down welfare state" (Bismarck); family-based social security systems; struggle of labor movement for social justice; charity-oriented solutions	Welfare transfers; bargaining between social partners; dissolution of family-based social security systems
"Justice type"	"Justice" imparted via traditional, relatively stable value contexts	"Justice" imparted via struggles between social classes	"Justice" imparted via welfare state
Pattern of organization and governance	Authoritarian-hierarchical, predemocratic patterns of organization and governance	Authoritarian-hierarchical, predemocratic patterns of organization and governance and development of countervailing powers (labor movement)	Democratic-majoritarian, hierarchical decision-making; neocorporatist arrangements

Economy - A Heuristic Overview	
Neoliberalism	Polycentric "network societies"
Narrowing of universalist principles to results of individual achievement (achievement-based justice) plus market "justice"; rejection of collective social security structures; advanced dissolution of collective (value) milieus	Renewed social conflict over principles of justice in social "spheres"; field of tension: universalist versus "sphere-bound" principles of justice; beginning conflict over "global justice"; continuation of individualization tendency accompanied by growing significance of network organizations
Free trade and market economy	Systemic competitiveness
Loss of governance by the state; inherent dynamics of the (world) market; loss of significance of labor unions	State as moderating and controlling agency; constraint to work out and implement principles of justice in networks and social subsystems; (world) market allocation; privatization of power (global firms)
Individual achievement of *homo oeconomicus*; subsidiarity; market allocation	Restructuring of welfare state; growing significance of the "Third Sector" and the company level; market allocation
"Justice" via market economy	"Justice" imparted via the constitutional state and complex bargaining processes in and between associations of civil society, (networked)firms, policy networks
democratic-majoritarian patterns of organization and governance; social self-organization; market governance	Governance pluralism: hierarchical, network-like and market-based patterns of organization and governance

The risk that networks will be confronted with bargaining blockades affecting possible alternative solutions whose costs and benefits are very difficult to determine (**core problem 4**) can likewise be countered by common solution-oriented action strategies and decision-making styles. Conflicts over fundamentally different alternative solutions, as a rule not accessible to the compromise formula of "a little of this, a little of that", are, it is true, likewise based on interest constellations characterized by the existence of individual and common interests, but, in terms of game theory, they correspond to the type defined by battle-of-the-sexes conflicts, which are more difficult to resolve than the prisoner's dilemma and the chicken-game constellation.

Here the communication between the actors concerned, the existence of contractual and legal security and a minimum of trust between the actors (i.e. the basic mechanisms needed to work out a joint solution and to defuse the prisoner's dilemma and the chicken-game constellation) are necessary but not sufficient conditions for averting the bargaining blockade that threatens. What is crucial is the capacity of the network actors to develop criteria of justice and distribution that can be used to evaluate different alternative solutions, some of which cannot be monetarized. Only in this way is it possible to develop a common problem-solving orientation and to prevent bargaining blockades.

The discussion of the concepts of justice of Rawls, Walzer, and Honneth led to a complex profile of what is required in terms of individuals, institutional structures, value patterns, and political principles of organization. This provides an orientation as regards the question as to the conditions under which it is possible to sustain the governance capacity of social subsystems and networks in which the actors are forced to develop successful discourses on justice if they are to solve battle-of-the-sexes conflicts. The way in which internal network interest conflicts are dealt with is not clearly determined by their institutional structure; it instead remains strongly dependent on the specific action orientations of the actors, the existing degree of trust or distrust in social relations, i.e. the concrete shape given to interpersonal relationships. Networks are thus not efficient per se. The mobilization of their problem-solving capacities (also) depends on the above-sketched deep structures of the societies in which they are anchored.

4.2   The Social Functional Logic of Networks

The thoughts discussed thus far lead to a reconstruction of the social functional logic of networks. Wherever this functional logic is unable to unfold, it is likely that networks will founder on the pitfalls of network governance worked out above. It has become clear that, in networks marked by interaction between actors with common and divergent interests, it is in many cases impossible to achieve a collective output solely on the basis of exchange orientations and individual rationales. The interaction typical for networks is bargaining. The decisive social mechanism that ensures the functioning of bargaining systems is the willingness of the actors to compromise.

Mayntz point to the significance of specific rules for the functioning of bargaining in networks (see Mayntz 1991). The observance of rules as a stabilizing element is not a factor specific to network organization, since the market as well as hierarchical organizations are also in need of rule systems. What is essential is the substantive content of the rules needed to govern the logic of compromise and bargaining in networks. Mayntz specifies four central network rules: fair exchange/just distribution of costs and benefits, reciprocity, restraint of one's own freedom of action, respect for the legitimate interests of other actors.

The rules constitute the social functional logic of networks; they are schematized in the following figure. The figure weights and categorizes the rules specified by Mayntz in terms of their functions.

The bargaining logic in networks presupposes actors capable of compromising, who respect the legitimate interests of the other actors (here we see signs of Walzer's *"art of separation"*), while they are at the same time engaged in seeking joint solutions (Walzer's *"art of connection"* of one's own and contrary interests). The problem-solving orientation is geared to a collective process of searching and learning keyed to a viable goal system. If the actors are prepared to compromise and in a position to develop a common problem-solving orientation, the concern will be to find forms of a fair balance and to distribute justly the costs and benefits that emerge from specific decisions. It was shown in the last chapter that this process of working out common rules of evaluation, distribution, justice and fairness is extremely demanding. If principles of fair exchange are to be achieved, the parties must be capable of dealing openly with conflicts, and this implies that actors are willing to restrict voluntarily their individual scopes of action in order to attain joint results. Any bargaining logic based on this pattern and geared to solving problems - i.e. to attempting to establish, through joint efforts, a goal system previously defined - is based on the functional principle of "reciprocity" and is dependent on the functional condition of "trust" between the network actors concerned. These two categories are superordinate to the other rules named.

4.2.1   Reciprocity as the Functional Principle of Networks Geared to Problem-solving

While negotiations based exclusively on individual-egoistic utility rationales are dominated by the exchange principle, network action strategies geared to problem-solving are guided by the principle of reciprocity, which, for the present, can be understood as a reciprocal process of give and take. The logic of reciprocity is the foundation on which the actors develop a joint problem-solving orientation, even though these actors may at the same time, and in addition to the others, also pursue conflicting interests. Reciprocity is the constitutive functional principle of network organizations.

Reciprocity can be distinguished from the exchange principle in three respects:

-   **Principles for the evaluation of give and take**: The principle of exchange is concerned with the equivalent value of exchanged goods or services. "Money" normally serves as the universal equivalent used to define exchange value. Reciprocity, on the other hand, is characterized by the fact that actors exchange their material goods, services, benefits, or intrinsic gratifications for **adequate or approximate equivalents**. This principle is applicable to the above-discussed battle-of-the-sexes problem, which is characterized in particular by the fact that alternative solutions that are difficult to measure - and as a rule cannot be expressed in terms of money - have to be weighed against one another.

- **The time dimension**: The traditional principle of exchange is defined as a one-off event that is concluded when the exchange has been completed. The principle of reciprocity, on the other hand, is, as a process of give and take, *"tied to lasting social relationships between the actors, to a common relationship history that extends into the past"* (Mahnkopf 1993, pp. 71 f.) as well as to the *"shadow of the future"* (see Axelrod 1984). This principle, too, is compatible with the institutional structures of network organizations.

- **The normative foundation**: The principle of exchange is for the most part governed by explicitly contractual relationships covered by contractual and legal security. Reciprocal relationships are often informal agreements, arrangements difficult to put into contract form, and it is thus **trust** in the stability of the social relationship and the cooperative, fair, reliable attitude of the others that constitutes the foundation of this type of interaction. This characteristic, too, is entirely compatible with the logic of networks.

Against this background, it become clear that the principle of reciprocity is not *one* of the rules supporting stability and efficiency in networks but the central functional principle under which the other rules (fair exchange, voluntary restriction of individual scopes of action, respect of the legitimate interests of the other actors) can be subsumed. And the principle of reciprocity is particularly interesting for the network discussion in that it does not describe symbiotic relationships but binds together solidarity and egoism and is thus wholly compatible with the core structure of networks, which link individual and common interests, cooperation and conflict to form a (potentially) productive, though tense, relationship structure.

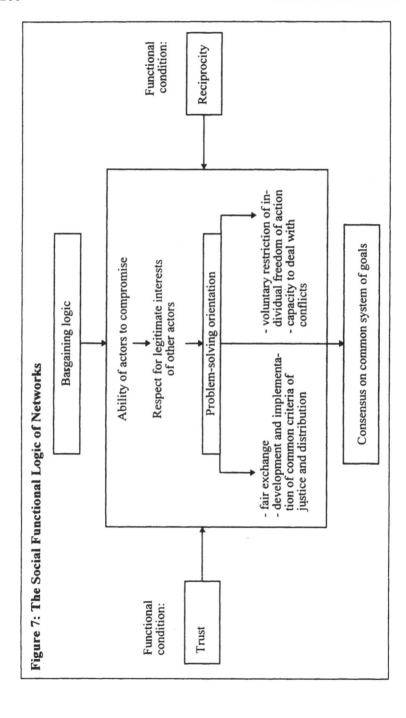

Figure 7: The Social Functional Logic of Networks

Reciprocity is a functional principle that presupposes the mutual social recognition of actors, as is emphasized by Honneth and Mead (Mead 1980; Honneth 1992, pp. 64 f. and 177), thus creating a sociomoral bonding agent in highly differentiated societies: reciprocity sets egoistic motives in motion, though it at the same time channels them in the interest of sustaining and optimizing the social system; and it does so by mobilizing among the actors additional motivations to gear their efforts to seeking joint solutions. Alvin Gouldner circumscribes this in the following way: *"Reciprocity demands that you, when others have fulfilled their status obligations to you, have for your part an additional second-order obligation (repayment) to fulfill your status obligations to them. In this sense it unites the attitude of gratitude with the attitude of rightfulness and adds a security margin to the question of the motivation to act accordingly"*. Gouldner accordingly understands the norm of reciprocity as a *"sort of supple filler that can be poured into the cracks of social structures and must, in a sense, serve as a bonding agent available for all purposes"* (Gouldner 1984, pp. 106 f.).

4.2.2   Trust as a Functional Condition of Network Governance

"If distrust is complete, cooperation will fail among free agents."
D. Gambetta (1988), p. 219

"Trust reduces complex realities far more quickly and economically than prediction, authority, or bargaining."
W.W. Powell (1990), p. 205

4.2.2.1   The Significance of Trust for the Reproducibility of Societies

The normative precondition for reciprocal relationships is a minimum of trust between actors. The significance of trust was addressed above in the context of the discussion on the "action orientations of actors in networks" in order to show that in the standard constellations (prisoner's dilemma, chicken game, battle of the sexes) problem-oriented solutions in networks cannot be reached without a minimum of trust among the actors. Trust is thus the general functional condition that permits problem-solving orientations based on reciprocal relationships between networks actor capable of compromising (see Figure 7).

The insight that trust is of crucial significance for the capacity to reproduce social relationships is, to be sure, neither new nor exclusively pertinent to networks. The patriarch of liberalism, Adam Smith, was, in contrast to many of his intellectual successors, entirely familiar with the importance of social ties and moral resources in capitalist economies and societies marked by division of labor. Smith demonstrated that competition in economy and society can avoid mutual destruction only when the relationships between actors and their attitude toward the observance of universally binding rules is dominated by a minimum of trust: "... *if there is any society among robbers and murderers, they must at least ... abstain from robbing and murdering one another"* (Smith [1759]/1976, p. 86). This argumentation of Smith's is taken up again by Niklas Luhmann, who likewise emphasizes that highly differentiated societies cannot function on the basis of generalized distrust of the kind typical for Western democracies.[44]

Generalized trust contributes to radically lowering control and transaction costs, which anyone can verify who has been in societies dominated by generalized distrust. If social rules are largely observed, the costs of justice, police, and other agencies of control and sanction decline.

Trust can be interpreted as one of essential determinants of social development in general. In his studies on the Protestant ethic, Max Weber observed that unscrupulousness keyed solely to self-interest and generalized distrust is more typical of precapitalist countries than of competition-oriented market economies. Put the other way around, this implies that market economies can survive only on the foundation of reasonably stabilized trust-based relationships between social actors. Market economies that function in an ambient of generalized distrust tend to degenerate into disintegrated societies in which the transaction costs for interaction between actors and the control efforts required to enforce rules are permanently on the rise and in this way gradually undermine the efficiency gains of competitive economies.

These issues cannot be gone into at any length here. It is, however, no doubt safe to assume that trust plays a greater role in networks geared to direct interaction between actors, development of a common problem-solving orientation, and reciprocal relationships than it does in hierarchical decision-making structures or in markets. Societies dominated by generalized distrust will no doubt be less able to mobilize the organizational advantages and governance potentials afforded by networks than will societies dominated by generalized distrust.

The following section will show that the usual method of public-choice theory is unable to decode the phenomenon of "trust". This will be followed by a discussion of the conditions for the emergence and reproduction of trust in societies.

4.2.2.2 The Limits of Public-choice Theory in Explaining the Phenomenon of "Trust"

In the context of public-choice theory, the first question posed to explain the conditions required for the emergence of "trust" is of course the question of the rational motives of actors. It is possible to explain against this background why, in competitive situations, the emergence of trust is undermined by one-sidedly egoistic orientations on the part of actors: the *homo oeconomicus* exploits free-rider opportunities. Exclusively individualist action orientations thus often constitute a barrier preventing the emergence of "trust". However, as was pointed out above, it is, in cases like the prisoner's dilemma and the chicken game, entirely conceivable for communication between actors to narrow the gap between individual and common interests. The *homo oeconomicus* of the world of public-choice theory is thus, under specific conditions, capable of developing trust-based relationships from individual utility rationales.

This argumentation is certainly not new, nor is it particularly original. Diego Gambetta point out that the emergence of trust does, however, not depend solely on the motives of particular actors, and even in cases in which trust and cooperative behavior in bargaining situations would lead to an increase of the individual utility of the persons concerned - i.e. we were, in "objective terms", dealing with rational motives for cooperative behavior - trust need not necessarily come about. Gambetta's argumentation implies that trust is anchored in naturally developed social relationships and cannot be reduced to utility rationales and rational motivations.

Gambetta argues as follows: "... *one of the most interesting ... lessons of game theory is that even if people's motives are not unquestioningly egoistic, cooperation will still encounter many obstacles. This is a much more striking result than that which shows that rationality in the pursuit of self-interest may not suffice*". He exemplifies his thesis with reference to the prisoner's dilemma: "... *the mere expectation that the second player might choose to defect can lead the first player to do so, if only in self-defence. The first player's anticipation of the second's defection may be based simply on the belief that the second player is unconditionally uncooperative. But, more tragically, it may also be based on the fear that the second player will not trust him to cooperate, and will defect as a direct result of this lack of trust. Thus the outcome converges on a sub-optimal equilibrium, even if both players might have been conditionally predisposed to cooperate*" (Gambetta 1988, p. 216; underlining in original).

Even when actors have motives to build trust, cooperative action strategies need not result, since the motives of the other actor or actors are nor known ("double contingency"). One possibility of remedying this problem is to create communication, though this alone is not enough, since even given communication there remains a questionable area that Gambetta discusses under the heading "lack of belief". This should not be confused with the motivation of the individual actors.

Even actors who want to build trust-based relationships may be prevented from doing so by two obstacles. The first obstacle can consist in the fact that one actor does not believe that all other actors are willing to show trust and cooperation and shies away from cooperative strategies for fear that the trust he advances will be exploited. The second obstacle is that a given actor not only has to trust that the others will behave cooperatively, he also has to believe that the others trust him.

Public-choice theory, with its one-dimensional concentration on utility rationales and motivational patterns beyond space and time, turns out against this background to be lacking in prognostic power. Whether or not trust and with it cooperativeness and the basis for reciprocal relationships will arise in identical bargaining and interest structures is largely a matter of the specific action orientations of actors, personal predispositions in specific actor constellations, institutional structures that encourage or discourage trust, and the universal system of norms and rules held by societies. A prisoner's-dilemma situation that would be easy to solve in a firm or a policy network marked by solid trust-based relationships can lead to blockades and suboptimal outcomes under social conditions that do not include trust.

In looking more exactly into the sources of trust, we must first inquire into the conditions under which trust is essential. This task amounts to clarifying the question of what is meant by "trust" in the first place. Two essential things must be noted here: first, blind trust and absolute distrust are apt to more the exception than the rule. Trust might accordingly be plotted along a continuum extending from 0 (absolute distrust) to 1 (absolute trust). Second - and here we get to the core of the significance of trust - trust is relevant in particular in situations marked by **ignorance and uncertainty** as regards the future activities of other actors that affect one's own options.[45] As an action resource, trust is required to do justice to a social reality in which uncertainty and ignorance and imperfect information play a major role in nearly all decision-making constellations.[46] "Trust" is thus of fundamental significance for the reproduction of societies. Shklar (1984, p. 151) argues exactly in this direction: *"Trust is a tentative and intrinsically fragile* *response to our ignorance, a way of coping with the limits of our fore-sight".*

4.2.2.3   Framework Conditions for the Emergence of "Trust"

Evolutionary views see trust as emerging in a historical process as a by-product, a result of chance events or cumulative learning processes and experience. Three evolutionary approaches can be distinguished.

1. We can point to authors like Hayek who interpret "trust" in market economies as a by-product of the process of social order (see Hayek 1978).

2. Axelrod argues entirely differently, though likewise in evolutionary categories (see Axelrod 1984). He attempts to show that trust can also emerge in situations originally characterized by a high level of distrust and lack of communication. Axelrod proceeds from the prisoner's di-lemma and plays through the variants of a case in which the same ac-tors are repeatedly forced to go through the same or similar prisoner's-dilemma situations. Examples would be peace talks between warring parties each of which doubts the other side's credibility; examples of less dramatic cases would be industrial action between employers and employees or efforts to reach solutions in networks in which distrust has become widespread. Axelrod then argues that trust-based relation-ships **can** arise in the course of time (*repeated prisoner's dilemma*) if two basic conditions are met: the parties concerned are unable to avoid confrontation, i.e. have only the choice to fight against one another or to cooperate; the actors know that they are in a situation that can persist and the outcome of which, i.e. the costs and benefits that may accrue in the future, are unknown and thus unpredictably high.

Under these conditions cooperation **can** come about within the context of generalized distrust, because the actors learn that persistent destruc-tiveness is expensive for all parties involved and only cooperation can show a way out of the dilemma. This process can, to be sure, be somewhat time-consuming, since distrust initially finds itself permanently confirmed, thus generating ever renewed distrust. Axelrod demonstrates his thoughts by pointing to the example of two warring parties who can find their way out of the vicious circle of mutual distrust only through cooperation (example: the peace process in the Middle East: Israel-PLO). When this will come about is of course impossible to predict. Axelrod speaks of "random signals" which initiate the transition from confrontation to cooperation. The transition is prepared for by

- an accumulation of knowledge on the constantly rising costs of destructive behavior,

- the insight that it is only by cooperative behavior and the development of mutual interests that the vicious circle of mutual destructiveness can be broken through or indeed transformed into a maximization of mutual utilities, and

- the objective circumstances in which parties are forced to recognize common interests and develop trust (which is of course easier to achieve in "normal industrial disputes" than between warring parties).

"Random signals" are set in motion by the accumulating costs caused to one another by the destructive behavior of the two disputing parties and the fact that both sides realize this. What is interesting about Axelrod's argumentation is that under the specific conditions cooperation can come about even in the context generalized distrust, i.e. trust is not always the condition for interaction and cooperation between actors, it can also be seen as its result (even under unfavorable conditions). Applied to the network problematic, societies with limited experience in cooperation between actors would thus also have a chance to engage in learning processes which, in the end, make it possible to establish networks. And Axelrod's argumentation is interesting for the network discussion for one other reason as well: the idea that trust-based relationships come about as a result of repeated cooperation, i.e. the knowledge of the persons concerned that it is necessary *"again and again to deal with one another"* (Axelrod 1984, p. 4), also defines the reality of networks which are, as a rule, marked by a reciprocal dependence on the part of the actors involved. This constellation, characterized by cooperation that has already proven its worth and the likelihood that this cooperation will continue in the future, encourages the emergence of trust. Market relationships are, in contrast, unable to generate integration of this sort. egoistic-rational actors will attempt to use one-time encounters in the marketplace to exploit the other party and refuse to cooperate. This is the reason why in industrial clusters marked by a minimum of permanent relationships between those involved (see the discussion on systemic competitiveness) it is impossible to reduce the relations between the actors involved to market processes of the type envisaged by the world of neoliberal theory.

3. Scharpf argues along similar lines. Interaction between actors in bargaining systems (networks) is normally conducted on the basis of imperfect information. And thus even slight risk aversion constitutes, in principle, a sufficient ground to display more or less distrustful behavior (see Scharpf 1993, pp. 74 ff.). It was pointed out in the last chapters that distrust between actors in the usual dilemma constellations leads to bargaining blockades and suboptimal outcomes. For Scharpf, trust is fueled by two sources. **On the one hand**, as in Axelrod, trust can be brought about by adjustment pressure. Networks come about as a rule because the actors, if they are to reach a given goal, are forced to rely on the specific inputs of the other persons involved, i.e. the costs of avoidance strategies are high. In view of the growing relevance of networks, which can operate efficiently only on the basis of reciprocal relationships, trust is developed through the "constraints of circumstances". If it proves impossible to create trust and solve problems in a network, many challenges will remain beyond the scope of the individual actors. Scharpf thus represents a functionally grounded optimism as regards the development of trust: if little or nothing works without trust, there develops in the course of time (i.e. evolution) an awareness of the necessity to build and sustain trust-based relationships. Scharpf does, though, also point out that the adjustment pressure directed toward trust-building can turn into generalized trust only if expectations are regularly confirmed in subsequent interactions. Organizational

structures (like networks) that are reliant on trust thus remain fragile and context-dependent.

On the other hand, There is an adjustment pressure operating in the direction of trust, and it does not emerge from specific interaction constellations (in networks, as in Schapf's first argument, or in repeated prisoner's dilemmas, as in Axelrod). Scharpf, referring to Charles Sabel, argues that, in view of the unattractive results invariably generated by distrust, it might be possible to postulate a universal human interest in building trust-based relationships, be it in networks, firms, organizations, or in private relationships (see Scharpf 1993, p. 74; Sabel 1992).

The evolutionary views of Scharpf and Axelrod demonstrate how trust **can** emerge in the form of processes under specific conditions. Whether cooperative, trust-based, or confrontational relationships emerge in the spontaneous process of social development, depends above all on whether the actors are predisposed to place basic trust in the possibilities afforded by trust-based relationships: *"The claim that cooperation can evolve without trust ... is inconceivable in relation to humans without at least a predisposition to trust: when the game has no history a cooperative move is essential to set it on the right track ..."* (Gambetta 1988).

If it is possible to assume basic confidence on the part of actors in the significance of "trust", there are some reasons for the optimistic arguments of the evolutionary view. So the question is what conditions are required for basic trust and what mechanisms are needed to stabilize it. In principle, four dimensions are important here: **first**, the value context and the social and moral resources at the disposal of societies; **second**, the stability of social relations and legal security; **third**, learning-by-doing mechanisms; **fourth**, institutional structures conducive to trust.

It was above all Weber who pointed to the significance of the **value patterns** (religions, moral standards, etc.) prevalent in societies. A minimum of trust can prevail in societies in which family ties safeguard social security and protect the individual from various risks or in highly differentiated societies with a marked social consensus in which individuals are protected against "life risks" and guaranteed equal opportunities and legal security. In the context of stable trust-oriented value patterns, it is easier for individuals, even under the conditions of imperfect information, to avoid "risk aversion", to advance their trust, in this way improving the chances for cooperative, reciprocal action orientations. Value patterns that encourage trust are anchored in the *deep structures* (Senghaas) or *ligatures* (Dahrendorf) of societies and can thus not be arbitrarily "created".

It is, however, controversial whether the advancing differentiation of society and processes of individualization are exhausting the moral resources that fuel the basic trust of actors. There are indications that the market economies have long lived on the reserves of social morality that developed prior to the capitalist revolution (e.g. family solidarity, premodern systems of social obligations, e.g. of the churches). There is also much that indicates that the neoliberal discourse since the mid-1980s, i.e. the cultural inflation of the egoistic-hedonistic *homo oeconomicus* has gone some way toward exhausting solidarity potentials in society. This is also indicated by the studies cited above that show that it is precisely economists geared to man seen in the image of public-choice theory who seek their orientation in free-rider strategies. On the other hand, patterns of organization and governance in economy and society call for new action orientations and actors who are capable of focusing at the same time on both individualistic and public-interest-oriented strategies. There is accordingly pressure operating in the direction of adjustment, and it finds expression in, among other things, the great variety of current discussions on the "bonding force" present in modern societies. It would appear that modern societies are gradually beginning to realize - and not for reasons of sentimentality but as a postulate of reason - that what they need for their reproduction is more than the sum total of the acts of egoistic utility maximizers. This process of growing awareness, supported by appropriate institutional structures, could well lead to a strengthening of systems of norms that encourage reciprocity and trust.

Stable social, economic, and welfare conditions, and, not least, legal security, constitute framework conditions favorable to the development of reciprocal, trust-based relationships, which work in conflict situations as well. On the other hand, it is difficult to build (or rebuild) trust-based relationships - i.e. trust in trust - in contexts marked by unstable socioeconomic conditions, a lack of legal security, and pronounced polarization between social groups. One example would be the rigidified dichotomies between state and economy, employers and labor unions, or human-rights groups and the system of justice in Chile in the years of the Pinochet dictatorship. The generalized distrust that built up here is proving difficult to overcome, now that the dictatorship is over, under democratic conditions. Wage conflicts, for instance, that are relatively simple to settle in stable democracies, can easily escalate and block cooperative problem-solving strategies under the conditions of generalized distrust (which have persisted in post-dictatorship Chile).[47] At the same time, however, Chile can look back to a tradition of democratic, enlightened value patterns that, disregarded by the military dictatorship, were still not fully eradicated. This is likely to be the reason why - despite the atmosphere of generalized distrust created by the military dictatorship - several social subsystems were able relatively quickly to develop cooperation-oriented relations between groups of actors once the transition to democracy was achieved (at the end of the 1980s), in contrast to some other postauthoritarian regimes which lacked any such historically anchored value context (see Mármora/Messner 1991b, Messner 1993b and 1993c).

The thoughts developed on the significance of social value contexts and socioeconomic stability for the emergence and stabilization of trust-based relationships underline the fact that trust, and with it reciprocal relationships, can not simply be "implemented". Social structures that encourage trust are in this sense something like lost historical property; Gambetta speaks of *"social luck"* (1988, p. 231). It is important here not to underestimate the forces of inertia in societies. Laws and policies can be altered quickly, grown value systems, moral concepts, i.e. basic trust, are, however, social variables that change only very slowly.

If societies have, or give rise to, basic trust, a minimum of trust capacity on the part of actors, this, like other behavioral patterns, can be stabilized and expanded by *learning by doing*, **repetition, and imitation**. Trust and the cooperative and reciprocal relationships built on it can be practiced: cooperation is stabilized by successful cooperative behavior; trust is reproduced and deepened by positive experience with trust. Hirschman points to the important fact that trust is one of the few goods that are not exhausted by being consumed, utilized, or used; quite on the contrary: *"Trust is depleted through not being used"* (Hirschman 1984, p. 92).

Trust can in the end be supported by **institutional structures**. Charles Sabel emphasizes the organizational dimension of trust-based relationships. He speaks in this context of the *"procedural character of trust"* (Sabel 1993, p. 92), which is to say that the institutional arrangements of a society can either encourage or undermine the development of trust-based relationships: favorable are organizational structures that, for instance, are characterized by relationships based on the rule of law, transparency of information, institutionalized monitoring mechanisms, consultations, high communication density, and reflexivity. The characteristics of an institutional structure that facilitates the formation of trust could be enriched by the six packages of factors noted by Michael Walzer as a way of describing the institutional contours of a society that - in his sense - faces up to the problem of justice. The normative foundations of a given society are not given by nature, they are a cultural achievement that must be sustained and are in need of corresponding institutions.

4.2.3   Dimensions of the Strategic Capacity of Network Actors and Networks

The efficiency of networks is based on the strategic capacity of the actors involved. The strategic capacity of actors in turn is based on consciously shaping decisions with regard to three dimensions. The following three points must be kept in mind if strategic orientations are to be developed:

- the **time dimension**, i.e. the *"generalized capacity for global maximization ... related to the future"*.[48] This point addresses the capacity of actors to make future-oriented decisions, to weigh and to assert future interests against immediate, often short-term and myopic present interests;

- the **goal dimension**, i.e., first, the capacity to weigh different alternative actions and to choose from them the one that appears most viable as a means of attaining the goal system aimed for, and, second, the capacity to adapt the goal system and the action strategies needed to attain it flexibly and quickly to rapidly changing framework conditions and requirements;

- the **interest dimension**, which refers to the capacity of actors to evaluate and (whenever possible) anticipate the strategies of other actors whose actions are important to attaining goals once set, and to do so with an eye to coordinating the action options available for the purpose.

However, strategic capacity does not automatically emerge against this background: there can be tradeoffs both in the time dimension and with regard to defining the goal to be aimed for. Divergent goal and time preferences that can be imagined will force actors to **set priorities**. For instance, it is not possible to aim for an arbitrary number of goals within a given period of time, and thus it becomes necessary to establish time hierarchies. Also, specific goals may conflict to some extent (e.g. fighting inflation and growth policies) or even collide; in both cases it is necessary to define the priorities of specific goals with respect to others. In other cases goals will prove unattainable when they run up against insurmountable power structures. The strategic capacity of actors accordingly depends fundamentally of their ability and willingness *"to accept, or to impose, these necessary sacrifices"* (Scharpf 1991b, p. 283).

If priorities are to be set, the necessary condition is a minimum of **expert knowledge concerning effective contexts** in the sphere under discussion. If such expert knowledge is available, strategic capacity will depend on whether the actors are able, under the real conditions facing them, to realize the **temporal, factual, and interest-related limitations on their activities**, perceive both concrete and restricted scopes of action, i.e. to embark, against this background, on a well-founded, nonvoluntarist strategy that will remain **stable within a predictable time frame**.

Actors involved in networks are additionally, and for the reasons cited, faced with the fact that they can usually only realize their interests in a network by cooperating with other actors on the basis of a problem-solving orientation worked out jointly. This restriction distinguishes them from actors who endeavor only to achieve their own individual "utility function". The latter can also try their hand with strategies that are geared - e.g. through the use of power resources - to realizing individual interests against the goals of other actors.

If we apply these thoughts on the strategic capacity of actors to the issue of the strategic capacity of networks, we are first faced with the question whether networks can be understood at all as "collective actors" with specifiable strategies. It can be said that networks, no less than organizations, firms, or states, are then perceived by third parties as engaging in actions and strategies, if they represent identifiable interests over a longer period of time and develop their activities as a social unit that evinces a certain measure of coherence and stability.

Following this argumentation, we must first note that the strategic capacity of networks builds on the specific efficiency and strategic capacity of the actors participating in them. A group of inefficient actors weak in strategic capacity will not be able to bring about a strong network. On the other hand, the existence of a group of strong actors does not yet imply any ability on their part to work productively together in a network. It might, for instance be imagined that precisely strong actors will tend to underestimate the possibilities and potentials that can emerge in networks on the basis of cooperation. There are examples enough of this phenomenon from the world of business. It is often the market leaders and traditional top corporations that insist too long on their autonomy and pay for this antiquated autonomy strategy by being outdistanced by new "networked firms".

A network is in any case always more than the sum of its parts. As a result of the reciprocal dependence of the actors on the governance resources of other actors, networks as actor groups are as a rule forced to develop joint **problem-solving orientations.** The capacity to develop a joint problem-solving orientation is accordingly an initial foundation of the strategic capacity of networks. Aside from the three dimensions outlined above that confront individual actors who want to develop strategic capacity, networks must take into account a fourth, **interpersonal dimension.** What is meant by this is the fact that networks must as overall systems be capable of identifying, and taking seriously, divergent time and goal preference as well as problems and approaches of the individual network actors, and they must also be able to focus **jointly formed interests** and integrate them within a viable action concept valid for the overall network.

This capacity to bring together internal potentials to form a strategy, while not losing sight of existing interest conflicts, presupposes that the actors are able to **compromise and solve conflicts** and that the networks have adequate **problem-solving mechanisms.** It is also important to recognize the limits of joint action and to concentrate cooperation in fields in which common strategies can be implemented. This process of focusing know-how can boost the creativity and problem-solving competence of a network as compared with the effectiveness of individual actors, though the ensuing increase in complexity, ever-present latent conflicts, and difficulties in finding compromises can also lead to paralysis and inability to act or structurally conservative orientations that can result - in the course of the process of compromise - from an exaggerated level of cognitive standardization within the network.

4.2.4 The "Radical Individualist": A Network Actor Doomed to Failure - The "Public-choice Society": Unsuited to Mobilizing the Governance Potential of Networks

As we have seen, the social functional logic of networks is grounded in principles situated beyond the premises of public-choice theory. Networks can fully harness their efficiency and problem-solving potentials only on the basis of a set of rules (willingness to compromise, respect for the legitimate interests of other actors) and the development of a solution-oriented decision style geared to the development and implementation of common criteria of justice and distribution, fair exchange, and voluntary restriction of individual scopes of action. Reciprocity is the functional principle of networks; yet a minimum of trust between the actors is the basic condition that has to be met if bargaining is to work in networks.

The "Radical Individualist" and the Functional Logic of Networks ·

This set of rules constitutes a framework that guarantees the capacity to act and to solve problems despite the existence side by side of common, individual, and conflicting interests. The "individual utility maximizer" of public-choice theory will be able to act successfully only in networks in which his individual interests and the common interests of the network are absolutely congruent. As soon as interest constellations occur that, as in the case of the battle-of-the-sexes situations discussed above, require agreement on common criteria of evaluation and justice, the development of a common problem-solving orientation, and curtailments of individual preferences, networks are faced with the serious risk of sterile "endless discussions" without an outcome, action blockades, or indeed the collapse of negotiations. The "egoistic utility maximizer" has as good as no reasons to abandon his preferences. The willingness to aim for joint problem-solving orientations and to gear individual action to compromise and reciprocity is beyond the scope of his rationale. And any interiorization of the action logic of the "utility maximizer" is evidently fertile soil for free-rider behaviors. This is indicated by the "experiments" that found that individuals whose view of the world and scientific methodology are keyed to the premises of public choice theory tend more in the direction of opportunistic behavior than others. This basic position thus constitutes an extremely unfavorable presupposition for action in networks.

"Public-choice Philosophy" and the Working Capacity of Networks

The working of networks is essentially dependent on the existence of trust between the actors involved. All three mixed-motive games discussed (prisoner's dilemma, chicken game, battle of the sexes) require a minimum of trust if the best possible solutions are to be reached. In all three cases the fear of opportunistic behavior on the part of the other actors, i.e. even a low level of risk aversion, will lead to obstruction of network dynamics.

If it is correct to say that network constructions gain significance in differentiated societies in that they constitute an organizational pattern that can, under certain conditions, work out solutions to problems that are beyond the reach of markets and hierarchies, then we can easily understand why it is that "value debates" are experiencing a heyday in all Western societies. It is becoming clear that the economic and social philosophy dominant since the 1980s in many industrialized and developing countries alike (neoliberalism ands public-choice theory) has given birth to a value concept that is difficult to reconcile with the demands that networks place on societies. At times, as was shown with reference to the conservative communitarians, this value discussion drifts off into a premodern romanticism which play off universalism and the liberal society against the integrative potentials of "communities" and particularist worldviews. At any rate, the revival of the value discussion reflects a crisis of the concept of the "egoistic utility maximizer" and the societies in which this concept is firmly anchored.

"Public-choice Societies" and the Working Capacity of Networks

The social functional logic of networks differs both from the action orientation of radical individualism and from any fusion of divergent interests in an integrated organization. Public-choice theory has no concept for the organizational type represented by the network, because it is able to comprehend collectives only as homogenized aggregates consisting of the preferences of members, who, as individuals, are not seen as having any autonomous intentionalities. From the perspective of public-choice theory, activities of social interest organizations in a policy field can be conceptualized only in terms of lobbyism and clientelism. This view was elucidated with reference to the studies published by Olson on the institutional sclerosis of industrial societies. Here, every actor, every organization is geared exclusively to injecting its own interests into the policy process, and seeing them realized. In the real world there are many examples of these phenomena. They are, however, not "necessary" phenomena but the result of specific action orientations that have been elevated to the status of a norm in public-choice theory and in radical free-marketeering worldviews.[49] My thesis is thus: The functioning of networks is undermined by radical-liberal norm structures that feature the "rational egoist" as a model. The "public-choice society" (as a theoretical ideal type) is thus limited in its "fitness for networks".

In societies one-sidedly oriented to radical liberalism and the premises of public-choice theory (e.g. the USA), social organizations tend more strongly to beleaguer the political sphere with lobbyism, thus accelerating tendencies toward an institutionalization of power and undercutting the latitudes open to the political sphere. Productive network formations that are able to harness individual and community interests to the goal of working to find collective solutions, and in doing so rely on resources such as trust, curtailment of individual scopes of action, skills in working out common criteria of justice and evaluation, and appropriate social institutions, will encounter unfavorable conditions in "public-choice societies". In societies in which radical-liberal theoretical concepts of society form part of the existing hegemonial order of values, network structures are accordingly, first, less likely to be found; second, are less likely to develop; and third, they will, when they do exist, be seriously threatened by a tendency to assume the role typical of lobbying organizations, thus falling short of the problem-solving potentials typical of networks. In short: Societies geared to public-choice theories are inadequately prepared for the demands posed by the "network society".

Societies that have traditions in social cooperation and concerted action between groups of actors or social classes aimed at solving social conflicts are more apt to be capable of harnessing the productive potentials of networks. This is of course not to say that no lobbyism will occur in these societies. The representation of particularist interests in pluralist societies is an important task of interest organizations. It might, however, be assumed that the norm and value systems of societies experienced in cooperation and concerted action (e.g. Japan, with its close links between state and industry; northern European countries, with their marked "social-democratic consensus", or Germany, with its experience with neocorporative political patterns) are more "compatible" with the functional logic of networks. That is to say, it is more likely that in such circumstances network-based cooperation will emerge beside policy forums concerned with the representation of particularist interests, and that these network-based organizations (in some cases the same ones) will be the ones concerned with elaborating solutions to common problems. These countries are likely to be faced with the challenge of cutting back the hierarchical patterns of concerted action and the exaggerated statist governance claims typically encountered in the past, of expanding the scopes open for social self-coordination (and for networks), and of adapting the functions of state-level governance to the new exigencies posed by "network societies".

Walzer's thoughts on harnessing dialectically the *"art of separation"* with the *"art of connection"* as sources of the social capacity for learning, transformation, and integration or Etzioni's assumption of a partial overlap of the *"ego with the whole"* amount to theoretical search processes that hold more promise for the analysis of network-like organizational patterns in societies than the dominant public-choice theories.

4.3   Procedures and Institutional Mechanisms for Strengthening the Problem-solving Orientation in Networks

The scope of action of networks is based on their institutional consolidation and the development of common views, orientations, and strategies on the part of the actors concerned. The chapter dealing with the institutional consolidation of networks pointed out that the individual architecture of networks is always situated in the field of forces delineated by disintegration (too weak ties) and overly dense relationships (too strong ties) (see core problem 3, Overview 6). In terms of their institutional structure, networks are confronted with three core problems:

-    The institutional consolidation of networks can lead to functional and cognitive straits and end up in collective conservatism. (core problem 2)

-    The development of a common identity and closer patterns of co-operation within networks can encourage intended and unintended externalizations of costs at the expense of the network environment (compromising at the expense of third parties). (core problem 5)

-    Networks can founder on their own inability to work out the common criteria of distribution and evaluation needed to judge possible alternative solutions. This problem is particularly relevant in battle-of-the-sexes constellations. (core problem 4)

In the first two cases (core problems 2 and 5), we are faced with the paradox that an important condition for the functioning of a network consists in enabling and advancing cooperation between the actors involved; exaggerated cooperation as a mechanism for coping with conflicts can, however, at the same time lead to the pathologies outlined above. The last chapters pointed out that the concern should never be cooperation "at any price". The concern must be, **first of all**, not to neutralize the force-field between cooperation and conflict, with its divergent views, perceptions, and search orientations, by harmonizing and "streamlining it; instead, the task at hand is to manage it. It is precisely this field of force that constitutes one of the essential sources of innovation. Productive conflicts must be harnessed to broaden the information base for decisions and to examine as closely as possible alternative scenarios, i.e. to encourage the broadest possible search and learning processes. Neutralizing the force-field surrounding conflict and cooperation in favor of simple cooperation is a recipe for losses in creativity.

Second, cooperation in a network must be geared to substantive goals and governance and target-formulation functions that can be realized; action in a network must be given a direction (e.g. in "regional conferences": strengthening a region's competitiveness). If efforts to define a substantive orientation of this sort fails, cooperation will become an end in itself, one that is most likely to ensure the continued existence of the network at any price and to safeguard the privileges of the actors involved (cognitive blockade, collective conservatism). Accordingly, the condition of the efficiency of network governance is a clear-cut definition of the tasks and goals of a network and the problem-solving orientation of the actors associated with it. This problem-solving orientation can be stabilized by actor self-restraint, but also by external control (e.g. by the state or the public).

The problem-solving orientation makes it easier to gear actor cooperation to targeted goals (e.g. strengthening a region's competitiveness), and it can thus be used as a gauge of network activity. An explicit definition of goals and a commitment of the actors to the imperative of a common problem-solving orientation (prior to any consideration of particularist interests) can contribute to attenuating the trend toward "collective conservatism" (e.g. option for subsidies for traditional industries in a network instead of for structural change and a strengthening of future-oriented industries) (core problem 2). Furthermore, it is possible to reduce any particularly unintended externalizations of costs at the expense of the network environment if there is an awareness of this inherent tendency and the corresponding problem-solving orientation gains the day (core problem 5). Networks that remain unaware of the potentially counterproductive, destructive consequences of their activities for their environment may be able to optimize their own subsystem, though in doing so they will contribute to fragmenting society.

A note must be added here: Whether the goal system aimed for is viable will often become visible only in retrospect. An example: Well-organized networks aimed at optimizing one-sidedly inward-looking industries, e.g. in Brazil, have failed not for internal reasons but because they were geared to an economic concept that proved to be a dead-end street. In the end, no network and no society is immune to this danger of looking primarily to the interests of projects not keyed to the future. The contribution that networks can make to reducing this danger of "misorientation" is that the collective learning processes, the focusing of know-how, and the ongoing discussion over divergent views which they entail increase the probability of a higher level of "collective intelligence".

The bargaining blockades that may occur if a network fails to decide in favor of one of a number of alternative solution-oriented approaches (core problem 4) result not from the paradox logic of cooperation in networks but from the difficulty involved in working out common criteria of distribution and evaluation. This problem area, too, can only be solved with the aid of problem-solving orientations on the part of network actors. Confrontational strategies and patterns of action based on exchange orientations lead in many cases - as was demonstrated - to bargaining blockades.

The question is what institutional mechanisms can contribute toward encouraging problem-solving orientations in networks and countering tendencies operating in the direction of stabilizing the power of compromises reached at the lowest possible denominator and geared to solving problems at the expense of third parties.

One of the first important considerations is that network actors must develop an awareness of the social dynamics and functional logic, the strengths and pitfalls of network organizations. This problem consciousness can doubtless be presupposed when, for instance, we look at the state of the discussion on network organization as an indicator: the scholarly and the policy-oriented literature on the network problematic breaks down into two camps (though there are some exceptions) which either romantically praise the potentials of the "collective reason" of networks or roundly dispute their action and problem-solving potentials. The current literature no doubt reflects accurately the way the chances and risks of network governance are perceived by potential network actors. The actors involved should therefore, in the initial phase of a network, gradually clarify the possibilities and limitations of network organization. Transparency is the best foundation on which to build targeted strategies to circumnavigate the shoals of network organization.

Three methods can be of use to encourage actors to develop a common problem-solving orientation:

1. **Procedural conditions** for bargaining, mechanisms for settling conflicts and mediating interests in networks should be coordinated and put in place as means of building trust between the actors and creating clear expectational horizons. The actors involved should not proceeded on the assumption that reciprocal relationships and common problem-solving orientations will emerge as it were automatically in a network. If discussions over binding rules (consultation of arbitrators in cases of conflict, recognition of the legitimate interests of others, etc.) are initiated before real conflicts have taken shape, the chances of averting bargaining blockades will increase accordingly. In other words, the main consideration is to translate the above-noted functional principles of network organization into mechanisms of anticipatory conflict solution and universally accepted rules.

2. **Communication processes concerning notions of evaluation, distribution, and fairness** should also, wherever possible, be initiated

prior to the emergence of real conflicts in order to diminish the likelihood of escalating conflicts and bargaining blockades.

3. Development of procedural conditions for reaching a fair compromise on costs and benefits stabilizes actor expectations ad ensures that reciprocity will remain a valid principle, thus making is possible to arrange for **subsequent tie-in deals**. This makes it possible to reach compromises that may burden some actors more than others and that may entail binding obligations to decide in the future in favor of the interests those bearing the major share of the present burdens. This pattern of decision-making tends to increase the flexibility of action in networks. Tie-in deals can constitute an instrument that can be used to reduce the pressure to find, for each individual case, a common denominator and a complete compromise of the interests concerned. Solution-oriented decisions are more likely under these conditions.

By stabilizing expectations, all three procedures contribute to introducing a future orientation into networks. Future orientation and "farsightedness" are important factors in overcoming the logic of the *"omnipresence of the present"* (Lechner 1994, p. 5) that tends to dominate market societies.

Even when networks succeed, on the basis of the procedures outlined, in creating stable expectations, harnessing the field of tension between conflict and cooperation, formulating common goals, and aiming concretely at realizing future orientations against well-organized present interests, the self-interests of the actors concerned will nevertheless have to be dealt with in each individual case.

It is possible to infer from the empirical findings of network research three methods that can contribute to influencing (not: neutralizing) the tense relationship between compromise of interests and problem-solving in favor of an interests in reaching solutions. Those active in networks are as a rule representatives of their organizations/firms. If a network fails to get beyond a pure representation of the particular interests (lobby logic), activities will remain at the level of the smallest common denominator and end up in collective conservatism. Scopes of action in a network can only unfold when the network is given a relatively free hand to formulate its approaches. Here we can once again point to cooperation of a variety of different regional actors pursuing the common goal of boosting the competitiveness of their industrial region. Strengthening competitiveness implies structural change. And it often proves possible to encourage such change when a network's goals can be detached somewhat from the individual utility rationales of the actors involved. If this is not done, the potential losers of the process of structural change will determine the pace and direction of network activities. Under these conditions a network can prove more a brake on the process of economic restructuring.

Political practice encounters this problem by setting up research and advisory institutions or expert councils that (can) provide for a measure of separation between problem analysis and expert proposals on the one hand and any possible consternation on the other. These institutions are (in principle) capable of working out solution-oriented analyses and action-oriented proposals. They can in this way take on important functions in the phase of policy preparation.

It is somewhat difficult to decouple decision-making competence and subjective willingness to accept the effects of decisions made in networks which, as a result of the distribution of governance resources over a number of actors, are geared to solving problems only via horizontal cooperation and coordination. One characteristic of networks is that in them decision-makers and those affected by such decisions are often one and the same person. To remain with the example referred to above: advisory institutions can cast light on problem analyses and action perspectives for a process of regional structural change, though they often are only in possession of partial information, codified knowledge. Practice-relevant detailed knowledge, *tacit knowledge* (e.g. on new challenges for universities and training institutions that develop in connection with the creation of new industries, environmental impacts, information on problems of implementation and control involved in the introduction of technical standards) are tied to the organizations and firms concerned and not readily accessible to research and advisory institutions.

Thus the question is under what conditions it may be possible to at least partially separate action motivations and action orientations in networks from the immediate interests of the organizations concerned. Against the background of empirical analyses, Renate Mayntz points to the following patterns of differentiation that can prove useful in implementing problem-solving orientations (Mayntz 1993):

1. One possibility would be an **institutional differentiation** into commissions and arenas in which it is possible to negotiate compromises of interest and solutions of problems separately. A differentiation between bodies at least implies the chance to develop subject-oriented solutions and to prevent the search matrix from being narrowed down too quickly by specific interests. This, however, does not imply that once the bodies are linked, i.e. in the process of decision-making, the problem-oriented view will prove able to win the day against the pressure to compromise interests.

2. We can also observe **situational differentiations** in which, even in constellations involving decision-makers who stand to be affected adversely, a problem-solving orientation is upheld. A development of this sort is no doubt more apt to come about in situations of deep crisis or under great external stress (e.g. in the context of structural adjustment measures of the World Bank in developing countries). Mayntz notes that in the situation of change entailed by German unification the members of the Science Council, asked to work out a proposal for restructuring the science system in the east and west of Germany, came up with a standard acceptable to all parties, one which rules out as inappropriate any insistence on preserving vested institutional interests. In other words, specific situations often offer the opportunity of defining collective decision-making situations as such, postponing the pursuit of self-interests, and aiming for solutions *"in the interest of the matter at hand"* (Mayntz 1993, p. 52).

3. One important consideration is that networks usually entail cooperation between the representatives of organizations. Organizations in turn are not monolithic structures; indeed, their structure consists of many different levels. Organizational sociology has determined that actors

within institutions often hold highly divergent action orientations. Crozier/Friedberg (1979) use the term *"zones of indifference"* to designate the action autonomy of members of organizations. This **differentiation of levels of identification** can be used in networks to strengthen concrete problem-solving orientations.

The decisive consideration is that, according to experience, professional experts (engineers, economists, etc.) are more strongly keyed to issue-related arguments than members of management hierarchies, who feel more committed to "their" organization. In other words, there are good reasons, at least in the phase of problem identification, situation analysis, and consideration of possible solutions, to leave the field over to professional experts in order to prevent any overly rapid narrowing down of views and search matrices, which can result from the inevitable clash of conflicting self-interests. Two examples: In innovation networks in which engineers from R&D departments of competing firms work together we often find that formal information barriers that exist between firms can be overcome at the level of direct expert interaction in the interest of cooperation keyed to innovation. Another interesting example is negotiations in international standardization organizations in the field of telecommunications aimed at developing technical standards to ensure the compatibility of different electronic systems. Here manufacturers and national telephone companies are represented by technical experts. These bodies, comparable with sectoral policy networks, are committed to finding, in joint cooperation, technically optimal solutions, and thus argue in purely technical terms. It is on this basis that solution-oriented action strategies can be developed; vested economic and political interests of the organizations involved play only a secondary role here.

Finally, it must be borne in mind that in the process of network development the organizations concerned become more "permeable"; demarcations between the inside world and the outside world begin to blur. The network logic is carried into the organizations involved, and at the same time the networks reflect, in various refractions, the interests and orientations of all persons involved as well as different external influences and "inherent necessities".

4.4   "Openness" of Network Structures as a Motor of Innovation

Close interaction between network actors, consensus orientation, and the elaboration of joint orientations and visions contribute to consolidating networks. Development of routines, common standards, expectations, and models creates counterbalances to the *"adhocracy"* (Mintzenberg/McHugh 1985) of market societies, reduces uncertainties over the future, and improves the conditions under which actors can develop a stable expectational horizon; and this facilitates the formation of strategic orientations, long-term modernization and innovation strategies. This process of interlinking actors and homogenizing their perceptions always entails at the same time the risk of functional and cognitive blockades. An interesting paradox takes shape: on the one hand, the collective elaboration of long-term orientations, models, and visions is, precisely under the conditions of great turbulence and uncertainty typical for complex societies, the *conditio sine qua non* for any innovative political formulation of structures and realization of future interests against present interests. On the other hand, ever more unified views and the necessary definition of and commitment to development corridors at the same time entail "artificial" reductions of complexity and marginalization of alternative solutions that might likewise have been practicable.

The longer and more successfully a well-organized network operates, remains within a given development corridor, thus optimizing the space defined by the corridor and increasing the density of interaction and communication there, the more strong will be its risk of closing itself off from its environment, of ignoring new challenges and risks and becoming self-referential. This process ends up in

-    organization myopia and ignorance of new development corridors,

-    externalization of costs (e.g. environmental, social costs) at the expense of the overall system (*"subsystem paternalism"*),[50]

-    clientelism and corruption,

- the exclusion of new actors, who might generate adjustment pressure, introduce new visions, and disrupt the existing balance in an interaction nexus that has rigidified into routine,

- rigidity that will prove more pronounced the more tight the originally loose ties between the actors were and that can, in the worst possible case, lead to the development of monopoly-like structures which threaten to eliminate the initial creativity of the organizational form *"between markets and hierarchies"*.

What is required if these tendencies (summarized in core problems 2 and 5 of network governance, Overview 6) are to be countered is "contradictory and corrective potential". On the one hand, a network can only be put under pressure and monitored "from outside" if the negative trends outlined above are rendered transparent and thus accessible to correction. The key role here is played by the openness of the political system, democratic public opinion, the media, or the state, which is in a position to monitor social networks or at least to influence the framework conditions under which they operate. On the other hand, network actors can easily counteract these tendencies - which are in the end counterproductive to their collective efficiency - by integrating conflict and corrective potential in their network-related activities. One might think here of including labor unions and environmental groups and experts in networks concerned with locational-policy issues as a means of avoiding the danger that their search process may be narrowed down to economic terms alone.

In view of the complexity, the risk of cognitive blockades and institutional rigidification, that networks have to deal with, "insubordinate outsiders", "troublemakers", "rule-breakers", and "interlopers" have to be understood as "exogenous learning incentives" and motors of innovation that can assume the following functions:

1. By introducing into networks *"external elements of meaning"* (Wiesenthal 1994, p. 148), it is possible to overcome their blindness for **creativity potentials beyond the defined development corridor and rigidified common models.** Troublemakers need not necessarily al-

ways be right, nor be what networks call for, but they can at any rate provide for cognitive mobility.

2. The critical potential in networks can assume **warning functions** and facilitate a rapid adjustment to changing conditions. Ecological movements and green parties played this role in western Europe in the 1980s. In many of his publication John Kenneth Galbraith has pointed to the crucial significance of counterbalances to dominant trends as an essential element of the capacity of societies for social learning, coining for this phenomenon the term *"countervailing powers"*.

3. The effective potential of "troublemakers", their articulation of perceptions and interpretations not covered by the received truths, can take on the shape of **cognitive innovation**. Far-reaching upheavals in particular (this is less the case for incremental changes) often occur beyond the scope defined by dominant expectations.

Complex, nontransparent, interdependent problems with which networks are confronted call for discontinuous, multiple interpretive efforts and views of the problem at hand. Institutionalizing "responsible disloyalty" by consciously integrating contradictory potentials in network architectures, and the readiness not to marginalize corrective potentials but to harness them productively as a potential sources of innovation, can contribute considerably to this end. What is essential is that conflicts and divergent perceptions not be permitted to lead to a disintegration or obstruction of communication contexts; they must remain communicable. In networks in which both public and private actors play important parts, the state has the function of providing for "counterbalances" as a means of controlling the inherent dynamics of particularist interests.

Integrating contradictory potentials within the world of networks, and the readiness of network actors to acknowledge them, can be facilitated by a phenomenon known in pluralism theory as *"overlapping membership"* (Truman 1951, pp. 157 ff.). The persons active in networks are representatives of organizations who, aside from organizational interests, also - sometimes even chiefly - bring to bargaining and decision-making processes their own professional interests and standards, thus facilitating issue- and solution-oriented strategies. And, what is more, individuals have "multiple identities" that they are unable to "discard" fully in their professional work. Chemical engineers are often at the same time members of environmental groups or victims of ecological damage; industrial representatives or union leaders are recipients of subsidies and taxpayers, etc. These multiple identities can strengthen the cognitive openness in networks and counteract *"subsystem paternalism"* (Habermas) and the tendency to narrow down search and learning processes in the course of the process of network consolidation.

4.5   The Significance of Networks in Phases of the Policy Process

Classical theory of the state assigns to the state the exclusive competence for formulating policies. Networks and policy formulation on the basis of horizontal coordination come about spontaneously or are initiated (by the state, but also by private organizations and/or firms) in social sectors in which hierarchical state-level governance has failed. Policy networks constitute, despite the forms of network failure outlined above, an organizational pattern suited to move into the vacuum that comes about when the state, in specific sectors, is no longer in possession of sufficient autonomy of action to govern society from its central position.

Critics of network governance argue that horizontal coordination among a great number of actors can entail high transaction costs and paralysis of the decision process. These arguments are correct (see core problems 1 and 2 of Overview 6); but in view of the growing number of policy fields in which the state has foundered on the complexity of the policy field to be governed and shaped and is thus forced to rely on cooperation with social actors, it is not a sufficient ground to decide against network governance. Growing differentiation of social subsectors leads to the development of independent, decentrally active organizations and subsystems (i.e. independence), while at the same time giving rise to increasing interdependence on the part of the actors concerned, who, if they are to tackle their tasks successfully and realize their goals, are forced to rely on interaction with others and the proper functioning of their environment. It is not only the state, many other social actors and organizations have also lost some of their autonomy of action in the permanent process of increasing social differentiation. This state of affairs can increasingly be observed in many fields of economic and locational policy as well as in environmental, social, and regional policy.

Now, the judgment (not to say prejudice) of many network critics is that the participation of an overly large number of actors in the process of political governance leads a priori to incapacitation. The chapter of this study on the limitations of network governance (**Problem of numbers**) showed that this problem does exist. What follows will show that the notion that in networks invariably all actors work together in an equal and balanced fashion in all phases of the policy process, jointly attending to all current tasks and thus faced with coordination problems that can hardly be coped with, fails to do justice to the organizational pattern represented by the network. Every policy process, ideally, runs through six phases (see Overview 5) in which definable governance functions have to be tackled, different groups of actors take on specific tasks, and specific governance instruments are of significance. The following presentation constitutes a woodcut-style description of an ideal-typical sequence of the policy process in a network. The point of departure is the case of a policy network in which state institutions work together with private actors.

1. Problem identification, assessment of problem relevance, analysis of effective contexts relevant to governance: This phase is concerned with the basic task of bringing together knowledge that is relevant to governance and distributed across a number of different actors; the aims here are, first, to place proposed policy projects on the broadest possible know-how footing and, second, to ensure that the participating organizations have a higher level of transparency, including for their own organizational activities. Governance relevant knowledge includes both technical/problem-oriented information, i.e. the "sifting through" of a great variety of possible interpretations and rival, conflicting perspectives, and precise knowledge of interests and power structures in a given policy field.

For stable networks this represents a permanent field of activities. It involves observing processes, changes, new requirements and checking into the need for adjustments at the level of specific policy fields. This collective learning process at the same time gives rise to know-how that can be used by the participating organizations to optimize their individual action strategies. One might also think here of ad hoc networks that are constituted (sometimes by state institutions as well) solely with the goal of pooling the knowledge resources of a variety of actors in the preparatory phase of a projected policy reform in order to heighten a policy project's chances of success.

The important thing in this phase is to initiate broad-based, common search and learning processes. It therefore makes sense to involve as many actors as possible who are in a position to contribute to this end. These are as a rule responsible state institutions, organizations that stand to be affected (firms, labor unions, social groups) or the interest organizations and federations representing them, functional institutions (R&D institutions, technically oriented sectoral institutions, etc.), and self-help organizations or citizens' initiatives, which, in contrast to established federations, are as a rule geared to one or a limited number of goals and exist for a limited period of time.

The state is disburdened by the work of networks. Its task is not to master the challenge (in many cases long since beyond its scope in any event) of accumulating comprehensive know-how in every single policy field in order to steer policy without any reference to the social actors concerned. The relief provided in this way makes it possible for the state to reduce bureaucracies that have invested much time and expense in accumulating the detailed information required to grasp the know-how available in society. Instead, the state takes on tasks involved in coordination, organization, and moderation in order to bring together actor knowledge in the policy-preparation process. The state can in this way concentrate more effectively on strategic, conceptual tasks (e.g.: in what direction is the process to be steered; technology assessment/"policy assessment"). Network organization is thus a concept that can be used to gain mastery of the "knowledge problem", one of the central problems of governance, and at the same time to avoid the errors made in the heyday of "rational policy planning", which consisted chiefly in building growing state bureaucracies to "gather information".

The function of nonstate actor groups consists in contributing relevant know-how. Their motivation to contribute such inputs is as a rule based on their own interest in the information of other actors as well as their need for an efficient environment and given framework conditions that they regard as pertinent, and it is often impossible shape these conditions without any network-based cooperation.

State institutions active in a network are also in need of **strategic knowledge** in order to be able to exercise their governance functions. Nonstate actors, in particular interest organizations, will always be torn between representing their own interests (lobbying) and actively cooperating with an eye to finding solutions in the network. One could, for instance, imagine that individual organizations might hold back strategically important knowledge in the hope of obtaining the information of other participants without divulging their own. For state institutions, disburdened of their need to gather detailed information of their own, two other fields of activity emerge: first, core ministerial-level tasks include the above-mentioned coordination and moderation functions as well as concentration on the development and realization of strategic orientations; second, ministries, supported by research and advisory institutions, must be able to provide contributions of their own to the process of problem perception and analysis of governance-relevant effective contexts so as to be in a position to assess the information provided by others, to be taken seriously as interlocutors, and to ensure that no one-sidedly power-based particularist interests are able push their interests through. Interfaced know-how can prove to be strategic knowledge here. Private network actors will as a rule have specific knowledge concerning their own organizations; building interfaced know-how is geared to focusing different inputs to form an overall strategy.

This perspective goes beyond governance-theoretical positions that reduce the role of the state to purely moderator functions. Without a "critical mass" of strategically relevant knowledge, a moderator will quickly find himself at the mercy of the best-organized interests - the "Olson phenomenon" could then pose a threat. Furthermore, the state is, as a democratically legitimated authority, in the last analysis obliged to take "overriding" aspects into account, while private networks will first of all (be able to) represent their own particularist interests and then - in the best case - overall sectoral viewpoints. State institutions should be able and willing to provide for solution-oriented search and learning processes in the policy-preparation phase. If "the state" assumes in a network a one-sidedly partisan approach not oriented to finding concrete solutions, the network organization will turn into a structure that may advance and perpetuate a society's power structures and rigidifications. Here, too, we see that networks can be instruments of both domination and power, that they can be used to integrate potentials for change and to postpone reform pressure, and that they can be a form of organization that can be used to focus the problem-solving potentials of a society, to facilitate and accelerate reforms.

This phase of the policy process is marked by a "soft", procedural governance consisting in bringing together the strategically important actors (high density of communications and information). This communication process between organizations that otherwise operate decentrally counters the fragmentation tendencies in specific policy fields by encouraging integration-friendly initiatives (bridging mechanisms).

2. Development of solution-oriented approaches: This process can, depending on the problem to be solved or the task to be formulated, prove very difficult (e.g. because alternative solutions are conceivable that affect network actors differently; battle-of-the-sexes constellations); yet it is also conceivable for common solution-oriented strategies to be developed on the basis of a problem analysis accepted by all parties. We can note here, with reference to Thompson (1967, pp. 54

ff.), that it is in general possible to distinguish in networks three types of coordination problem and the patterns of solution corresponding to them.

The first case is concerned with coordination problems that can be solved by **standardization**. Examples would be the establishment of technical standards, emission limits, industrial safety rules, quality standards. The establishment of standards can in many cases entail conflict. Then, however, the actors, using the new framework conditions they have defined, are in a position to shape the remaining options completely autonomously. In this case, network coordination ends when the binding standards have been defined. The task that remains is for state-level or private institutions to monitor and control compliance with the framework agreed upon.

The second case is concerned with **"sequential interdependence"**. The matter involved here is to set priorities in a network and to establish time sequences. One example of this would be defining the time-related coordination and priorities required to develop physical and nonphysical infrastructure in an economic region. Firms and organizations can plan for the long term when the priorities and time sequences of infrastructure development have been reliably defined. Thompson speaks in this connection of **"coordination by plan"**, through joint development of **"decision schedules"**. On the basis of the coordination processes initiated in a network, the actors can operate autonomously in the future; transaction-cost-intensive coordination in the network is thus limited, in this case as well, to the phase of orientation and coordination in the policy-formulation process.

In the third case, Thompson speaks of a "reciprocal interdependence" that can be mastered only by **"coordination by mutual adjustment"**. Here the decision-making possibilities of the actors involved are dependent on the behavior of the other actors. In the world of the economy, for instance, reciprocal interdependence can be found in company networks organized on the basis of just-in-time concepts, thus making the output of the one actor into input of the others and, in addition, requiring precise time coordination. In the field of locational policy, regional development concepts coordinated between relevant actor groups fall under this category. The aim of the coordination strategy is to go beyond common priorities and long-term orientations and undertake efforts aimed at jointly shaping structures; activities of firms, federations, state-level promotion institutions, research and advisory institutions mesh to advance a region's structural development. The network attempts to engage in continuous "coordination by adjustment" in that, first, it is rightly assumed that only continuous interpersonal and interorganizational cooperation between the strategically relevant actors can come to terms with the "permanent task" of shaping regional locational policy and, second, permanent coordination between relevant policy fields (e.g. transportation infrastructure, qualification, innovation and technology, the environment and energy, cultural infrastructure) should form the basis of any sustainable locational policy. The development of solution-oriented approaches is - in contrast to the first two variants - a "moving target". Implementation of these long-term strategies calls for development of a common problem-solving orientation in a network and is for that reason, as was noted in the last chapters, a demanding project.

Working out alternative solutions is based on the broad-based accumulative learning process of the first policy phase, which ensures a high level of information. In formulating concrete alternative solutions, it will as a rule make sense at this point to focus on the strategically important actor groups instead of all persons concerned. The course this process takes depends essentially on whether the actors are able to master the demands entailed by innovative governance - which were worked out in the last chapters. If they meet with failure, it is likely that either especially well-organized particularist interests will gain the day and only suboptimal results will be achieved, or that an action blockade will be the result.

No doubt, one key factor in encouraging the development of reasonable and appropriate solutions is to engage independent experts along with the strategically relevant private actor groups (looking at regional structural policy, e.g. firms, labor unions, and federations) as a means of preventing any one-sided prevalence of particularist interests. Apart from its moderator function, the state has in this sequence the task of developing, on the basis of the information and problem analyses worked out in the first phase, orientations and objectives, and thus of assuming a governance function more active than in the first policy phase. In addition, it can also be crucial for the state to exercise arbitration functions in order, for instance, to prevent the emergence of interest blockades and to strengthen weaker actors who have important concerns. This policy sequence is also dominated by soft, procedural governance mechanisms.

3. Definition of policies: The definition of policies is seldom a collective act of a network. Responsibilities are here clearly reassigned. It will as a rule be state institutions that, by means of legislation, directives, or administrative acts - i.e. "hard forms of governance" - will create new framework conditions or initiate structural change. It is, however, also conceivable that private actors might assume voluntary obligations, e.g. firms in the environmental sector, or modifications of curricula in vocational training institutions or universities, resulting from search and learning processes in policy networks.

In the first phase of the policy process, the important thing is to accumulate governance-relevant knowledge and to focus problem-solving potentials, in this way creating the frameworks and preconditions required to develop governance capacity in complex policy fields in the first place and to enhance the effectiveness of policies. A network is not a substitute for the state institutions that now are expected to take decisions and to assume responsibility for them; networks instead serve to imbed such institutions in social structures. Conversely, private, decentrally operating actors are integrated within sectoral structures as a means of making them into active partners in the process of shaping policy. The goal is to include a variety of particularist interests in collective policy-shaping and problem-solving structures.

This organizational pattern can contribute to counteracting ubiquitous fragmentation tendencies (the danger posed by the "Luhmann trap"), to compensating for the erosion of state-level governance capacity, and to come to adequate terms with the actual functional interdependencies in the policy fields that reflect the simultaneous loss of autonomy on the part of state and nonstate actors (Thompson's *reciprocal interdependence*).

Apart from the concrete policy decisions that result from work in a policy network, a variety of "secondary effects" are conceivable which can also contribute to boosting a society's problem-solving capacity. It is only when the narrow analysis of political governance processes as a task of the state has been overcome that we can begin to see that, based on collective search and learning processes in the first two phases, a great variety of private actors can, by rethinking the action strategies they have as decentrally operating organizations or firms, contribute to solving sectoral or policy-field problems. To remain with the example of regional conferences: Apart from the task of expanding physical and nonphysical infrastructure, which can be done in a more targeted fashion when collective search processes are involved than by means of traditional top-down industrial and structural policies, it is conceivable, first, for firms or organizations to use their participation in a network to accelerate their own learning processes and imitation efforts and to better harness their **endogenous creativity and problem-solving potentials** (e.g. improvement of workforce qualification, initiation of environmental measures). Second, it is conceivable for network actors to recognize and mobilize for the first time their **collective creativity potentials** by cooperating on a continuous basis. This, for instance, would imply that firms, once they have gathered experience in cooperation in networks, would be better able to cooperate more intensively with training institutions and to forge on with incremental modernization measures than they were previously (as self-referential firms), or that innovation centers might cooperate more strongly with universities and firms in order to more closely interlink basic research and applied research and to improve the company-level implementation of research findings.

We might, accordingly, imagine the emergence of a "sectoral structure" (cluster) which many actors are interested, and involved, in advancing, whereas beforehand this "structure" consisted of a variety of decentrally operating firms and organizations and responsibility for the "overall structure" was shifted onto "the (overburdened) state". If it proves possible to strengthen the self-organization capacity of actors and to awaken in them, beside their specific self-interests, common interests and responsibilities, this will entail an increase in the competence of individual actors and the problem-solving capacity of society as a whole. It would also disburden the state, thus strengthening its governance capacity.

4. Policy implementation: Here we can distinguish two variants: First, the state can take on the implementation function, e.g. when the concern is to alter framework conditions, to define standards and guidelines, i.e. for the legislative to modify legal regulations or to develop new state institutions. The difference between this and classical hierarchical, state-level governance consists in such cases in the "mere" fact that the political interventions are based on the collective "spadework" done by a policy network.

Second, one might think of cases in which the state delegates its implementation functions to networks. This can make sense when an implementation of state projects by public institutions would be very expensive or require great efforts to monitor (e.g. in company-level industrial safety, environmental and health standards in companies), cases in which implementation or monitoring tasks can better be exercised by labor unions or chambers of industry and commerce, or where policies cannot be effectively implemented without the cooperation of the parties concerned (e.g. the dual system of vocational training). The state retains "final control" in these cases in which the implementation of policies is delegated to social actors and their organizations.

5. Evaluation of the impacts of policies and monitoring of success: Collective policy preparation and the (possible) participation of parties concerned in the implementation process boost the degree of well-founded information possessed by all persons involved. Along with the classical methods in which success is monitored by state institutions, expert opinions, etc., the chances for "systemic monitoring of success" can be improved in this way. In other words, joint policy preparation can provide the basis for monitoring processes concerning policy impacts. Seen in terms of regional conferences, this would mean that, just as in the sequence of policy preparation, the follow-up phase in a network (as an overall structure) and by individual network actors (as parties concerned) could again make use of collective search and learning processes (soft, procedural governance) to accompany and advance the policy-formulation process by continuously evaluating the effects of policies.

6. Corrections: Corrections would then be the consequence of continuous monitoring of success and the begin of a process of renewed incremental change. Phases 5 and 6 are thus carried over into the next sequence of problem identification, assessment of problem relevance, and analysis of effective contexts (phase 1).

This schematic description of the activities of a policy network in an ideal-typical policy process makes one thing clear: the type of network governance in individual sequences reveals different

- **organizational patterns** (extending from broad participation of many actors in the first phase, and the collaboration of strategically relevant actors in the second phase, to the possibility of autonomous decisions taken by the state institution responsible, i.e. quasi-classical hierarchical governance, in the third phase);

- **functions that network actors must fulfill** (state functions of standardization, coordination, organization, moderation, arbitration, and monitoring - depending on the tasks to be dealt with in the policy phase in question - direct participation of the actors concerned in the governance process via collective search and learning processes in the first or the fourth phase, and the task of monitoring the state); and

- **governance media**: (from soft, procedural media to the hard, regimented instruments of governance).

Network governance would thus - in contrast to widespread prejudices - not mean that "everyone is at all time responsible for everything". It has also become clear that, aside from the policy process outlined and the policies directly resulting from it, what is decisive is the "secondary effects" of network cooperation. The self-organization capacity of the actors in a policy field or sector and their goal-directed interaction complement and focus the "intelligence" and creativity of the individual actors and create possibilities to contain the potential fragmentation and nonintended effects of decentral action. It is in this way that the continual shaping of structures, "reflexible modernization" (Beck) and goal-directed governance becomes conceivable.

4.6   The Network Cycle - The Efficiency of the Network Society with Reference to the Governance of Incremental and Radical Social Change

Network theory discusses two dichotomous views on the significance of networks. The one side emphasizes the governance achievements of networks and ascribes to them a higher collective intelligence. The other side sees networks as crippling, power-based communities of interests that contribute to the immobility and paralysis of modern societies. Olson's argumentation on the rigidification tendencies in societies characterized by strong social organizations points in this direction (the issues addressed here are core problems 1 and 2, Overview 7). Grabher seeks to refute the "myth" of the creativity of network with reference to the example of the German Ruhr district: *"First, the consequence of the at times feudal relations of dependence between dominant coal and steel corporations and the regional supplier industry was sensitive shortcomings in the so-called boundary-spanning functions ... Second, the relationships, stable in the long term, encouraged the development of common orientations, of a shared technical jargon, of common bargaining procedures, indeed, in the end, of a common worldview that blocked reorganization measures at a juncture when the region was still in possession of sufficient adjustment leeway"* (Grabher 1994, p. 79).

Both views are one-sided. The fact is that there is empirical evidence that supports both arguments. There exist in reality both dynamic networks and structurally conservative networks that defend privileges and vested interests.

It was pointed out above that the logic of networks has an inherent trend toward social, cognitive, and political obstruction (see core problems 2 and 3). This trend can be attenuated by a joint problem-solving orientation on the part of the actors and an openness of networks for "contradictory potential". It will be argued below that there can be no optimal "once and for all" equilibrium and permanent balance between the capacities for conflict and consensus, no orientation in terms of both self-interests and joint problem-solving or consolidating internal structures and openness. Nor can the above-sketched mechanisms geared to optimizing network governance lead to any complete neutralization of the tendency toward social and cognitive obstruction anchored in the logic of networks. It instead makes sense to grasp the development of a network as a cycle comparable with the dynamics of economic or product cycles.

As patterns of social organization, policy networks are a component of the socioeconomic development process. Socioeconomic development can be described in terms of cycles in which specific types of accumulation or technical paradigms and the social and production structures attendant upon them gain ground, unfold, are exhausted, and, finally, are replaced by altered, new socioeconomic patterns of organization and production. Socioeconomic development is accordingly not a linear process; and by the same token the development of networks cannot be seen as a linear process, either.

A network cycle breaks down into three phases: the **dynamic phase** in which a development corridor, once embarked upon, is shaped and consolidated (incremental modernization); the **phase of exhaustion** in which a development corridor reaches its limits and is successively faced with social and cognitive obstructions; the **phase of upheaval** in which new orientations must win the day and a new development corridor is called for (radical change). These phases will be characterized in the following section.

4.6.1   The Dynamic Phase of a Network Cycle

The **first phase** begins once a social consensus on a basic development orientation has been achieved (e.g. in Latin America at the beginning of the 1990s: reorientation from a strategy of import substitution toward an outward-looking orientation), or once the new orientation has been pushed through by a functioning social coalition, possibly even by an authoritarian state (e.g. the "economic revolution" of the Pinochet regime). It is also possible for radical techno-organizational innovations to initiate a fundamental and irreversible restructuring of economy and society (e.g. the transition to Fordist mass production in Western Europe in the 1940s/50s). In the following sequence in which a socioeconomic development corridor is formulated and consolidated, the strengths of network organization can then unfold.

In the dynamic development phase the task is to give shape to the economic, social and environmental framework conditions and corresponding regulations, to develop a viable institutional setting and a social coalition broad enough to bear the expanding development concept and to ensure its legitimacy. Both the state and the business world contribute their share to the dynamics of development; but as the discussion on "systemic competitiveness" noted, a comprehensive mobilization of society is required to advance the framing of new structures in the various economic and social sectors and to be able to identify new challenges and risks and respond correctly to them.

In this phase networks are extremely efficient organizational patterns that, thanks to their ability to rapidly exchange information, focus knowledge, creativity, and problem-solving potentials, as well as to bring individual and system interests into line and to channel social search processes, are capable of accelerating both individual and collective learning processes. Network actors contribute to shaping their common environment (economic sector, region, policy field) - a task that, in view of the complexity of modern societies, can be mastered neither by individual organizations or firms nor by state organizations working on their own.

It is particularly important that network structures, in the phase in which a development corridor is being formulated, improve the chances for rapid learning process on the part of social actors by contributing to establishing and broadening common orientations and goal-directed search processes and generally heighten the density of information and interaction between actor groups. Popper rightly points out that the capacity of actors to build a common horizon of expectations is a central condition for any accelerated individual and collective learning processes (Popper 1994).

A "solid horizon of expectations" and strategic orientations in terms of a goal system facilitate the development of individual and collective action strategies, and help reduce complexity and recognize regularities - "without direction" learning is hardly conceivable. It is only goal-directed learning, i.e. learning keyed to a frame of reference, that makes it possible to formulate, and - if necessary - falsify, expectations and to aim for, or correct, the appropriate action options. The network is a mechanism that, first, favors the development of a common horizon of expectations and strategic orientations and, second, contributes to the "inscription" of common orientations, "network interests", into the goal systems of the individual network actors. This breaks up the purely self-interest-oriented perspective of actors and organizations. In a network, firms become familiar with the views of labor unions, education/training institutions, state actors, etc. (and vice versa), work together with them to find solutions to common problems, and they are at the same time sensitized to the task of taking into account self-interests, the (possible conflicting) interests of others, and common interests of the network, even in formulating their individual action strategies (as firms, unions, universities, ministries). This dynamic contributes to the process of steadying, stabilizing, and shaping a development corridor that has been set out upon. At the same time close interaction-based relationships encourage imitative learning, which Popper describes, beside goal-directed learning processes keyed to "expectational horizons", as the second possibility for rapid learning.

Aside from learning processes and the use of network-governed structural development, the emergence of reciprocal, trust-based behavioral patterns between network actors and the development of common problem-solving orientations can constitute an institutional framework in which it is possible to deal productively with conflicts and process different types of problem perceptions. Network structures and their social functional logic can also contribute to attenuating the tendencies toward an accelerated fragmentation of social systems and the risk of subsystem self-referentiality pointed out by Luhmann. In other words, networks contribute to social integration.

In the dynamic phase of framing a development corridor, the network characteristics outlined by Grabher at the level of regional economic zones (coordination between large firms and suppliers, development of an infrastructure keyed to a regional economy, focusing of personal relationships between strategically relevant actors, development of common perspectives, establishment of bargaining procedures for dealing with conflicts, etc.) prove extraordinarily functional. This process involves at the same time an improvement of the external economies of firms and a strengthening of the social cohesion of the region concerned. Strengthening the capacity for social self-organization and focusing social potentials in networks can play a role in compensating for reductions of state-level governance capacity and complementing or correcting the logic of the market. The success of the industrial districts in northern Italy is based on this dynamic.

Due to a governance potential distributed over a number of actors, both the shape given to an economic location and appropriate incremental institutional modernization can as a rule only be advanced on the basis of functioning network structures. Networks are accordingly important motors of development in complex societies in which not only the economy but also the political and social institutions are permanently exposed to new challenges and must be further developed on a continuous basis.

It must be noted here that networks are not at all per se "development-friendly" in the phase in which a development corridor has been embarked upon. In fact it is possible that dynamic, efficient networks will be geared to nonviable goal systems (e.g. the one-sided model of im-

port substitution in Latin America; the development concept of the industrialized countries, which is ecologically untenable over the long
run) or that networks may, highly successfully, pursue "perverse" goals
(e.g. the Mafia).

4.6.2   The Phase of Exhaustion of the Network Cycle

In the **second phase** of the network cycle the until then positive, devel-
opment-stimulating, interaction-based relationships gradually turn into
development blockades. It is here that Grabher's arguments gain cogency. The chapter on the ambivalent consequences of the institutional
consolidation of networks worked out the mechanisms on which Grabher's empirical observations are based: in the course of the institutional
consolidation of the alliance of actors, a network's compromise orientation implies a retardative logic that leads to collective conservatism;
functional obstructions become more likely in that any deviation from
the development corridor embarked upon may violate the interests of
strategically important actors, thus threatening the network's precarious
stability. The growing standardization of perspectives, symbiotic relationships, and "exaggerated" social cohesion lead to constricted cognitive perception. The process of internal network stabilization tends in
the direction of hermetic closure.

These trends and signs of exhaustion are inherent in the dynamics of
networks. An interesting phenomenon appears here. A network is a
structure that can contribute to bridging the a priori self-referentiality
of all subsystems, as seen by Luhmann, and the lack of communication
between them. In networks, organizations that otherwise operate decentrally manage to coordinate their coordination activities. In their dynamic phase, network structures create communication channels between autonomous actor groups and organizations and are in this way
able to overcome their self-referentiality. In their phase of exhaustion,
characterized as it is by a tendency toward cognitive standardization
and hermetic closure, the Luhmann problematic reappears, as it were

"at a higher level". The network itself now threatens to fall victim to the "Luhmann trap".

It is not rare for once highly successful networks to run into major problems in correcting their development corridors. It is considerably more difficult to modify policies, institutions, and even networks once they have been accepted and shaped by a broad coalition of actors, and have also entailed benefits for all the actors involved. The past success takes on the character of a drag on development in that the network actors are inclined to continue on the basis of patterns that have until now proven successful (institutional structures, forms of cooperation, distribution structures). Precisely networks that, in the first phase of their cycle, were able to integrate broad constellations of actors and possessed a great degree of legitimacy in formulating policy are now faced with the profoundest of crises - end up in a situation of immobility. This blockade mechanism affecting once-successful networks holds the key to success for late- or newcomers who are able, at the onset of a new development cycle, to seize the chance to quickly formulate new structures, without being encumbered by the "shadow of the past".

The Ruhr district is an instructive example for illustrating this development logic. The paralytic phenomena sketched by Grabher for this economic region followed a phase of huge success experienced by a network consisting of corporations, the state, labor unions, and intermediary institutions in the period dominated by heavy industry. Not networks themselves are the problem, it is instead the paradox that the stability and the governance achievements of the network and the dynamics of structure-building in the phase of development and consolidation of a development corridor lay, in the end, the foundation for a shift in the precarious relationship between too narrow and too dense patterns of interaction, between stability and change in the direction of social and cognitive obstruction, thus encouraging collective structural conservatism.

Beside the "shadow of success", a growing "path dependency" gains ascendancy in the course of a network cycle. What is meant by this is that the effort required to implement changes in routinized networks

continues to increase, since established modes of operation, governance instruments, interpretive schemas, and vested interests and compromise structures bearing on the distribution of power or costs and
benefits stemming from network decisions that have come about in the
first phase of the network cycle, providing for stability and balance, are
now difficult to question.

Networks thus represent efficient organizational patterns in the phase
in which development corridors are formulated and incremental modernization is realized. The trend toward increasingly narrow, standardized relationship structures exhausts the innovative power of networks
(second phase). A networks strengths turn into weaknesses when the
challenge at hand is radical change, fundamental changes of course, a
modification of the overall goal system, the need to leave a development corridor (third phase).

4.6.3   The Phase of Upheaval of a Network Cycle

The third phase of the network cycles sees the two pillars of a network's functional logic undermined:

-   A network's **bargaining and compromise logic, trust-based re-
    lationships** facilitate step-by-step reforms. In phases of radical
    economic and social change, however, there are always winners
    and losers; new actor constellations need to develop, old patterns
    of interaction dissolve, trust-based relationships must be aban-
    doned.

    In phases of upheaval it become increasingly more difficult for
    network actors to develop a common **problem-solving orienta-
    tion**. The process of incremental change, is, it is true, also familiar
    with costs and benefits of decisions, although compromises are
    still possible here as a result of the reciprocal dependence of the
    actors and relatively stable framework conditions. Networks are
    effective in coming to terms with limited turbulences. But radical
    change alters the goal system aimed for, framework conditions are

revised and restructured, new development corridors are embarked upon, the interests of actors significant until then (during the transition from import substitution to a world-market orientation, for instance, the entrepreneurs geared to the domestic market; during the transition from resource- and energy-intensive industry to an economy based on services and information, heavy industry) are sharply curtailed. The process of comprehensive change undermines the second pillar of the efficiency of networks - the capacity to develop problem-solving orientations that are supported by all actors concerned. In the process of radical change, new socially relevant actors and newly constituted networks are concerned with working out common problem-solving orientations and building a modified and stable horizon of expectations.

The process of upheaval can be delayed for some time if the traditional network structure has operated successfully and/or was anchored solidly. Social search and learning processes are now impeded by the established structures, which are an expression of past and present interests, not, however, of future orientations. In the phase of radical change the social functional logic of networks is invalidated or gradually eroded, until new development corridors have emerged, and they in turn are successfully shaped by newly constituted networks.

Grabher describes this problematic with reference to the Ruhr district. Further examples can be observed in Latin America in the context of the transition from import substitution to an outward-looking orientation, Here, too, success has been met with, or is being met with (e.g. in Brazil and Argentina or Uruguay [see Meyer-Stamer 1994, Kosacoff 1993, Snoeck et al. 1994, Messner 1993]), by networks of well-organized actors groups (e.g. inward looking firms, government employees) in blocking steps aimed at reform, securing privileges, and establishing a culture of "cortoplasmo" that impedes economic and social reorientations. Uruguay is a particularly instructive example of a well-organized and at the same time completely blocked social system. The established and strategically relevant groups of actors and networks have for some time been incapable of advancing development-friendly policies, though they have been strong enough to block reforms and obstruct the development of change-oriented coalitions of actors. Olson's concept of "institutional sclerosis" is entirely applicable to this state of affairs.

The thoughts presented here make it plain that the "we-must-all-pull-together" rhetoric that is frequently encounted in network theories, as well as the notion it implies of a network society based on consensus, balance, and harmony, proceed from a mistaken, because linear, understanding of development. The response due to the "consensus theorists" on the one hand and those on the other that reject network solutions and other forms of concerted action with reference to its allegedly crippling effects per se is that given by Niels Bohr, who distinguished between two types of truth: on the one hand, the truth of *"plain and simple facts"*, the opposite of which is obviously wrong (Bohr 1949, p. 240). For Bohr, however, there are other *"deeper truths whose opposite also contains a deep truth"*. The harmony-oriented "consensus theorists" and the fundamentalist "network critics" proceed on the assumption that they have formulated "clear truths", though what they deliver is more like a good example of "deep truths".

Social development takes place, as the presentation of the network cycles illustrates, in waves, is characterized by phases of relative stability in which networks conducive to cooperation may constitute motors of development, but also in sequences in which necessary breaks and restarts are initiated by deep conflicts and crises, social discord and the breakdown of established network structures; here, the *"active society"* may turn into a *"blocked society"*.

4.6.4 Three Patterns of Acceleration of the Process of Change Leading to New Development Corridors

In the phase of upheaval of the network cycle, there are in principle three conceivable possibilities of breaking up the social, cognitive, and political blockades marking the "phase of exhaustion". The following reform-friendly initiatives often overlap.

First, outside pressure can force networks and blocked actor constellations to take action and work for change. Examples would be the outside pressure exerted in developing countries by the International Monetary Fund and the World Bank within the framework of structural adjustment programs or social movements in the industrialized countries that carry future-oriented themes into established policy networks and generate pressure for reform.

Second, it is conceivable that a higher-level agency, in the rule the state, could restrict the scopes of action of blocked networks one-sidedly geared to securing privileges and, in phases of upheaval, impose classical forms of **hierarchical governance**. Examples of this would be "top-down" structural adjustment programs in developing countries conceived to circumvent the particularist interests of various social groups.

What speaks for a procedure of this sort is the fact that it is often impossible to bring about a broad consensus on policies entailing first and foremost social costs which must be distributed, and that the inclusion of a great number of actors, e.g. of existing but cognitively obstructed networks, in the process of policy preparation may lead to half-hearted, less effective reforms. One need only point out how difficult it is in Germany in the mid-1990s to implement reforms of the existing health-care system with and against well-organized pressure groups (such as medical federations, health-insurance funds). This background allows us to understand why authoritarian regimes are sometimes more able to initiate processes of radical social change than democratic political systems in which well-organized networks have a substantial influence potential, which can prove to be a positive potential in phases of dynamic development, though it can by the same token turn out to be a blockade potential in phases of upheaval.

Five basic arguments can be cited both against the strategy of using classical hierarchical governance to get through phases of upheaval and - even more decidedly - against authoritarian patterns of problem-solving:

1. The decisions of an "insulated state" may either founder on the **complexity** of the reforms to be tackled or prove to be "too simple" in that the state may have to rely on the know-how of actors against whose vested interests the reforms are to be implemented (**knowledge problem**). In the case of structural adjustment, this might apply for the know-how or business federations that would e.g. be required to reduced customs tariffs in such a way as to take into account the actual response potential of the firms concerned. In addition, there is the trivial argument that hierarchical agencies of governance, e.g. the autonomous state, are apt to make mistakes as a result of the limited information available to them (e.g. as concerns the development corridor to be embarked upon or the pace of reform). On the other hand, the "intelligence" that network structures and social interest organizations can harness to monitor the state consists precisely in the fact that they institutionalize distrust of "higher" insights, backroom resolutions, or unilaterally defined notions of the public interest.

2. When far-reaching reforms are called for, the state is forced to rely on its **legitimacy** vis-à-vis strategically significant actors. Any massive loss of legitimacy can lead to a situation in which an initial phase of reform will frustrate successive steps toward reform. It is thus, for instance, conceivable in the former socialist states that rapid privatization or strict austerity programs, as reasonable as they may be in macroeconomic terms, may give rise to social distortions, which in turn will lead to losses of legitimacy that make further reform more difficult.

3. The state is faced with the fundamental dilemma that is may be expedient, in a phase of upheaval, to seek distance from groups of social actors and their specific particularist interests, whereas the subsequent phase of consolidation can hold promise of success only when strategically relevant actor groups are again successfully tied into policy networks designed to formulate a new development corridor. In the phase between upheaval and subsequent consolidation of a new development corridor, the state thus invariably moves in a **difficult field of force defined by hierarchical governance** - as an instrument to be used to overcome particularist interests intent on obstructing reform - and the efforts required to **constitute new, viable policy networks.** *"... it is*

useful to distinguish between the politics of initiation and the politics of consolidation, since the two phases of reform demand a somewhat different balance between state autonomy and the representation of interests. Given the problems of collective action outlined, reform initiatives are more likely where and when political institutions insulate politicians and their technocratic allies from particular interest group constraints, at least in the short run. The consolidation of reform, by contrast, involves stabilizing expectations around a new set of incentives and convincing economic agents that they cannot be reversed at the discretion of individual decision makers" (Haggard/Kaufman 1992, p. 19).

4. Authoritarian regimes have a marked tendency to **obstruct**, following the phase of change, the mobilization of social creativity so important to the phase of consolidation and to **block** the development of viable networks consisting of public and private actors. This tends to hamper the task of shaping new structures. Leffler describes this state of affairs in connection with his analysis of structural adjustment processes in African states. Countries that had successfully implemented structural adjustment programs "from the top down" (e.g. Ghana) were, in a second reform sequence, confronted by an "adjustment dilemma": *"In terms of time, authoritarian regimes can far more effectively decree a change in framework conditions, which, however, is not at all the case when we look at the sustainability of the reform process. ... [S]ystems of authoritarian rule seem, from a given point on, to run up against concrete limits to their scopes of action and implementation, since the implementation of sectoral and individual measures of a structural adjustment programs are very largely dependent on a mobilization of social groups"* (Leffler 1994, p. 3). The same state of affairs could be described for Chile. The military regime under Pinochet was able to push through a new macroeconomic framework against the resistance of nearly all social forces. But, as a result of the political and social polarizations induced by the regime, there was little progress in the area of mesopolicy (e.g. industrial and technology policy, decentralization, regional locational policy), which relies decisively on the ability to focus social forces. This is apt to be the most important reason why it proved impossible to give rise to an efficient industrial lo-

cation, and the "Chilean export model" has until now been based on exports of raw materials and agricultural goods.

5. **State institutions** are often integrated within existing social networks, or indeed protagonists of policy networks. In phases of social upheaval, they for this reason often constitute not the solution but **an element of the problem** itself. The close association with social actors required as a result of a mutual dependence on the governance resources of other actors can undermine the state's relative autonomy to such an extent that the state is no longer able to exercise its corrective and supervisory functions.

The question whether in phases of radical change the state is able to make any substantial contribution to overcoming social, cognitive, and political blockades is, in the last analysis, one that can be answered only empirically. It might be pointed out that, for instance, the Korean state succeeded, in the difficult phase of economic adjustment it was faced with at the beginning of the 1980s, in asserting its autonomy vis-à-vis particularist interests and at the same time in playing a key role in social networks, in particular together with the strategically relevant firms. In the South Korean case, the key condition was a high level of action and governance competence on the part of the state, which has not "exhausted its role" in the policy networks but continues to pursue an autonomous, future-oriented strategy: "*... (in Korea) state autonomy and embeddedness were two sides of the same coin. The institutional cohesiveness of the state apparatus enhanced the capacity of elites to set the policy agenda and to construct exchanges with the private sector on terms that were consistent with broad policy objectives. At the same time, embeddedness allowed government agencies to monitor and assess private sector responses and to adjust policy goals in face of new information*" (Haggard/Kaufman 1992, p. 24). These conditions are of course not given in many countries.

The **third** variant that can be used to initiate and accelerate change is based on the mobilization of the self-transformation capacities inherent in networks. It can at least not be ruled out that networks in the period of transition from the second to the third phase of the network cycle will generate potential for change on their own initiative. The basic condition required to mobilize inherent forces to overcome incidental social, cognitive, and political blockades is likely to be that network actors refrain from subscribing to an exaggerated "we-are-as-always-pulling-together" ideology and instead pay attention to the retardative aspects inherent in network structures. There is no doubt that it is difficult to develop an enlightened-pragmatic perspective of this type against the weight of inertial forces. The elaboration of the conditions required for the networks to constitute themselves, to consolidate and develop problem-solving capacities, has shown that that networks must first of all be able to create a substantial measure of social cohesion. The conditions constitutive for network efficiency in the first phase of the cycle thus make it difficult to develop the distance to the original functional principles required in the phase of exhaustion.

It is possible to strengthen the autonomous capacity of network actors to de-block rigidified structures when the actors are permitted, in the first phase of the cycle, a relative large measure of openness and conflict potential so that they can avoid any narrowing down of their cognitive capacities. It should also be possible for networks, as early as in the phase of their inception, to attempt to anticipate future signs of exhaustion, eroding trust mechanisms, and necessary changes that will force them to abandon the balances and compromises on which power and distribution in a network are based. It should prove possible to bring into the common problem-solving orientation in the process of development, as one of its dimensions, a willingness on the part of the actors to identify as early as possible symptoms of paralysis and signs of social, cognitive, and political blockades. One component of the common action orientation would be to monitor such trends; the network would, as it were, learn to protect itself from its own pathologies.

No doubt, even networks capable of "reflexible modernization" will be faced with hard conflicts of interests in their "hour of truth". Powerful actor groups will attempt to use the network structure to achieve their own interests. To come back to the example of the Ruhr district cited so often already: heavy industry was long successful in mobilizing the loyalty of the established network to gain huge subsidies. Nevertheless, a network that, in its constitutive phase, sets itself the task of observing its own blockade tendencies has better chances to prolong the initial phase of the network cycle and to abbreviate both the second phase and the period of radical change. The chances of anchoring in a network a problem-solving orientation conceived along these lines are not at all bad: at the outset of the cycle the actors involved are unaware of who will belong to the group of winners or losers of the beginning cycle. At the same time, all actors involved in the constitutive phase of a network will be interested both in prolonging as far as possible the dynamic sequence of the cycle and avoiding pathologies.

Going one step further, it may be assumed that societies in which policy networks play an important role and the above-described forms of "self-reflexivity" gain ascendancy will possess a higher level of problem-solving competence in phases of radical change than societies in which the state, as an autonomous crisis manager, is forced to act against a variety of particularist interests; what is meant here are, in other words, societies in which the "Olson logic" is deeply anchored. The functional logic of networks socializes (the most favorable case assumed here) the actors involved inasmuch as they are willing to take account of possibly conflicting interests of others as well as common interests touching upon the policy field to be shaped. Functioning networks are, as was shown by the discussions conducted with reference to Scharpf, Rawls, Walzer, and Honneth, based both on highly differentiated institutional structures characterized by a variety of checks and balances and on demanding normative orientations and action strategies that can be reproduced only on the basis of a minimum of "generalized trust" between social actors, tolerance, and the capacity of actors to deal with conflicts in a fashion oriented to solving problems. Should it prove possible to anchor a social milieu of this type in network societies, it can at the same time prove possible to diminish the risk of social disintegration invariably present, in latent form, in phases of upheaval.

Public-choice-oriented individuals will tend to opt for polarization and lobbying struggles in phases of upheaval. Network actors accustomed to balancing divergent interests and interpreting themselves as part of an overall system (an economic sector, a policy field) are more apt to be capable of overcoming purely defensive, structurally conservative action strategies aimed at stabilizing established privileges and encountering the exigencies posed by change by searching for offensive options. True, the integrative problem-solving mechanisms in networks tend to erode in periods of crisis. But a practiced "culture of problem-solving orientations" and a permanent process of learning to compromise and deal with conflicts, and a routinized acknowledgment, consideration, and coordination of individual interests, the interests of other actors, and overriding interests can favor the development of a "culture of change" and compromise even in phases of upheaval. The main consideration here is thus the development of a social milieu that refrains from structurally decoupling individual interests and collective and public interests. True, in phases of radical change there are winners and losers and network structures will break down. But if the dimension of the social functional logic of network governance can be anchored in society, this can strengthen overall social problem-solving capacities and avoid social disintegration. Societies that are able to develop compromise mechanisms to protect and reintegrate losers in periods of radical change may need more time for reorientation, but in doing so they are creating the social-integrative foundations for efficient network governance in the development sequence following the period of upheaval.

The capacity of networks to strengthen their own self-responsibility vis-à-vis overall social processes and mobilize potentials for change in the second and third phase of rigidification and exhaustion can be intensified, encouraged, or even compelled by the use of outside pressure, control, and incentive. Outside pressure can, for instance stem from state initiative, a vigilant publicity, or social movements. To this extent, the three mechanisms discussed (outside pressure, "strong state", mobilization of the transformation potential of networks), which can operate in the phase of radical change in the direction defining a new development corridor.

Finally, a remark of considerable significance. While actors in modern societies act continuously under great turbulence and uncertainty, and, as in the economy, cycles of change in the political sphere appear to be growing shorter, incremental change and modernization remain the rule and far-reaching upheavals the exception. Since networks have their clear-cut strengths as patterns of organization in the processing of complexity and in coming to terms procedurally with incremental modernization, it is time to reflect, both theoretically and practically, about instruments that can be used to diminish retardative mechanisms in networks - knowing well that in the last analysis the network cycle cannot, for the reasons cited, be neutralized.

4.7   On the Complementarity of Network Coordination and State-level Governance in the Network Society

The focus on the dynamics of network governance should not lead us to neglect either the existence of hierarchical mechanisms or the role of the state. The discussion on the network cycle pointed to the overlap between the governance functions of networks and the state. The further course of the study has further noted that the maintenance of social governance capacity is dependent in many areas on the existence of efficient networks and that scopes of state action can often be preserved only by delegating classical governance functions to intermediary institutions within the "Third Sector". This makes plain the limits faced by hierarchical governance by the state.

This view will be now expanded to show that that this relationship of dependence, or, better, complementarity, holds true in both directions. In many areas the performance and problem-solving capacity of networks remains bound up with effective hierarchical coordination mechanisms. Four of the five core problems of network governance worked out above (see Overview 6) can be attenuated by imbedding horizontal self-coordination in hierarchical structures and providing for specific interventions by state institutions.

The danger posed by decision blockades in a network due to the **development of veto positions** (core problem 1) can be reduced by providing state organizational aids for weak network actors. Czada in particular has pointed out in his studies that the state often is autonomous enough to determine (or indeed create) the actors who act in policy networks (Czada 1983 and 1992). Moreover, state agencies in policy networks are particularly able to set rules for bargaining modes, thus ruling out or limiting any opportunistic actions on the part of individual actors, when the bargaining concerned is compulsory bargaining and/or the network actors are forced to rely on state governance resources.[51] In spite of the loss of its absolute action autonomy, the state is in many cases entirely able to take on functions involving arbitration and formulation as a means of balancing out power asymmetries and bringing overall social decision-making criteria into networks.

Also, it is possible, by integrating self-coordination in hierarchical structures, to defuse the tendencies toward structurally conservative strategies, **cognitive and functional blockades** (core problem 2), and the risk - due to a lack of the common evaluation and justice criteria needed to decide between alternative solutions (core problem 4) - of obstruction of bargaining in networks. The state's task is to introduce overall social decision-making criteria into networks or to use appropriate control mechanisms to break up self-referential tendencies or to prevent particularist decisions. If the state is to assume these arbitration functions, the state-level actors, be they directly involved in policy networks or addressees of proposed solutions and concepts prepared by nonstate actors, need not be completely integrated within the - necessarily chiefly self-referential, particularist, and myopic - "network logic"; they should instead always be in a position to take into account the impacts of activities that a specific policy field has on its environment. This "public-interest-oriented" perspective cannot simply be presupposed on the part of private actors. The state is to this extent not simply *primus inter pares*, it must be allotted specific tasks.

An additional intervention mechanism comes about when networks, in the phase of policy preparation, develop concepts and instruments that are then presented to state agencies for decision, or at least have to be coordinated with them. This mechanism entails for network actors a constraint to develop solutions "compatible with the public interest". In many areas it is such that compromises worked out in networks are subsequently examined by higher-level agencies and then transformed into binding legislation by parliamentary decision. The state thus often has the chance to compel fair negotiations and block obviously opportunistic strategies developed in or by networks. That is to say, it is often the state that creates the context and the framework conditions required for horizontal self-coordination. These possibilities of state influence are of course most pronounced when the nonstate network actors are forced to rely on state governance resources (e.g. legislative competence, availability of financial resources and democratic legitimacy).

State intervention can be particularly important in networks when the network actors either understand each other "too well" (and thus tend to "close off" the network and externalize costs at the expense of third parties) or fail to understand each other (e.g. in a network in which environmental groups and industry are forced to work out compromises). The state's task is then to bring the parties to one table (system of compulsory bargaining) or to function as an arbitrator or authority in charge of setting rules.

The state also has monitoring, control, and supervisory functions aimed at preventing any externalization of costs of network bargaining at the expense of other subsystems of society as a whole (core problem 5) or limiting tendencies toward social fragmentation that can be accelerated by the process of network formation. The state must develop competences in the spheres of "interface management" and interdependence management if it is to be able to assert itself at the interfaces between networks and society as a whole and intervene in the sense of governance.

The state can assume these functions only under the condition that it (as a rule) gears its activities to the public interest. If we impute a priori opportunistic behavior to the state, or if we are dealing with societies largely marked by corrupt state institutions, network societies will degenerate into a type of organization that might perhaps best be termed "clan societies". Clan societies are dominated by the networks that are best organized and endowed with the power resources most relevant in strategic terms. The phenomena of institutional sclerosis and the rule of particularist pressure groups described by Olson as well as Luhmann's process of growing social fragmentation and the cold logic of subsystem self-referentiality gain real power under these specific conditions.

Aside from the normative preconditions for effective state action in network societies, the state must also be able to competently assume to governance functions outlined above by taking on the role of "**interface and interdependence manager**". This means that the network society entails for the state a task profile that differs distinctly from that of the leviathan in the model world of classical theory of the state. State institutions are (as a rule) no longer able to autonomously shape the entire policy process independently of society.

The crisis of the "planning state" of the 1970s and 1980s (in western and northern Europe as well as in other regions of the world such as Latin America) consisted in the fact that this type of state, with its traditional intervention mechanisms, was no longer able to come to terms with the new challenges posed by highly differentiated societies. Wherever states were unwilling to accept their loss of absolute governance autonomy and attempted to compensate for the reduction of their scopes of action by building additional state institutions and harnessing the governance instruments that they still had in the framework of the old concept of governance, what emerged were (as was the case in many Latin American countries) omnipresent states that were at the same time weak. The response to the crisis of the planning state consisted of deregulation concepts of neoliberal provenance, which, in many areas, did help to overcome state-level development blockades - to be sure, at the cost of accelerating tendencies toward social fragmentation and disintegration. Both governance concepts proved unable to come to terms with the altered basic structures of complex societies.

The post-statist and post-neoliberal area is experiencing a gain in the significance of state-level governance functions designed to integrate policy networks within the overall process of social development, and to monitor them, without fundamentally challenging their action autonomy. The social actors active in networks function as agencies of control vis-à-vis the state and at the same time become partners of cooperation in the policy process, though they also have to be curbed if "network egoisms" are to be prevented; and, in the last analysis, it is the task of state institutions to monitor the overall process of social development and to limit fragmentation. As "interface and interdependence manager", the state must assume the tasks that were discussed in connection with the discussion in the political and administrative sciences on the "cooperative state" and the "development of the Third Sector". The state takes on

- **tasks of coordination, organization, and moderation**, e.g. in order, networked with other social actors, to advance the search for solutions to problems;

- **functions involving mediation** between conflicting parties, e.g. in order to strengthen the self-organizational capacity in social subsystems that are endangered by interest blockades or to contribute to developing common goals and the acceptance of policies;

- **monitoring tasks**, e.g. in connection with the delegation of public tasks to nonstate institutions, e.g. to check whether they have met with success;

- **initiator and orientation functions**, e.g. as a means of realizing future interests against present interests of "injecting" overall social interests and problem areas into social subsystems (e.g. the economy) that tend, self-referentially, to orient themselves exclusively in terms of their own rationality criteria (e.g. growth, profit) and not to perceive external effects (e.g. environmental problems); the state thus has the task of integrating network activities, which are invariably particularist, within development process compatible with overall social interests (management of interdependence);

- **corrective functions**; e.g. for the state to strengthen the self-organizational capacity of weak social actors by providing them with financial or institutional aids that enable them to build up checks-and-balances functions.

The network society gives rise to an organizational pattern in which (modified) state governance mechanisms interact with horizontal self-coordination. The pattern of organization can contribute to coming to terms with the phenomenon of "divided autonomies" and the reciprocal dependence of social actors on the governance resources of others. Scharpf speaks aptly of "self-coordination in the shadow of hierarchy" (Scharpf 1993c, pp. 145 ff.). There is no doubt that hierarchical coordination, defined as autonomous problem-solving and central political governance, loses significance in complex societies. Yet in many cases horizontal self-coordination in networks remains imbedded in hierarchical structures. Scharpf comes to the conclusion: *"... this suggests a conceptual distinction between hierarchical forms of organization on the one hand, and hierarchical coordination on the other. While the latter may not often be employed in practice, hierarchical organization is still ubiquitous in the real world, and it continues to serve important functions in facilitating agreement and in controlling opportunism even when it is not used to achieve hierarchical coordination"* (Scharpf 1993c, pp. 146 f.).

Social development dynamics emerge in the parallelogram of forces consisting of participation, efficiency, consensus, and control. The two supporting and complementary pillars of the governance capacity of society are participation (of the social subsystems) and control. Wherever control becomes dominant and overly powerful, there develop "overgoverned societies"; where the level of control is low, i.e. the state's governance capacity is weak, while at the same time the organizational capacity of the subsystems is high and their participation in the social governance process is great, there emerge ungoverned or "undergoverned societies": "the risk that the state and society will be colonized by pressure groups".

The argumentation can be summarized as follows: The efficiency and governance capacity in societies is based on the governance competence of the state, with its altered profile of tasks as "interface and interdependence manager", as well as on active social networks both able and willing to engage in mutual coordination, networks that bring their problem-solving capacities into the process of overall social governance. "Strong state" and "strong society" are complementary terms. This study has discussed at length the fact that this complementarity of state governance competence and social problem-solving capacity does not emerge automatically in the development process, bound up as it instead is with complex normative preconditions, institutional conditions, and practice in the uses of a broad palette of governance instruments. Governance capacity in networks must be continuously stabilized and further developed - it is always at risk.

Part IV Social Governance Capacity and International Competitiveness

CHAPTER 1   Attempt at a Résumé and an Outlook: Contours of a Synthetic View of the New Organizational and Governance Pluralism in Network Societies

"...every work, regardless of what type it may be, knows more than it says and wants more than it knows."
Friedrich Schlegel, cited after E. Behler (ed.), Kritische Friedrich-Schlegel-Ausgabe, vol. II, Paderborn/Munich/Vienna 1958, p. 140

Here no attempt will be made to synthesize once again the great variety of approaches discussed on the course of the study. The intention is instead - in a first step - to present the present state of governance theory in the context of the network discussion. A second step will develop a structural picture of differentiated networks societies. This will entail referring, in brief form, to the conflicting views of Helmut Willke, Bernhard Peters, and Jürgen Habermas.

1.1   The State of Governance Theory in the Context of the Network Discussion

At the end of Chapter 3 (Part II) on "Neoconservative and (neo)liberal discourses on the crisis of the state", three central complexes were isolated that pose governance problems: the problems of complexity, power structures, and motivation (see Overview 2). Following the discussion of the new theoretical approaches to governance, in particular network theories, we are now faced with the question of how to assess the problems.

As regards the **problem of complexity**, it can be noted that network organizations (can) compensate for some *"functional gaps of state policy"* (Schmalz-Bruns 1994, p. 19) and hierarchical governance. Networks are capable of distinctly improving both problem perception and the assessment and processing of problems in advance of political interventions and the implementation of policies. In the growing number of cases in which governance-relevant resources are distributed across different actors, networks are a form of organization that offers greater problem-solving potentials than hierarchical decision-making systems. Aside from this dimension, the complexity problem conceals the phenomenon, emphasized in particular by Luhmann, of the simultaneously increasing self-referentiality of subsystems (or organizations) and interdependencies between social subsystems. Based on his restrictive assumption of self-referentiality on the part of subsystems (dominance of independence), Luhmann regards any attempt to master the interdependence problem by means of political governance as naive.

The network discussion has, however, shown that the functional logic of network governance is geared to making possible intersystemic or interorganizational communication. Though it is true that hierarchical decision-making and governance systems are less and less capable of autonomously influencing the dynamics of "self-purposed" subsystems. Policy networks that come about as a result of the reciprocal dependence of the actors on action resources held by others can, however, prove capable of articulating together the logic of independence and the logic of interdependence. The actors involved in networks are forced to (and learn to) to coordinate their own interests and action logics with those of other participants. The present study has shown that the state is often involved in networks, or at least able to influence their framework conditions or rules (*"self-coordination in the shadow of hierarchy"* - Scharpf 1993c, p. 145). The complexity problem is accordingly not solved by the existence of network structures, though it can be tackled more effectively by them than it can on the basis of the instruments of intervention available to the statist planning optimism of the past or the neoliberal and neoconservative strategies that have been under discussion since the end of the 1970s as the solution to the crisis of the state.

The **problem of power structures**, which, basically, involves both the danger that the state may be colonized by well-organized particularist interests and thematized the fact that society is clearly dominated by a limited number of actor groups, cannot be solved by network structures. Two fundamental findings may, however, be noted here. **First**, network structures give rise to a sort of "systemic control". Pressure groups, regardless of how well organized they may be, are as a rule reliant on resources held by other actors, and phenomena of absolute power are thus apt more to be the exception. It is precisely societies in the stage of growing differentiation that are marked by a loss of action autonomy on the part of nearly all actors; "divided sovereignties" are the rule, absolute sovereignty of an organization, an enterprise over all other actors is the exception. This does not imply "balances of power", though it does open up scopes of action, and it points to the necessity of installing the right checks and balances in constellations of social relations as a means of counteracting the tendency for power structures to form.

Second, and this point is particularly important to the network discussion, it has been pointed out that the dynamics - noted by Olson - involved in a growing siege of the state by particularist interests tend to gain sway in societies primarily geared to the normative structure often termed the "egoistic individual". Productive networks are based on a functional logic (reciprocity, trust, the ability to compromise and deal with conflicts) that is hardly compatible with the normative premises of radical liberalism. This implies two things: on the one hand, the problem-solving potentials of networks cannot be optimally utilized in societies in which the normative framework of public-choice theory, the *"egoism principle"* (Etzioni 1994), is deeply rooted. This means that governance problems will remain unsolved in complex policy fields in which state and market fail and only mechanisms of horizontal self-coordination open up paths to solving problems. On the other hand, the tendencies toward growing social differentiation and increasing self-organizational capacities on the part of society are irreversible. That is to say, the number of groups capable of articulation is on the increase. In societies in which the normative value system of "egoistic individualism" is dominant, the group interests capable of articulation are translated into complex lobbying systems that can contribute to blocking the political system (Olson phenomenon).

The task of mobilizing the problem-solving know-how of social groups and tying it into policy networks is a question of an action orientation of actors geared to the joint solution of problems. Individual, common, and conflicting interests must be articulated. It was shown that this network logic is situated beyond the logic of public choice. This means that the growing number of efficient actors in societies that prove able to anchor the functional logic of productive networks can contribute to strengthening society's problem-solving capacities (the **active society**). In societies that fail in this task, the growing number of efficient actors (who, as strong lobbyist groups, will look only to their own interests) encourages a "siege" of the state and successively weakens the state capacity to act (the **blocked society**). The problem of power structures would, in other words, only intensify under these conditions; the likely result would be the institutional sclerosis of which Olson speaks.

The **motivation problem** can be circumscribed with keywords such as individualization tendencies, desolidarization, social fragmentation; governance capacities restricted by the breakdown of common orientations and action dispositions on the part of social actors. Dubiel synthesized this phenomenon as follows: *"What in earlier times provided, almost naturally, cohesion among citizens is today, everywhere and inexorably, dissolving. And the seat of this consumption is evidently the institutions of market society and liberal democracy themselves. Indeed, stability has been drawing on a moral capital that it cannot itself produce within its institutions"* (Dubiel 1994).

On this point, the following can be said with reference to the network discussion: There is no doubt that the breakdown of the bonding power of valid values and orientation in modern and modernizing societies is continuing. It is precisely because of the state's loss of action autonomy, the erosion of social *"bonding forces"* (Dahrendorf), and the growing self-organizational capacity of society that the *"de-moralization of action dispositions under the sign of a liberal individualism"* (Schmalz-Bruns 1994, p. 23) is linked with an increasing need for *re-*

sponsibly ethical mass orientations. If the state were, in many areas, losing its autonomy of action, i.e. if the governance capacity in society were growing increasingly dependent on governance activities "from below", and the individuals in networks were, in many cases, reliant on common discourses on justice in order to remain capable of solving problems, while at the same time people were becoming less and less capable of developing common orientations and activities, the future of network societies would, indeed, not look good.

At least one important trend running counter to the often-emphasized individualization tendencies can be made out: the existence of networks in which the actors involved (must) provide joint governance efforts, i.e. the "inherent necessities of the network society", as it were, can play a role in developing collective problem-solving orientations and competence as well as a collective sense of responsibility. The discussions on the crisis of the "egoistic individual" (as a concept counter to the individual oriented to the public interest), which can be observed in all industrialized societies, and the lively discussions on "justice" (see Rawls, Walzer, Honneth) point in the direction of a re-foundation of the *"moral resources"* (Honneth) of complex societies. In the (day-to-day) political debate, this important discussion has until now (unfortunately) been conducted actively, in essence, only by the (neo)conservative side, and then for the most part with a backward-looking orientation. The democratic left has until now had little to say about this field.

The increasing significance of networks has led, in connection with these considerations, to an additional problem complex associated with governance. The constitution of policy networks makes it possible to rationalize them "internally" and heighten their problem-solving competence in specific fields, though it also involves the danger of **overall social disintegration** when subsystems become independent and coordination processes between networks fail. If a tendency of this sort prevails, there is a danger that self-referential, powerful policy networks will solve their problems at the expense of third parties/society, marginalizing less well-organized and weaker interests in doing so. We are here again confronted with the interdependence-dependence problem with which societies have to learn to come to terms. This point will be taken up again below.

The discussion of the structures of network societies has made it clear that governance capacity comes about in a multistage social context of mediation: market, state, horizontal self-organization in networks, and the interlinkage of hierarchical and network-like governance complement one another in the forms worked out above. Beside law, power, and money as the classical governance media, the flow of information and the capacity of social actor groups and policy arenas to communicate with one another is gaining in significance. This view implies that it is time to break away from the notion of an institutionally concentrated, homogenized, and linear policy process. Problem perception, problem assessment, development of solutions, and implementation of policies turn out to be *"graduated processes referring back to one another in a number of stages"* (Schmalz-Bruns 1994, p. 27) and leading to decisions and solutions.

The traditional institutions of political governance (parliament, administration) are not supplanted but, on the contrary, complemented by the deliberated policy processes discussed here. Active societies can be created through the reciprocal effects of parliamentary activities, problem-solving efforts of state-level institutions (which modify their functions and engage more intensively in functions associated with coordination, organization, moderation, and initiative and corrective activities - instead of "top-down" central governance) as well as by shaping societies in accordance with the needs of networks. Mechanisms of mutual control and cooperation are strengthened in the context of an organizational and governance pluralism of this sort, and it can in this way prove possible to address long-term community interests and to impart more force to them vis-à-vis short-term and particularist interests.

The problem-solving and governance competence of societies is accordingly more and more strongly bound up with their capacity to reflect permanently on social issues and to engage in continuous processes of adjustment. The fact that this multistage system of social governance is based not only on appropriate institutional structures but at the same time also on the "normative capital" of a society was pointed out in particular in connection with the discussion on the social functional logic of networks. Networks by no means generate a priori a high level of collective intelligence, as was shown by the discussion of the pitfalls of network governance. Societies that see themselves confronted with the challenge of complementing market- and state-level governance with forms of horizontal self-coordination and network organization, e.g. in order to strengthen the systemic competitiveness of their economies by developing an efficient mesodimension, are at the same time faced with great challenges. These apply both to the institutional design of the state, the economy, and social organizations, to say nothing of the action orientations of the actors involved and their strategic capacities. The view often put forward in the development discussion that, following a period of unilateral fixation on the state (e.g. in Latin America) the concern is now primarily to mobilize social development potentials (e.g. NGOs) often overlooks the fact that developing countries often are as good as without developed markets and are marked by a weak state and weak social actors lacking sufficient strategic capacity. The concern can accordingly not be to develop one of these dimensions at the expense of others.

The Great Challenge: How to Succeed with the Project of Social Integration?

Habermas correctly notes: "If a decentered society were no longer able to preserve its unity, it would not profit by an increase in the complexity of its parts, and would, as an entity, fall victim to their gains in complexity." But how is social integration possible in societies in which "there is no (more) place where problems relevant to the reproduction of society as a whole can be perceived and dealt with?" (Habermas 1992, p. 416) This problem entails two pitfalls that confront highly differentiated societies and which I, in the course of this study, have termed the "Olson phenomenon" and the "Luhmann trap".

Olson describes the danger that the state may be besieged by powerful interest organizations, a process which undermines the state's capacity to act and leads to institutional sclerosis. It was shown that this phenomenon is not a natural law in modern societies and that it occurs when interest groups gear their activities one-sidedly to a "lobby logic" (based on the normative system of public-choice theory) and societies fail (in the sense of complementariness, not substitution) to create moorings for the "network logic" worked out above. For Olson, blockade mechanisms result from the activities of specific interest organizations. In societies increasingly characterized by network structures, this problem might pose itself at the level of networks that undermine the state's capacity to act. A good example would be the "Ruhr cartel" discussed above.

The Luhmann trap occurs when the active field between growing independence (of networks) and interdependence (between networks) breaks down and the subsystems go their own ways, become self-referential. This problem can result on the one hand from the "Olson phenomenon": powerful networks develop particularist behaviors, disregard the impacts of their activity on their environment, and the state is unable, or unwilling, to take on, or provide for, the coordination and harmonization activities required between the social subsystems. On the other hand, the possibility cannot be ruled out that the dynamics of the process of social differentiation will overtax the capacity of both the state and social actors to act as "interface managers", and this can give rise to disintegration problems.

1.2   An Enlightened Systems-theoretical View - and its Black Holes: The Conception of Helmut Willke

The problem of integration in highly differentiated societies is also acknowledged by the "enlightened" systems theorist Helmut Willke: *"Quasi-natural development* (in societies in the process of increasing differentiation) *can lead into evolutionary impasses, or worse; it is limited to local optimization"* (Willke 1992a, p. 143). What he first makes plain is how the problem cannot be solved: *"... in the active so-ciety, the creation of order is no longer only a ... problem* (of the state). *Social order is only possible on the basis of a specific interplay of autonomous actors, fraught with presuppositions. Social order on the basis of hierarchy and planning is as antiquated as the liberalist for-mula of order based on evolution has become dangerous."*[1]

But how does Willke imagine the "interplay, fraught with presupposi-tions", of the actors as a means of averting the danger of social disinte-gration? What he is looking for is no less than an equivalent of the greatness that *"in simpler times was termed commonweal, public inter-est, or indeed as raison d'état"* (Willke 1992a, p. 136). He develops an interesting idea that proceeds from the core thesis advanced by Norbert Elias on the "Process of Civilization". Elias had argued that civiliza-tion, or culture, can acquire substance only when psychic, social, and institutional conditions are created that make it possible to replace the "external constraint" of the absolutist state on individuals with "self-constraint" and "affect moderation" of individuals. Where this fails, societies threaten to disintegrate, since it is impossible to hold together societies based on division of labor with the means of external con-straint. Elias explains the increasing self-control and moderation of human affects with reference to the constantly increasing densification of the chains of action in societies marked by division of labor.

Willke now applies this argumentation to network societies: social disintegration is to be avoided by the *"self-binding"* of the subsystems (networks). This self-binding is seen as the means through which *"organized subsystems are able to transcend their limited subsystem rationalities in the name of their own interest in global maximization and strategic action"* (Willke 1992a, p. 139), in this way rendering hi-erarchical governance superfluous. The notion of self-binding of net-works is in general an important element in conceiving any integration of network societies. Elias, referring to the action orientations of indi-viduals, had already presented a consistent concept of the significance of such social mechanisms in securing the existence of societies char-acterized by division of labor. If individuals and networks fail to inter-nalize a minimum of *"affect moderation"* and control of individual behavior as far as its impacts on third parties and the community as a whole are concerned, the *"Process of Civilization"* is jeopardized.

Willke presents an important argument to explain the emergence of this mechanism of self-binding in networks and other social subsystems. Since the state has in many areas irreversibly lost shares of its action autonomy and groups of social actors successively realize this state of affairs, the subsystems must learn to assume responsibility for themselves and their environment that has otherwise been laid at the doorstep of the state. The tendencies that can be observed in the field locational policy are a clear indication of the correctness of Willke's thesis. The shaping of structures in the mesodimension by a variety of private and public actors is a reflex of the loss of the state's action autonomy in this policy field and a sign of the inability of firms to optimize their business environment on a completely autonomous basis. Willke's argument thus has a real core. Yet he fails to mention that fact that this form of self-binding in an enlightened self-interest is likely only when reciprocal dependencies emerge between the specific subsystems. That is to say, the firms and institutions of an industrial cluster assume policy-shaping functions aimed at improving competitiveness; the important task of mobilizing self-coordination potentials is, however, not referred to the impacts of cluster activities on the environment or social problems, because (and as long as) negative effects of company behavior on the environment and social development do not generate negative impacts on the action potentials of the economic actors involved.

A second argument that reinforced the assumption of the emergence of self-binding in networks appears to me to be more significant. In the organizational structure of networks and their functional logic there are inherent mechanisms that favor the development of "collective responsibility". Conventional social theory sees individuals, but also collective actors (organizations, interest groups, firms) as invariably oriented to representing their own particularist interests. The state is responsible for the community and the public interest. Particularist interests and public interests as well as their representation are accordingly clearly distinct. The organization of networks is a new type of social order inasmuch as it constitutes a collective actor structure in which the interests of those involved are not fused to form a homogeneous overall interest. Networks are concerned precisely with coordinating and articulating individual interests as well as conflicting and common interests. The functioning of networks confronts their actors with major challenges. The organization of networks is a conflictual and fragile project, and - a very important point - it represents a field of learning aimed at bringing about what Willke designates as the "capacity for self-binding".

For Elias, the process of civilization, beside the growing self-control capacity of humans, is linked with the emergence of the state monopoly of power. Elias saw the following problem: in societies characterized by division of labor, the individuals are compelled to control their effects through the fact of their being imbedded in extensive chains of action. On the other hand, however, extensive chains of action can also lead to apathy toward the results of one's own actions as well as to normative indifference.[2] Elias therefore sees the state, qua agency of control, as an important stabilization factor complementing the moderation of the affects in societies characterized by division of labor.

Willke, too, complements his concept of self-binding with reflections on the role of the state. It is seen as developing into the *"supervisory state"* and exercising *"contextual governance"* (Willke 1992a, pp. 335 ff.). His initial premise is that the political system is, as a matter of principle, equivalent to all other functional systems, and for that reason it is impossible for the state to engage in any hierarchical governance of social subsystems. Willke succeeds in clearly formulating the tasks that the supervisory state must assume: *"The function of supervision is to cast light on what the actors were unable to see in the process of the original decision. ... Supervision (acts) as a process of reflection in which the unavoidable blind spots and myopias of the decision process are made distinct in some functional system and tentatively treated as contingent"* (Willke 1992a, p. 336).

Less clear is how the state, as *primus inter pares*, is supposed to be able to master these tasks. The manner in which what Willke calls contextual governance is concretized is somewhat less satisfactory: *"In*

essence, contextual governance means the reflexive decentral govern-
ance of the contextual conditions of all subsystems and autonomous
self-governance of the internal processes of each individual subsystem"
(Willke 1992a, p. 341). Here the vocabulary of systems theory is obviously used to express what in usual parlance is known as formulating
framework conditions. Willke does not get any further here than the
administrative scientists who have contributed, at a much more concrete level, to a redefinition of the workings of the state. His view of
the state remains behind the level reached by network theories and the
notion of the complementarity of hierarchical governance and horizontal self-coordination developed in the present study. The question of
the mechanisms of social integration is more than difficult to answer
with Willke's conceptions of society and supervisory state.

The Black Holes of Enlightened Systems Theory

Willke gets caught up in the snares of systems theory. On the one hand,
he insists on subsystem autonomy, the self-binding capacity of subsystems and the assumption that the state is not capable of governing
them: "In the logic of operative autonomy it makes considerably more
sense for a system to set, within its own operational mode, the constraints which, according to its own perception of its environment, are
compatible with other systems in this environment than to permit other
systems to dictate restrictions **whose language** and **rationality it cannot judge**" (Willke 1992a, p 332; emphasis by D.M.).

On the other hand, Willke argues that social integration is possible only
when *"a minimum of common orientation or vision"* (Willke 1992a, p.
341) exists between the subsystems, and he even notes that the subsystems have to be capable of forming *"consensus"* in the intersystemic
communicative relationships between them (Willke 1992a, p. 419).
These shared factors come about, the astonished reader is given to understand, in the process of decentral contextual governance, and they
lead to a phenomenon that seems quite ill suited to the world of self-
referential subsystems, incapable as they are of intersystemic communication: *"Here we are concerned with a new type of rule. For the first*

time, these rules are no longer anchored in the subsystems but emerge at the system level from the active and intentional interplay of the parts, which want to combine to form an emergent overall system. This type of rule is the material from which decentral contextual govern-ance, as a technique of political supervision, can develop. ... It must therefore also be noted for complex societies that the deep structure of the order is bound to the grammar of understandable information"(!) (Willke 1992a, pp. 345 f.; emphasis by D.M.). How, by virtue of what intermediary mechanisms, common rules can "emerge" from semanti-cally closed systems and autopoietic subsystems can overcome the logic of pure self-reference is a secret not divulged by Willke.

It can be noted that this attempt of an enlightened systems theorist to solve the problems involved in the mediation between the inherent dy-namics of social subsystems and the overall system turns out to be un-satisfactory. This should be kept in mind in that it is no doubt an impor-tant merit of systems theory to have worked out the phenomenon of the simultaneous increase of independence and interdependence and, in doing so, of having analyzed one of the crucial cores of the governance problematic that had until then been diffusely circumscribed. As I noted in connection with Luhmann, his questions are more interesting, and lead us further, than his answers. This is likewise true for Willke's recent work, though it should also be noted that he at least addresses the issues stemming from the concrete conclusions arrived at by the theory of autopoiesis for a practice-relevant theory of society.

The present study shares Willke's thoughts on the necessity of self-binding and self-control of subsystems. But Willke's ideas on the insti-tutional embedding of the principle of self-binding are not convincing. So what remains as the hard core of his argumentation is only the hope of self-responsibility on the part of subsystems. Three points must, in my opinion, be criticized here in order then to address again the issue of the basic structures and organizational principles of highly differen-tiated societies which are conducive to integration and, with reference to Peters and Habermas, to outline a more promising theoretical direc-tion of inquiry.

But to come to the three points of criticism: **First**, Willke is unable to explain on the basis of his systems-theoretical premises how it is that consensus, common rules, and, in the end, an overall system can emerge in the process defined by the interaction of self-referential subsystems. It is interesting that there are in actual societies - despite the undeniable tendency of subsystems to become independent - mechanisms that are capable of creating social integration. In his references to the possibility of common rules shared by the subsystems and the "emergence" of an overall system, Willke confirms this state of affairs, but without working out the mechanisms behind it. The process of social integration remains a black box.

Second, in Willke the integration of subsystems within an overall social context is not referred back to values, norms, and interests. The intersystemic communication processes are reduced cognitively to producing technical integration. Social integration becomes a purely technocratic problem for which experts from the individual subsystems are responsible who inform one another of the modes of operation of the individual subsystems as a means of avoiding self-referential blindness. Habermas rightly points out that what Willke describes under the headings of supervisory state and decentral contextual governance has the smack of management literature (Habermas 1992, p. 420). As *primus inter pares*, the state is reduced to the role of the moderating training instructor; the public sphere, parliamentary checks and balances, or the question of legitimacy do not occur in Willke. His view of the overall architecture of modern societies recalls the relatively simple intermediary mechanisms used by pluralism theorists of the 1950s and 1960s to describe the working of democracies under the rule of law. The pluralism theorists see states of social equilibrium as being automatically generated by elections and formulation of policy by parliaments. For Willke all that is needed, in the end, to create social integration is exchange between the subsystems, supported by the moderating state. The place of the "political market" of the theories of pluralism is taken by the technocratic rule of subsystem managers; Habermas aptly speaks in this context of *"systems paternalism"*.

Third, Willke's governance discussion, arbitrarily and exclusively geared to functional coordination, is inappropriate for two reasons. On the one hand, the structural social picture sketched by Willke is under-complex and unrealistic in that for him the expert discourses of system representatives are in no way linked to the variety of existing social structures (parliaments, democratic public opinion). On the other hand, however, his conclusions are counterproductive in purely cognitive terms. If complex social problems are to be solved, there is a need both to mobilize professional expert knowledge and to tie such coordination efforts into processes of deliberative politics. Reference was made to this point in the discussion of the role of "troublemakers" as motors of innovation in networks. Willke's *"corporative society"* ("Ständegesell-schaft") (Habermas 1992, p. 426), in contrast, threatens to suffocate form the invariably limited and narrow-minded rationality of subsystem experts.

1.3   Theoretical Search Process with an Eye to Jürgen Habermas and Bernhard Peters

Bernhard Peters and, picking up on some of his ideas, Jürgen Habermas have succeeded in convincingly conceptualizing the multistage process of decision-making and problem-solving in highly differentiated socie-ties (Peters 1993, pp. 344 ff., and Habermas 1992, pp. 429 ff.). The heuristic concept developed by them (see the visualization in Figure 8 is suited to summarize the components of the theory of governance de-veloped by the present study at the level of overall social patterns of organization and governance.

The core area of the political system is constituted by the institutional complexes of administration, including government, the legal system, and the institutions in which democratic public opinion and the demo-cratic will are formed. The core area of the political system, marked as it is by formal decision-making competence and real prerogatives vis-à-vis the ramified structure of the periphery of the political system, is thus not monolithic but institutionally heterogeneous and porous. Now, how is social complexity processed within the political system? It is first of all important that action-related competences and tasks are differently distributed within the core area. The legal system is responsible for the control and enforcement of an overall system of rules governing society; it provides for a routinized processing of conflicts between social actors. A functioning legal system furthermore constitutes a crucial basis for stabilizing a minimum of trust in society. It thus contributes to dealing with conflicts, the key components and (potential) motors of the development of modern societies, conflicts that might otherwise accelerate the erosion of social stability. Moreover, a minimum of generalized trust between social actors is the *sine qua non* of the capacity of complex societies to reproduce themselves.

The parliamentary complex involved in the democratic formation of public opinion and the political will is largely open to perceiving and addressing social problems, although the price it must pay for this sensibility is a level of problem-solving competence that is low in comparison with that possessed by the field of administration. The two complexes of the political system are thus complementary and at the same time marked by a certain tension. The administrative complex incorporates specific governance and problem-solving knowledge, and the actors involved here tend to harbor a sectorally narrow-minded, particularist view of things. And this is what they should do, too, if they are to effectively represent the interests of their policy field against those of other policy fields. The actors and institutions involved in the formation of the democratic will "observe" the development in individual policy arenas and must link it with the development dynamics at work in society as a whole. These actors and institutions thus have a control function vis-à-vis the particularist views of the specialists of the administrative sector. The latter are frequently apt to see the smooth course of their policy-shaping activities obstructed, and with good reason, too, by interventions on the part of the "generalists". The core of the political system is accordingly not at all a monolithic block.

At the periphery of the political system there is a nexus consisting of a great variety of institutions that are for the most part endowed with self-administrative rights or delegated sovereign and control functions

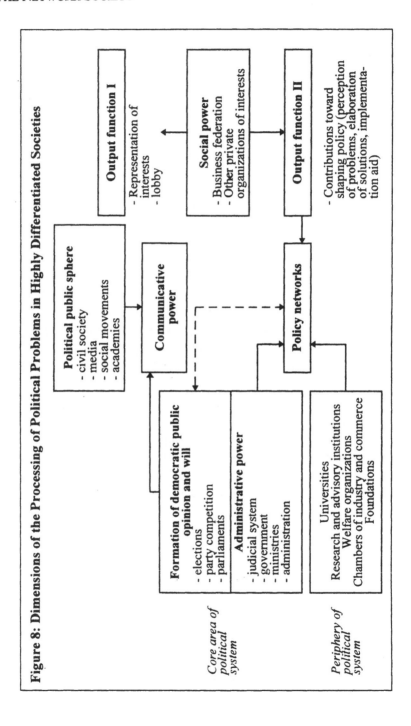

Figure 8: Dimensions of the Processing of Political Problems in Highly Differentiated Societies

(universities, advisory institutions, chambers of industry and commerce, foundations, welfare associations). These public or semi-public intermediary institutions support the administrative complex in the course of the policy process: it is here that specialized and professional know-how crucial to any analysis of effective governance-relevant contexts is accumulated; the implementation of policies can in part be delegated to these institutions. It seems to me that these institutions are constantly gaining relevance in the face of the growing significance of knowledge as a governance resource and its circulation in society. There is also a second argument: against the background of the argumentation developed above, it must be assumed that the institutions of administrative power will in the future have to (or at least should) concentrate more and more on their roles as moderators, organizers, and "interface managers" and spend less time than in the past in accumulating detailed information on the sectors to be governed. This detailed knowledge should be processed, stored, and fed into the policy process by the intermediary institutions on the periphery of the political system. Government, administration, and ministries could then concentrate on the tasks of strategic governance and would be relieved of the weighty burden of preparing and processing information.

In society, "social power" is organized in private federations, organizations, and interest groups. The organizations of the complex of social power have a twofold and tension-laden output function. They act on the one hand as pressure groups and lobbies, and they articulate their particular problems, interests, or needs, stake out political claims, and attempt to gain sway on the political decision-making process. This is the type of activity that Olson had in mind in speaking of institutional sclerosis. On the other hand, organizations (sometimes the same ones) in this sphere provide contributions to the formulation of policy. They heighten the perception of problems, possess governance-relevant knowledge, cooperate in policy networks in developing policies, or assist in the process of implementation.

Policy networks focused on specific policy fields and sectors are as a rule constituted through the interplay of public and specialized administrations (ministries, public authorities), intermediary institutions on the periphery of the political system, and organizations of social power which (with their second output function) are involved in the process of political governance. The course of the present study has made it clear how these policy networks emerge and what functional logics and development dynamics are characteristic of them. The central significance of network structures for the process of social governance is mentioned only in passing by Peters and Habermas, though it is especially underlined in the context of the present study. Willke's vision of social governance is reduced to the interplay within this "expert triangle".

The output function of the organizations in the sphere of social power involved a complicated field of force in that the "recipients" of policy are here, as it were, fused with its "suppliers". It was noted above that other authors are as a rule only concerned with one of these two functions: Olson concentrates one-sidedly on the first output function (representation of interests, lobbying), while the neocorporatists are primarily concerned with the second output function (contributions to the shaping of policy).

Beside the core areas of the political system as well as its periphery and the organization of social power, the second sphere is that of the formation of public opinion. This includes on the one hand the media and on the other the various organizations of civil society (e.g. social movements, citizens' initiatives, academies) that contribute to shaping public opinion and have become specialized in gaining public influence, providing warning signals, and controlling administrative power. The actors in this sphere are for the most part not directly involved in the formulation of policy, even though it is no longer seldom for e.g. environmental organizations to participate in policy networks. Seen in comparison to the actors involved in the complexes of public and semi-public administration and social power, the contribution of the political public sphere is primarily to perceive social problems, to thematize them, and to feed them into the core areas of the political system, while their actual problem-processing capacity is of course small.

Habermas subsumes the actors of the political public sphere and the democratic decision-making process under the category of *"communicative power"*: The concept "communicative power" expresses (*idealiter*) the deliberative mode of the conflict of opinions in these institutions concerning "public affairs", while the other sectors of societies are as a rule concerned with activities in specialized fields.

To describe the process of decision-making, Peters (1993) works with a model of a floodgate. Binding decisions, when they are to be implemented with authority, are directed through the channels of the ramified core area of the political system. Peters emphasizes that the legitimacy of decisions is dependent on the processes in which public opinion and the political will are formed in society and in parliament. To concretize this, it should be added that the organizations of civil society and public decision-making also have the important function of perceiving and articulating problems, that, in other words these organizations are crucial actors for both legitimatory and cognitive reasons. While the specialized institutions of the administrative complex and of social power possess key knowledge bearing on the solution of problems, they are often marked by limited views of their specific working fields. The task of the organizations of the sphere of communicative power is therefore to introduce, against the narrowness of outlook marking specialists and particularist interest groups, *"practical reason"*, higher -level points of view (e.g. moral orientations, trendsetting political decisions) into the problem-solving process.

Peters fails to articulate sufficiently clearly the fact that the level at which social problems are processed and solved is also reliant on the close interlinkage (in his metaphor: open floodgates) between the administrative sectors and the private organizations (of social power). In a great number of problem areas, the prospects of successful governance are poor if the governance resources of these two complexes are not combined. In addition, Habermas and Peters both largely disregard the possibility of horizontal self-coordination on the part of social actors.

Despite the modifications of the views of Peters and Habermas and the different weighting given here to the individual sectors of society in the governance process, the image of the floodgate is useful in grasping the complex, overlapping filters and control mechanisms in the process of problem-processing: The manifold communications flowing in circular or in opposite directions serve to disburden the official circulation system (i.e. the core area of the political system) of some of its un-avoidable complexity by breaking down problems. A key consideration both from the standpoint of legitimacy (or democracy theory) and in terms of governance-related functional (cognitive) considerations is that processes of change can be initiated from different spheres of so-ciety. In contrast to simplistic and idealized models of the cycle of democratic power, Habermas and Peters reconstruct the process of political governance in the triangle defined by **communicative power** (including the political public sphere and the institutions involved in forming democratic public opinion and framing the democratic will), **administrative power**, and **social power**. And in doing so they leave open the question how, in concrete cases, the overall system of political governance operates. While e.g. the neocorporatists, or indeed Olson, believe to be able to discern a linear and necessary development logic of governance in modern societies, Habermas and Peters make it clear that the question whether the above-outlined system of "countervailing powers", operates

- through decisions legitimated by democratic control,

- in the sense of a compromise of interests,

- through cognitive openness and high levels of communicative density between the three power centers of society, or

- by controlling powerful groups of actors and strengthening weak groups

is an empirical one.

A great variety of different developments are conceivable. In countries in which powerful interest organizations from the sphere of social power are active in the sense of lobbying, the political system can be blocked or colonized; such societies will also be confronted with governance problems in that in a number of policy fields it will prove more than difficult to deal effectively with decision-making tasks without any efficient policy networks, and they are as a rule reliant on the solution-oriented participation of the intermediary institutions of the private sector. This is the realm of institutional sclerosis described by Olson.

Another possibility is that the power of the administrative complex and the social power of the intermediary structures acting on the core area might "join forces and go it alone", close themselves off to "outside" influences, thus insulating themselves from communicative power ("dictatorship of the mesodimension", which is no longer tied into the overall social context). If this happens, the probable outcome is network failure.

Such tendencies toward proliferation of power can at least be limited by control and influence exercised by the sphere of communicative power. Whether this proves successful will in turn depend on the effectiveness and articulate capacity of the actors from the public sphere and the effectiveness of parliamentary organizations. The crucial consideration is whether these actors fulfill their admonitory role as sensitive detectors. The strength or weakness of communicative power in a society is determined by a great number of factors: the political culture, the strategic capacity of the actors involved, institutional rules that can promote or impede the influence potentials of the organizations of civil society, and the structure of the media landscape.

One might of course also think of opposite cases: strong organizations from the sphere of communicative power can, in concrete cases, be in a position to obstruct necessary adjustment measures and reforms for protracted periods of time. The case of Uruguay is instructive here. An analysis noted that here urgently required economic reforms were long blocked by the structural conservatism of the organizations of communicative power. Constellations of this type are likely when societies are faced with the challenge of breaking with a model of accumulation that was formerly successful (or formerly successful subsegments of a social formation) from which many groups of actors and social classes have profited in the past. The shadows of the past preclude any orientation in terms of the future.

The heuristic model of Habermas and Peters can help in structuring this multiplicity of dynamics and is compatible with the views developed in the present study. The macroinstitutional design of highly differentiated polities is characterized by an overlap of different patterns of organization and governance, while theories from the social sciences for the most part attempt to localize **one** tape of social order as the central type of governance. The planning optimists pointed to the state, the neocorporatists to the triad of state, capital, and labor, Olson to the combination of free market economy and authoritarian state, Luhmann and Willke to the self-organizing capacity of the subsystems, and some network theorists to the collective intelligence of network organizations. The present study has made it clear that modern societies are dominated by a pluralism of organization and governance.

This multiplicity of complementary and overlapping organizational patterns and forms of governance does not, of course, imply any arbitrariness. The present study has worked out **on the one hand** the strengths, weaknesses, and determinants of the various patterns of organization and forms of governance and their functions in processing discernible problem constellations in the individual phases of the policy process and as regards dealing with the incremental or radical process of social and/or economic change. **On the other hand**, the study has shown that societies are confronted with a diverse catalogue of challenges. Highly differentiated societies are concerned with enhancing the problem-solving competences in subsystems (e.g. strengthening systemic competitiveness), protecting the autonomies and development potentials of a limited number of highly significant subsystems that are either weak or difficult to organize (e.g. culture, poor population groups) from the dominance of other social subsystems (Walzer's *"art of separation"*), and managing the interfaces between the subsystems so as to prevent social fragmentation and disintegration (Walzer's *"art of connection"*). This can only succeed when visions and social priorities are developed and aimed for in the governance process, without unilaterally orienting society as a whole to a goal system (competitiveness versus the environment versus the problem of poverty versus democratization), thus giving rise to undesirable developments.

The question of the integrative capacity of complex societies cannot be answered in any conclusive and clear-cut manner. Willke attempt to develop a "formula of integration" is reductionist in nature. The subsystems of a highly differentiated society do not automatically jell to form a symbiotic whole. The tense relationship between subsystem interdependence and the danger of growing subsystem independence, which can also end up in self-referentiality, remains fragile: *"There is no 'functionalist explanation' of the genesis of social structures and mechanisms that ensures that functions are fulfilled. ... The functions fulfilled by individual subsystems and the conditions of the compatibility between them can only be empirically ascertained, not 'derived'"* (Peters 1993, p. 401). Social integration and political governance are constituted in the above-sketched floodgate system, in the combined action and mutual control of the organizations of society. Money, i.e. "the invisible hand of the market", and administrative power represent structure-building mechanisms of social integration. Both mechanisms are bound up with structures of communicative power, the dynamics and development logic of which are fed through their ties to the lifeworld, the democratic process in which public opinion and the political will are formed, and the political public sphere. Integration itself consists of the interlinkage between these different social levels and the manner in which (action-related or functional) imperatives of different origins are processed.

The structure and the development and organization of institutions involved in solving social problems are collective learning processes that often operate along the lines of trial and error. The heroic assumption of any absolute capacity on the part of the political system to plan and shape policy must be abandoned. The more or less complete surrender of governance called for by theories of a neoliberal hue likewise leads to a dead end. Societies are capable of managing a great number of adjustments to constantly changing environments, and they are called upon to produce and to further develop directions, orientations, and visions to which the governance process can be keyed. Both Karl

Deutsch and Popper have emphatically pointed out that any "direc-
tionless" learning on the part of individuals, collective actors, and societies can proceeded only very gradually. The ability to engage in a
social discourse on the direction of the development to be embarked
upon is therefore of central significance.

Societies that wish to move in the direction outlined will have to reflect
on the institutional design most conducive to collective learning. The
present study has worked out some indications of the structure of any
such design conducive to learning and development. It was also pointed
out that the dynamics of institutional systems is highly dependent on
the moral resources and the systems of values and rules available to
societies. Criteria for problem dimensions and solutions to problems
are also defined culturally, are based on civilizatory standards that can
be modified in the context of social learning processes or by outside
pressure, though little is known of their structures and dynamics.
Money, policy instruments, and physical infrastructures can easily be
copied or transferred, e.g. in the framework of development cooperation - though this is not the case with trust and patterns of reciprocity.
The governance and problem-solving capacity of societies is accordingly dependent on an extremely complex interplay of factors that
touch upon the basic structures of society.

The current development-related discussion on "good governance" is
making it plain how the extremely important topic of governance capacity in societies is transformed myopically into day-to-day politics.
Now that one-sidedly market-centered governance concepts have
proven counterproductive, the World Bank and related agencies have
begun thinking about a redefinition of the role of the state. But the discussion and the policies resulting from it are unilaterally focused on
purely technocratic issues (e.g. reduction of bureaucracies, monitoring
the success of state activities; formal rule of law existent or not). As a
rule, extremely simple and idealistic pluralism-theoretical models of
democracy serve as a foil here. It should have become clear that the
thoughts on boosting the problem-solving and governance capacity of
developing countries, countries in transformation, and of course also

industrialized countries must be discussed within a far more complex frame of reference.

CHAPTER 2   Conclusions Drown from the Governance Discussion on the Concept of "Systemic Competitiveness"

A good number of cross-references were made to the topic of competitiveness during the course of this study. It was pointed out that it is not only in the economic sphere that a "New Production Paradigm" has emerged; the basic structures of society are also in the midst of a profound process of change that is not accessible to conceptualization with the means offered by classical theories of governance and the state. A multiplicity of new patterns of organization and governance has emerged beside hierarchical governance of society by the state. A new sociotechnological-organizational paradigm appears to be gaining ground. The following chapter will recapitulate the four levels of the concept of systemic competitiveness and work out the various governance-relevant challenges that are developing in this context.

2.1   The Macrolevel as the Framework for the Development of Competitiveness: The Primacy of Hierarchical Governance

As regards the task of creating a stable macroeconomic framework capable of securing competitiveness and encouraging exports, in may be noted that in this policy field the state still has an action monopoly. The macrolevel is dominated by the logic of hierarchical governance. The efficiency of this action arena depends crucially on the competence of the individually responsible administrative institutions of the political system as well as on public and private advisory institutions (e.g. economic research institutions). Macroeconomic reforms are first and foremost a technocratic problem. This is shown by the experience of the past 15 years of structural adjustment in the developing countries.

A relatively small staff of experts is in charge of preparing and formulating the adjustment programs.

In view of the state's action monopoly in shaping macroeconomic framework conditions, three reservations are important: **First**, and in contrast to neoliberal concepts, it is important to underline the close connection between macroeconomic reforms and the microlevel constituted by the firms concerned. Macroeconomic reforms that fail to take proper account of the response and adjustment potential available at the microlevel defined by firms and seek to implement textbook structural adjustment programs can trigger exaggerated adjustment processes and contribute to destroying industries that have modernization potential. The empirical experience gathered from many Latin American economies, or indeed from the new, eastern regions of Germany, represent material that can be instructive in illustrating this point. That is to say, the shape given to the macroeconomic framework conditions is - in particular in the phase of radical economic change - dependent on profound know-how on the economic structure, the level of productivity in the various sectors, and the specific modernization potential available. This knowledge must be processed by organizations on the periphery of the political system, or be available from the federations and advisory institutions of the private sector.

Second, Legitimacy problems must be anticipated in the face of incisive corrections of course, e.g. during the transition from an inward-looking orientation to one geared to the world market, a problem faced by many developing countries, or in the face of the process of restructuring taking the countries in transition from planned to market economies, or indeed in industrialized countries that are losing their competitiveness and are forced to adjust to the new challenges posed by the world market. The first problem posed by structural adjustment processes is how the costs are to be distributed. Many adjustment programs, e.g. in Latin America, fail due to the inability of the governments and other strategic groups to bring about a consensus on the distribution of the costs involved. In other words, in phases of crisis and radical change even macroeconomic reforms are bound up with the specific forms of organization and integration mechanisms available in these societies, and these reforms therefore go beyond any pure technocratic policy management. In these phases the relationship between the state administrative complex, the organizations of the political public sphere, and the (democratic) process of forming public opinion and the political will gain in significance. Macroeconomic reforms are as good as impossible to realize in societies in which an interplay between these levels is unable to create political stability and an action orientation on the part of strategic actors that is geared to solving problems. However, it is nevertheless true that hierarchical governance is still largely intact in this policy field in phases of relative stability in which macroeconomic policy is engaged in as a matter of course.

Third, the scopes of action available at the macrolevel are decisively weakened by the globalization of the economy. Keynesian demand management is practically ruled out in an open national economy. The sovereignty of governments and central banks in matters of interest-rate policy is restricted by the activities of the international financial markets, and the scopes of exchange-rate policies are sharply curtailed by speculative capital flows in the global currency markets. Governance problems result at the macrolevel, i.e. primarily due to the partial loss of national sovereignty as far as action is concerned. It is likely that the globalization of the economy is contributing in the national economies to a leveling of policy patterns as far as the formulation of macroeconomic framework conditions is concerned. What this implies is that it is hardly possible to develop specific competitive advantages at the level of macropolicy, even though naturally weaker economies will be hit harder by world-economic deformations and fluctuations than more strong ones.

National macroeconomic policy is not at all rendered superfluous by the state of affairs outlined above. It is still true that macroeconomic policies can encourage or impede the development of competitiveness. The challenges posed for macropolicy by the process of globalization can, however, not be met exclusively at the national level. The international level is likewise plagued by reform and governance deficiencies: **On the one hand,** the world economy, like a national economy, needs an organizational framework, in particular to prevent misallocations.

Coordination processes, at least, are achieved at the level of international trade policy, regardless of how these process may be judged in detail. The international financial markets are, however, totally under-governed, encourage purely speculative capital movements, and undermine the stabilization efforts of many weaker economies on the international scale. **On the other hand**, the future will experience an increase of coordination efforts in the field of macroeconomic policy in economic regions such as the European Union, NAFTA, or MERCOSUR. There are governance potentials at this multilateral level that are not yet exhausted.

2.2   The Mesolevel as the Locus at which Dynamic Competitive Advantages are Created: The World of Network Governance

The governance and problem-solving requirements at the mesolevel differ fundamentally from the challenges and scopes of action encountered at the macrolevel; this goes for

- the number and type or actors and organizations involved;

- the levels of intervention (local, regional, national);

- the specific patterns of organization, problem-solving, and governance involved;

- the functional logic (dominant in network structures);

- the strategic and problem-solving capacities needed by the actors and organizations involved, and the institutional design of society;

- the significance of the dominant system of norms and the action orientations of the actors in strengthening problem-solving competence in this field;

- the scope of mesopolicies, and

- their significance for the development of systemic competitiveness.

These problem dimensions have been analyzed in depth in the course of the present study: the mesolevel is the world of network structures, the horizontal self-coordination, and the interplay of hierarchical and network-like governance (self-coordination in the shadow of hierarchy). The reason for the dominance of network-based governance mechanisms in the mesodimension is a broad distribution of governance resources (capacity to perceive problems, knowledge on effective governance-relevant contexts, competence in the field of implementation). The mesodimension is characterized by the phenomenon of "divided sovereignties", which affects state-level institutions, firms, and intermediary institutions alike. Any shaping of an industrial location with the aid of a set of different technology-, innovation-, training-, industrial-structural, and regional-policy measures is thus forced to rely on a close interlinkage of actors from the micro- and mesolevels. The mesolevel is characterized by cooperation between actors from state administration (from the local to the regional level), the institutions on the periphery of the political system (e.g. advisory, technology, and training institutions), and public or private intermediary institutions (e.g. chambers of industry and commerce, federations). Interaction gives rise to cumulative learning processes that intensify the efficiency of both the actors concerned and the mesodimension itself.

Both the patterns of organization, problem-solving and governance specific to the mesodimension and the functional logic of network governance and the resultant challenges to the strategic and problem-solving capacity of the actors involved, the institutional design of society, the significance of the dominant system of norms, and the action orientations of the actors need not be presented again here; the same goes for the efficiency potentials of network governance and their pitfalls. These issues have already been discussed at length.

But three points will be commented on by way of conclusion:

1. The relationship between the mesolevel and the metalevel: Various patterns of organization and governance overlap at the mesolevel. The ability to shape this dimension depends on the organizational and strategic capacity of a variety of actors. The discussion of the functional logic of network-like governance and the network cycle made it clear that the efficiency of the mesodimension is closely linked to the deep structures of the society concerned, and thus, at the same time, with the metalevel. The mesodimension in concerned with

-   optimizing the efficiency of the subsystems involved (firms, clusters of firms, federations of capital, labor etc., interest groups, the functional institutions on the periphery of the political system, state administrations at the core of the political system);

-   coordination of these subsystem to generate synergy effects and focus broadly distributed governance resources, without undermining the creativity and relative autonomy of the actors concerned, and here

-   it is important to find a balance between individual, conflictual, and common interests.

There is also a need for a system of countervailing powers to prevent any externalization of (ecological, social, and economic) meso-network costs at the expense of society as well as for specific action orientations on the part of actors. The shaping of the mesodimension therefore poses extremely great demands on society and is very difficult for countries in the process of development or transformation to implement. If the three dimensions already discussed are disregarded, the shape given to the macrodimension is a technocratic problem. The process of shaping the mesodimension is, on the other hand, a test case for the organizational and governance capacity of the societies concerned. This has proven to be the case in 15 years of structural adjustment in developing countries. True, some countries have attained macroeconomic stabilization, but few have succeeded in improving their locational conditions, either because they lack suitable concepts for shaping the mesodimension (e.g. the attempts made are often too technocratic in nature, neglecting "bottom-up" structuring by the persons concerned) or because the social actors are unable to implement more complex patterns of organization and governance. In addition, social disintegration tendencies tend to hamper the development of common problem-solving capacities.

This problem complex is particularly weighty in that is becoming clearer and clearer that countries in the process of development and transformation that pursue an economic strategy geared exclusively to macroeconomic reforms and neglecting the task of shaping the meso-dimension tend to fail as export-oriented economies or exporters of raw materials and agricultural products.[3] This danger also threatens societies that fail to meet the institutional-organizational demands posed at the mesolevel. Studies conducted by the author in Argentina and Bolivia, for instance, showed that neither country has a lack of institutions and diverse initiatives at the mesolevel. On the contrary, structurally weak Bolivia is faced with a critical problem in its innumerable institutions and projects aimed at strengthening the country's technological competence. These institutions and projects are, however, completely isolated from one another, are as a rule developed far from the productive sector, tend strongly to counteract one another, and in the last analysis are themselves proving to be an organizational and development problem.[4]

Aside from actor weakness there are additional pitfalls that can frustrate the implementation of mesopolicies. In successful economies close cooperation between strategically relevant actors in networks has proven to be a productive force (see: The functional logic of networks, Overview 7). Many problems encountered at the mesolevel can be solved only in networks and similarly interlinked systems. It can, however, prove unfeasible to copy these organizational concepts in other societies

-   because the actors involved are geared solely to lobbyist orientations and are unable to develop any common problem-solving orientations (effect: "Olson phenomenon");

-   because there is a lack of historical experience with methods of compromising and processing conflicts and network structures therefore tend to end up in endless disagreement; or

-   because a lack of due process of law is hampering the formation of "generalized trust" between actors, one of the important conditions for the development of network governance.

2. The scope of the policies and private activities in the mesodimension: In contrast to macroeconomic reforms, the scope of which is restricted by the globalization of the economy, the mesodimension is a space that has greater latitudes for creative activity and a growing significance. If it is correct that efficiency at the mesolevel comes about through cooperation between actors and the local, regional, and national dimensions are not losing their significance here, indeed if this dimension holds *national competitive advantages* (Porter), i.e. the development of competitive advantages is bound up with the quality of industrial locations, then the challenges posed by mesopolicies are great, though the scopes open for formulating them are likewise great. It is of course possible to harness external potentials (foreign know-how, participation in international technology networks) , but the mesodimension, as an institutional structure, remains geographically restricted, can neither be exported nor imported. Geographical agglomeration effects are encourage in particular by the network-like patterns of organization and governance dominant at the mesolevel.

3. The significance of the mesodimension for the development of systemic competitiveness: While policies at the macrolevel are becoming increasingly similar throughout the world, the industrial locations of individual countries differ considerable. The "design" of industrial locations is shaped above all by the institutional landscape at the mesolevel. It is here that **institutional and organizational competitive advantages**, specific organizational patterns and national profiles emerge on which competitive advantages are built and that are very difficult for other competitors to copy. This argument should be given more weight with an eye to the thoughts presented by the present study on the complex institutional-organizational challenges posed to the actors by the mesospace and the development of strongly context-dependent dynamics in the network-like structures of the mesospace. This view contrasts sharply with the supposition of authors like Knieper (1993), who argues that the world economy is giving rise to increasingly "faceless", uniform industrial locations and that investment decisions are thus geared more and more to specific wage levels and tax rates.

It is more likely that, due precisely to global competition, very differ-ent, specifically national patterns of competition will develop in the world economy. Those economies will prove to be especially success-ful that do not attempt solely to imitate tried and proven patterns, even though creative imitation can **initiate** economic "catch-up" processes. Sustainable competitive advantages do not result from competition for a given number of niches but are based on the process of specialization and development of new niches (e.g. products, technologies and insti-tutional patterns). This thought proceeds from theories of dynamic evolution. Classical evolution theory is dominated by the notion that those systems prevail that are able to solve the problem of competition by capturing one niche or a fixed system of niches. Seen in this way, the world of competition is a world of violent struggle. Theories of dy-namic evolution, in contrast, advance the thesis that (social or eco-nomic) niche systems are in a process of constant change, that new ar-eas can constantly be opened up beside existing niche systems, and that the appearance of constantly new settings gives rise to new differences and thus to new chances of specialization. I think it is correct to say that even the world economy is not a zero-sum game, that, indeed, the challenge facing countries is to develop specific, efficient organiza-tional patterns to improve their industrial locations. Or, as Böhret cor-rectly notes: *"You can't pass somebody by remaining in his footsteps"* (Böhret 1990, p. 195).

2.3   The "New Production Paradigm" at the Microlevel: The World of Clusters

The new challenges at the micro-, the company level, were discussed in the context of theories of competitiveness. The first crucial factor here is the interaction between the microlevel and the mesolevel. A further fact that can be noted is an interesting convergence of the governance needs at the microlevel and in social policy networks. Both spheres display phenomena of "divided sovereignty", increasing complexity, decreasing scopes of hierarchical governance - or a redefinition of the governance tasks to mastered "from above", and a growing significance of mechanisms of horizontal self-organization and network structures.

These tendencies have been examined in depth for the social sphere. Similar tendencies are in evidence at the microlevel. Firms are introducing market mechanisms (profit centers), corporate headquarters are delegating governance functions to lower levels and themselves taking on moderator and interface-manager tasks, firm are being integrated in supplier systems and technology networks, all of which can boost efficiency, while at the same time causing a situation of tension between independence and interdependence. At the microlevel the challenge of strengthening competitiveness is primarily a problem of organization and governance.

2.4 Organizational and Governance Pluralism at the Metalevel: Social Governance Capacity as a Condition for Economic Efficiency and Development

Building systemic competitiveness is based on a pattern of social organization characterized by

- **a strengthening of market forces** by reducing overregulation and bureaucratic development blockades and creating stable macroeconomic framework conditions;

- **disburdening the state and boosting its efficiency** by strengthening market forces and delegating governance tasks to nonstate actors, interlinking public and private actors, and strengthening subsidiary principles, developing social mechanisms for compromising and dealing with conflicts, and building sectoral networks;

- **strengthening social capacities for self-organization**, a condition for the development of viable patterns of social organization and complex forms of governance;

- **embedding the market** within efficient institutional systems with the aim of optimizing economic development potentials and correcting the (socially ands ecologically) destructive tendencies of the market economy system.

It is against this background that we can see emerging the contours of a "competitive cooperative system", a market economy corrected and intensified by discourse, interlinkage, and networking. The market acts as a motor of rationalization and development, the state takes on the role as the motor of overall social and economic networking, social actors interact in networks as a means of pursuing their own interests, dealing with conflicting interests, and realizing common interests together with other actors by focusing their forces. The principles of competition, countervailing powers, and cooperation have to be brought into a state of balance. An "organized society" of this sort can, under given circumstances that were worked out above, mutate to form a "blocked society" or develop into a "formed society" when society as a whole is geared to an unduly narrow goal system (e.g. economic abbreviation of the challenge of building competitive advantages).

The concept of a pluralism of organization and governance in network societies has been used here to circumscribe a type of society that differs fundamentally from the Fordist model. This pattern of organization and governance poses great challenges to social actors. The attempt made here, in contrast to Willke and proceeding from Peters and Habermas, to outline the direction of a synthetic perspective of the dynamics of network societies has made it plain that the challenges to counties to aim for international competitiveness and that the development problem can generally be conceptualized as a problem of social organizational and governance capacity. This result is important, not least to development research, in that, until recently (and in influential theories and the writings of important authors), the development problem has been reduced primarily to capital insufficiencies or a lack of market-friendly framework conditions.

Notes

Introduction and Formulation of the Problem

1   This first point of departure is not worked out in detail in the present study. On this topic, see the author's country studies on Uruguay, Chile, Argentina, and South Korea (as a contrast case). These studies were produced at the German Development Institute in the context of further studies by Klaus Esser, Wolfgang Hillebrand, and Jörg Meyer-Stamer on *advanced developing countries*. The theoretical-conceptual considerations developed in the present study also refer basically to industrialized and/or advanced developing countries as well as countries in transformation. On the failure of import substitution, see Esser at al. (1992, 1993, 1996). The most brilliant and earliest study on the causes of the failure of one-sided import substitution was published by Fernando Fajnzylber (1984). See Messner/Meyer-Stamer (1994) for a comparison between Latin American and Eastern European countries and Mármora/Messner (1992) for a comparison between Latin American and Asian economies.

Part I

1   See the country and sectoral studies (referred under Literature) by Esser, Hillebrand, Meyer-Stamer, and Messner.

2   Tobin (1978). This issue will be taken up below.

3   One instructive example is the structural adjustment process in South Korea at the beginning of the 1960s. The transition from import substitution to a world-market orientation was flanked by big financial transfers from the US. Only in this way was it possible to combine a restrictive antiinflationary monetary policy with comprehensive investment programs aimed at modernizing the infrastructure. See Messner (1988).

4   This governance-theoretical dimension of mesopolicy is, for instance, left completely out of the picture in Peters' (1981) standard work on mesoeconomics.

5   The basic policy areas in the mesodimension (training/advanced training, research and technology, trade policy, financial-sector development, environmental policies) are discussed at length in Esser et al. (1996). R.B. Reich (1993) likewise points to crucial significance of these factors for national economic development.

6   Industrial sites and economic agglomeration centers can of course also develop on a transnational basis. Thus, for example, there are signs that between western and eastern Europe a division of labor is emerging that is comparable with that which existed between the highly industrialized counties of western Europe and the economies of the southern hemisphere in the 1960s and 1970s. High-tech production in the most advanced countries is linked with the relocation of wage-intensive

and less demanding production sectors to the "cut-rate" industrial locations of neighboring countries or regions.

7   See in particular the excellent overview of German research and technology policy in Meyer-Krahmer/Kuntze (1992).

8   In addition, there is in the European Union, as well as, in an incipient phase, e.g. in MERCOSUR, also a multilateral dimension of technology policy that cannot be discussed at any greater length here.

9   See the studies by Altvater listed in the bibliography.

10 See Hübner (1991). The studies published by regulation theorists are for the most part concerned with change at the macrolevel of society (e.g. restructuring of the welfare state; emergence of new types of industrial relations), but without paying much attention to the inherent dynamics of social structures and their society-related functional logics.

Part II

1   CEPAL (1990). See also Mármora/Messner (1991).

2   For an overview, see Lancaster (1993), Moore (1993), Killick (1994), Williamson/Young (1994).

3   Willke (1992(b), pp. 17 ff.) is right in pointing out that Hegel's understanding of the state was based more on a regulative idea than a description of actual circumstances. Hegel speaks in many places of the state as *"a spiritual entity"*, as *"moral spirit"*. The task of the Hegelian state is to ensure the unity of a system in which centrifugal forces, driven by industrialization and the growing division of labor, were becoming ever more apparent. The discussion of the state in Hegel is thus a reflection on the difficult relationship between "state and society". In his distinction between state, civil society, and family, and in his elevation of the state to the level of the center instituting unity, Hegel already thematized what until today has constituted the core of the discussion in the social sciences over the relationship between state and society: How is possible to conceive the unity of a society which is engaged in a permanent process of differentiation and fragmentation? Both conservative and Marxist critics of Hegel have fallen short of the separation of state and society in that they have simply negated the significance and the evolutionary fact of the increasing differentiation of society. While the former interpret the inherent dynamics of civil society as an assault on the *"Myth of the State"* (thus Dahrendorf, 1965, pp. 225 ff.) and yearn for a return to the absolute state (e.g. Schmitt, 1940), Marxist theorists have looked to an overcoming of the state of separation into state and society, down to the extinction of the state.

4   Klawitter (1992), p. 194. Klawitter refers to an older edition of Hegel's *"Grundlinien der Philosphie des Rechts"* (Hegel, 1970).

5   For an overview, see Nuscheler/Steffani (1972), Fraenkel (1972, Erdmann (1988); see Dahl (1956), Lindblom (1965) on the discussion in the US.

6   See the overview in Eisfeld (1985). For a critical appraisal of pluralism theories, see Habermas (1992), pp. 399 ff., Schubert (1989), pp. 19 ff.

7   Kremendahl (1977), p. 263; see also Dahl (1965, pp. 130 ff.), Bently (1967, p. 169), Lindblom (1965).

8   Some authors who have provided important contributions to the discussion on political planning: Koch/Senghaas (1970), Lau (1975), Mayntz/Scharpf (1973); critical views: Tenbruck (1972), Volk (1970).

9   Offe (1987), p. 310.

10 Mayntz (1987), p. 97; see Mayntz et al. (1978) for a more in-depth presentation.

11 Mayntz (1987), pp. 97 f.; Bardach/Kagan (1982), Hood (1976) pursue a similar line of argumentation.

12 Scharpf (1972), pp. 173 f. Scharpf's more recent studies abandon any hope of being able to fulfill these three conditions and in this way ensuring optimal coordination. The present study will go into this problem in more depth.

13 The connection between the loss of the planning illusion and the "career" of the term "governance" is also illustrated by the fact that this term seldom occurred in the literature of the social sciences until the end of the 1960s. See Mayntz (1987, p. 91).

14 See Lang (1970); Schwegler/Roth (1992). Cybernetics analyzes control circuits in terms of a database reproduced under certain given conditions in order to be able to implement technical innovations in a microcosm analyzed, mathematically formalized, and clearly demarcated in such a way that they will function permanently (Klawitter 1992, pp. 200 f.). Such initial conditions are not met by the relations between state and society. The governance concept borrowed from technology and the natural sciences must thus be defined in terms of the social sciences if it is to operationalized for research in this field.

15 Kielmannsegg (1977), p. 144. See the volumes on the topic of governability edited by Hennis (1977 and 1979).

16 Olson (1982, p. 65). Be it noted here in passing that the rent-seeking discussion introduced quite similar lines of argument in the debate on deregulation. For a key example, see Buchanan et al. (1980).

17 Olson (1982), pp. 165 ff. Reference may here be made in passing to the innumerable cases of kleptocratic rule by authoritarian regimes which, unfettered by democratic control, are dedicated primarily to their own self-enrichment.

18 Luhmann (1992), pp. 66 ff. Luhmann sees as *"partial or subsystems"* areas with relatively clear *"guiding orientations"*, which have established themselves as autonomous systems with relatively stable boundaries vis-à-vis society and other

subsystems. The examples he cites include religion, law, economy, science, politics, and the educational system.

19 Willke 1987.

20 Hartwich 1987.

21 Streeck/Schmitter (1985). These authors assign *"spontaneous solidarity"* to the communities as their functional principle. Others have pointed out that solidarity is more an action resource than a principle of governance.

22 Simon (1983). Giddens (1992, p. 208) speaks of *"flexible contracts"* between actors as a means of emphasizing the procedural character of problem-solving.

Part III

1   For an overview see Powell (1990), Marin/Mayntz (1991), and the articles in the "European Journal of Political Research" (Feb. 1992).

2   See Smith (1987). On the constitution and significance of "experts" in modern societies, see Hitzler (1994).

3   Renate Mayntz (1987) distinguished four complexes of causes that can lead to failure of efforts aimed at governance (see: part II, chapter 4.3): problems bound up with knowledge, implementation, motivation, and governance capacities. These distinctions are useful for addressing causes of problems from the perspective of the system to be governed (governance capacity problems), the governance actors (knowledge problem), and the actors to be influenced (motivation and implementation problems). The significance of all four problem areas are in the last analysis closely linked to the - as it were - overriding complexity problem.

4   Hayek (1945, p. 254; emphasis in original) writes: *"If we possess all the relevant information, if we can start out from a given system of preferences, and if we command the complete knowledge of available means, the problem which remains is purely one of logic ... This, however, is emphatically **not** the problem which society faces."*

5   **Rational-choice theory** proceeds on the assumption that individuals take choice-related acts that are subject to a rationality calculation. Here, rationality means that an individual, faced with a choice between different alternatives, will decide in factor of the one that is most beneficial to him. In judging the choice it is unimportant whether the decision was "correct" in hindsight. Nor is it presupposed that the individual was comprehensively informed and familiar with all conceivable alternatives of action. The approach plainly and simply assumes that the individual chooses the option that seems to him the most advantageous. The rational-choice approach was developed within the framework of neoliberal economic theory as a means of analyzing individual decisions on the supply and demand of private goods. **Public-choice theory** applies this analysis of individual decisions to poli-

tics, and here the focal point is the question of how, on the basis of individual utility maximization, collective goods are provided or not provided. Important authors
include Buchanan/Tollison (1972), Cao-Garcia (1983), and Coleman (1990).
Kirsch (1993, p. 8), himself an enlightened representative of Public Choice, rightly
points to the circular character of the concept of rationality involved: "... *the individual chooses the best alternative; and: the best alternative is the one that he
chooses...* "

6   Bentham (1960), quoted after Etzioni (1988), p. 6. Important representatives of
     this notion of the *home oeconomicus* include Friedman, Hayek, and Nozick.

7   See Holmstrom (1979), Wolf (1987), Cook/Wood (1989). In organizational the-
     ory, on the other hand, there are empirically validated studies that come to the
     finding that there is no systematic difference in the efficiency of profit-oriented
     enterprises, nonprofit organizations, and public institutions. In Simon's (1991, p.
     30) eyes the decisive question is: "... *what motivates real people in real organiza-
     tion?* " He himself seeks answers to this question in the field defined by organiza-
     tional goals, identification of actors with these goals, variously efficient patterns of
     coordination in organizations, material and social (in the sense of recognition, etc.)
     incentives, and control.

8   Frey (1994), p. 137. One the most prominent representatives of a position of this
     type is the 1992 Nobel laureate Gary Becker. See Becker (1992).

9   Within public-choice theory, Brennan/Buchanan (1993) belong to the representa-
     tives of *"constitutional political economists"* who at least make the effort to reflect
     how the *"egoistic and predatory energy of the state"* can be contained through in-
     centives and control mechanisms or by institutionalizing party competition.

10   Etzioni (1988), p. 5. Etzioni does not object to the assumption of public choice
     theory stating that the behavior of individuals, organizations, communities, and
     societies is purposively rational, rejecting instead the universal assumption of
     egoistical-rational action orientations. See also Elster (1986 and 1991).

11   See Honneth (1993), p. 16. There are of course still authors on both sides who are
     not to be found along the "line of convergence" sketched above. Conservative rep-
     resentatives who can be see as strictly antilibertarian would, for instance, include
     Michael Sandel and Alasdair MacIntyre. On this point see the articles in Honneth
     (1993).

12   This distinction is made by Honneth (1993, p. 14).

13   On the communitarianism discussion, see Zahlmann (1992), Walzer (1992), Hon-
     neth (1993).

14   Important representatives include Pappi (1987 and 1993), Laumann/Knoke (1987).

15   They define seven forms of networks: state directed, concertation, pressure plural-
     ism, clientele pluralism, parantela pluralism, industry dominant pressure pluralism.

16 See Powell (1990), who speaks of organizational forms *"beyond markets and hierarchies"* in order to underline the specific quality of network structures and distance himself from e.g. Williamson (1990), who describes networks as a hybrid form between markets and hierarchies.

17 According to Williamson, network-like structures are aimed for when on the one hand transaction costs of market solutions are too high because of asset specificity and on the other hand the transaction costs of a fully integrated organization are likewise too high.

18 Streeck (1991) points out that *"institutionally rich societies"* are characterized more by a high level of social cohesion and political efficiency than societies that (like e.g. the UK under Thatcher) are geared to the paradigm of *"institutional minimalism"* (p. 22). This statement must be formulated more precisely by noting that organizational diversity (i.e. the existence of an *"active society"*) is a necessary, but by no means sufficient, condition for dynamic social development.

19 Six core problems can be discerned in the extensive literature on market failure (for an overview see Hayek (1952), de Vroey (1991), Kirsch et al. (1982). **First**, the market can lead to an imperfect allocation of resources when, due to their positions of power, individual market participants find it impossible to pay other participants compensation for negative external effects or claim payment for services either not rendered or insufficiently rendered (imperfect competition). **Second**, allocation via the market is generally not possible when private ownership rights cannot be claimed for realized goals that have come about as the consequence of a decision (nonvalidity of the exclusion principle). In this case the public sphere/the collective must step in for the nonexistent market. **Third**, market failure occurs when the use of a good by a consumer does not lead to a reduction of its utility that another consumer may derive from the good (noncompeting consumption). **Fourth**, even in the case that the first three problem areas may be ruled out, the market serves as an allocative principle for goods whose value can be expressed in prices, which, for instance, is very difficult, indeed often impossible, in appraising ecological goods. These four core problems are as a rule acknowledged by traditional, (neo)liberal economists. In addition, **fifth**, the market provides - with the reservations noted - for supplies of goods, but not for distributive justice. **Sixth**, the market is not only an allocation mechanism but also, as Marx (1981) and Polanyi (1978) have shown, a "social relation." The market it not efficient if it is not imbedded in specific institutions and they are not anchored in the value patterns of social actors.

20 Coase (1960). The preconditions that Coase posits for the operation of his theorem are often not specified: first, transaction costs are disregarded and, second, distribution-related issues are ignored.

21 The discussion that follows is based essentially on Scharpf (1991); see also Scharpf (1992b) and (1993a).

22 These center for the most part on John Rawls' Theory of Justice (1971 and 1973), which will be discussed in more detail below. In the current discussion on justice - see e.g. Dahrendorf (1992), Tugendhat (1993), and Honneth (1994) - the positions of the individual theorists - from Nozick' radical-liberal position to the views of the conservative wing of communitarianism (for an overview see Honneth 1993) - are frequently defined with an eye to Rawls.

23 Honneth (1994, p. 12) uses this term to thematize the action orientations and moral orientations of actors that constitute the foundation of the reproduction of complex, modern societies.

24 Thus, for instance, Riegraf (1993) shows that schemes of corporate headquarters aimed at promoting women's chances can fail as a result of active and passive forms of obstruction on the part of some of the persons affected. Similar phenomena concerning the limits of hierarchical governance are described by Naschold (1992 and 1993) for the dependence of state institutions on the willingness of social actors to cooperate in the process of policy formulation and implementation; Reichard (1994) does so with reference to local policy, Krumbein (1991) in the context of regional structural policy, Messner et al. (1991) in an analysis of the development of sectoral policies and institutions in Chilean industry, and Jürgens et al. (1989) for the implementation of new production concepts in the auto industry.

25 Crozier/Friedberg (1979), p. 41. Giddens (1992), in his "Constitution of Society", pp. 313 ff., argues along similar lines: see also Kiessling (1988), pp. 156 ff.

26 One example would be the "Ruhr cartel" consisting of heavy industry, state government, and labor unions in North Rhine-Westphalia. It was, for almost two decades, able to prevent future-oriented economic restructuring measure in the region and to push through solutions for which third parties (the taxpayer) had to foot the bill. See Grabher (1994), pp. 79 ff.; Voelzkow (1991), Drüke/Burmeister (1991).

27 See the studies in Honneth (1993). One of the most prominent representatives of the conservative communitarians is Robert Bellah. See Bellah et al. (1985).

28 Dubiel (1991) and (1993). For an overview, see Rödel's collective publication (1990), especially the article by Gauchet, to which Dubiel refers.

29 It is interesting in this connection that Popper does not play off personal responsibility and individualism against collective identities and group solidarity. Instead, group responsibility, i.e. the individual's responsibility for the consequences of his acts, constitutes the foundation of a nondestructive individualism (1980, p. 232). It is not by chance that these thoughts recall the categorical imperative of Kant, to whom Popper dedicated his life-work, "The Open Society".

30 Hirschman (1994), p. 301. Hirschman refers to Lindblom's classical essay "The Science of Muddling Through" (1959).

31 Hirschman (1994) distinguishes between "divisible", more-or-less conflicts" (distributional conflicts) that are in principle easier to resolve through the "art of compromise and bargaining" than "indivisible", "either-or conflicts" (e.g. disputes

over multicultural societies versus homogeneous societies, conflicts surrounding the abortion issue). The latter conflict type may easily bear the seeds of what Hirschman *"solvents"* or *"dynamite"*. But Hirschman also points out that conflicts with which societies have not yet learned to come to terms are often initially labeled *"indivisible"*, *"either-or problems"*. Hirschman: *"These conflicts can be understood only gradually, as we live through them"* (p. 304).

32 See Scharpf (1991a), pp. 63 ff. Etzioni (1994) argues along similar lines.

33 There are of course interest constellations displaying a basic structure that leads, as it were, "objectively" to unalterable or unmodifiable relationship patterns. The competition of two interested parties for **one** scarce and indivisible good can be solved only in the form of a zero-sum game. The competitive situations changes as soon as time is introduced as a dimension and the future holds similar decisions concerning scarce goods. In this case, assuming a corresponding action orientation on the part of the actors involved, cooperation and compromise become possible. Moreover, in the "real world" it is entirely possible for scientific, political, or ideological interpretations of interest constellations to change radically. If, in the Marxist discussion, the relationship between labor and capital was long regarded as fundamentally antagonistic (in terms of game theory: zero-sum game), today hardly anyone will dispute the fact that there is room for compromise and cooperation in bargaining between employers and labor unions (in terms of game theory: mixed-motive games are possible - if not necessary).

34 Situations in which there are "objectively correct" decisions are accordingly not subsumed under the category "battle of the sexes." One conceivable case would be a dispute between two persons over the best way to invest savings, when the two persons share the goal of saving together. The optimal savings investment could be determined at a given point of time, given absolute market transparency. In reality, however, the conflicts accessible to "objective decision" decrease. The real issues more often turn out to be those concerned with evaluation, distribution, and justice.

35 See e.g. Kenis/Schneider (1991), Marin (1990). As a rule network theorists do not distinguish between different constellations of interests and relationship patterns on the part of actors.

36 An example: a network of actors in a region scheduled for structural change in industry decides in favor of modernizing old industries or developing new ones. It is difficult to find an objectively correct solution. Even once the required scientific expertise has been reviewed, the ultimate issue will be to jointly define criteria of evaluation and justice. Both solutions would presumable entail social and ecological costs, and these would have to be analyzed and weighted. It is only in the timeless and spaceless world of neoliberalism that there are always objectively correct allocative decisions.

37 See Rawls (1971 and 1993); see Kersting (1993) for an overview and introduction.

38 Rawls' concept of equal opportunity thus goes beyond the Pareto optimality generally accepted in economics. Rawls' theory provides for redistribution to improve the position of poor population groups, and these may also mean that those who have much will have to relinquish some of it for the benefit of others.

39 Rawls here delineates himself in particular from utilitarian positions that seek orientation solely in terms of the overall utility of decisions. Rawls (1994, p. 147) writes: *"It may perhaps be useful, but not just, that some have less* **so that** *other are better off"* (Italics by D.M.). Rawls' theory centers on the individual with his rights, not the abstract "overall system interest".

40 All in all, Walzer distinguishes eleven spheres of justice: membership, family, security and welfare, money and goods, offices/administration, hard work, leisure, education and training, kinship and love, divine grace (meaning "happiness"), and political power.

41 It should be noted that it is not only here that Walzer (1992, pp. 51 ff.) switches to universalist motives situated upstream of his "sphere-bound" principles of justice (see the interpretation of Buchstein/Schmalz-Bruns (1992, pp. 380 ff.)). At the same time, his fundamental critique aims precisely at Rawls' attempt to justify universalist core principles, a point noted, to this extent rightly, by Walzer's critics. It is thus against his actual intention that Walzer's arguments can indeed be linked up with Rawls' logic - though they nonetheless go beyond it.

42 Externally, Walzer calls for defense against claims made by specific subsystem environments that could overburden the world of the "members." In these passages Walzer at times comes close to the narrow and particularist worlds of conservative communitarians; but there are also many convinced "progressive" dependence theorists who would have little trouble subscribing to this idea of Walzer's if it were applied to North-South relations. Yet in this issue Walzer underestimates the productive effects of "disruptions" from outside, which can heighten the ability of social systems or "spheres" to learn and boost their creativity. It is certainly correct that any system can be overburden by great external pressure.

43 Honneth (1994a), p. 86. Honneth specifies three levels at which individuals are forced to compete for recognition: love and friendship, legal recognition as citizens, social recognition of one's own individual achievements.

44 See Luhmann (1988). Gambetta (1988, p. 219) argues in the same direction: *"If distrust is complete, cooperation will fail among free agents. Furthermore, if trust exists only unilaterally cooperation may also fail, and if it is blind it may constitute rather an incentive to deception."*

45 Gambetta (1988, p. 219) defines as follows "trust" against the background of the thoughts outlined above: *"..., trusting a person means believing that when offered the chance, he or she is not likely to behave in a way that is damaging to us, and trust will* **typically** *be relevant when at least one party is free to disappoint the other, free enough to avoid a risky relationship,* **and** *constrained enough to consider that relationship is an attractive option. In short, trust is implicated in most*

human experience, if of course to widely different degrees" (Underlining in original).

46 Of course trust differs in significance in different contexts. In functioning states under the rule of law, trust in the law is necessarily greater than in corrupt regimes. Trust in the law also strengthens trust between individuals. For orthodox neoliberal theorists, on the other hand, trust has no role to play because their model world presupposes perfect information and transparency. While Adam Smith differentiated very precisely between model world and reality, the model-based theoretical assumptions of "modern" public-choice analysts take on a life of their own and are confused with real dynamics in real societies.

47 I.e. even "proofs" that specific conflicts can be settled on the basis of cooperative, solution-oriented strategies are not of much help in a context of generalized distrust. "Proofs" from the past - from the perspective of distrust - are not evidence that trust will be sanctioned, and not exploited, in the future. Gambetta (1988, p. 234) writes: *"... deep distrust is very difficult to invalidate through experience ..."* What we see here are indications of a self-fulfilling-prophecy logic.

48 Elster (1979), p. 4. Elster, however, reduces strategic capacity to the dimension of future orientation.

49 See e.g. the excellent study by Azpiau and Nochteff on the social deep effects of the neoliberal hegemony prevalent in Argentina since the 1980s. See also the country studies of Argentina, Chile, Uruguay in Hurtienne et al. (1994) and Tironi (1990) and Montero (1993) on Chile.

50 Habermas (1992, p. 427) coins this term to describe the autonomization of social subsystems vis-à-vis their environment.

51 One example would be the regional conferences just discussed. As a rule, compromises on the part of actors are the condition for state policy initiatives building on them. In other words, state agencies establish bargaining rules. The regional conferences in some regions of the state of North-Rhine Westphalia are compulsory bargaining systems inasmuch as state activities are, as a matter of principle, bound to previous initiatives, incentives, or concepts worked out by the regional conferences. The task of analyzing effective contexts and problem dimensions and working out proposals for solutions are thus (bindingly) delegated to the actors involved, thus focusing their tacit knowledge and channeling it into policy proposals. The activities of the policy network nonetheless are conducted under the auspices of state institutions.

Part IV

1 Willke (1992a), p. 143. In using this formulation Willke is also criticizing Luhmann's position.

2   König (1993, p. 459) rightly point out that the Holocaust, as systematic mass mur-
     der, was possible only in a modern society marked by division of labor.

3   Bolivia would be an example of the case of "successful stabilization without de-
     velopment;" see Messner (1993). Chile is an example of a country that has suc-
     ceeded in mobilizing resources-based exports on the basis of a clever macro-
     economic management, but without (at least until now) making the transition to
     more pronouncedly technology- and knowledge-based productive base, since lacks
     efficient structures in the mesospace. See the studies Chile by Messner and Scholz,
     bibliography.

4   See the author's studies (1993d and 1993e) on strengthening technological compe-
     tence in Bolivia and Argentina and the study by Hillebrand/Messner/Meyer-Stamer
     (1993), based on five additional country analyses, on the strengthening of techno-
     logical competence in developing countries (Zimbabwe, Tanzania, Indonesia,
     Thailand, Singapore).

Bibliography

Abromeit, H. / U. Jürgens (eds.): *Die politische Logik wirtschaftlichen Handelns*, Berlin 1992

Alchian, A.A. / H. Demsetz: "Production, Information Costs and Economic Organization", in: *American Economic Review*, 1972, No. 62

Aldrich, H.: *Resource Dependence und Interorganizational Relations*, Berlin 1975

Altmann, N. / D. Sauer: *Systemische Rationalisierung und Zuliefererindustrie*, Frankfurt, New York 1989

Altvater, E.: *Sachzwang Weltmarkt*, Hamburg 1987

-: *Die Zukunft des Marktes*, Münster 1991

-: "Stammwesen im globalen Dorf", in: *Blätter für deutsche und internationale Politik*, 1992, No. 5

-: "Gewinner und Verlierer, Entwicklung als 'Niederauffahrt'". *Blätter des Informationszentrums Dritte Welt*, 1993, No. 191

-: "Die Ordnung rationaler Weltbeherrschung oder: Ein Wettbewerb von Zauberlehrlingen", in: *PROKLA-Zeitschrift für kritische Sozialwissenschaft*, 1994a, No. 95

-: "Beschäftigungpolitik jenseits von Nationalstaat und 'Arbeitsintensität'", in: *WSI-Mitteilungen*, 1994b, No. 6

Altvater, E. / K. Hübner / M. Stanger: *Alternative Wirtschaftspolitik jenseits des Keynesianismus*, Opladen 1983

Amin, A.: "The Globalization of the Economy. An Erosion of Regional Networks", in: G. Grabher (ed.), *The Embedded Firm*, London 1993

Antal, A.B.: *Corporate Social Performance*, Frankfurt 1992

Arrow, K.: *Gift and Exchanges. Philosophy and Public Affairs*, 1972, No. 1

-: "The Production and Distribution of Knowledge", in: G. Silverberg / L. Soete (eds.), *The Economics of Growth and Technical Change*, Aldershot 1994

Asheim, B.: "The Role of Industrial Districts in the Application, Adaption and Diffusion of Technology in Developed Countries". Discussion paper presented at an UNCTAD / GTZ seminar, 16/17 Nov., 1992, Geneva 1992

Ashoff, G.: "Rent-Seeking: Zur Relevanz eines relativ neuen Konzeptes in der ökonomischen Theorie der Politik und der entwicklungstheoretischen Diskussion", *Vierteljahresberichte*, 1988, No. 112

Atkinson, M.M. / W.D. Coleman: "Corporatism and Industrial Policy", in: A. Cawson (ed.), *Organized Interests and the State*, London 1985

-: "Strong States and Weak States. Sectoral Policy Networks in Advanced Capitalist Economies", in: *British Journal of Political Science*, Vol. 19, 1989, No. 1

Audretsch, D.B.: "Small Business in Industrial Economics. The New Learning", Discussion paper, Wissenschaftszentrum Berlin (WZB), Berlin 1992a

-: "Größe von Unternehmen", in: *WZB-Mitteilungen*, 1992b, No. 58

Augé, M.: *Orte und Nicht-Orte*, Frankfurt 1994

Axelrod, R: *The Evolution of Cooperation*, New York 1984

Azpiasu, D. / H. Nochteff: *El desarrollo ausente. Restricciones al desarrollo, neoconservadorismo y elite económica en la Argentina*, Buenos Aires 1994

Bachrach, B.: *Die Theorie demokratischer Eliteherrschaft*, Frankfurt 1967

Badura, P.: *Staatsrecht*, Munich 1986

Baeza, M.F.: *Las Instituciones de Gobierno y las Políticas de Desarrollo en América Latina*, Heidelberg 1989

Banfield, E.C.: *The Moral Basis of Backward Societies*, New York 1958

Barber, B.: *The Logic and Limits of Trust*, New Brunswick 1983

Bardach, E. / R.A. Kagan: *The Problem of Regulatory Unreasonableness*, Philadelphia 1982

Becattini, G.: "Sectors and/or Districts", in: E. Goodman et al. (eds.), *Small Firms and Industrial Districts in Italy*, London 1989

-: "The Marshallian Industrial District as a Socio-economic Notion", in: F. Pyke et al. (eds.), *Industrial Districts and Inter-Firm Co-Operation in Italy*, Geneva 1990

Beck, U.: *Die Neuerfindung des Politischen*, Frankfurt 1993

Becker, G.S.: "Habits, Addictions and Tradition", in: *Kyklos*, 1992, No. 45

Bellah, R., et al.: *Habits of the Heard. Individualism and Commitment in American Life*, Berkeley 1985

Bendel, K: "Funktionale Differenzierung und gesellschaftliche Rationalität", in: *Zeitschrift für Soziologie*, 1993, No. 4

Bennett, C.J. / M. Howlett: "The Lessons of Learning. Reconciling Theories of Policy Learning and Policy Change", in: *Policy Science*, 1992, No. 3

Benson, J.K.: "The Interorganizational Network or a Political Economy", in: *Administrative Science Quarterly*, 1975, No. 20

Bentham, J.: *An Introduction to the Principles of Morals and Legislation*, Oxford 1960

Bentley, A.: *The Process of Government*, Cambridge 1967

Benz, A.: "Politisch-administrative Strukturen und Institutionen", in: Th. Ellwein et. al. (eds.), *Jahrbuch zur Staats- und Verwaltungswissenschaft*, Baden-Baden 1987

-: "Mehr-Ebenen-Verflechtung. Politische Prozesse in verbundenen Entscheidungsarenen", Max-Planck-Institut für Gesellschaftsforschung, Discussion paper, Cologne 1991

-: "Zusammenarbeit zwischen den Norddeutschen Bundesländern", in: A. Benz et al. (eds.), *Horizontale Politikverflechtung*, Frankfurt 1992

Benz, A. / F.W. Scharpf / R. Zintl: "Horizontale Politikverflechtung", *Schriften des Max-Planck-Instituts für Gesellschaftsforschung*, Cologne 1992

Bermbach, U.: "Politische Institutionen und gesellschaftlicher Wandel. Zum Institutionenverständnis im politischen Denken der Neuzeit", in: H.H. Hartwich (ed.), *Macht und Ohnmacht politischer Institutionen*, Opladen 1988

Bernholz, P.: "Constitutions as Governance Structures. The Political Foundations of Secure Markets", in: *Journal of Institutional and Theoretical Economics*, Vol. 1, 1993

Bernschneider, W. / G. Schindler / J. Schüller: "Industriepolitik in Baden-Württemberg und Bayern", in: U. Jürgens / W. Krumbein (eds.), *Industriepolitische Strategien*, Berlin 1991

Best, M.: *The New Competition*, Cambridge 1990

Beyme, C. v.: *Theorie der Politik im 20. Jahrhundert*, Frankfurt 1991

Beyme, K.: "Methodische Ansätze politikwissenschaftlicher Forschung", in: K. Beyme (ed.), *Die politischen Theorien der Gegenwart II*, Opladen 1992

-: "Grundbegriffe der politischen Theorie", in: K. Beyme (ed.), *Die politischen Theorien der Gegenwart III*, Opladen 1992

-: "Der Zusammenbruch des Sozialismus und die Folgen für die sozialwissenschaftliche Theoriebildung", Wissenschaftszentrum Berlin, in: *WZB-Mitteilungen*, 1994, No. 63

-: "Der Nationalstaat", in: *WZB-Mitteilungen*, 1992, No. 56

Bitran C.E. / P.E. Saavedra: "Algunas Reflexiones en Torno al Rol Regulador y Empresarial del Estado", in: O. Muños Goma (ed.), *Hacia el estado regulador*, Santiago 1993

Bobbio, N.: *Die Zukunft der Demokratie*, Berlin 1988

Bodemer, K.: "Uruguay: Zwischen Systemblockade und zaghaften Reformansätzen", in: K. Bodemer et al. (eds.), *Uruguay*, Hamburg 1993

Böhret, C.: *Entscheidungshilfen für die Regierung, Modelle, Instrumente, Probleme*, Opladen 1970

-: *Folgen*, Opladen 1990

Bohr, N.: "Discussion with Einstein", in: P.A. Schlipp (ed.), *Albert Einstein: Philosopher-Scientist*, Evanston 1949

Bonus, H.: "The Evolving Science of Organization", in: *Journal of Institutional and Theoretical Economics*, 1993, No. 1

Brennan, G. / J.M. Buchanan: *Die Begründung von Regeln*, Tübingen 1993

Brinkerhoff, D.W. / A.A. Goldsmith: "Promoting the Sustainability of Development Institutions. A Framework for Strategy", in: *World Development*, Vol. 20, 1992, No. 3

Brodkin, E.Z.: *Towards a Structural Theory of Action*, New York 1982

Brücker, H.: *Privatisierung in Ostdeutschland. Eine institutionenökonomische Analyse*, Dissertation am Fachbereich Wirtschaftswissenschaften der J.-W.-v.-Goethe-Universität, Frankfurt 1993

Brunkhorst, H.: "Die Krise der Demokratie", in: *Frankfurter Rundschau*, Dokumentation, Feb. 5, 1994

Brusco, S.: "Small Firms and Industrial Districts. The Experience of Italy", in: D. Keeble / E. Wever (eds.), *New Firms and Regional Development in Europe*, London 1986

-: "The Idea of the Industrial District. Its Genesis", in: F. Pyke et al. (eds.), *Industrial Districts and Inter-Firm Co-Operation in Italy*, Geneva 1990

Brusco, S. / M. Pezzini: "Small-scale Enterprise in the Ideology of the Italian Left", in: F. Pyke et al. (eds.), *Industrial Districts and Inter-Firm Co-Operation in Italy*, Geneva 1990

Brusco, S. / E. Righi: "Local Government, Industrial Policy and Social Consensus. The Case of Modena", in: *Economy and Society*, No. 18, Routledge 1989

Brutti, P. / F. Calistri: "Industrial Districts and the Unions", in: F. Pyke et al. (eds.), *Industrial Districts and Inter-Firm Co-Operation in Italy*, Geneva 1990

Buchanan, J.M.: "Choosing what to choose", in: *Journal of Institutional and Theoretical Economics*, 1994, No. 1

Buchanan, J.M., et al. (eds.): *Towards a Theory of the Rent-Seeking Society*, London 1980

Buchanan, J.M. / R.D. Tallison (eds.): *Theory of Public Choice*, Ann Arbor 1972

Buchstein, H. / R. Schmalz-Bruns: "Gerechtigkeit als Demokratie. Zur politischen Philosophie von Michael Walzer", in: *Politische Vierteljahresschrift*, 1992, No. 3

Buci-Glucksmann, C. / G. Therborn: *Der sozialdemokratische Staat*, Hamburg 1982

Bühl, W.: "Die Dynamik sozialer Konflikte in katastrophentheoretischer Darstellung", in: *Kölner Zeitschrift für Sozialpolitik*, 1984, No. 4

-: "Grenzen der Autopoieses", in: *Kölner Zeitschrift für Sozialpolitik*, 1987, No. 4

-: "Sozialwissenschaften jenseits des Gleichgewichtspfades", in: *Soziale Welt*, 1989, No. 1/2

Cao-Garcia, R.J.: *Explorations Toward an Economic Theory of Political Systems*, London 1983

Capecchi, V.: "A History of Flexible Specialization and Industrial Districts in Emilia-Romagna", in: F. Pyke et al. (eds.), *Industrial Districts and Inter-Firm Co-Operation in Italy*, Geneva 1990

Carliner, G.: "Industrial Policies for Emerging Industries", in: P.R. Krugman (ed.), *Strategic Trade Policy*, Cambridge 1987

Carter, J.: *Keeping Faith - Memories of a President*, New York 1983

Castillo, M. / M. Dini / C. Maggi: "Reorganización industrial y estrategias competitivas in Chile", Santiago 1994 (mimeo)

Cawson, A.: "Conclusion: Some Implications for State Theory", in: A. Cawson (ed.), *Organized Interests and the State*, London 1985

-: "Varieties of Corporatism: the Importance of the Meso-level of Interest Intermediation", in: A. Cawson (ed.), *Organized Interests and the State*, London 1985

-: *Corporatism and Political Theory*, Oxford 1986

Chandler, A.D.: *The Visible Hand*, Cambridge 1977

Chinitz, B.: *Contracts in Agglomeration*, New York, Pittsburgh 1961

Chisholm, D.: *Coordination without Hierarchy*, Berkeley 1989

Coase, R.H.: "The Problem of Social Cost", in: *Journal of Law and Economics*, 1960, No. 3

Colclough, Ch.: "Who Should Learn to Pay? An Assessment of Neo-liberal Approaches to Education Policy", *IDS Development Studies Series*, Oxford 1992

Colclough, Ch. / J. Manor (eds.): *States or Markets? Neo-liberalism and the Development Policy Debate*, Oxford 1992

Coleman, J.: *Introduction to Mathematical Sociology*, New York 1964

Coleman, J.S.: *Foundations of Social Theory*, London 1990

Collins, R.: "Is 1980s Sociology in the Doldrums?", in: *American Journal of Sociology*, Vol. 91, 1986, No. 6

Collis, D.J.: "The Machine Tool Industry and Industrial Policy", 1955-82, in: A.M. Spence / H.A. Hazard (eds.), *International Competitiveness*, Oxford 1988

Cook, B.J. / B.D. Wood: "Principal-Agent Models of Political Control of Bureaucracy", in: *American Political Science Review*, 1989, No. 83

-: "Principal-Agent Models of Political Control of Bureaucracy", in: *American Political Science Review*, 1989, No. 83

Crozier, M.: *La société bloqueé*, Paris 1970

Crozier, M. / E. Friedberg: *Macht und Organisation*, Königstein 1979

Czada, R.: "Konsensbedingungen und Auswirkungen neokorporatistischer Politikentwicklung", in: *Journal für Sozialforschung*, Vol. 23, 1983, No. 4

-: "Der Staat als wirtschaftender Akteur", in: H. Abromeit / U. Jürgens (eds.), *Die politische Logik wirtschaftlichen Handelns*, Berlin 1992

Czada, R. / M.G. Schmidt: "Einleitung: Verhandlungsdemokratie", in: R. Czada / M.G. Schmidt (eds.), *Verhandlungsdemokratie, Interessenvermittlung, Regierbarkeit*, Opladen 1993

Dahl, R.: *A Preface to Democratic Theory*, Chicago 1956

Dahrendorf, R.: *Soziale Klassen und Klassenkonfikt in der industriellen Gesellschaft*, Frankfurt 1957

-: *Lebenschancen. Anläufe zur sozialen und politischen Theorie*, Frankfurt 1979

-: *Der moderne soziale Konflikt*, Stuttgart 1992

-: "Ich bleibe ein radikaler Liberaler", in: *Die Zeit*, 27 August 1993

Dammann, K. / D. Grunow / K.P. Japp: "Theorie der Verwaltungswissenschaft - nach mehr als einem Vierteljahrhundert", in: K. Dammann et al. (eds.), *Die Verwaltung des politischen Systems*, Opladen 1994

De Alessi, L.: "The Evolving Science of Organization", in: *Journal of Institutional and Theoretical Economics*, 1993, No. 1

De Vroey, M.: "Der Markt - von wegen einfach", in: *PROKLA-Zeitschrift für kritische Sozialwissenschaft*, 1991, No. 82

Dearborn, D.C. / H.A. Simon: "Selective Perception: the Identifications of Executives", in: *Sociometry*, 1958, No. 21

Dettling, W.: "Und der Zukunft gar nicht zugewandt", in: *Die Zeit*, 22 July, 1994

Deutsch, K.: *The Nerves of Government*, New York 1963

-: *Politische Kybernetik*, Freiburg 1969

-: "Zur Handlungs- und Lernkapazität politischer Systeme", in: H. Lenk (ed.), *Handlungstheorien interdisziplinär*, Munich 1977

Dewatripont, M.: "Institutional Choice. A Contract-Theoretic Approach", in: *Journal of Institutional and Theoretical Economics*, 1993, No. 1

Dickens, W.T.: "The Economic Consequences of Economic Dissonance", in: G.A. Allerlof (ed.), *An Economic Theorist's Book of Tales*, Cambridge 1984

Diederich, N. / U. Hilpert: "Staatliche Politik und nicht-intendierte Konsequenzen", in: H.H. Hartwich (ed.), *Macht und Ohnmacht politischer Institutionen*, Opladen 1988

Dijk, M.P. v.: "The Interrelation between Industrial Districts and Technological Capability Development", Discussion paper presented at an UNCTAD / GTZ seminar on "The Role of Industrial Districts in the Application, Adaptation and Diffusion of Technology", 16/17 Nov., 1992, Geneva 1992

Dosi, G. / K. Pavitt / L. Soete: *The Economics of Technical Change and International Trade*, New York 1990

Downs, A.: *An Economic Theory of Democracy*, New York 1957

Dror, Y.: *Public Policy-Making*, San Francisco 1968

Drüke, H. / K. Burmeister: "NRW - Das sozialdemokratische Modell einer Industriepolitik?", in: U. Jürgens / W. Krumbein (eds.), *Industriepolitische Strategien*, Berlin 1991

Dubiel, H.: "Zivilreligion in der Massendemokratie", in: *Soziale Welt*, 1990, No. 2

-: *Konsens oder Konflikt*, Frankfurt 1991

-: "Das ethische Minimum", in: *Süddeutsche Zeitung*, 27/28 March, 1993

Dunning, J.H.: "The Global Economy, Domestic Governance, Strategies and Transnational Corporations. Interactions and Policy Implications", in: *Transnational Corporations*, Vol. 1, 1992, No. 3

Durkheim, E.: "Über soziale Arbeitsteilung", *Studie über die Organisation höherer Gesellschaften*, Frankfurt 1988

-: *Über die Teilung der sozialen Arbeit*, Frankfurt 1977

Dyke, C.: *Philosophy of Economics*, New York 1981

Eder, K.: "Prozedurale Rationalität. Moderne Rechtsentwicklung jenseits von formaler Rationalisierung", in: *Zeitschrift für Rechtssoziologie*, 1986, No. 1

Ehrenberg, R.G. / R.S. Smith: *Modern Labour Economics. Theory and Public Policy*, Glenview 1982

Einem, E. v.: "Industriepolitik: Anmerkungen zu einem kontroversen Begriff", in: U. Jürgens / W. Krumbein (eds.), *Industriepolitische Strategien*, Berlin 1991

Eisfeld, R.: "Pluralismus", in: D. Nohlen / R.O. Schultze (eds.), *Politikwissenschaft*, Munich 1985

Elias, N.: *Über den Prozeß der Zivilisation*, 2 vols., Frankfurt 1969

-: *Was ist Soziologie?*, Munich 1981

-: *Die Gesellschaft der Individuen*, Frankfurt 1987

Ellwein, T.: *Politik und Planung*, Stuttgart 1968

Elster, J.: "Ulyses and the Sirens". *Studies on Rationality and Irrationality*, Cambridge 1979

-: "The Possibility of Rational Politics", in: D. Held (ed.), *Political Theory Today*, Oxford 1991

-: "The Market and the Forum", in: J. Elster / A. Hylland (eds.), *Foundation of Social Choice Theory*, Cambridge 1986

Elwert, G.: "Wenn das Geld zur Macht fließt. Korruption in Afrika", in: *Entwicklung und Zusammenarbeit*, Vol. 34, 1993, No. 3

Engels, B.: "Die strukturellen Ursachen der Korruption", in: *Entwicklung und Zusammenarbeit*, Vol. 34, 1993, No. 3

Erdmann, H.: *Neopluralismus und Gewaltenteilung*, Leverkusen 1988

Eschenburg, T.: *Herrschaft der Verbände*, Stuttgart 1963

-: *Das Jahrhundert der Verbände*, Berlin 1989

Esser, J.: "Staat und Markt", in: I. Fetscher / H. Münkler (eds.), *Politikwissenschaft*, Hamburg 1985

-: "Staat und Markt", in: I. Fetscher / H. Münkler (eds.), *Politikwissenschaft*, Reinbek 1990

Esser, K.: "Perú. Una salida de la crisis", Working paper, GDI, Berlin 1989

-: "Development of a Competitive Strategy. A Challenge to the Countries of Latin America in the 1990s", Working paper, GDI, Berlin 1991

-: "Latin America - Industrialization without Vision", in: K. Esser / W. Hillebrand / D. Messner / J. Meyer-Stamer: *International Competitiveness in Latin America and East Asia*, London 1993

-: *Wettbewerbsorientierung und Integrationsdynamik*, GDI, Berlin 1994

-: "Neue Konzepte zum Erfolg. Die wirtschaftlichen Herausforderungen Lateinamerikas in den 90er Jahren", in: D. Junker / D. Nohlen / H. Sangmeister (eds.), *Latein-amerika am Ende des 20. Jahrhunderts*, Munich 1994

Esser, K., et al.: "Argentinien. Zum industriepolitischen Suchprozeß", Working paper, GDI, Berlin 1989

Esser, K. / W. Hillebrand / D. Messner / J. Meyer-Stamer: *International Competitiveness in Latin America and East Asia*, London 1993

-: *Systemic Competitiveness - New Governance Patterns for Industrial Development*, London 1996

Esser, K. / W. Hillebrand / E. Kürzinger/ D. Messner / J. Meyer-Stamer: *América Latina. Hacia una estrategia competitiva*, GDI, Berlin 1992

Etzioni, A.: *A Comparative Analysis of Complex Organizations*, New York 1961

-: *The Active Society*, New York 1968

-: *The Moral Dimension. Towards a New Economic*, New York 1988

-: *Jenseits des Egoismus-Prinzips*, Stuttgart 1994

Eucken, W.: *Grundsätze der Wirtschaftspolitik*, Reinbek 1959

Evans, P.: "A Comparative Political Economy Perspective on the Third World State", in: *Sociological Forum*, 1989, No. 4

-: "The State as Problem and Solution? Predation, Embedded Autonomy, and Structural Change", in: S. Haggard / R.R. Kaufman (eds.), *The Politics of Economic Adjustment*, Princeton 1992

Evans, P., et al.: *Bringing the State Back in*, Cambridge 1985

Fajnzylber, F.: *América Latina. La industrialización trunca*, Santiago 1984

Feick, D.: "Regulation", in: A. Görlitz / R. Prätorius (eds.), *Handbuch Politikwissenschaft*, Reinbek 1987

Forsthoff, E.: *Der Staat der Industriegesellschaft*, Munich 1971

Fraenkel, E.: "Um die Verfassung 1932", in: F. Nuscheler / W. Steffani (eds.), *Pluralismus*, Munich 1972

Freeman, C.: *Technology Policy and Economic Performance*, New York 1987

-: "Formal Scientific and Technological Institutions in the National System of Innovation", in: B. Lundvall (ed.), *National Systems of Innovation*, London 1992

Frey, S.B.: "Moral and Institutional Constraints", in: *Journal of Institutional and Theoretical Economics*, 1994, No. 150

Fröbel, F., et al.: *Die neue internationale Arbeitsteilung*, Reinbek 1977

-: *Umbruch in der Weltwirtschaft*, Reinbek 1986

Fronia, J.: "Möglichkeiten der EG zur Koordinierung regionaler Industriepolitiken", in: U. Jürgens / W. Krumbein (eds.), *Industriepolitische Strategien*, Berlin 1991

Fürst, D.: "Die Neubelebung der Staatsdiskussion. Veränderte Anforderungen an Regierung und Verwaltung in westlichen Industriegesellschaften", in: Th. Ellwein et. al. (eds.), *Jahrbuch zur Staats- und Verwaltungswissenschaft*, Baden-Baden 1987

Fürst, D., et al.: "Regionalverbände im Vergleich. Entwicklungssteuerung in Verdichtungsräumen", in: J.J. Hesse (ed.), *Schriften zur kommunalen Wissenschaft und Praxis*, Vol. 4, Baden-Baden 1990

Galbraith, J.K.: *American Capitalism*, Boston 1956

-: *The New Industrial State*, Boston 1987

-: *Die Wirtschaft der Bankrotteure*, Hamburg 1992

Gambetta, D.: "Can we Trust Trust?", in: D. Gambetta (ed.), *Trust*, New York 1988

Ganssmann, H.: "Sind soziale Rechte universalisierbar?", in: *Zeitschrift für Soziologie*, 1993, No. 5

Garreton, M.A. / M. Espinosa: "¿Reforma del Estado o cambio en la Matriz socio-política?", FLACSO, Documento de Trabajo, Santiago 1992

Gauchet, C.: "Die totalitäre Erfahrung und das Denken des Politischen", in: U. Rödel (ed.), *Autonome Gesellschaft und libertäre Demokratie*, Frankfurt 1992

Gerstein, D.R.: "Durkheim's Paradigm. Reconstructing a Social Theory", in: R. Collins (ed.), *Sociological Theory*, San Francisco 1983

Giddens, A.: *Die Konstitution der Gesellschaft*, Frankfurt 1992

Giersch, H.: "Das größere Übel", in: *Wirtschaftswoche*, 1994, No. 33

Glagow, M. (ed.): *Gesellschaftssteuerung zwischen Korporatismus und Subsidiarität*, Bielefeld 1984

Glasmeier, H.J.: *Durchstaatlichung und Selbstorganisation der Gesellschaft*, Munich 1984

Gocht, W. / J. Meyer-Stamer: *Stärkung technologischer Kompetenz in Simbabwe*, GDI, Berlin 1993

-: *Stärkung technologischer Kompetenz in Tansania*, GDI, Berlin 1993

Gollop, F.M.: "Analysis of the Productivity Slowdown. Evidence for a Sector-Biased or Sector-Neutral Industrial Strategy", in: W.J. Baumol / K. McLennan (eds.), *Productivity Growth and US Competitiveness*, New York 1985

Grabher, G.: *De-Industrialisierung oder Neo-Industrialisierung*, Berlin 1988

-: "On the Weakness of Strong Ties. The Ambivalent Role of Inter-Firm Relations in the Decline and Reorganization of the Ruhr", Discussion paper, Wissenschafts-zentrum Berlin, Forschungsschwerpunkt Arbeitsmarkt und Beschäftigung, Berlin 1990

-: "Against De-Industrialisation. A Strategy for Old Industrial Areas", in: E. Matzner / W. Streeck (eds.), *Beyond Keynesianism*, Worcester 1991

-: "Rediscovering the Social in the Economics of Interfirm Relations", in: G. Grabher (ed.), *The Embedded Firm*, London 1993

-: "The Weakness of Strong Ties, The Lock-in of Regional Development in the Ruhr Area", in: G. Grabher (ed.), *The Embedded Firm*, London 1993

-: *Lob der Verschwendung*, Berlin 1994

Grande, E.: "Die neue Architektur des Staates", in: R. Czada / M.G. Schmidt (eds.), *Verhandlungsdemokratie, Interessenvermittlung, Regierbarkeit*, Opladen 1993

Granovetter, M.: "The Strength of Weak Ties", in: *American Journal of Sociology*, 1973, No. 6

-: "The Strength of Weak Ties. A Network Theory Revisited", in: R. Collins (ed.), *Sociological Theory*, San Francisco 1983

-: "Economic Action and Social Structure. The Problem of Embeddedness", in: *American Journal of Sociology*, 1985, No. 91

Gretschmann, K.: *Steuerungsprobleme der Staatswirtschaft*, Berlin 1981

Groom, A.J.R.: "No Compromise. Problem-Solving in a Theoretical Perspective", in: *International Social Science Journal*, 1991, No. 127

Grossman, G.M.: "Strategic Export Promotion. A Critique", in: Paul R. Krugman (ed.), *Strategic Trade Policy and the New International Economics*, Cambridge 1987

Habermas, J.: *Zur Rekonstruktion des historischen Materialismus*, Frankfurt 1976

-: *Theorie kommunikativen Handelns*, Vol. 1/2, Frankfurt 1981

-: *Faktizität und Geltung*, Frankfurt 1992

Haggard, S. / R. Kaufman: "Institutions and Economic Adjustment", in: S. Haggard / R. Kaufman (eds.), *The Politics of Economic Adjustment*, Princeton 1992

Hahn, F.: "Die Relevanz der allgemeinen Gleichgewichtstheorie für die Transformation zentral geplanter Wirtschaften", in: *PROKLA-Zeitschrift für kritische Sozialwissenschaft*, 1994, No. 94

Hakansson, H. / J. Johanson: "The Network as a Governance Structure. Interfirm Cooperation beyond Markets and Hierarchies", in: G. Grabher (ed.), *The Embedded Firm*, London 1993

Hall, P.A.: *Governing the Economy. The Politics of State Intervention in Britain and France*, New York 1986

Hanf, K.: "The Implementation of Regulatory Policy. Enforcement as Bargaining", in: *European Journal of Political Research*, 1982, No. 10

Hanf, K. / L. O'Toole: "Networks, Implementation Structures and the Management of Inter-Organizational Relations", in: *European Journal of Political Research*, 1992, No. 21

Hannig, A. / M. Witt: "Financial Sector Development. Economic versus Social Policies", Discussion paper, GDI, Berlin 1993

Harrison, B.: "Industrial Districts: Old Wine in New Bottles", in: *Regional Studies*, 1992, No. 5

Hartwich, H.H.: "Zentrale Fragen der Politikwissenschaft in der Diskussion. Einige Wahrnehmungen", in: H.H. Hartwich (ed.), *Policy-Forschung in der Bundesrepublik Deutschland*, Opladen 1985

-: "Die Suche nach einer wirklichkeitsnahen Lehre vom Staat", in: *Aus Politik und Zeitgeschichte*, 1987, No. 46/47

-: *Macht und Ohnmacht politischer Institutionen*, Opladen 1989

Hayek, F.A. v.: "The Use of Knowledge in Society", in: *American Economic Review*, Vol. 35, 1945, No. 4

-: *Individualismus und wirtschaftliche Ordnung*, Zurich 1952

-: "The Theory of Complex Phenomena", in: F.A. v. Hayek (ed.), *Studies in Philosophy, Politics and Economics*, London 1967

-: *The Three Sources of Human Values*, London 1978

Heclo, H.: "Issue Networks and the Executive Establishment", in: A. King (ed.), *The New American Political System*, Washington 1978

Hegel, G.W.F.: *Grundlinien der Philosophie des Rechts*, Theorie Werkausgabe, Frankfurt 1970

Hegner, F.: "Solidarity and Hierarchy. Institutional Arrangement for the Coordination of Actions", in: F.X. Kaufmann et al. (eds.), *Guidance, Control and Evaluation in the Public Sector*, Berlin, New York 1986

Heidenreich, M. / G. Schmidt (eds.): *International vergleichende Organisationsforschung*, Opladen 1991

Heine, J.: "¿Reforma o Status-Quo? Dilemas y Desafíos del Estado en Chile", in: *Revista de Ciencia Política*, Vol. XV, Instituto de Ciencia Política, Santiago 1993

Heinze, R.G. / H. Voelzkow: "Regionalisierung der Strukturpolitik in Nordrhein-Westfalen", in: B. Blanke (ed.), *Staat und Stadt*, Opladen 1991

Held, D.: "Democracy, the Nation-State and the Global System", in: *Economy and Society*, 1991, No. 20

Heller, H.: *Staatslehre*, Tübingen 1983

Hennis, W.: "Zur Begründung der Fragestellungen", in: W. Hennis et al. (eds.), *Regierbarkeit*, Vol. 1, Stuttgart 1977

Hennis, W., et al. (eds.): *Regierbarkeit*, Vol. 1, Stuttgart 1977

-: *Regierbarkeit*, Vol. 2, Stuttgart 1979

Héritier, A. (ed.): *Policy-Analyse*, Opladen 1993

Hesse, J.J.: "Die Neubelebung der Staatsdiskussion", in: T. Ellwein et al. (eds.), *Jahrbuch zur Staats- und Verwaltungswissenschaft*, Baden-Baden 1987

Hillebrand, W.: *Industrielle und technologische Anschlußstrategien in teilindustrialisierten Ländern*, GDI, Berlin 1991

-: *Stärkung technologischer Kompetenz in Indonesien*, GDI, Berlin 1993

-: *Stärkung technologischer Kompetenz in Thailand*, GDI, Berlin 1993

Hillebrand, W., et al.: *Technological Modernization in Small and Medium Industries in Korea with Special Emphasis on the Role of International Enterprise Cooperation*, GDI, Berlin 1992

Hillebrand, W. / D. Messner / J. Meyer-Stamer: *Strengthening Technological Capability in Developing Countries. Lessons from German Technical Cooperation*, GDI, Berlin 1994

Hilpert, H.G.: "Japanische Industriepolitik", in: *ifo-Schnelldienst*, 1993, No. 17/18

Hinterberger, F. / M. Hüther: "Von Smith bis Hayek und zurück", in: *Jahrbuch für Nationalökonomie und Statistik*, 1993, No. 3/4

Hirsch, F.: *Social Limits of Growth*, London 1977

Hirsch, J.: *Wissenschaftlich-technischer Fortschritt und politisches System*, Frankfurt 1970

Hirschman, A.O.: *The Strategy of Economic Development*, Princeton 1958

-: "Against Parsimony", in: *American Economic Review*, Vol. 74, 1984, No. 3

-: *Entwicklung, Markt und Moral. Abweichende Betrachtungen*, Munich 1989

-: *Denken gegen die Zukunft*, Munich 1992

-: "Die Rhetorik der Reaktion", in: *Deutsche Zeitschrift für Philosophie*, 1993, No. 6

-: "Wieviel Gemeinsinn braucht die liberale Gesellschaft?", in: *Leviathan*, 1994, No. 2

Hitzler, R., et al.: *Expertenwissen*, Opladen 1994

Hollingsworth, J.R.: "The Governance of American Manufacturing Sectors. The Logic of Coordination and Control", Max-Planck-Institut für Gesellschaftsforschung, Discussion paper, Cologne 1990

Hollingsworth, J.R. / L.N. Lindberg: "The Governance of the American Economy. The Role of Markets, Clans, Hierarchies, and Associative Behaviour", in: W. Streeck / Ph.C. Schmitter (eds.), *Private Interest Government. Beyond Market and State*, London 1985

Holmstrom, B.: "Moral Hazard and Observability", in: *Bell Journal of Economics*, Vol. 10, 1979, No. 1

Honneth, A.: *Kritik der Macht*, Frankfurt 1989

-: *Kampf um Anerkennung*, Frankfurt 1992

-: "Kommunitarismus", in: A. Honneth (ed.), *Kommunitarismus*, Frankfurt 1993

-: "Das Andere der Gerechtigkeit", in: *Deutsche Zeitschrift für Philosophie*, 1994, No. 2

-: "Die soziale Dynamik von Mißachtung", in: *Leviathan*, 1994, No. 1

Hood, C.C.: *The Limits of Administration*, London 1976

Hotz-Hart, B.: "Comparative Research and New Technology. Modernization in Three Industrial Relations Systems", in: R. Hyman / W. Streeck (eds.), *New Technology and Industrial Relations*, Oxford 1988

Hucke, J.: "Implementing Environmental Regulations in the Federal Republic of Germany", in: *Policy Studies Journal*, 1982, No. 1

Hucke, J. / H. Wollmann (eds.): *Dezentrale Technologiepolitik?*, Basel 1989

Hübner, K.: *Theorie der Regulation*, Berlin 1989

-: "Ökonomische Theorie und osteuropäische Transformation", in: *PROKLA-Zeitschrift für kritische Sozialwissenschaft*, 1992, No. 89

Humphrey, J.: "New Technologies, Flexible Automation, Work Organisation and Employment in Manufacturing", in: International Labour Organisation (ed.), *World Employment Programme*, Working paper, Geneva 1992

Hurtienne, T.: *Theoriegeschichtliche Grundlagen des sozialökonomischen Entwicklungsdenkens*, Vol. 2, Saarbrücken 1984

-: "Fordismustheorie, Entwicklungstheorie und Dritte Welt", in: *Peripherie*, 1986, No. 22/23

-: "Gibt es für den verschuldeten Kapitalismus einen Weg aus der Krise?", in: E. Altvater et al. (eds.), *Die Armut der Nationen*, Berlin 1987

Hurtienne, T. / D. Messner: "Neue Konzepte von Wettbewerbsfähigkeit", in: B. Töpper / U. Müller-Plantenberg (eds.), *Transformationen im südlichen Lateinamerika*, Hamburg 1994

Hurtienne, T. / L. Mármora / D. Messner / U. Müller-Plantenberg / B. Töpper (eds.): *Cambio de rumbo en el cono sur - Crisis y oportunidades*, Caracas 1994

Hyman, R. / W. Streeck: "Editors' Introduction", in: R. Hyman / W. Streeck (eds.), *New Technology and Industrial Relations*, Oxford 1988

IDS Bulletin: *Flexible Specialization. A New View on Small Industry?*, No. 3, 1992

Imai, K. / Itami, H.: "Interpenetration of Organization and Market", in: K.B. Clark et al. (eds.), *The Uneasy Alliance*, New York 1984

Jacobs, S.H.: "Controlling Government Regulation. A New Self-Discipline", in: *The OECD Observer*, 1992, No. 175

Jann, W.: "Prozesse öffentlicher Problemverarbeitung", in: Th. Ellwein et al. (eds.), *Jahrbuch zur Staats- und Verwaltungswissenschaft*, Baden-Baden 1987

Jessop, B.: "Corporatism, Parliamentarism and Social Democracy", in: G. Lehmbruch / P.C. Schmitter (eds.), *Trends toward Corporatist Intermediation*, London 1979

Johanson, J. / L.G. Mattson: "Interorganizational Relations in Industrial Systems", in: *International Journal of Management and Organization*, 1989, No. 1

Johnson, B.: "Towards a New Approach to National Systems of Innovation", in: B.-A. Lundvall (ed.), *National Systems of Innovation*, London 1992

Johnston, R., et al.: *Technology Strategies in Australian Industry*, Canberra 1990

Jonas, H.: *Das Prinzip Verantwortung. Versuch einer Ethik für die technologische Zivilisation*, Frankfurt 1979

Jordan, A.G. / J. Richardson: "Overcrowded Policy-making. Some British and European Reflections", in: *Journal of Theoretical Politics*, 1983, No. 2

Jürgens, U.: "Entwicklungslinien der staatstheoretischen Diskussion seit den 70er Jahren", in: *Aus Politik und Zeitgeschichte*, 1990, No. 10

Jürgens, U., et al.: *Moderne Zeiten in der Automobilindustrie*, Berlin 1989

Kaiser, J.H.: *Planung I*, Baden-Baden 1965

Kaldor, N.: "Welfare Propositions of Economics and Inter-Personal Comparison of Utility", in: *The Economic Journal*, 1939, No. 49

Kanter, A.: *Bureaucracy Politics in the Pentagon*, Washington 1971

Katzenstein, P.J.: *Between Power and Plenty. Foreign Economic Policies of Advanced Industrial States*, Madison 1978

-: *Corporation and Change*, London 1984

Kaufmann, F.X.: *Steuerung wohlfahrtsstaatlicher Abläufe durch Recht*, Bielefeld 1985

-: "Diskurse über Staatsaufgaben", Max-Planck-Institut für Gesellschaftsforschung, Discussion paper, Cologne 1991

Keck, O.: "Die neue Institutionalisierung in der Theorie der Internationalen Politik", in: *Politische Vierteljahresschriften*, 1991, No. 4

-: *Information, Macht und gesellschaftliche Rationalität*, Baden-Baden 1993

Keller, B.: "Interessenorganisation und Interessenvermittlung", in: *Kölner Zeitschrift für Soziologie und Sozialpsychologie*, Vol. 42, 1990, No. 3

Kelley, H.H. / J.W. Thibaut: *Interpersonal Relations*, New York 1978

Killick, T.: "East-Asian Miracles and Development Ideology", in: *Development Policy Review*, 1994, No. 12

Kenis, P.: "The Preconditions for Policy Networks. Some Findings from a Three-Country Study on Industrial Restructuring", in: B. Marin / R. Mayntz (eds.), *Policy Networks*, Frankfurt 1991

394   THE NETWORK SOCIETY

Kenis, P. / V. Schneider: "Policy Networks and Policy Analysis", in: B. Marin / R. Mayntz (eds.), *Policy Networks*, Frankfurt 1991

Kersting, W.: *John Rawls: Zur Einführung*, Hamburg 1993

Khan, M. / M. Knight: "Fund-supported Adjustment Program and Economic Growth", *IMF-occasional paper*, No. 41, Washington 1985

Kielmansegg, P.: "Organisierte Interessen als 'Gegenregierungen'"?, in: W. Hennis et al. (eds.), *Regierbarkeit*, Vol. 2, Stuttgart 1979

Kiessling, B.: *Kritik der Giddenschen Sozialtheorie*, Frankfurt 1988

Kirsch, G.: *Neue Politische Ökonomie*, Düsseldorf 1993

Kirsch, G. et al.: *Jenseits von Markt und Macht*, Baden-Baden 1982

Kitschelt, H.: "Materiale Politisierung der Produktion", in: *Zeitschrift für Soziologie*, Vol. 14, 1985, No. 3

-: "Industrial Governance Structures, Innovation Strategies, and the Case of Japan. Sectoral or Cross-national Comparative Analysis?", in: *International Organization*, Vol. 45, 1991, No. 4

Klages, H.: *Planungspolitik*, Stuttgart 1971

Klawitter, J.: "Staatstheorie als Steuerungstheorie?", in: H. Busshoff (ed.), *Politische Steuerung*, Baden-Baden 1992

Kleinert, H.: "Die Krise der Politik", in: *Politik und Zeitgeschichte*, 1992, No. 35

Kley, R.: "F.A. Hayeks Idee einer spontanen sozialen Ordnung. Eine kritische Analyse", in: *Kölner Zeitschrift für Soziologie und Sozialpsychologie*, Vol. 44, 1992, No. 1

Knie, A. / S. Helmers: "Organisationen und Institutionen in der Technikentwicklung. Organisationskultur, Leitbilder und Stand der Technik", in: *Soziale Welt*, 1991, No. 4

Knieper, R.: *Nationale Souveränität. Versuch über Ende und Anfang einer Weltordnung*, Frankfurt 1991

-: "Staat und Nationalstaat", in: *PROKLA-Zeitschrift für kritische Sozialwissenschaft*, 1993, No. 90

Knorr Cetina, K.: "Zur Unterkomplexität der Differenzierungstheorie", in: *Zeitschrift für Soziologie*, 1992, No. 6

Koch, C. / D. Senghaas (eds.): *Texte zur Technokratiediskussion*, Frankfurt 1970

König, H.: "Dieter Senghaas und die Zivilisationstheorie", in: *Leviathan*, 1993, No. 4

Kolatek, C.: *Informational Networks and Regional Business Potential. An Economic Analysis for Japan*, Berlin 1993

Kosacoff, B.: *El desafío de la competitividad. La industria argentina en transformación*, Buenos Aires 1993

Krauch, H. (ed.): *Systemanalyse der Regierung und Verwaltung*, Freiburg 1971

Kremendahl, H.: *Pluralismustheorie in Deutschland*, Leverkusen 1977

Krohn, W. / G. Küppers: "Rekursives Durcheinander", in: *Kursbuch*, No. 89, 1989

Krueger, A.O.: "The Political Economy of the Rent-Seeking Society", in: *American Economic Society*, 1973, No. 3

Krumbein, W.: "Industriepolitik. Die Chance einer Integration von Wirtschafts- und Gesellschaftspolitik", in: U. Jürgens / W. Krumbein (eds.), *Industriepolitische Strategien*, Berlin 1991

-: "Industrie- und Regionalisierungspolitik in Niedersachsen", in: U. Bullmann (ed.), *Die Politik der Dritten Ebene*, Baden-Baden 1994

Kuran, T.: "The Tenacious Past. Theories of Personal and Collective Conservatism", in: *Journal of Economic Behaviour and Organization*, 1988, No. 10

Lachenmann, G.: *Social Movements and Civil Society in West Africa*, GDI, Berlin 1992

Lachenmann, G., et al.: *Bauernorganisation und Selbsthilfe im Senegal*, GDI, Berlin 1990

Lahera, E.: "Gestión pública para el desarrollo nacional", in: *Revista de Ciencia Política*, Instituto de Ciencia Política, Vol. XV, Santiago 1993

Lancaster, C.: "Governance and Development: The Views from Washington", in: *IDS Bulletin*, Vol. 24, 1993, No. 1

Lang, E.: *Zu einer Kybernetischen Staatslehre*, Salzburg, Munich 1970

Lash, S. / J. Urry: *The End of Organized Capitalism*, Buckinghamshire 1987

Lau, C.: *Theorien gesellschaftlicher Planung*, Stuttgart 1975

Laumann, E.O., et al.: "Organizations in Political Action. Representing Interests in National Policy Making", in: B. Marin / R. Mayntz (eds.), *Policy Networks*, Frankfurt 1991

Laumann, E.O. / D. Knoke: *The Organizational State*, Madison 1987

Lax, D.A. / J.K. Sebenius: *The Manager as Negotiator*, New York 1986

Lechner, N.: "Reflexión acerca del Estado Democrático", FLACSO, Documentos de Trabajo, Santiago 1992

-: "Las Sombras del Mañana", in: *Colección Estudios Cieplan*, 1993, No. 37

-: "Market Society and the Changing Patterns of Politics", Discussion paper for the 16th *Weltpolitologenkongreß*, 21-25 August, 1994 in Berlin, Berlin 1994

Leffler, U.: *Stärkung von Partizipation und Selbsthilfe im Zusammenhang mit Struk-turanpassungsmaßnahmen in Afrika*, GDI, Berlin 1994

Lehmbruch, G.: "Liberal Corporatism and Party Government", in: *Comparative Political Studies*, Vol. 10, 1977, No. 1

-: "Wandlungen der Interessenpolitik im liberalen Korporatismus", in: U. v. Alemann / R.G. Heinze (eds.), *Verbände und Staat*, Opladen 1979

-: "Concertation and the Structure of Corporatist Networks", in: J.H. Goldthorpe (ed.), *Order and Conflict in Contemporary Capitalism*, Oxford 1984

-: "Politische Institutionen als Determinanten der Politikentwicklung und -durchführung. Was leisten politische Institutionen?", in: H.H. Hartwich (ed.), *Macht und Ohnmacht politischer Institutionen*, Opladen 1988

Lehmbruch, G. / P.C. Schmitter (eds.): *Trends Toward Corporatist Intermediation*, London 1979

Lehner, F.: "Pluralismus, Paradigmen und Erkenntnisfortschritt in der Politikwissenschaft", in: H.H. Hartwich (ed.), *Policy-Forschung in der Bundesrepublik Deutschland*, Opladen 1985

-: "Interest Intermediation, Institutional Structures and Public Policy", in: H. Keman / H. Paloheimo / P.F. Whiteley (eds.), *Coping with the Economic Crisis*, London 1987

-: "Neue Politische Ökonomie", in: A. Görlitz / R. Prätorius (eds.), *Handbuch Politikwissenschaft*, Reinbek 1987

-: "Institutionelle Determinanten der Wirtschaftspolitik in westlichen Demokratien, Ansätze und Elemente einer systematischen Theorie", in: H.H. Hartwich (ed.), *Macht und Ohnmacht politischer Institutionen*, Opladen 1988

-: "The Institutional Control of Organized Interest Intermediation", in: R. Czada / A. Windhoff-Héritier (eds.), *Political Choice. Institutions, Rules and Limits of Rationality*, Frankfurt 1991

Lehner, F. / K. Schubert / B. Geile: "Die strukturelle Rationalität regulativer Wirtschaftspolitik", in: *Politische Vierteljahresschrift*, 1983, No. 4

Leibenstein, H.: "Organizational Economics and Institutions as Missing Elements. An Economic Development Analysis", in: *World Development*, 1989, No. 17

Lerch, W.: "Industriepolitik im Saarland - ein neues Politikmodell oder traditioneller Korporatismus?", in: U. Jürgens / W. Krumbein (eds.), *Industriepolitische Strategien*, Berlin 1991

Levi, M.: *Of Rule and Revenue*, Berkeley 1988

Levitt, T.: *The Third Sector*, London 1973

Lindblom, C.E.: *Politics and Markets*, New York 1977

-: "The Science of Muddling Through", in: *Public Administration Review*, 1959, No. 19

-: *The Intelligence of Democracy*, New York 1965

-: *Politics and Markets*, New York 1977

Lindenberg, S.: "Contractual Relations and Weak Solidarity", in: *Journal of Institutional and Theoretical Economics*, 1988, No. 144

Lipp, W.: "Autopoiesis biologisch, Autopoiesis soziologisch. Wohin führt Luhmanns Paradigmenwechsel?", in: *Kölner Zeitschrift für Soziologie und Sozialpsychologie*, Vol. 39, 1987, No. 3

Lompe, K.: *Gesellschaftspolitik und Planung*, Freiburg 1971

Luhmann, N.: *Politische Theorie im Wohlfahrtsstaat*, Munich 1981

-: *Soziale Systeme. Grundriß einer allgemeinen Theorie*, Frankfurt 1984

-: "The Autopoiesis of Social Systems", in: F. Geyer / J. v.d. Zouwen (eds.), *Sociocybernetic Paradoxes*, Beverly Hills 1986

-: "Systeme verstehen Systeme", in: N. Luhmann / K. Schorr (eds.), *Zwischen Intransparenz und Verstehen*, Frankfurt 1986

-: "Familiarity, Confidence, Trust: Problems and Alternatives", in: D. Gambetta (ed.), *Trust: Making and Breaking Cooperative Relations*, Oxford 1988

-: "Steuerbarkeit - Streitgespräch mit F.W. Scharpf", in: H.H. Hartwich (ed.), *Macht und Ohnmacht politischer Institutionen*, Opladen 1989

-: *Beobachtungen der Moderne*, Opladen 1992

-: *Das Recht der Gesellschaft*, Frankfurt 1993

Lundvall, B.A.: "Innovation as an Interactive Process", in: G. Dosi et al. (eds.), *Technical Change and Economic Theory*, London, New York 1988

-: *National Systems of Innovation*, London 1992

-: "Explaining Interfirm Cooperation and Innovation. Limits of the Transaction-Cost Approach", in: G. Grabher (ed.), *The Embedded Firm*, London 1993

Maggi, C.: *Decentralización territorial y competitividad: El caso de Chile*, GDI, Berlin 1994

Mahnkopf, B.: "Soziale Grenzen fordistischer Regulation", in: B. Mahnkopf (ed.), *Der gewendete Kapitalismus*, Münster 1988

-: "Markt, Hierarchie und soziale Beziehungen", in: N. Beckenbach / W. v. Treeck (eds.), *Umbrüche der gesellschaftlichen Arbeit*, Düsseldorf 1993

Maier, Ch.S.: "Preconditions for Corporatism", in: J.H. Goldthorpe (ed.), *Order and Conflict in Contemporary Capitalism*, Oxford 1984

Makropoulos, M.: "Möglichkeitsbändigungen. Disziplin und Versicherung als Konzepte zur sozialen Steuerung von Kontingenz", in: *Soziale Welt*, 1990, No. 4

Mandell, M.P.: "Intergovernmental Management in Interorganizational Networks", in: *International Journal of Public Administration*, 1988, No. 11

Mann, S.: *Macht und Ohnmacht der Verbände*, Baden-Baden 1994

Manor, J.: "Politics and the Neo-liberals", *IDS Development Studies Series*, Oxford 1992

March, J.G. / J.P. Olsen: *Rediscovering Institutions. The Organizational Basis of Politics*, New York 1989

March, J.G. / H.A. Simon: *Organizations*, New York 1958

Marhill, T.H.: *Class, Citizenship and Social Development*, Westport 1976

Marin, B. (ed.): *Generalized Poitical Exchange*, Frankfurt 1990

Marin, B. / R. Mayntz (eds.): *Policy Networks*, Frankfurt 1991

Marks, G.: *Structural Policy, European Integration and the State*, Chapel Hill 1991

Mármora, L.: "Sustainable Development and soziale Gerechtigkeit", in: *PROKLA-Zeitschrift für kritische Sozialwissenschaft*, 1992, No. 86

-: "Soziale Gerechtigkeit und Weltmarktintegration am Beispiel Lateinamerika", in: W. Hein (ed.), *Umbruch in der Weltgesellschaft*, Hamburg 1994

Mármora, L. / D. Messner: "Chile im lateinamerikanischen Kontext. Ein Modell für Demokratisierung und Entwicklung?", in: J. Ensignia / D. Nolte (eds.), *Modellfall Chile*, Hamburg 1991

-: "La integración de Argentina, Brazil y Uruguay: concepciones, objectivism resultadism", in: *Comercio Exterior*, Vol. 41, 1991, No. 2

-: "Zur Kritik eindimensionaler Entwicklungskonzepte", in: *PROKLA-Zeitschrift für kritische Sozialwissenschaft*, 1991, No. 82

-: "Der Abstieg Argentiniens und der Aufstieg Südkoreas", in: *Zeitschrift für Lateinamerika*, No. 40/41, Vienna 1991

-: *Jenseits von Etatismus und Neoliberalismus. Zur aktuellen Steuerungsdiskussion am Beispiel Argentinien und Südkorea*, Hamburg 1992

Marshall, A.: *Principles of Economics*, 5th edition (first appeared in 1890), Basingstoke 1986

Martinsen, R.: "Theorien politischer Steuerung. Auf der Suche nach dem Dritten Weg", in: K. Grimmer et al. (eds.), *Politische Techniksteuerung*, Opladen 1992

Marwell, G. / R.F. Ames: "Economists Free Ride, Does Anyone Else?", in: *Journal of Public Economics*, 1991, No. 15

Marx, K.: "Zur Judenfrage", *Marx-Engels-Werke*, Vol. 1, Berlin 1964

-: "Das Kapital", Vol. 1 - 3, *Marx-Engels-Werke*, 23, 24, 25, Berlin 1981

Matz, U.: "Der überforderte Staat", in: W. Hennis (ed.), *Regierbarkeit*, Vol. 1, Stuttgart 1977

Matzner, E.: "Policies, Institutions and Employment Performance", in: E. Matzner / W. Streeck (eds.), *Beyond Keynesianism*, Worcester 1991

Matzner, E. / W. Streeck: "Introduction: Towards a Socio-Economics of Employment in a Post-Keynesian Economy", in: E. Matzner / W. Streeck (eds.), *Beyond Keynesianism*, Aldershot 1991

Mayer, J.M.: "'Wann sind Paketlösungen machbar?'. Eine konstruktive Kritik an F.W. Scharpfs Konzept", in: *Politische Vierteljahresschrift*, 1994, No. 3

Mayntz, R.: "Die gesellschaftliche Dynamik als theoretische Herausforderung", in: B. Lutz (ed.), *Soziologie und gesellschaftliche Entwicklung*, Frankfurt 1985

-: "Politische Steuerung und gesellschaftliche Steuerungsprobleme. Anmerkungen zu einem theoretischen Paradigma", in: Th. Ellwein / J.J. Hesse et. al. (eds.), *Jahrbuch zur Staats- und Verwaltungswissenschaft*, Baden-Baden 1987

-: "Modernization and the Logic of Interorganizational Networks", Max-Planck-Institut für Gesellschaftsforschung, Discussion paper 91/8, Cologne 1991

-: "Interessenverbände und Gemeinwohl", in: R. Mayntz (ed.), *Verbände zwischen Mitgliederinteressen und Gemeinwohl*, Gütersloh 1992

-: "Policy-Netzwerke und die Logik von Verhandlungssystemen", in: A. Héritier (ed.), *Policy-Analyse*, Opladen 1993

Mayntz, R., et al.: *Vollzugsprobleme der Umweltpolitik, Materialien zur Umweltforschung*, Wiesbaden 1978

Mayntz, R. / B. Nedelmann: "Eigendynamische soziale Prozesse", in: *Kölner Zeitschrift für Soziologie und Sozialpsychologie*, Vol. 39, 1987, No. 4

Mayntz, R. / F. Neidhardt: "Parlamentskultur. Handlungsorientierungen von Bundestagsabgeordneten", in: *Zeitschrift für Parlamentsfragen*, Vol. 20, 1989

Mayntz, R. / F.W. Scharpf: *Planungsorganisation*, Munich 1973

Mc Connell, G.: *Private Power and American Democracy*, New York 1966

Mead, G.H.: Gesammelte Aufsätze, Vol. 1, Frankfurt 1980

-: Gesammelte Aufsätze, Vol. 2, Frankfurt 1983

Meller, P.: "La apertura comercial chilena", in: *Colección Estudios de CIEPLAN*, No. 35, Santiago 1992

Messner, D.: "Südkorea. Kontrastfall in der Verschuldungskrise, Streitfall in der entwicklungstheoretischen Debatte", in: *Peripherie*, 1988, No. 33/34

-: *Von der Importsubstitution zur weltmarktorientierten Spezialisierung*, GDI, Berlin 1990

-: "Die Herausbildung von Wettbewerbsfähigkeit als gesellschaftlicher Such- und Lernprozeß", in: K. Esser et al., *Neue Determinanten internationaler Wettbewerbsfähigkeit*, GDI, Berlin 1992

-: "Die südkoreanische Erfolgsstory und der Staat. Von der Allmacht des Entwicklungsstaates zur Krise des hierarchischen Steuerungsmodells", in: *Vierteljahresberichte*, 1992, No. 130

-: "Der schwierige Weg aus der Krise des binnenmarktorientierten Industrialisierungsmodells". Das Beispiel Uruguay, in: K. Bodemer et al. (eds.), *Uruguay*, Hamburg 1993a

-: "Búsqueda de competitividad en la industria maderera chilena", in: *Revista de la CEPAL*, 1993b, No. 49

-: "New Directions in Chilean Economic Policy", in: *Economics*, 1993c, No. 48

-: *Stärkung technologischer Kompetenz in Bolivien*, GDI, Berlin 1993d

-: *Stärkung technologischer Kompetenz in Argentinien*, GDI, Berlin 1993e

-: "Südkorea", in: D. Nohlen / F. Nuscheler (eds.), *Handbuch Dritte Welt*, Vol. 8, Bonn 1994a

-: "Lateinamerika auf der Suche nach einem neuen Entwicklungsmodell", in: *Zeitschrift für sozialdemokratische Politik und Wirtschaft*, 1994b, No. 76

-: "Chile - Exitos y nuevos retos", Discussion paper, No. SE310-108-94, Deutsche Stiftung für internationale Entwicklung, Berlin 1994c

-: "Fallstricke und Grenzen der Netzwerksteuerung", in: *PROKLA-Zeitschrift für kritische Sozialwissenschaft*, 1994d, No. 97

Messner, D., et al.: *Weltmarktorientierung und Aufbau von Wettbewerbsvorteilen in Chile. Das Beispiel der Holzwirtschaft*, GDI, Berlin 1991

Messner, D. / J. Meyer-Stamer: "Die nationale Basis internationaler Wettbewerbsfähigkeit", in: *Nord-Süd-aktuell*, 1993, No. 1

-: "Systemic Competitiveness. Lessons from Latin America and Beyond. Perspectives for Eastern Europe", in: *European Journal of Development Research*, Vol. 6, 1994, No. 1

Messner, D. / F. Nuscheler: "Global Governance", Policy paper 2/1996, Foundation Development and Peace, Bonn 1996   .

Messner, D. / I. Scholz: "Wirtschaftlilche Entwicklungsdynamik und gesellschaftliche Modernisierungsblockaden in Chile", in: *Nord-Süd aktuell*, 1996, No. 1

Messner, F.: "Das Konzept nachhaltiger Entwicklung im Dilemma internationaler Regimebildung", in: *Peripherie*, 1993, No. 51/52

Meyer, T.: *Die Transformation des Politischen*, Frankfurt 1994

Meyer-Krahmer, F. (ed.): *Innovationsökonomie und Technologiepolitik. Forschungsansätze und politische Konsequenzen*, Heidelberg 1993

Meyer-Krahmer, F. / U. Kuntze: "Bestandsaufnahme der Forschungs- und Technologiepolitik", in: K. Grimmer et al. (eds.), *Politische Techniksteuerung*, Opladen 1992

Meyer-Stamer, J.: "Mit Mikroelektronik zum 'Best Practice'?", in: *Peripherie*, 1990, No. 38

-: *From Import Substitution to International Competitiveness. Brazil's Informatics Industry at the Crossroads*, GDI, Berlin 1990

-: "Kompetenter Staat, wettbewerbsfähige Unternehmen. Die Schaffung dynamischer komparativer Vorteile in der ostasiatischen Elektronikindustrie", in: *Nord-Süd-aktuell*, 1991, No. 1

-: "Staatlich-private Forschungskooperation in der Elektronik", in: *Vierteljahresberichte*, 1993, No. 131

-: *Technologie und industrielle Wettbewerbsfähigkeit: Allgemeine Überlegungen und Erfahrungen aus Brasilien*, Berlin 1996

-: "Taiwan - die anhaltende Erfolgsstory", in: *Internationale Politik und Gesellschaft*, 1994, No. 1

-: "Micro-level Innovation and Competitiveness", in: *World Development*, 1995, No. 1

Meyer-Stamer, J., et al.: *Comprehensive Modernization on the Shop Floor. A Case Study on the Brazilian Machinery Industry*, GDI, Berlin 1991

Michalski, W.: "Leitlinien für eine Politik der positiven Strukturanpassung", in: *Beihefte für Konjunkturpolitik*, 1985, No. 31

Middlemass, K.: *Politics and Industrial Society*, London 1979

Migdal, J.: *Strong Societies and Weak States*, Princeton 1988

Miller, G.J. / T.M. Moe: "The Positive Theory of Hierarchies", in: H.F. Weinberg (ed.), *Political Science*, New York 1986

Mills, C.W.: *The Power Elite*, New York 1956

Mintzberg, H. / A. Mc Hugh: "Strategy Formation in an Adhocracy", in: *Administrative Science Quarterly*, 1985, No. 2

Mjoset, L.: "The Limits of Neoclassical Institutionalism", in: *Journal of Peace Research*, 1985, No. 22

Montero, C.: "El actor empresarial en transición", in: *Colección Estudios CIEPLAN*, No. 37, Santiago 1993

Moore, M.: "Declining to Learn from the East? The World Bank on 'Governance and Development'", in: *IDS Bulletin*, Vol. 24, 1993, No. 1

Müller, H.P. / M. Schmid: "Arbeitsteilung, Solidarität und Moral. Eine werkgeschichtliche und systematische Einführung in die 'Arbeitsteilung' von Emile Durkheim", in: E. Durkheim, *Über soziale Arbeitsteilung*, Frankfurt 1992

Müller, K.: "'Katastrophen', 'Chaos' und 'Selbstorganisation'", in: *PROKLA-Zeitschrift für kritische Wissenschaft*, 1992, No. 88

Müller, W. / C. Neusüss: "Die Sozialstaatsillusion", in: *Sozialistische Politik*, 1969, No. 2

Muñoz Goma, O.: *Hacia el Estado moderador*, Santiago 1993

Muñoz Goma, O. (ed.): *Después de las privatizaciones. Hacia el Estado regulador*, Santiago 1993

Muñoz Goma, O. / C. Celedon: "Chile en Transición. Estrategia Económica y Política", in: *Revista de Ciencia Política*, Instituto de Ciencia Política, Vol. XV, Santiago 1993

Murray, R.: *Local Space. Europe and the New Regionalism*, Manchester 1991

Murswieck, A.: "Policy-Forschung und politische Institutionenanalyse", in: H.H. Hartwich (ed.), *Policy-Forschung in der Bundesrepublik Deutschland*, Opladen 1985

Nadvi, K.: "Flexible Specialization, Industrial Districts and Employment in Pakistan", ILO, Paper No: 232, Geneva 1992

Nadvi, K. / H. Schmitz: "Industrial Clusters in Less Developed Countries: A Review of Experiences and Research Agenda", IDS, Discussion paper 339, Sussex 1994

Narr, W.D.: "Communitarians: Zahnlose Kritik", in: *PROKLA-Zeitschrift für kritische Sozialwissenschaft*, 1992, No. 87

-: "Recht - Demokratie - Weltgesellschaft", in: *PROKLA-Zeitschrift für kritische Sozialwissenschaft*, 1994, No. 94

-: "Recht - Demokratie - Weltgesellschaft, Teil II", in: *PROKLA-Zeitschrift für kritische Sozialwissenschaft*, 1994, No. 95

Naschhold, F.: "Politik und politische Institutionen in neokorporatistischen und Public-Choice-Ansätzen. Anmerkungen zu einem Theorieprogramm", in: H.H. Hartwich (ed.), *Macht und Ohnmacht politischer Institutionen*, Opladen 1989

-: "Soziotechnische Modernisierungspolitik in der Bundesrepublik", in: U. Fricke (ed.), *Jahrbuch Arbeit und Technik*, Bonn 1990

-: "Soziotechnische Modernisierungspolitik in der Bundesrepublik", in: *Jahrbuch Arbeit und Technik*, Bonn 1990

-: *Den Wandel organisieren*, Berlin 1992

-: "Organization Development, National Programs in the Context of International Competition", in: F. Naschold et al. (eds.), *Constructing the New Industrial Society*, Maastricht 1993

Naschold, F., et al. (eds.): *Constructing the New Industrial Society*, Assen, Maastricht 1993

Nelson, R.R.: "What has been the Matter with Neoclassical Growth Theory?", in: G. Silverberg / L. Soete (eds.), *The Economics of Growth and Technical Change*, Aldershot 1994

Nitsch, M.: "Vom Nutzen des institutionalistischen Ansatzes für die Entwicklungsökonomie", in: H. Körner (ed.), *Zur Analyse von Institutionen im Entwicklungsprozeß und in der internationalen Zusammenarbeit*, Berlin 1989

North, D.: *Structure and Change in Economic History*, New York 1981

Nozick, R.: *Anarchy, State, and Utopia*, New York 1974

Nuscheler, F. / W. Steffani (eds.): *Pluralismus*, Munich 1972

O'Toole, L.J. / R.S. Montjoy: "Interorganizational Policy Implementation. A Theoretical Perspective", in: *Public Administration Review*, 1984, No. 6

OECD / TEP: *Technology in a Changing World*, Paris 1991

-: *Technology and the Economy. The Key Relationship*, Paris 1992

Offe, C.: "Politische Herrschaft und Klassenverhältnisse. Zur Analyse spätkapitalistischer Gesellschaftssysteme", in: R. Kress / D. Senghaas (eds.), *Politikwissenschaft. Eine Erfahrung und ihre Probleme*, Frankfurt 1969

-: "Das politische Dilemma der Technokratie", in: C. Koch / D. Senghaas (eds.), *Texte zur Technokratiediskussion*, Frankfurt 1970

-: *Berufsbildungsreform*, Frankfurt 1975

-: "Die Utopie der Null-Option. Modernität und Modernisierung als politische Gütekriterien", in: J. Berger (ed.), *Soziale Welt*, Göttingen 1985

-: "Die Staatstheorie auf der Suche nach ihrem Gegenstand. Beobachtungen zur aktuellen Diskusssion", in: Th. Ellwein et al. (eds.), *Jahrbuch zur Staats- und Verwaltungswissenschaft*, Baden-Baden 1987

-: "Fessel und Bremse. Moralische und institutionelle Aspekte intelligenter Selbstbeschränkung", in: A. Honneth et al. (eds.), *Zwischenbetrachtungen, Jürgen Habermas zum 60. Geburtstag*, Frankfurt 1989

-: "Das Dilemma der Gleichzeitigkeit", in: *Merkur*, Vol. 45, 1991, No. 4

Ohamae, K.: "The Rise of the Region State", in: *Foreign Affairs*, 1993, No. 2

Olson, M.: *Die Logik des kollektiven Handelns*, Tübingen 1968

-: *The Rise and Decline of Nations*, New Haven 1982

-: *Umfassende Ökonomie*, Tübingen 1991

Ostrom, E.: "An Agenda for the Study of Institutions", in: G. Tullock (ed.), *Public Choice*, New York 1986

-: *Governing the Commons*, Cambridge 1990

Ouchi, W.G.: "Bureaucracies, Markets, and Clans", in: *Administrative Science Quarterly*, 1980, No. 25

Panitch, L.: "The Development of Corporatism in Liberal Democracies", in: *Comparative Political Studies*, 1977, No. 1

-: "Recent Theoretization of Corporatism", in: *British Journal of Sociology*, 1980, No. 2

Papcke, S.: "Auf dem Weg in eine Gesellschaft ohne Staat?", in: *Gewerkschaftliche Monatshefte*, 1993, No. 2

Pappi, F.U. (ed.): *Methoden der Netzwerkanalyse*, Munich 1987

-: "Policy-Netze: Erscheinungsform moderner Politiksteuerung oder methodischer Ansatz?", in: A. Hériter (ed.), *Policy-Analyse*, Opladen 1993

Parsons, T.: *The Structure of Social Action*, New York 1968

Perroux, F.: "Note sur la notion de 'pole de criossance'", in: *Economie Appliquée*, 1955, No. 2

Perrow, Ch.: "Eine Gesellschaft von Organisationen", in: *Journal für Sozialforschung*, Vol. 28, 1989, No. 1

Peters, B.: *Die Integration moderner Gesellschaften*, Frankfurt 1993

Peters, H.-R.: *Grundlagen der Mesoökonomie und Strukturpolitik*, Bern 1981

Peters, T.J.: *Thriving on Chaos. Handbook for a Management Revolution*, New York 1987

Piore, M.J. / Ch.F. Sabel: *Das Ende der Massenproduktion*, Berlin 1984

Platteau, J.P.: "Behind the Market Stage. Where Real Societies Exist", in: *Journal of Development Studies*, 1994, No. 3

Polanyi, K.: *The Great Transformation*, Frankfurt 1978

-: *Ökonomie und Gesellschaft*, Frankfurt 1979

Pollak, D.: "Das Ende einer Organisationsgesellschaft", in: *Zeitschrift für Soziologie*, 1990, No. 19

Poon, A.: "Flexible Specialization and Small Size. The Case of the Carribbean Tourism", in: *World Development*, 1990, No. 1

Popper, K.R.: *Die offene Gesellschaft und ihre Feinde*, Vol. 1/2, Munich 1980

-: *Ausgangspunkte*, Hamburg 1994

Popper, K.R. / J. Eccles: *The Self and its Brain. An Argument for Interactionism*, Heidelberg 1977

Porter, M.: *The Competitive Advantage of Nations*, New York 1990

Powell, W.W.: *The Nonprofit Sector*, New Haven 1987

Powell, W.W.: "Neither Market nor Hierarchy. Network Forms of Organization", in: *Research in Organizational Behavior*, 1990, No. 12

Pyke, F., et al. (eds.): *Industrial Districts and Inter-Firm Co-Operation in Italy*, Geneva 1990

Pyke, F. / W. Sengenberger (eds.): *Industrial Districts and Local Economic Regeneration*, Geneva 1992

Qualmann, R.: "Bedingungen der Wettbewerbsfähigkeit kleiner Unternehmen. Eine kritische Analyse der Konzeption der Industrial Districts", Diplomarbeit am FB Wirtschaftswissenschaft der Universität Tübingen, Tübingen 1993

Rammert, W.: "Wer oder was steuert den technischen Fortschritt?", in: *Soziale Welt*, Vol. 43, 1992, No. 1

Rawls, J.: *A Theory of Justice*, Oxford 1971

-: *Die Idee des politischen Liberalismus*, Frankfurt 1992

-: *Political Liberalism*, New York 1993

-: "Der Hauptgedanke der Theorie der Gerechtigkeit", in: H. Münckler (ed.), *Politisches Denken im 20. Jahrhundert*, Munich 1994

Regionalkonferenz Ostwestfalen-Lippe: *Mittelfristiges Entwicklungskonzept für die Region Ostwestfalen-Lippe*, Detmold 1991

Reich, R. B.: *Die neue Weltwirtschaft*, Frankfurt 1994

Reichard, C.: *Umdenken im Rathaus*, Berlin 1994

Rhodes, R.A.W.: "Policy Networks. A British Perspective", in: *Journal of Theoretical Politics*, 1990, No. 2

Riegraf, B.: *Frauenförderung. Alibi oder Aufbruch zur Chancengleichheit*, Berlin 1993

Ritter, E.H.: "Der kooperative Staat", in: *Archiv des öffentlichen Rechts*, 1979, No. 104

-: "Staatliche Steuerung bei vermindertem Rationalitätsanspruch? Zur Praxis der politischen Planung in der Bundesrepublik Deutschland", in: Th. Ellwein et al. (eds.), *Jahrbuch zur Staats- und Verwaltungswissenschaft*, Baden-Baden 1987

Rödel, U. (ed.): *Autonome Gesellschaft und Libertäre Demokratie*, Frankfurt 1990

Ronge, V.: "Politökonomische Planungsforschung", in: V. Ronge / G. Schmieg (eds.), *Politische Planung in Theorie und Praxis*, Munich 1971

-: *Am Staat vorbei. Politik der Selbstregulierung von Kapital und Arbeit*, Frankfurt 1980

-: "Der Dritte Sektor zwischen Markt und Staat", in: H.H. Hartwich (ed.), *Macht und Ohnmacht politischer Institutionen*, Opladen 1988

-: "Politische Steuerung - innerhalb und außerhalb der Systemtheorie", in: K. Damman et al. (eds.), *Die Verwaltung des politischen Systems*, Opladen 1994

Rosewitz, B. / U. Schimank: *Verselbständigung und politische Steuerbarkeit gesellschaftlicher Teilsysteme*, Frankfurt 1988

Sabel, C.F.: "Studied Trust. Building New Forms of Cooperation in Volatile Economy, in": F. Romo / R. Swedberg (eds.), *Human Relations and Readings in Economic Sociology*, New York 1991

-: "Studied Trust. New Forms of Co-Operation in a Volatile Economy", in: F. Pyke / W. Sengenberger (eds.), *Industrial Districts and Local Economic Regeneration*, Geneva 1992

-: *The Reemergence of Regional Economies*, Wissenschaftszentrum, Berlin 1989

-: "Constitutional Ordening in Historical Context", in: F.W. Scharpf (ed.), *Games in Hierarchies and Networks*, Frankfurt 1993

Salomon, L.M.: "The Rise of the Nonprofit Sector", in: *Foreign Affairs*, 1994, No. 3

Sangmeister, H.: "Die Spielregeln des Systems, Korruption in Lateinamerika", *in: Entwicklung und Zusammenarbeit*, Vol. 34, 1993, No. 3

Sartre, J.P.: *Marxismus und Existenzialismus*, Reinbek 1964

Scharpf, F.W.: *Demokratietheorie zwischen Utopie und Anpassung*, Konstanz 1970

-: "Planung als politischer Prozeß", in: *Die Verwaltung*, 1971, No. 4

-: "Komplexität als Schranke der politischen Planung", in: *Politische Vierteljahresschriften*, 1972, No. 4

-: *Politische Durchsetzbarkeit innerer Reformen*, Göttingen 1974

-: "Die Politikverflechtungs-Falle. Europäische Integration und deutscher Föderalismus im Vergleich", in: *Politische Vierteljahresschrift*, 1985, No. 4

-: "Plädoyer für einen aufgeklärten Institutionalismus", in: H.H. Hartwich (ed.), *Policy-Forschung in der Bundesrepublik Deutschland*, Opladen 1985

-: "Grenzen der institutionellen Reform", in: Th. Ellwein et al. (eds.), *Jahrbuch zur Staats- und Verwaltungswissenschaft*, Baden-Baden 1987

-: *Sozialdemokratische Krisenpolitik in Europa*, Frankfurt, New York 1987

-: "A Game-Theoretical Interpretation of Inflation and Unemployment", in: *Journal of Public Policy*, 1988a, No. 7

-: "Von Fug und Unfug institutioneller Erklärungen", in: *Politische Vierteljahresschrift*, Vol. 29, 1988, No. 2

-: "Decision Rules, Decision Styles and Policy Choices", in: *Journal of Theoretical Politics*, 1989, No. 1

-: "Politische Steuerung und politische Institutionen", in: H.H. Hartwich (ed.), *Macht und Ohnmacht politischer Institutionen*, Opladen 1989b

-: "Koordination durch Verhandlungssysteme. Analytische Konzepte und institutionelle Lösungen am Beispiel der Zusammenarbeit zwischen zwei Bundesländern", Max-Planck-Institut für Gesellschaftsforschung, Discussion paper, Cologne 1991

-: "Political Institutions, Decision Styles, and Policy Choices", in: R. Czada / A. Windhoff-Héritier (eds.), *Political Choice*, Frankfurt 1991a

-: "Games Real Actors Could Play. The Challenge of Complexity", in: *Journal of Theoretical Politics*, 1991b, No. 3

-: "Wege aus der Sackgasse. Europa: Zentralisierung und Dezentralisierung", in: *WZB-Mitteilungen*, No. 56, Berlin 1992

-: "Zur Theorie von Verhandlungssystemen", in: A. Benz et al. (eds.), *Horizontale Politikverflechtung*, Frankfurt 1992a

-: "Koordination durch Verhandlungssysteme. Analytische Konzepte und institutionelle Lösungen", in: A. Benz et al. (eds.), *Horizontale Politikverflechtung*, Frankfurt 1992b

-: "Positive und negative Koordination in Verhandlungssystemen", in: A. Héritier (ed.), *Policy-Analyse*, Opladen 1993a

-: "Games in Hierarchies and Networks", in: F.W. Scharpf (ed.), *Games in Hierarchies and Networks*, Frankfurt 1993b

-: "Coordination in Hierarchies and Networks", in: F.W. Scharpf (ed.), *Games in Hierarchies and Networks*, Frankfurt 1993c

-: "Versuch über Demokratie im verhandelnden Staat", in: R. Czada / M.G. Schmidt (eds.), *Verhandlungsdemokratie, Interessenvermittlung und Regierbarkeit*, Opladen 1993d

Scharpf, F.W. / A. Benz: "Kooperation als Alternative zur Neugliederung", in: J.J. Hesse (ed.), *Schriften zur Innenpolitik und zur kommunalen Wissenschaft*, Vol. 6, Baden-Baden 1991

Schenk, K.E.: "Die neue Institutionenökonomie. Ein Überblick über wichtige Elemente und Probleme der Weiterentwicklung", in: *Zeitschrift für Wirtschafts- und Sozialwissenschaften*, 1992, No. 112

Schmalz-Bruns, R.: *Ansätze und Perspektiven der Institutionentheorie*, Wiesbaden 1989

-: "Die Konturen eines neuen Liberalismus. Zur Debatte um Liberalismus, Kommunitarismus und Civil Society", in: *Politische Vierteljahresschriften*, 1992, No. 4

-: "Zivile Gesellschaft und reflexive Demokratie", in: *Neue soziale Bewegungen*, 1994, No. 1

Schmidt, G.: "Die neue institutionelle Ökonomie", in: *Leviathan*, 1989, No. 3

-: "Zur politischen Logik wirtschaftlichen Handelns", in: H. Abromeit / U. Jürgens (eds.), *Die politische Logik wirtschaftlichen Handelns*, Berlin 1992

Schmitt, C.: *Positionen und Begriffe im Kampf mit Weimar, Geneva, Versailles 1931*, Hamburg 1940

-: *Die geistesgeschichtliche Lage des heutigen Parlamentarismus*, Hamburg 1969

Schmitter, P.C.: "Still the Century of Corporatism", in: *Review of Politics*, Vol. 36, 1974, No. 1

-: "Neokorporatismus: Überlegungen zur bisherigen Theorie und zur weiteren Praxis", in: U. v. Alemann (ed.), *Neokorporatismus*, Frankfurt 1981

Schmitz, H.: "On the Clustering of Small Firms", in: *IDS Bulletin*, 1992, No. 3

Schmitz, H. / T. Hewitt: "Learning to Raise Infants. A Case-study in Industrial Policy", *IDS Development Studies Series*, Oxford 1992

Schmitz, H. / B. Musyck: "Industrial Districts in Europe", IDS, Brighton 1993

Scholz, I., et al.: *Ökologische Produktauflagen in der EU als Herausforderung für Entwicklungsländerexporte. Beispiel Chile*, GDI, Berlin 1994

Schubert, K.: "Politics and Economic Regulation", in: F. Castles / F. Lehner / M. Schmidt (eds.), *Managing Mixed Economies*, Berlin 1988

-: "Interessenvermittlung und staatliche Regulation", *Studien zur Sozialwissenschaft*, Opladen 1989

Schumpeter, J.A.: *The Theory of Economic Development*, Cambridge 1934

-: *Kapitalismus, Sozialismus und Demokratie*, Bern 1950

Schuppert, G.F.: "Markt, Staat, Dritter Sektor - oder noch mehr? Sektorspezifische Steuerungsprobleme ausdifferenzierter Staatlichkeit", in: Th. Ellwein et al. (eds.), *Jahrbuch zur Staats- und Verwaltungswissenschaft*, Baden-Baden 1989

-: "Zur Neubelebung der Staatsdiskussion. Entzauberung des Staates oder 'Bringing the State back in?'", in: *Der Staat*, Vol. 28, 1989, No. 1

Schwegler, H. / G. Roth: *Steuerung, Steuerbarkeit und Steuerungsfähigkeit komplexer Systeme*, Cologne 1992

Schweizer, U.: "Institutional Choice. A Contract-Theoretic Approach", in: *Journal of Institutional and Theoretical Economics*, 1993, No. 1

Scitovsky, T.: "Two Concepts of External Economies", in: A.N. Agarwala / S.P. Singh (eds.), *The Economics of Underdevelopment*, Oxford 1963

Seibel, W.: "Erfolgreich scheiternde Organisationen. Zur politischen Ökonomie des Organisationsversagens", *Politische Vierteljahresschrift*, 1991, No. 3

Selten, R.: "Institutional Utilitarianism", in: F.X. Kaufmann et al. (eds.), *Guidance, Control, and Evaluation*, Berlin 1986

Semmler, W.: "Markt- und nichtmarktförmige Regulierung", in: *PROKLA-Zeitschrift für kritische Sozialwissenschaft*, 1991, No. 82

Sen, A.: *Poverty and Famines*, Oxford 1981

Shapiro, H. / L. Taylor: "The State and Industrial Stategy", in: *World Development*, Vol. 18, 1990, No. 6

Shiratori, M.: *Development Assistance to Developing Countries. Japanese Model more Relevant than Simple Marketism*, World Bank Tokyo Office, Tokio 1992

Shklar, J.N.: *Ordinary Vices*, Harvard 1984

Shonfield, A.: *Geplanter Kapitalismus*, Cologne, Berlin 1968

Shubik, M.: *Game Theory in the Social Science*, Cambridge 1987

Simon, H.A.: "The Organization of Complex Systems", in: H.H. Pattee (ed.), *Hierarchy Theory. The Challenge of Complex Systems*, New York 1973

-: *Reason in Human Affairs*, Stanford 1983

-: "Organizations and Markets", in: *Journal of Economic Perspectives*, 1991, No. 5

-: *Homo rationalis*, Frankfurt 1993

Simon, K.: "Subsidiarität als Rahmenbedingung für Entwicklung", in: K. Simon et al. (eds.), *Subsidiarität in der Entwicklungszusammenarbeit. Dezentralisierung und Verwaltungsreform*, Baden-Baden 1993

Simonis, G.: "Forschungsstrategische Überlegungen zur politischen Techniksteuerung", in: K. Grimmer et al. (eds.), *Politische Techniksteuerung*, Opladen 1992

Smith, A.: *The Theory of Moral Sentiments*, Oxford 1976

Smith, C.S.: "Networks of Influence", in: M. Bulmer (ed.), *Social Science Research and Government*, Cambridge 1987

Snoeck, M., et al.: "Uruguay", in: B. Töpper / U. Müller-Plantenberg (eds.), *Transformation im südlichen Lateinamerika*, Frankfurt 1994

Sorensen, A.: "Korruption und die Interessen der Wirtschaft", in: *Entwicklung und Zusammenarbeit*, Vol. 34, 1993, No. 3

Soto, H. de: *The Other Path*, New York 1989

Spencer, H.: "Die Evolutionstheorie", in: H.P. Dreitzel (ed.), *Sozialer Wandel*, Berlin 1972

Srubar, I.: "Variants of the Transformation Process in Central Europe", in: *Zeitschrift für Soziologie*, 1994, No. 3

Stern, K.: *Das Staatsrecht in der Bundesrepublik Deutschland: Grundbegriffe und Grundlagen des Staatsrechts*, Vol. 1, Munich 1984

Stewart, F. / E. Ghani: "How Significant Are Externalities for Development?", in: *World Development*, Vol. 19, 1991, No. 6

Stopford, J.M. / S. Strange / J.S. Henley: *Rival States, Rival Firms. Competition for World Market Shares*, Cambridge 1992

Storper, M. / A.J. Scott: "The Geographical Foundation and Social Regulation of Flexible Specialization Production Complexes", in: J. Wolch / M. Dear (eds.), *The Power of Geography*, Boston 1989

Streeck, W.: "Interest Heterogeneity and Organizing Capacity - Two Class Logics of Collective Action?", in: R. Czada / A. Windhoff-Héritier (eds.), *Political Choice. Institutions, Rules and Limits of Rationality*, Frankfurt 1991

-: "On the Institutional Conditions of Diversified Quality Production", in: E. Matzner / W. Streeck (eds.), *Beyond Keynesianism*, Worcester 1991

Streeck, W. / P.C. Schmitter: "Gemeinschaft, Markt und Staat - und die Verbände?", in: *Journal für Sozialforschung*, 1985, No. 1

-: "Community, Market, State - and Associations? The Prospective Contribution of Interest Governance to Social Order", in: W. Streeck / P.C. Schmitter (eds.), *Private Interest Government*, London 1985

Streeck, W. / P.C. Schmitter (eds.): *Private Interest Government - Boyond Market and States*, Beverly Hills 1985

Street, J.H.: "Estructuras e instituciones: una puente hacia la teoría del desarrollo", in: El Trimestre Económico, 1967, No. 136

Streeten, P.: "Interdependence and Integration of the World Economy. The Role of States and Firms", in: *Transnational Corporations*, Vol. 1, 1992, No. 1

Sydow, J.: *Strategische Netzwerke*, Wiesbaden 1992

Tallard, M.: "Bargaining over New Technology. A Comparison of France and West Germany", in: R. Hyman / W. Streeck (eds.), *New Technology and Industrial Relations*, Oxford 1988

Tenbruck, F.: *Zur Kritik der planenden Vernunft*, Freiburg, Munich 1972

Teubner, G.: "Die Vielköpfige Hydra. Netzwerke als kollektive Akteure höherer Ordnung", in: W. Krohn / G. Küppers (eds.), *Emergenz. Die Entstehung von Ordnung, Organisation und Bedeutung*, Frankfurt 1992

Teubner, G. / H. Willke: "Kontext und Autonomie", in: *Zeitschrift für Rechtssoziologie*, 1984, No. 1

Therborn, G.: "Lessons from 'Corporatist' Theorizations", in: J. Pekkarinen et al. (eds.), *Social Corporatism*, Oxford 1992

Thompson, J.D.: *Organizations in Action*, New York 1967

Thorelli, H.B.: "Networks. Between Markets and Hierarchies", in: *Strategic Management Journal*, 1986, No. 7

Thoss, R.: "Ansatzpunkte einer systemkonformen Investitionslenkung", in: Bestens et al. (eds.), *Investitionslenkung - Bedrohung der Marktwirtschaft?*, Cologne 1975

Tironi, E.: *Chile: Autoritarismo, modernización y marginalidad*, Santiago 1990

Tobin, J.: "A Proposal for International Monetary Reform", in: *Eastern Economic Journal*, 1978, No. 4

Tocqueville, A. de: *Über die Demokratie in Amerika*, Stuttgart 1959

Tönnis, F.: *Gemeinschaft und Gesellschaft* (first appeared in 1935), Darmstadt 1979

Toye, J.: "Is There a New Political Economy of Development?", *IDS Development Studies Series*, Clarendon Press, Oxford 1992

Traxler, F. / B. Unger: "Institutionelle Erfolgsbedingungen wirtschaftlichen Strukturwandels", in: *Wirtschaft und Gesellschaft*, Vol. 16, 1990, No. 2

Trebilock, A., et al.: *Towards Social Dialogue*, ILO, Geneva 1994

Truman, D.B.: *The Governmental Process*, New York 1951

Tugendhat, E.: *Vorlesung über Ethik*, Frankfurt 1993

Velez-Ibanez, G.: *Bonds of Mutual Trust*, Brunswick 1983

Voelzkow, H.: "Organisatorisch-institutionelle Aspekte einer regionalen Industriepolitik - illustriert am Beispiel Nordrhein-Westfalen", in: U. Jürgens / W. Krumbein (eds.), *Industriepolitische Strategien*, Berlin 1991

Volk, E.: *Rationalität und Herrschaft*, Berlin 1970

Vollrath, E.: "Institutionenwandel als Rationalisierungsprozeß bei Max Weber", in: H.H. Hartwich (ed.), *Macht und Ohnmacht politischer Institutionen*, Opladen 1988

Waarden, F. v.: "Dimensions and Types of Policy Networks", in: *European Journal of Political Research*, 1992, No. 21

Wade, R.: *Governing the Market*, Princeton 1990

412   THE NETWORK SOCIETY

Walzer, M.: *Zivile Gesellschaft und amerikanische Demokratie*, Berlin 1992a

-: *Sphären der Gerechtigkeit*, Frankfurt 1992b

-: "Die Kommunitaristische Kritik am Liberalismus", in: A. Honneth (ed.), *Kommuni-tarismus*, Frankfurt 1993

-: "Moralischer Minimalismus", in: *Deutsche Zeitschrift für Philosophie*, 1994, No. 1

Weber, M.: Gesammelte Aufsätze zur Religionssoziologie, Tübingen 1947

-: *Wirtschaft und Gesellschaft*, Tübingen 1956

-: *Soziologische Grundbegriffe*, Tübingen 1960

Weingast, B.R.: "Constitutions as Governance Structures. The Political Foundations of Secure Markets", in: *Journal of Institutional and Theoretical Economics*, Vol. 149, 1993, No. 1

Weisbrod, B.A.: *The Nonprofit Economy*, Cambridge 1988

-: "Rewarding Performance that is Hard to Measure. The Private Non-profit Sector", in: *Science*, 1989, No. 244

Weiss, D.: "Institutionelle Aspekte der Selbstblockierung von Reformpolitiken. Fall-studie Ägypten, in: *Konjunkturpolitik*, 1992, No. 1

Wellman, B.: "Structural Analysis. From Method and Methaphor to Theory and Sub-stance", in: B. Wellmann / S.D. Berkowitz (eds.), *Social Structures*, Cambridge 1988

Widmaier, H.P.: "Wirtschaftliche Logik politischen Handels? Eine Kritik ökono-mischer Positionen", in: H. Abromeit / U. Jürgens (eds.), *Die politische Logik wirtschaftlichen Handelns*, Berlin 1992

Wiesenthal, H.: "Sturz in die Moderne. Der Sonderstatus der DDR in den Transforma-tionsprozessen in Osteuropa", in: M. Brie / D. Klein (eds.), *Zwischen den Zeiten*, Hamburg 1992

" Lernchancen der Risikogesellschaft", in: *Leviathan*, 1994, No. 1

Wiggins, S.N.: "Institutional Choice. A Contract-Theoretic Approach", in: *Journal of Institutional and Theoretical Economics*, Vol. 149, 1993, No. 1

Wilks, S. / M. Wright: *Government - Industry Relations. States, Sectors, and Net-works*, Oxford 1987

Williamson, D. / T. Young: "Governance, the World Bank and Liberal Theory", in: *Political Studies*, 1994, No. 1

Williamson, O.E.: *Die ökonomischen Institutionen des Kapitalismus*, Tübingen 1990

-: "The Evolving Science of Organization", in: *Journal of Institutional and Theoretical Economics*, Vol. 149, 1993, No. 1

Williamson, O.E. / W.G. Ouchi: "The Markets and Hierarchies and Visible Hand Perspectives", in: A.H. v. Ven / W.F. Joyce (eds.), *Perspectives on Organization Design and Behavior*, New York 1981

Willke, H.: "Entzauberung des Staates. Grundlinien einer systemtheoretischen Argumentation", in: Th. Ellwein et al. (eds.), *Jahrbuch zur Staats- und Verwaltungswissenschaft*, Baden-Baden 1987

-: "Institution", in: A. Görlitz / R. Prätorius (eds.), *Handbuch Politikwissenschaft, Rowohlts Enzyklopädie*, Reinbek 1987

-: "Systemtheorie entwickelter Gesellschaften", in: K. Hurrelmann (ed.), *Grundlagentexte Soziologie*, Cologne 1989

-: *Die Ironie des Staates*, Frankfurt 1992a

-: "Prinzipien politischer Supervision", in: H. Busshoff (ed.), *Politische Steuerung*, Baden-Baden 1992b

-: "Staat und Gesellschaft", in: K. Damman et al. (eds.), *Die Verwaltung des politischen Systems*, Opladen 1994

Winkler, J.T.: "Corporatism", in: *Archives Européennes de Sociologie*, Vol. 17, 1976, No. 1

Wolf, C.: *Markets or Governments*, Cambridge 1987

Wolff, R.P.: "Jenseits der Toleranz", in: R.P. Wolff / B. Moore / H. Marcuse (eds.), *Kritik der reinen Toleranz*, Frankfurt 1966

Womack, J.P., et al.: *The Machine that Changed the World*, New York 1990

Zahlmann, C. (ed.): *Kommunitarismus in der Diskussion*, Berlin 1992

Zeitlin, J.: "Local Industrial Strategies. Introduction", in: *Economy and Society*, Vol. 18, 1989, No. 4

Zintl, R.: "Kooperation und die Aufteilung des Kooperationsgewinns bei horizontaler Politikverflechtung", Max-Planck-Institut für Gesellschaftsforschung, Discussion paper, Cologne 1991

*For Product Safety Concerns and Information please contact
our EU representative GPSR@taylorandfrancis.com Taylor & Francis
Verlag GmbH, Kaufingerstraße 24, 80331 München, Germany*

T - #0079 - 270225 - C0 - 229/152/23 - PB - 9780714644028 - Gloss Lamination